AF505692

Front Lines

MATERIAL TEXTS

Front Lines

SOLDIERS' WRITING IN THE EARLY
MODERN HISPANIC WORLD

Miguel Martínez

PENN

UNIVERSITY OF PENNSYLVANIA PRESS   *Philadelphia*

THIS BOOK IS MADE POSSIBLE BY A COLLABORATIVE GRANT
FROM THE ANDREW W. MELLON FOUNDATION.

Published by
University of Pennsylvania Press
Philadelphia, Pennsylvania 19104-4112
www.upenn.edu/pennpress

Printed in the United States of America on
acid-free paper

10 9 8 7 6 5 4 3 2 1

A Cataloging-in-Publication record is available from
the Library of Congress

ISBN 978-0-8122-4842-5

CONTENTS

AGI   Archivo General de Indias. Accessed through PARES:
         Portal de Archivos Españoles.
AGS   Archivo General de Simancas. GyM: Guerra y Marina.
BAE   *Biblioteca de Autores Españoles*. 305 vols. Madrid: M.
         D. Rivadeneyra, 1846–1999.
BNE   Biblioteca Nacional de España.
CODOIN   *Colección de Documentos Inéditos para la Historia de
         España*. 112 vols. Madrid: Impr. de la Viuda de Calero,
         1842–95.
HSA   Hispanic Society of America.
JCB   John Carter Brown Library.
RAH   Real Academia de la Historia.

Front Lines

Introduction

The Muses' Comrades

. . . then Cretheus, friend of the Muses, the Muses' comrade,
Cretheus, always dear to his heart the song and lyre,
Turning a verse to the taut string, always singing
Of cavalry, weapons, wars and the men who fight them.

—VIRGIL, *Aeneid*

Virgil was the son of a tinker and he was the best of Italian poets.

—PEDRO MEXÍA, *Silva de varia lección*

It has been remarked that soldiers do not inherit letters but conquer them.[1] Against all odds, the rank-and-file soldiers of early modern Spain participated in the production, distribution, and consumption of a remarkably innovative set of works on war that have been almost completely neglected by literary and historical scholarship. The soldiers of Italian garrisons and North African presidios, on colonial American frontiers and in the traveling military camps of northern Europe, read and wrote epic poems, chronicles, ballads, pamphlets, and autobiographies—the stories of the very same wars in which they participated as rank-and-file fighters and witnesses. These Spanish *soldados pláticos*, professional soldiers conversant with war, turned into *soldados curiosos*, inclined to letters, by engaging in a wide variety of writing and reading practices. Furthermore, it was precisely the vast network of spaces articulated around the political and military institutions of an ever-expanding and struggling Spanish empire that facilitated the global circulation of the men themselves and of their textual production, and constituted what I call "a soldierly republic of letters." The lines they wrote on the front provide a critical view from below on state violence and imperial expansionism. It is their perspective that grounds this book, a cultural history of Spain's imperial wars as told by the common men who fought them.

Front Lines develops two symmetrical lines of argument. On the one hand, it exposes how the European military revolution—a locus of intense scholarly debate and a powerful historiographical narrative of modernization linked to state-building, imperialism, and globalization—affected literary practices. In this sense, I contend that the common soldiery of the Spanish armies played a key role in shaping Renaissance literary culture. These men reinvented classical genres such as the epic, produced new regimes of truth for historical writing, experimented with innovative poetic idioms and objects for the lyric, and created new autobiographical subjectivities. On the other hand, I explore the ways in which these varied and enriched literary traditions allowed soldiers to question received values and ideas about the social logic of warfare, the ethics of violence, and the legitimacy of imperial aggression.

The questions that drive my analysis aim at exploring the multiple and vexed relations between literary culture and imperial warfare in the early modern period. How does war affect the production, dissemination, and consumption of different literary genres and products? How do practices of warfare, such as recruitment and military socialization, discipline, war reporting, and worldwide travel, affect early modern literary practice? How does literature represent, legitimize, or oppose colonial violence? What is the social articulation of the different views and representations of war? How does what the observers witness on the battlefield unsettle their previous ideas and values about war? Soldierly writing, I argue, intensely interrogates the nature, means, goals, and consequences of war and empire. The voices of the common soldiers thus provide a privileged place from which to explore these questions, which are no less pressing today than they were in the early modern period. *Front Lines* contributes to the cultural history of war and violence, contesting a powerful historiographical narrative about Spain's Golden Age that has long assumed an unproblematic harmony between sword and pen, between the empire, its soldiers, and military literature.

Notions about the theme of "arms and letters" have indeed structured some of the most durable discourses on the Spanish Golden Age and Spain's imperial past.[2] The story of the Golden Age usually conflates, intentionally or not, cultural productivity and splendor with imperial grandeur. Take the greatest Spanish writer of the period, Miguel de Cervantes. The bodily mutilation he suffered in Lepanto, where an arquebus shot destroyed one of his hands, was for a long time a metonymy of Cervantes's "exemplary and heroic life" and remains an icon of the vexed relation between war and writing, between political and cultural history, to which "Golden Age" as a historiographical narrative refers. Lope de Vega, more his enemy than friend, conventionally praised the novelist by saying that his crippled hand had turned the lead of the cannon shots at Lepanto's mythic battle into diamantine lines of poetry, playing on the two meanings of *versos*.[3] This study draws from an important body of scholarship that, in the last decades, has explored this complex alchemic economy of arms and letters and provided a more nuanced vision of the relation between war and culture and between soldiers and the states that employed them.[4] In addition to Cervantes, many other writers of Golden Age Spain served in war, from commoners like Bartolomé de Torres Naharro, Bernal Díaz del Castillo, Alonso de Contreras, and Juan Rufo to those belonging to the higher or lower echelons of the nobility like Garcilaso de la Vega, Francisco de Aldana, Alonso de Ercilla, and Bernardo de Vargas Machuca, among many others. In addition to revisiting these soldier authors, this study examines the lives and writings of forgotten or unknown ones, such as Baltasar del Hierro, Alonso de Salamanca, Cristóbal Rodríguez Alva, Sancho de Londoño, and Emanuel Antunes, as well as a cohort of anonymous soldiers. Despite the pervasiveness of the theme of the pen and the sword in Golden Age literature and scholarship, the specific, material relation between the practice of war and the practice of literature has not been fully interrogated in all of its sociocultural dimensions.

The new practices and social spaces, global and local, of Renaissance warfare are largely the result of the military revolution. Since Michael Roberts formulated the concept in 1955, historians have disagreed about its nature, chronology, and relevance.[5] Despite the vastness and complexity of this scholarship, most specialists would nevertheless agree that during the early modern period the practice of war underwent substantial transformations in Europe, which could be briefly summarized as "larger numbers, greater permanence, and a new firepower."[6] Although a far from linear and coherent process, it is possible to single out some pivotal moments that radically transformed the ways war was waged and understood. The pike and pikemen formations as used by the Swiss from the 1470s had a key role in the gradual decline of the traditional aristocratic men-at-arms of heavy cavalry as the decisive units in battle: between the battles of Fornovo (1495) and Pavia (1525) the proportion of infantry to cavalry shifted from 1:1 to 6:1.[7] The widespread use of gunpowder and the improvement of artillery led to important developments in military architecture and engineering, which in turn led to further innovations in firepower and to a substantial transformation of tactics and strategy. Trench warfare developed around the protracted sieges of strategic cities. Grand field battles remained important, to be sure, but the bulk of combat was now carried out in the form of skirmishes, raids, ambushes, and attrition warfare. Armies required more manpower than ever before in order to successfully implement military policy. The logistics of warfare thus became more complex as campaigns grew longer and tighter, thus requiring important adjustments in recruiting, training, discipline, and the structure of command.[8]

The technologies, social spaces, and practices of early modern imperial warfare helped bring together a community of interests, a public for "the matters of war," that became the foundation for new writing and reading practices, new genres, and new material ways of distribution and appropriation. My account turns the "society of soldiers," as some military historians have referred to the peculiar forms of social and institutional organization of early modern armies, into a soldierly republic of letters.[9] This peculiar republic facilitated, for instance, the collection and publication of *romances* or ballads, the translation of some of the most important literary works in Renaissance Europe, and the circulation and exchange of all sorts of cultural materials in multiple languages. In the soldiers' republic of letters, the shared tent became a makeshift literary academy. The chain of command occasionally provided alternative structures for literary patronage. The army's baggage train carried books from Antwerp to Barcelona, from Milan to Tunis, from Seville to Santiago de Chile or Manila. While the Habsburg territories in Europe, together with their neighboring lands, have been deemed "the heartland of the military revolution," the dynasty's imperial ambitions made the soldiers' republic reach quite far.[10]

The soldiers' discourse on war entailed a proud affirmation of their public relevance as the backbone of imperial Spain. But by celebrating the honor and valor of fighting comrades, they pitted themselves against the ascendancy of a nobility that, since the early sixteenth century, had partially abandoned its traditional military role. Class and professional bonds often overrode ostensibly stronger allegiances such as ethnic and national loyalties, complicating the relationship between soldiers and the kings, countries, or empires they were hired to serve. The late sixteenth-century sonnets and epistles of the poet-soldier Andrés Rey de Artieda, published in 1605, do not depict his comrades as the proud agents of the empire but rather as its cursed victims. In Alonso de Ercilla's famous epic poem *La Araucana* (1569–90), which recounts imperial military efforts to defeat a successful indigenous rebellion in Chile, the poet and participating soldier took sides with the enemy he was supposed to be fighting on the battlefield. The longest episode in the *Breve suma de la vida y hechos de Diego García de Paredes* (1533), one of the first Renaissance autobiographies written by a soldier, is not one of the historically crucial battles of the Italian Wars he witnessed and in which he fought but a tavern brawl in which he viciously killed or maimed insulting thugs and prostitutes. The commoner Baltasar del Hierro did not recount in his short epic published in 1560 the wars against the Ottomans in which he served but instead narrated the successful mutiny of his comrades-in-arms against Spanish imperial authority in the North African fortress they were expected to defend.

Soldierly discourse oftentimes eroded imperial certainties and assumptions. As Adam McKeown has argued about Elizabethan writing soldiers, Spanish servicemen very often "used [their] authority as veterans to question not only the state's rationale for waging war but also the role of war in creating relations between the state and its subjects."[11] The social, cultural, national, and religious heterogeneity of the spaces of war, together with the porosity of the borders and contact zones in which the soldiers spent most of their daily lives, facilitated unexpected exchanges and solidarities. The same comradeship that was necessary to boost combat morale and unit cohesion allowed for dangerous sociabilities and rebellious confraternization. The structures that enabled the waging of war also allowed for the material production and circulation of soldierly texts that many times opposed those very same structures. These writings voiced criticism of the soldiers' military superiors and of imperial policies, while publicizing their exploitative working conditions and establishing solidarities among the troops that often led to mutiny and massive desertion.

The myriad pens and mouths of common soldiers had indeed many stories to tell about war and empire, oftentimes at odds with those told by their superiors, whether back home or on the front. Their stories were told in "the small voice of history," in Ranajit Guha's apt phrase.

And, albeit occasionally, we certainly find in their texts "the voice of a defiant subalternity committed to writing its own history."[12] Early modern soldiers made a particularly compelling effort, against the burden of partial literacies and the lack of cultural capital, to become authors and to understand in their own terms the imperial wars in which they fought. Although hawkish warmongering had a place in the writings and sayings of common soldiers, attitudes toward imperial warfare, toward its glories and horrors, vary widely, from enthusiastic support to frontal opposition, from skepticism to indifference. The chaotic tumult of war, the agitation of combat, the exhilaration of victory, the misery of defeat, the extreme material deprivation of life at war, and the challenges of the veteran back home all formed part of the thematic repertoire of soldierly writing.

Whether in the strictly coded form of a classical epic or in the swift and protean ephemerality of political gossip, whether in an autobiographical manuscript or in a printed broadside ballad, *plático* soldiers aspired to participate in the *pláticas* (conversations) of public discourse. They constructed their social and political identities, individually and collectively, by telling their stories to themselves and to others. And the often clamorous, rowdy voices of common, sometimes marginal soldiers were frequently perceived by authorities as suspiciously heterodox and disruptive of the social order. The type of the veteran *soldado roto* (broken soldier) did indeed pose problems of order and discipline. The figure of the *bravo* or *valentón* (braggart), idling in the streets of early modern Madrid, became a popular hero, a dangerous (counter)model of social behavior and public speech. Furthermore, the codes and ethos of military masculinity often conspired to offer alternative textual conceptualizations of affective relations, sometimes in sharp contrast to the traditions of Petrarchan love, Ciceronian friendship, or Virgilian filial piety.

The first chapter provides a detailed portrayal of the social and cultural world of these writing soldiers. "The Soldiers' Republic of Letters" gathers a wealth of testimonies about the widespread presence of literature and the dissemination of literate practices among the common fighting men of the Habsburg monarchy. I first show that literacy rates were significantly higher among soldiers, regardless of their social background, than among their civilian peers, and I explore the material conditions under which soldierly writing and reading took place while in deployment. Next I examine the global circulation and reception of texts throughout the spaces of war and the role that these spaces played in the shaping of publics and reading practices in the army. Finally, the chapter traces the relation between oral and written culture in the soldiers' republic of letters, establishing connections between war news and the early modern public sphere.

From this point, the organization of my argument combines a flexible geographical and chronological structure with attention to corresponding shifts in literary genre. Beginning with the Wars of Italy (1494–1559), the second chapter ("The Truth About War") focuses on a new group of Spanish poems written in ottava rima and divided in cantos that, in contrast to the fictional self-awareness of previous traditions of European heroic writing, claimed to offer realistic and accurate eyewitness accounts of the multiple contemporary wars of the Habsburg empire. These new Spanish epics established a sharp opposition to the textual tradition of chivalric romance from which they partially derived and, by claiming to tell "the truth about war," generated new understandings of the means and nature of armed strife and imperial violence. Building on Michael Murrin's illuminating insights about the new "relation between poetic and real war," I argue that this corpus of *gunpowder epics*, by authors such as Jerónimo Sempere, Jerónimo Jiménez de Urrea, Juan Rufo, and Miguel Giner, became the poetry of the new war, the specialized genre of the soldierly class, the proletarians of warfare.[13]

The third chapter, "Rebellion, Captivity, and Survival," focuses on the early modern Mediterranean conflicts between the Habsburgs and the Ottomans, particularly in North Africa, as experienced by the fighting and writing rank and file. Grounded in archival documentation, this chapter also brings to light several previously unknown or forgotten texts written by common soldiers that provide compelling articulations of rebellion and captivity, and of personal and collective defeat. First, the epic poems and ballads of Baltasar del Hierro reveal the shifting political and religious allegiances of the common soldiery in the face of conflict and prolonged contact across cultures. Next, the chapter explores the relation between epic and autobiography, and the heroics of survival and authorship, in the poetry and military treatises of a Spanish soldier captured by the Turks in the 1574 Ottoman conquest of La Goleta and Tunis.

"New World War," the fourth chapter, considers the soldierly texts produced in the New World during the wars of conquest. The Arauco War in Chile prompted a massive amount of discourse, perhaps unmatched in any other part of the Indies, during the sixteenth and seventeenth centuries, mostly by fighting soldiers. The challenge for contemporaries was to understand why the seemingly almighty Spanish empire had failed to defeat the Mapuche in southern Chile. This American experience effectively shattered some of the most defining and dearly held self-representations of Spanish imperial soldiery, representations that had been consistently elaborated on the European and Mediterranean fronts of the empire. Among the authors and works considered here are Pedro de Valdivia's letters, Bernardo de Vargas Machuca's *Milicia y descripción de las Indias* (1599), and Alonso de Ercilla's *La Araucana* (1569–90), together with a wealth of heterogeneous writings by Melchor Xufré del Águila, Santiago de Tesillo, and other anonymous colonial soldiers.

The last chapter, "Home from War," focuses on the experiences of the mutilated, the deserters, and the discharged in their conflicted returns to civil society. Often depicted as picaresque and even criminal, the voices of the returning soldier did indeed pose significant problems to the city's public order and the state's military policies. This chapter analyzes, on the one hand, the war ballads and lyrical languages produced and circulated in Europe's battlefields, particularly in the Netherlands, which helped publicize the soldiers' extenuating conditions of service in one of the longest and bloodiest wars of the period. On the other hand, it explores the group of well-known personal narratives by veterans, mainly Diego García de Paredes's *Breve suma* and Alonso de Contreras's *Discurso de mi vida*, in which they strived to produce proud and convincing autobiographical subjectivities. These bold first-person narratives openly defied the authority of the state and ended up questioning the thin lines between legitimate and illegitimate violence.

The overall argument of the present book is particularly concerned with what can be called the Icarian logic of soldierly writing. In a masterful study of popular culture, James Amelang uses the myth of Icarus, "the classic symbol of punishment for popular overreaching," as a powerful class allegory to understand subaltern forms of authorship and literary practice in early modern Europe.[14] The son of an artisan, Daedalus, Icarus attempts to fly too high, with man-made wings and against his father's counsel, and meets his demise as a punishment for his insolent hubris. Just like the artisans who took up the pen and wrote, against all odds and expectations, writing soldiers made ample use of "the images of flight, and the language of trespass and intrusion" that have been found revealing in the autobiographies of craftsmen.[15] This myth is a powerful story about arrogance and failed ambitions, but it is also about audacious disobedience and self-determination. The usual moral message is deeply rooted in a social conservatism that assumes that, just as mortals do not fly, artisans—or soldiers—do not write.

As we will see, soldiers, like Icarus or Phaeton, did indeed disobey. They deserted, rebelled, switched sides, abstained from fighting, killed officers, defied kings, and insulted popes. Their writing, like their behavior, was too often mutinous. Some early modern mutinies lasted long enough to transform what can be understood as an early labor strike into significant improvement of soldierly life, if rarely long lasting. And while hardly conceived as large-scale political action, soldierly self-organization and protest ended up many times challenging imperial designs. In contrast, some soldiers told the story of the relative failure of their class and of the early modern army as a set of practices and structures that could have allowed the popular classes of Spain to thrive and dispute political and social power. In either case, the stories they wrote and read narrate the struggle for survival and daring human endeavor, suffering and triumph. Their legacies in the long run will, moreover, shed light on the modern cultural and political history of warfare and war writing.

The fact that many of the texts I discuss in this book have remained hidden in the archive for so long speaks to canonical inertias in a discipline that has nonetheless striven to incorporate a varied array of texts that had been traditionally stripped of meaning and value. But more important, it reveals the scholarly unease, the humanistic unwillingness to understand war as an inextricable part of culture in the early modern age—and perhaps in other periods of human history. As Fernand Braudel argued, "War is not simply the antithesis of civilization" but a constitutive part of it.[16] This is far from arguing, as some conservative military historians do, that war is "the father of us all" or an ahistorical "tragic, nearly inevitable aspect of human existence."[17] Nor is it a celebration of the cultural productivity of violence. Quite the opposite: this argument is instead meant to stress the need for historians to account for "the cultural location of war."[18] It is an attempt to recover the ways in which the common people have tried to understand and give meaning—multiple and conflicted meanings—to the apparently meaningless irrationality of war. War is a discursive phenomenon with its own logic as much as it is an illogical, unutterable calamity, and many of its dimensions can only be understood by paying attention to the texts written by those who experienced it first-hand. Every war story participates in previous narrative structures, ideas, and ideological framing held in common, and the texts written by serving soldiers are not exempt from these preexisting discursive frames.[19] They are not more transparent, real, or authentic than any other textual product; they are not free from the cultural mediations that organize *experience*, a concept memorably scrutinized by Joan Scott.[20] But "for those who experience war first hand," Adam McKeown rightly points out, "the tortured process of negotiating a set of conflicted and deeply personal relations to war through another set of conflicted discourses about war in order to arrive at a meaningful narrative is especially pronounced."[21]

In dialogue with Foucault's "Nietzsche, Genealogy, History," the French historian Arlette Farge insists on the need to recover the *things said* (les choses dites) about the wars of the past as a means to avoid the interpretation of war as an eternal fatality, as some kind of recurring damnation alien to the rationality of human action: "To study war and its moments as sayable articulated events is the best way to show the reasons why they have been possible, and thus, how those events could have escaped that possibility." Moreover, to study the things said about war, the discursive formation the soldiers themselves called "las cosas de guerra" (the matters of war), will help us "to understand its recurrence, not to *rejoice* on its evolution, but to realize that other scenarios have been possible, with different rationalities and passions. Always keeping in mind that in any case, what has happened could have not taken place."[22]

The recovery of the eyewitness's gaze, the perspective of the killer and the survivor, the victor and the defeated, allows us to restore the contingency of imperial war and history. The soldiers' specialized languages shaped a down-to-earth representation of war that avoids some of the most common traps of modern discourse on violence, such as its association with the sublime or the transcendental, sometimes even theological, understanding of the causes of armed conflict. Providence or God's corrective punishments had little to do with the killing of men by men. Writers from the field very often identified the commanders or imperial officials that were responsible for wrong strategic decisions and offered alternative courses of action that could have avoided defeat, captivity, or carnage. Against its apparent excess, inevitability, and irrationality, war is a thoroughly human affair, and those who conduct it, from the emperor to the lowest pikeman, are entirely human. This is why the multiple voices of the early modern common soldiery, from the epic intonation of the victorious hero to the autobiographical whisper of the defeated captive or the mutinous political rumor of the returning veteran, invite us to engage with Farge's ultimately ethical proposal of historicization.[23]

In a fleeting moment of the *Iliad*, we hear the best soldier of all time, Achilles, playing his lyre and singing about "men's deeds of renown" to his dear comrade Patroclus.[24] In this intriguing mise-en-abyme the bard and his hero become ambiguously conflated. The greatest poet of antiquity seems to dress up for a moment, however short-lived, in warrior guise, and the coarse warrior poses briefly as the persuasive epic poet. The move would be imitated and taken further by Homer's most daring competitor. In book 9 of the *Aeneid*, in the roar of battle, Turnus sneaks into the Trojan camp just before Pandarus closes the gates to their Latin enemies. Among the scores of fleeing Trojans that Turnus viciously kills—Alcander, Halius, Prytanis, Noëmon, Lynceus, and others—we are told about a certain Cretheus, "friend of the Muses, the Muses' comrade." Like all of the *Aeneid*'s secondary characters, this soldier is granted a fugitive moment of glory in Virgil's war tale. Uniquely among all of Turnus's victims, however, Virgil takes the time to give a fully developed portrait of Cretheus as devoted poet, "always dear to his heart the song and lyre," and always singing "of cavalry, weapons, wars and the men who fight them."[25] The close parallelism between this verse ("arma uirum pugnasque canebat") and the *Aeneid*'s proposition ("Arma uirumque cano") forces the reader to make the connection: Cretheus, the soldier-poet, unmistakably resembles Virgil himself.

Unlike his compatriots and predecessors Naevius and Ennius, the founders of Roman epic, Virgil never served as a soldier.[26] Yet for Pedro Mexía, one of the most widely read authors of sixteenth-century Spain, the poet was the best example of "how those who are born to humble parents and lineages should follow the example of men who from lowly beginnings rose to great status."[27] The son of a tinker, as Mexía read in Suetonius, this figure of Virgil was particularly well suited for our Icarian soldiers who, against all expectations about their kind, rose above their status in daring literary flight to write the songs of their lives and travails. This book tells the story of the Spanish historical counterparts of Virgil's fictional Cretheus, the frontline comrades of the Muses who wrote about weapons, wars, and the men who fought them.

CHAPTER I

The Soldiers' Republic of Letters

CLASS AND LITERACY

Miguel de Cervantes, a veteran soldier himself, knew it all too well when he talked about his comrades: "No one is poorer in their misery, because they depend on their wretched pay, which arrives too late or never at all, and thus they are forced to subsist with whatever they can get with their own hands at the risk of their lives and their conscience" (No hay ninguno más pobre en la misma pobreza, porque está atenido a la miseria de su paga, que viene o tarde o nunca, o a lo que garbeare por sus manos, con notable peligro de su vida o de su conciencia).[1] It seems obvious that it was not only the rank structure and discipline of the army that provided Karl Marx with an old military analogy in his description of the emergent industrial proletariat: soldiering, as precariously salaried mass labor, was always associated with poverty, whether as a way to escape it or, more often, to tragically perpetuate it.[2]

Early modern imperial warfare was not an aristocratic business but a rather plebeian one. Ragged soldiers, not elegant courtiers, were the protagonists of both the military revolution and Iberian imperial expansion. According to the commoner Bernal Díaz del Castillo, Mexico was conquered by "a fleet of poor men" (nuestra armada era de hombres pobres), and for Gaspar Correia, an imperial official and chronicler of Portuguese Asia, India had been similarly gained with "the blood of the poor and humble folk" (o sangue dos pobres e homens pequenos)—even if the king favored the nobility when distributing his grace.[3] For the Venetian military engineer Giulio Savorgnan in 1572, men enlisted in the army "to escape from being craftsmen, working in a shop; to avoid criminal sentence; to see new things; to pursue honour." But the latter are very few: "the rest," he added, "join in the hope of having enough to live on and a bit over for shoes or some other trifle that will make life supportable."[4]

Most early modern soldiers were thus lowborn young men who found in the profession of arms the most plausible path to survival or social promotion, whether as salaried workers in the European wars or as aspirants to a share of the wealth from a colonial expeditionary force. In the case of Spain, the human resources of the empire's armies were also largely drawn from the popular classes of the multiple nations of the Habsburg composite monarchy.[5] Additionally, the army was one of the institutions in which the *limpieza de sangre* statutes were never legislated; racial or ethnoreligious ancestry never played a role in recruitment, which made it easier for large sections of the Iberian population to enroll.[6] Steady salary, however paltry, and the promise of plunder were indeed the main reasons for most recruits to join the army, since it "offered the starving poor one of their few chances of survival."[7]

How could, then, an army of poor men, largely formed of peasants, artisans, fugitives, and unemployed youth, provide shelter for a republic of letters?[8] How could these men read and write, let alone compose complex war narratives in verse and prose? Soldiers, after all, have traditionally been counted among "those who live on the margins of literacy,"[9] which explains why historians Marie-Christine Rodríguez and Bartolomé Bennassar, in one of the most comprehensive studies of literacy rates in early modern Spain, included soldiers under the same rubric as vagabonds, beggars, sailors, and actors.[10]

Some evidence exists, if scant, that allows us to suggest that the skills of reading and writing must have been more widespread among rank-and-file soldiers, whatever their social extraction, than among their civilian peers. In the late sixteenth century, one in three soldiers who made a will before dying at Santiago de Compostela's Hospital Real could sign his name.[11] One among them seemed to have prepared himself carefully for death, as in 1581 he owned a book of hours and a *Contemptus mundi*, two kinds of books that circulated widely among the popular classes as well as among the soldierly commons.[12] By the middle of the following century, these rates seem to have increased: seven out of nine soldiers could sign their will with their name in Madrid in 1650.[13] When set against these data, Cervantes's story about a veteran lieutenant who writes the *Dialogue of the Dogs* in Valladolid's Hospital de la Resurrección while convalescing from syphilis would not seem to "exceed all imagination."[14]

In contrast with these intriguing but insufficient glimpses into literacy rates among Spain's soldiers, surveys of conquistadores in the New World are strikingly systematic and reliable. It is well-known that the social status of almost all conquistadores, even the most eminent, was hardly distinguished. The vast majority of them were commoners of different trades, although some of the leaders belonged to the lineages of the destitute gentry or marginal *hidalguía*. Only about 120 of the 2,200 men who participated in the campaigns conducting the conquest of Tenochtitlán in 1519–21 were hidalgos, and yet "most of these conquistadors, hidalgo or not, could read and write."[15] Of the 318 of Cortés's men whose signatures can still be read in the company's petition sent from the newly founded Veracruz on June 20, 1519, up to 75 percent must have been literate, even though only 4–8 percent were of noble origin.[16] Strikingly similar figures have been estimated in the case of Tierra Firme, Chile, and New Granada, where 70–80 percent of the soldiers seem to have been at least partially literate.[17] In the case of the conquest of Peru, the leader Francisco Pizarro was illegitimately born—as were most of his brothers—to a humble peasant's daughter and remained illiterate all his life.[18] Of the 168 conquerors of the Inca empire under his command, however, a total of 108 could sign their name, which amounts to around 77 percent of Lockhart's "men of Cajamarca."[19] Of these 108, 51 were "definitely literate," while for the remaining 57 who could sign their name, we cannot fully ascertain the extent of their skills—although, as Lockhart points out, signing one's name in the sixteenth century meant some formal instruction, however basic, in reading and writing. Among the literate conquistadores of Peru were Pedro Cieza de León and Francisco de Xerez, both chroniclers of their uneducated captain's military exploits and soldiers themselves. Cieza was the son of a shopkeeper from the small town of Llerena, while Xerez was a poor commoner, "low, vile, and of little account."[20] Among the seemingly boorish conquistadores there appear to have been many who could read and write, even among those of humble extraction.

Scholarship on popular literacies, the history of the book, and popular culture has long shown that literacy was much more widespread among the laboring classes of early modern Europe and Spain than it was once thought.[21] To be sure, literacy and cultural capital were unequally distributed, which structured and hierarchized the social world in various ways. It is misleading, however, to assume that this distribution flawlessly overlapped with class distinctions and socioprofessional status.[22] At least two historical processes with wide-ranging consequences, namely the printing and educational revolutions, helped alter the social distribution of cultural capital and of written matter beginning in the early sixteenth century, resulting in a substantial increase in literacy rates across class boundaries.[23] Both historical processes converged to offer the lower classes of early modern Spain a path, however tortuous, to social promotion and public relevance; and in this regard, as far as my argument is concerned, they go hand in hand with the massive incorporation of the popular classes into the army as a result of the military revolution.

The expansion of literacy and the partial democratization of written culture have indeed a lot to do with the transformations brought about by movable type.[24] The new abundance of printed matter and its agile circulation made all layers of society more familiar with the written word, even those who did not know how to read or write. The rise of cheap print in Renaissance Europe, moreover, made it possible for large numbers of people to purchase its products. It is certainly true that some books remained an expensive luxury for common soldiers with their paltry salaries, even when printed in affordable and unpretentious formats. The price of the first edition of Alonso de Ercilla's *La Araucana* (Madrid: Pierres Cossin, 1569), for example, amounted to eighty-four maravedíes (twenty-eight sheets or *pliegos* at three maravedíes per sheet), which equaled more than two days of pay, and close to 9 percent of a pikeman's monthly salary. The percentage would be significantly lower for an experienced arquebusier with some *ventajas* (wage supplements paid to good soldiers) and even lower for a respectable, experienced officer. Despite its apparently high cost, *La Araucana* circulated widely among the common soldiers of the Spanish armies, as I will show. Yet by comparison, the products of popular print, particularly one-sheet *pliegos de cordel*, were produced cheaply and massively and were thus much more accessible for the pockets of common soldiers. According to the notes of Renaissance collector Hernando Colón in the 1500s–1530s, most single-sheet pliegos would sell for as little as one or two maravedíes or quatrines, a remarkably low price that would allow soldiers to purchase between 1,000 and 1,200 one-sheet pliegos with one month's pay. In 1540, for instance, a one-sheet *pliego* seems to have been cheaper than a loaf of bread or a half-dozen eggs.[25] The printed word was by then affordable for almost anyone.

The circulation of printed matter among the soldiers, as in other social groups, enhanced awareness of the written word in general and of the technologies and practices of writing itself, which fostered rather than inhibited the production and distribution of manuscript texts.[26] The death inventory of Diego García de Paredes (1533), one of the most famous soldiers of Renaissance Europe, included four printed items: a book of prayers, a book of hours (like that of the anonymous soldier at Santiago's hospital), a Bible, and Caesar's *Commentarii*.[27] The paucity of Paredes's printed library, which resembles that of many early modern soldiers, contrasts with the abundance of his manuscript papers. Up to eight items in his inventory refer vaguely to loose sheets, unbound quires, and notebooks containing different kinds of writings "by his own hand" (de su propia mano). The mention of the portable writing desk (*escribanía*) and the note-taking device, perhaps erasable, known as *libro de memorias* confirms that writing was an everyday activity for soldiers like him.[28] Indeed, it was among these autograph papers that his *Breve suma de la vida y hechos de Diego García de Paredes*, one of the first autobiographies written by a soldier in Renaissance Europe and arguably one of the first nonfiction memoirs of any kind written in Spanish, was found.[29]

The spread of the printing press and its products also contributed to make literacy a desirable goal among larger social sectors. While the costs of learning basic reading and writing skills remained high throughout the period for the Spanish poor, there were abundant alternatives that allowed them to achieve literacy. Parish priests and ordained relatives taught many destitute children for free. Some religious orders, such as the Franciscans and, especially, the Jesuits, also provided free instruction at different levels. Municipal councils in many towns and cities across Castile subsidized schools and supervised the activities of private masters. The children of poor parents could also attend school *de limosna*, by paying only a fraction of tuition, according to what they could afford.[30] During the sixteenth century, this is how some of the Muses' comrades, like many other commoners, learned their first letters in childhood, as they themselves will often record.

In his many lives, Miguel Piedrola was a tinker (as was Virgil's father) and a nobleman, a captive and a wandering troubadour, a soldier and a prophet. Born a commoner, Piedrola learned his first letters with an unnamed priest. Later on, he abandoned the tinker's apprenticeship to go serve another priest who gave him a vessel of holy water (*acetre*), "which is the way they help poor boys pay for their studies" by using it to beg for alms from door to door: "With the money I got, I paid for grammar lessons," that is, Latin. Then he went on to serve as a soldier for many years in the Mediterranean and was taken captive on several occasions. He claimed to be a prophet like those he read about in the Old Testament of a Bible he bought from a bookseller in Naples. The soldier-prophet, as he became widely known, wrote letters and prophecies to the king and the pope, and for a while he seemed to have enjoyed credit among followers and opponents alike. Eventually, however, the Inquisition charged Piedrola with sedition against the king and "usurpation of divine and celestial authority."[31] The paths to literacy may be tortuous for a soldier, but as this case shows, the ability to read and write often turned soldiers into a threat to authority and the social order.

Other writing soldiers provided similar accounts of their childhood schooling. In his autobiography, soldier Jerónimo de Pasamonte recounted how his legal guardian, a maternal uncle and a priest, taught him some Latin (*gramática*). Similarly, while he does not make explicit mention of his education, rank-and-file soldier Miguel de Castro was mentored in Valladolid by a friend of his uncle, who was also a priest and a *licenciado* (university graduate). Alonso de Contreras, the son of commoners, attended the school of one of those proverbially cruel masters of primary letters in Madrid around 1590. Contreras "escribía de ocho renglones," referring to the "renglón de a ocho," the "first size with which the teaching of writing starts" (tamaño primero con que se empieza a enseñar a escribir), when he had to end his education abruptly because of a violent feud he had with a richer classmate.[32] As I will discuss later, some poor boys—future soldiers— learned how to kill as soon as they learned how to write.

Most writing soldiers thus seem to have become literate before they joined the army. The spaces of war attracted men familiar with the written word and even skilled in the arts of the pen, and the urban origin of many recruits, as profiled by Ian Thompson, might also help explain the higher literacy rates among soldiers.[33] Though harder to document, it is also very likely that other soldiers learned how to read and write after enlistment. There are aspects of military life, such as disciplinary socialization, military idle time or *otium*, and the practice of war reporting that may have contributed to the spread of literacy among serving soldiers, regardless of their social background. Written documentation was a familiar presence in the everyday lives of Renaissance soldiers. From the moment a soldier enrolled—*asienta plaza*—and was required to sign his name in the company's books to the moment he was paid or discharged a series of complex administrative operations were mediated by the technologies and materials of writing and record keeping. Scribes, auditors, accountants, and paymasters, as we see in Cervantes's vivid account in *El licenciado Vidriera*, were some of the clerks who supported the Renaissance army as the highly complex assemblage of techniques and structures.[34] The *bandos* or ordinances that governed military life were published in the spaces of war in manuscript or even printed form, and every soldier was required to abide by them under the threat of severe punishment.[35] Moreover, Spanish and Latin American archives contain hundreds of thousands of documents that soldiers carried around folded in their pockets or in tin cans, as did the fictional lieutenant Mellado in Francisco de Quevedo's *Buscón* and the anonymous soldier of the ballad "Mirando estaba el retrato."[36] *Cédulas, memoriales, informaciones, testamentos,* and *probanzas,* usually written by professional notaries but occasionally autographed by the soldiers themselves, were the main instruments of interlocution between the soldier and the imperial military authorities. They attested to their professional achievements and military services to the crown. They enabled rank-and-file poor soldiers to request *mercedes* or rewards, offices, and occasional financial support (*ayudas de costa*). The presence of the written word in the spaces of war was more than quotidian; it constituted its very structure and enabled its functioning.

Other practices and institutions of army life must have also encouraged illiterate soldiers to engage with written culture. It is not unlikely that in the idle time of presidio life or in the winter quarters some soldiers could have learned how to read from literate comrades, whether gratis or for a low fee. In literature, *camaradas* are often depicted in fluent and everyday conversation about "matters of war." The *camarada* or camarade (the source of the English "comrade") was a rather informal association among three to six fellow soldiers who agreed to share lodging and meals, significantly reducing living expenses for the permanently underpaid rank and file.[37] The term, referring either to one of its members or to the group as a whole, was defined precisely by Covarrubias: "Roommate who eats and sleeps in the same lodging.

The word is used by soldiers and it is as much as saying companion and intimate friend, who is in the same company" (Compañero
de cámara, que come y duerme en una misma posada. Este término
se usa entre soldados, y vale compañero y amigo familiar, que está
en la misma compañía).[38] This form of institutionalized friendship
allowed for a peculiar sociability based on strong bonds of brotherhood and intimate conversation but also fostered lettered practices
and the circulation of literary materials. The material culture of sharing among comrades multiplied the potential readers of a book, like
those "*Hours of Our Lady* and a Garcilaso without commentary"
that the fictional Tomás Rodaja, "the son of a poor peasant," "carried
in the pockets of his breeches" when boarding a Neapolitan galley on
the way to Genoa (unas *Horas de Nuestra Señora* y un Garcilaso sin
comento, que en las dos faldriqueras llevaba).[39] Soldier-poet Cristóbal
de Virués found shelter against gossip and mockery in the intimacy of
the camarade, which facilitated the exchange of poems with a fellow
curioso soldier, also a poetry aficionado. Furthermore, literary skills
could occasionally help soldiers make their way to the captain's camarade, where they were expected to partake in a sort of improvised literary academy, according to soldier-poet Andrés Rey de Artieda in
1605.[40]

Rey de Artieda is a case in point to better understand the relation
between class, literacy, and the soldiers' republic of letters. Born in
Valencia in the late 1540s to a notary from Aragon, the poet experienced a combination of letters and arms in his youth, spending alter-
nate periods of time in the classroom and on the front lines of Italy,
the Mediterranean, and the Low Countries.[41] He also went to college,
which was rare even for a literate soldier. Rey de Artieda's epistles and
sonnets represent with painstaking detail the everyday life of military
friendship in the social spaces of early modern warfare. The poem titled
"To the Soldiers' Meal" (A una comida de soldados) depicts the joyful
conviviality of a soldierly camarade gathering at the Neapolitan port
of Barletta, feasting on salad and walnuts, drinking wine, and toast-
ing the appointment of one of them as corporal (*cabo de escuadra*),
the lowest rank for non-commanding officers in an infantry corps. In
another sonnet, "To a comrade of captain Antonio Vázquez" (A un soldado camarada del capitán Antonio Vázquez), Rey de Artieda satirizes
a soldier for being "skilled" in eating and drinking, skipping watches,
and caring only about his personal belongings, all to the detriment of
his fellow comrades. More important, however, is the fact that Rey

de Artieda included some of his comrades' poems with his own when he published his collection of military lyric. Antonio Vázquez himself is represented in Rey de Artieda's generously all-embracing collection with four sonnets on different topics, including a few about one of the most beloved themes of soldier-poets: prostitutes.[42] These poems must have been collected by his comrade Rey de Artieda throughout the years of a long and sustained military career—forty-seven years for Artieda—since Vázquez is disparately titled soldier, captain, and sergeant major in different pieces. But Vázquez is not the only comrade-poet in Rey de Artieda's collection. Some Cascajares—an unmistakably plebeian name—contributed poems, as did some well-known Valencian and Aragonese courtiers and humanists.[43] Rey de Artieda's book, while legally published under his name, is a highly collaborative one in which the author not only decided to print some of his best friends' military poems but also depicted them in scenes of soldierly intimacy and friendly conversation and participating in a vibrant literary activity in the spaces of war. The social spaces of early modern warfare contributed to the creation of a "network of popular sociability" that multiplied the effects of the printing revolution and facilitated an increasingly intimate familiarity with the written word.[44]

Indeed, soldierly comradeship was oftentimes mediated through writing. After the mutiny of Dunkirk was settled in 1594, the accountants of the army used some of the soldiers' testaments to set the record straight on what had been agreed between the striking infantrymen and the Habsburg military and political authorities. Soldiers often named fellow soldiers as their executors, like Domingo Hernández, who chose "his comrades [camaradas] Francisco Xuárez and Hernando de Guevara, soldiers in my company [soldados en mi compañía]," as the people in charge of carrying out the terms of his last will. It was a common practice among single men who shared in the same camarade to bequeath their overdue pay to each other in case of death, as did the Portuguese Pedro Hernández to his Castilian comrade Bartolomé González, both infantrymen participating in the same mutiny. Other soldiers wrote or signed on behalf of their illiterate brothers-in-arms: "Because I do not know how to write I asked the above mentioned witness Juan Ramírez, to sign it on my behalf" (porque yo no sé escribir rogué al dicho Juan Ramírez, testigo, que lo firmase por mi mano), says Ginés de Escames. And in the case of Luis Gómez, no fewer than eight fellow soldiers signed their names as witnesses at their friend's deathbed.[45] The bonds between brothers-in-arms, between "godfathers and godsons" (padrino[s] y ahijado[s])—as Juan Rufo refers to the relationship between comrades—were indeed many times articulated or mediated through witnessing and writing.[46]

Executing or bearing witness to a brother-in-arms' will, as did these sixteenth-century soldiers of Dunkirk, was much like writing stories about fallen comrades. Writing against oblivion, the most classical and time-honored justification of literary enunciation itself, was acutely felt in a society based on bonds of friendship, comradeship, and shared suffering. Composing war stories was the ultimate act of solidarity and respect among fellow soldiers. An economy of reputation, by which the fame and honor of individual soldiers relied on testimonies, both oral and written, of comrades-in-arms, regulated relations between those who had been killed and those who survived. The impulse to give account of oneself and one's comrades gave way to many front lines that, written from the battlefield, would keep alive the memory of many common infantrymen and their deeds in the republic of soldiers.

WRITING ON THE BATTLEFIELD

According to a one of the censors of Santiago de Tesillo's *Epítome chileno, ideas contra la paz*, published in Lima in 1648, the soldier writes "painting his commas with lead, inking his pen with gunpowder, drawing his words with shots and his lines with lances" (matizando sus comas con plomo, su pluma con pólvora, sus palabras con tiros y sus renglones con lanzas).[47] In contrast with Garcilaso de la Vega's symmetrically ordered alternation of the sword and the pen, "ora la espada, ora la pluma," the trope entails now a radicalization of the contiguity of arms and letters, a total conflation of the practice of writing and the practice of modern warfare.[48] Lead, gunpowder, shots, and pikes are metaphorically used to write the history of their very usage on the battlefield. Arms double their function as instruments of violence and the material support of writing, symbolically eliminating any distance between things and words, between textual and military culture, between the practice and the representation of warfare. By the middle of the seventeenth century the material cultures of writing and fighting had become indistinguishably equated in a powerful trope.

Despite the precariousness of military life, pen, ink, and paper, manuscript and printed matter, were found in large quantities in the baggage train of every early modern army and constituted an integral part of the soldier's daily life and material culture. Juan de Oznaya, a plebeian arquebusier who fought in the Wars of Italy and wrote about them, reveals the wealth of paper in his description of the Renaissance tactic of *encamisada*. The soldiers of an *encamisada* were detailed to storm an enemy position at night wearing white shirts (*camisas*) on top of their defensive arms in order to be recognized by their fellow combatants in the dark while they took advantage of the surprise factor.[49] "Tonight," says Oznaya, recollecting the orders of a commander, "you will wear shirts on top of your arms and go where the squadrons are formed" (Todos armados y con camisas encima de las armas o vestidos, salgáis donde se hicieren los escuadrones), but if the cloth of shirts or tents were not enough, the soldiers "will take two sheets of paper from that to be found in the camp and make a kind of mantle or cloak to whiten themselves and be recognized" (si no bastare, de dos pliegos de papel de lo que en todo el campo se hallare, harán unos capotines o sambenitillos con los que blanqueen por ser conocidos).[50] Paper and other basic tools of writing were as important for the military revolution as other enabling technologies readily associated with it, such as gunpowder and military engineering. And even far from the rich and cultured cities of Lombardy, the materiality of writing provided fighting soldiers in the farthest frontier of Spain's empire with a language to describe the shocking realities of the New World. During Pedro de Valdivia's first military expedition to Chile, the soldier Jerónimo de Vivar observed how the indigenous peoples of the northern coast built rafts with the skin of sea lions, which they pressed and folded "just like sheets of paper are folded" (como está un pliego de papel doblado).[51] In the second half of the sixteenth century, arquebusiers used paper in their ramrods and musketeers started to fabricate paper cartridges containing gunpowder and bullets in order to accelerate the loading of their guns.[52]

In August 1590, poet and infantry captain Andrés Rey de Artieda was instructed to raise a company in his native Valencia. In the book used to record the plebeian names of several dozens of young recruits, we find a wealth of calligraphic exercises, presumably by the company's scribe or by Artieda himself (Figures 1 and 2). Written rehearsals of epistolary formulae and random names of unidentified men not enrolled in the company fill the numerous blank pages of a notebook that carries with it the marks of the commerce of war. Perhaps to kill time while waiting for new recruits to show up at the drummer's call in a public square, one writer has drafted the first two lines of a ballad: "Dressed with our colors / in green and silver flowers" (De nuestro color vestido / de verde y flores de plata). The lines belong originally to a Moorish ballad, "Romance del gallardo Arbolán," turned *a lo divino* to sing the Nativity. The original ("A la jineta vestido / de verde y flores de plata") was first published anonymously in *Flor de varios romances nuevos y canciones* (Huesca, 1589), barely one year before Artieda's company book was drafted, and was later gathered in the *Romancero general* of 1600.[53] This particular example vividly illustrates not only the instrumental role of the technologies of writing in the constitution of the early modern armies but also the close rapport, the intimate contiguity of military and literary practices, in the society of soldiers.

The availability of the most basic writing materials and familiarity with the written word still do not suffice to fully articulate the soldiers' republic of letters, a site for the organized production, distribution, consumption, and discussion of literary texts. We have, however, numerous testimonies to the intensity of literary practices, which were widespread and unexceptional among the soldiers of Habsburg armies and amid the roar of war. When editing the poems written by his brother Francisco, Cosme de Aldana listed the titles of the many other texts that he had not been able to recover because they were "lost in war, where he always carried them" (perdidas en la guerra, do siempre las traía).[54] He was able, however, to recover and publish a substantial collection of Francisco's poems in Milan in 1589, a second one in Madrid two years later, and three more reprints in Spain's capital and the Low Countries, an editorial trajectory that closely follows the soldiers' roads throughout Europe. An infantry captain like Aldana, Cristóbal de Virués is best known for his *Monserrate*, an epic poem printed in 1588 recounting the legends of hermit Juan Garín. When Virués's friend Baltasar de Escobar, a humanist and diplomat at the Roman curia, received a copy, he encouraged him to "bring to light the lyric poems that, gathered in your drafts, have escaped the storms and dangers of your honorable military pilgrimages" (sacar las rimas que se hallaren recogidas por los borradores que se han escapado de las borrascas y peligros de sus honrosas peregrinaciones militares).[55] Some did indeed survive and were eventually collected in *Obras trágicas y líricas del capitán Cristóbal de Virués* (Madrid: Alonso Martín, 1609). Despite war's pressures on cultural activity, literary traffic was intense, and the backpacks of some soldiers, like

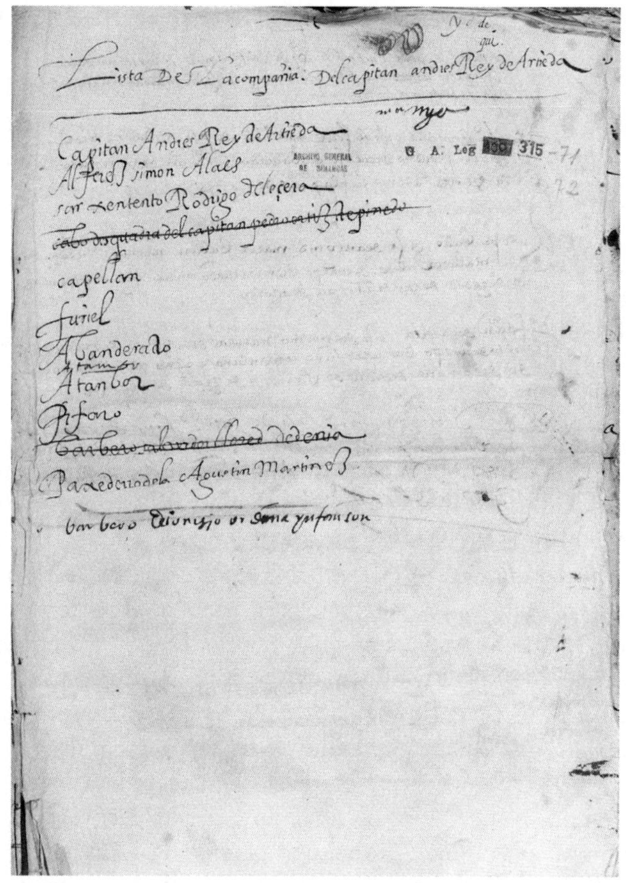

Figure 1. *Lista de la compañía del capitán Andrés Rey de Artieda*, August 1590. España, Ministerio de Cultura, AGS, GyM leg. 315, fol. 71.

Tomás Rodaja's *faldriqueras,* seem to have carried at least as many sonnets as *licencias* or recommendation letters.

Virués and Aldana are among the best-known writing soldiers of the period. Both of them came from the lower nobility, were well educated, and were raised to the position of infantry captains. Despite their rank and privileged background, however, they were no exception. Martín García Cerezeda, an arquebusier from Córdoba, very likely of plebeian background, wrote his voluminous *Tratado de las campañas del Emperador Carlos V* "in the times that I was idle while serving in the army" (en los tiempos que en la milicia fallaba

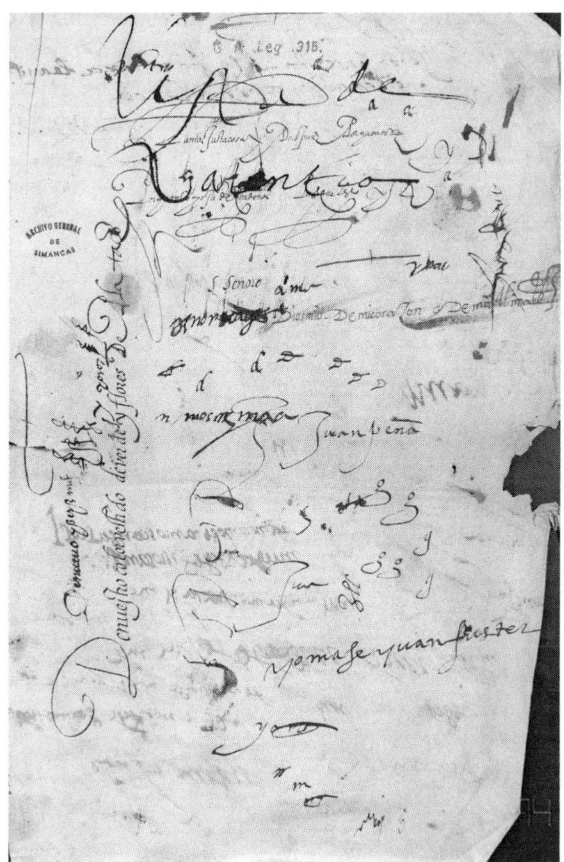

Figure 2. "De nuestro color vestido / de verde y flores de plata." *Lista de la compañía del capitán Andrés Rey de Artieda*, August 1590. España, Ministerio de Cultura, AGS, GyM leg. 315, fol. 1.

ociosidad).[56] His work narrates year by year, almost month by month, and with painstaking detail, the many military campaigns in which he participated as a rank-and-file soldier from 1522 to 1545, giving testimony to the radical transformations of warfare during the years of the Italian Wars and the Mediterranean conflict with the Ottomans in the first half of the century. García Cerezeda reproaches "the many excellent pens, both in philosophy and poetry, that I have seen and see every day in this most glorious army" (muy excelentes plumas, ansí en filosofía como en poesía, que he visto e veo cada el día en este felicísimo ejército) for not writing about the war they were waging and thus justifies his own firsthand narrative of these crucial events.[57] While apparently more inclined to poetry and philosophy, and not focused on recounting the war they were fighting, writers were not particularly uncommon among the ranks of Charles V's troops.

In his *Vida y hechos del emperador Carlos V*, royal chronicler Prudencio de Sandoval confirms the literary activity of this sizable group of soldiers inclined to letters (*soldados curiosos*), many of them anonymous, who provided commanders and historians alike with fresh reports from the field.[58] For the section on the campaigns against the Schmalkaldic league during 1546–47, Sandoval relied heavily on D. Luis de Ávila y Zúñiga's *Comentario de la guerra de Alemaña* (Venice: Thomás de Gornoça, 1548). Count by birth and marquis by marriage, Luis de Ávila y Zúñiga was one of the emperor's closest collaborators, a splendid courtier, an experienced military commander, and a respected historian.[59] His relation with Charles V was so intimate that His Majesty considered him a "witness to my thoughts" (testigo de mis pensamientos).[60] His *Comentario*, the most Caesarian of all military texts produced in Renaissance Spain, had sixteen editions in six years and almost immediate translations into Italian, Dutch, French, English, and Latin. It was arguably the most popular European book on the Schmalkaldic War and one of the most widely praised and read works of history in Spanish. The authority and popularity of the *Comentario* notwithstanding, Sandoval complemented this source "with some manuscript reports that the curious soldiers in the imperial camp carefully wrote and sent to Spain" (relaciones escritas de mano por soldados curiosos que andaban en el campo imperial que las escribían con cuidado y enviaban a España). Sandoval states that one of these reports, written by an anonymous soldier who recounted "what he saw, most of it on horse, as it happened" (lo que vio y que la mayor parte de ello lo escribía a caballo como iba ello pasando), is in fact identical to Luis de Ávila's second chapter. Since the soldier signed his account on November 11, 1547, allegedly antedating the first edition of the *Comentario*, Sandoval claims that this part of D. Luis's book borrows this anonymous soldier's account.[61]

There is no reason not to believe the scrupulous Sandoval, always transparent and thorough when assessing the sources of his monumental history of Charles V's reign, for which he profitably used and acknowledged Ávila y Zúñiga's praiseworthy work.[62] His testimony also restores the protagonism of the rank and file not only in fighting the wars, as they claimed repeatedly, but also in recounting them. Caesarian, noble captains writing with their pen what they fought with their swords were accompanied by anonymous soldiers in their common attempts to record the experience of war and make sense of it. Sometimes their respective accounts of imperial violence would resemble each other, but many other times they would radically differ. Whether by commanders or rank-and-file soldiers, all these testimonies suggest that writing and reading were widespread practices in Renaissance armies and in the spaces of war.

Moreover, relying on the eyewitness accounts of *curious* writing soldiers seems to have been simply natural for historians. The idea that soldierly texts produced on the battlefield were the principal sources for the writing of reliable history would eventually become naturalized among humanists and professional historians. When reflecting on the differences between writing general and particular histories, the highly respected humanist Bartolomé Leonardo de Argensola wrote that many historical events worth recounting remain unknown "because those who fought on those occasions only wrote in passing about them, leaving most of it for general histories, and their writings are not found when they are required" (porque remitiéndolas para las historias generales, no se escriben cuando suceden sino de paso por los que militaron en ellas, y cuando son menester sus escritos, no parecen).[63] For Argensola, the voice of the eyewitness soldier writing from the battlefield is the main source and ultimate guarantee of authority for historiographical discourse.

Presidios and marching camps provided a locus of enunciation, both real and metaphorical, for the writing soldier. The long periods of inactivity for garrisoned soldiers increased the appeal of reading, writing, and discussing literature as entertainment in the often dull life of the military. Baltasar de Vargas, a veteran soldier of the Naples *tercio* in the Duke of Alba's journey on the Spanish road in 1567, wrote his *Breve relación en octava rima de la jornada que ha hecho el Señor Duque de Alba* "in this idle life of the presidio" (en esta ociosidad del presidio).[64] This text narrates the journey with a wealth of detail about the logistics of deployment of an early modern army, paying a lot of attention to operations required to lodge, feed, move, and protect the army. The heroic actions of this brief epic are the duke's diligent dispatch of messengers, his negotiations with local lords and merchants, the precautions of secretaries, overseers (*veedores*), and accountants, the timely distribution of paychecks, and the agile transportation of the army's artillery train through the Alps. Although called "the veteran Vargas" by a comrade contributing a preliminary poem, he deems himself a greenhorn in poetry (en la poesía soy novicio).[65] Amateurism at writing is again set against their professionalism as soldiers. They make explicit the discrepancy between their public persona and their writing practice, between their profession of war and their tentative poetic endeavors, continuously thematizing a tension between fighting and writing that they nonetheless exploit to their benefit. The link between the symbolic capital of the professional participant soldier and the discursive authority of a text on the matters of war became so naturalized that when the clergyman Lorenzo de Zamora published his *Primera parte de la Historia de Sagunto, Numancia y Carthago* in 1589, he excused himself for writing on war, however ancient, not having any experience on the matter, "since I can assure you that not only have I not ever been to war, but even a private brawl I have never witnessed" (que te puedo jurar que no solamente no me he hallado en guerras, pero ni aun he visto riña particular ninguna).[66]

The transoceanic fleets that supported imperial warfare were not unfit spaces for writing on the matters of war either. The Portuguese poet and soldier Luís de Camões wrote part of *Os Lusíadas* (1572) while traveling and battling all along the Portuguese colonial possessions in the East and claimed to have saved his "sea-drenched Epic Song" (os cantos . . . molhados) from a shipwreck in the South China Sea by holding in his hands the actual sheets on which it was written.[67] Similarly, the common soldier and poet Gaspar García de Alarcón rhetorically asked the readers of his epic poem *La victoriosa conquista . . . de los Azores* (1585) "that they excuse the flaws of the work because I could not depart from the truth and because it was written at war, in the middle of the ocean; and because the military art that I practice is very different from that of writing in verse, with little study, little experience, and little time" (que me tomen en descuento el no poder salir de la verdad a que va arrimada, y escrita en un golfo, y parte della en la guerra. Y cuán diferente es el arte de milicia que profeso al componer en metro, con poco estudio, menos experiencia, no muy ayudado del tiempo).[68] The conventionally humble *excusatio* against the potential *murmuradores* or critics is indeed a proud defense of his professional role and of his military experience in the Marquis of Santa Cruz's naval campaign against the French fleet of Philippe Strozzi during the wars that followed the Habsburg conquest of Portugal in the early 1580s.

Many of the better-known chronicles and *relaciones* from the colonial American context were written by major and minor figures in the liminal spaces of the war of conquest in the new territories. The writing of war narratives was by no means limited to the leaders of the expeditions, such as Hernán Cortés. On the contrary, it was a widespread practice and was one of the main war genres in the soldiers' republic of letters. Most famous among them, Bernal Díaz del Castillo took up the pen in his *Historia verdadera de la conquista de la Nueva España* in order to counter the accounts written by historians far from the field that exaggerated the role of the leaders in the accomplishments of the conquest.[69] The chronicler of the conquest of Peru, the plebeian soldier Pedro Cieza de León, attributed the faults of his chronicle of Peru to his "pocas letras" and to his "being too absorbed in the business of war." "Many times," he continues, "when most soldiers rested, I exhausted myself writing. The roughness of the mentioned lands, mountains, and rivers, the intolerable hunger and necessity, none of this ever prevented me from dutifully following my two occupations, writing and serving my company and my captain" (Muchas veces, cuando los otros soldados descansaban, cansaba yo escribiendo. Mas ni esto, ni las asperezas de tierras, montañas y ríos ya dichos, intolerables hambres y necesidades, nunca bastaban para estorbar mis dos oficios de escribir y seguir a mi bandera y capitán sin hacer falta).[70] Perhaps the most emblematic and dramatic example of this gesture linking the practice of writing to the battlefield is Alonso de Ercilla's prologue to his first *Araucana* of 1569. Although this work was published more than ten years after his return from the Chilean frontier, the poet claims to have written his powerfully realistic stanzas "amid the very war, in the very marches and sieges, often writing on leather because of the lack of paper, and on scraps of letters so small that barely six lines fit, all of which made it rather difficult to put everything together later" (en la misma guerra y en los mismos pasos y sitios, escribiendo muchas veces en cuero por falta de papel, y en pedazos de cartas, algunos tan pequeños que apenas cabían seis versos, que no me costó después poco trabajo juntarlos).[71] The representation of the practice of writing in the most distant spaces of the imperial frontier is a powerful rhetorical device to produce discursive authority, determining the enunciative structure and truth-value of soldierly texts in very important ways. The legitimacy of Ercilla's poem is clearly linked to the detailed description of those rare moments provided by military *otium*, as in García Cerezeda's case, "stolen" (hurtados) from the professional exercise of warfare. The very inadequacy of the "pasos y sitios" for the intellectual practice of writing and the material precariousness of those pieces of paper and leather—"poor diapers"—make his firsthand account "truer" (más verdadero), even if those pieces do not fit the eight lines required to compose an *octava real*, the basic metrical unit of Renaissance epic.[72] The image of the soldier writing on the battlefield becomes the documentary and symbolic foundation of the historical authenticity of the soldierly text. The representation of the personal practice of war—"I am a soldier and I was there"—authorizes the poetic or narrative voice of a social subject whose discursive legitimacy relies on his military expertise and his direct contact with the spaces of war rather than on humanistic erudition, nobility, service at court, or inventive genius.

Critics have often taken these assertions, particularly Ercilla's, to be conventionally rhetorical at best, or plainly false. "One of the romantic fictions regarding the accounts of conquests in the Indies," says Rolena Adorno, "is that they were written at night in military encampments by soldier-hidalgos who, with quill in hand, bravely ignored the intimidating sounds of enemy war cries and drums. Hernán Cortés and Alonso de Ercilla y Zúñiga are among the authors who create this familiar impression."[73] Adorno's skepticism about the truth of the Caesarian image of the soldier simultaneously fighting and writing on the battlefield is a standard and healthy reminder of the long tradition of a particular literary convention. While acknowledging the "retrospective quality" of most soldierly writing,[74] evidence supports my contention here that this trope refers to actual practices in the spaces of war, both in the New World and the Old, that gained prominence over the period. For the first *Araucana* of 1569, Ercilla's brother-in-arms, the veteran captain Juan Gómez, wrote an *aprobación* where he legally testified that Ercilla was seen, by him and everyone else, "serving your majesty in that war, where he publicly wrote this book" (vi a don Alonso de Ercilla servir a Su Majestad en aquella guerra, donde públicamente escribió este libro).[75] Writing in the spaces of war was common, as we have seen, and the public nature of this practice in the case of Ercilla seems to make it a prestigious, collective activity and an integral part of the socialization processes of the Renaissance soldiery. Furthermore, our doubts about the actual truth of some of these statements should not prevent us from realizing the way in which they associate the authority of the written text with its material production, with the immediacy and urgency of imperial warfare and frontier spaces, with the contingencies of a military expedition on the Chilean frontier or of a sea journey from Macau to Goa.

In addition to providing evidence for the intensity of literary practice in the spaces of war, the discussion thus far has made it clear that for these writing soldiers the construction of discursive authority is based upon the fundamental link between the soldier's own enunciation, the material conditions of the battlefield, and the professional practices and institutions of the military corporation. The elaboration of this contiguity of pen and sword, of writing and fighting, is not always free of tension, but it will be crucial for understanding the rhetorical appeal of these texts for the society of soldiers. Moreover, the urgency of in situ writing, the material ephemerality of the soldierly text, is also important in understanding the memorializing drive of much of the heroic textual production on war. For "those who live dying" (los que moriendo vivimos), as veteran Torres Naharro put it, leaving a trace of who they were in writing must have been a particularly pressing impulse.[76]

Cristóbal Rodríguez Alva, a soldier who fought in Italy and the Netherlands during the last years of the sixteenth century, held the matter of his epic poem *La inquieta Flandes* (1594) to "have been entirely seen by my eyes" (es toda obra por mis ojos vista), as did many other soldiers who offered their own firsthand accounts of their and their comrades' exploits, but he also claimed that the lines of his poem were "watered with the blood of my veins, and written among the arms and the furor of death" (regada con la sangre de mis venas y escrita en medio de armas y furor de muerte).[77] However rhetorical, the image is a powerful reminder of the dire conditions under which soldiers carried out their daily lives. The wrecking of the body in the spaces of war, whether actual or metaphorical, threatens to disintegrate the very material support of soldierly narratives. The fragile materiality of the text is, like the bodies of soldier-poets, always threatened by the ravages of war. Writing on the front line entailed a sort of precarious survival amid the violent urgencies and unpredictable contingencies of early modern warfare.

TRAVELING TEXTS

Ercilla did indeed manage to preserve those pieces of *authentic* writing produced amid the roar of war. He brought them back to the metropolis from the farthest frontier of the empire and put them together in print. In the prologue discussed earlier, published in the first *Araucana* of 1569, Ercilla appealed to a public of fellow warriors who shared the same socioprofessional spaces, the many "keen to the matters of war" who "were present to many of the events that I narrate here" (aficionados a las cosas de guerra; que se hallaron en muchas cosas de las que aquí escribo) and who were taken to be the final guarantors of the truth so carefully produced by the Caesarian rhetoric of the fighting and writing soldier.[78] Which is to say that soldiers usually expected fellow soldiers to read their texts. We know that some of the brothers-in-arms who were present in the brutal war of Chile did indeed get to read the poem. Some of them even used it as legal proof of their participation in the conquest of Chile, referring to Ercilla's poetic stanzas as some kind of *probanza de mérito*, a witness's sworn testimony to one's deeds.[79] Irving Leonard suggested that *La Araucana* was a popular read on the ships of the *carrera de Indias*, while the poem also circulated widely among the soldiers of the army of Flanders, back on the European war stage, as we will see in detail in Chapter 4.[80] The highly organized military practices, agents, and institutions of the Spanish Habsburgs provided the material basis for the fast circulation and consumption of cultural products among the curious soldiers. While the previous section focused on the production of textual materials in the spaces of war, the pages that follow will revolve around reading and exchanging in a soldierly republic of letters that was quickly becoming global.

Soldiers were usually the first to reach the edge of the empire and the last to leave, so they had a particularly intense and concrete experience of imperial space. Regardless of specific itineraries and military careers, soldiers often experienced extended travel across several territories of the empire. When the soldiers of the second Cambodia Campaign of 1594 faced a larger Ming Chinese army in Churdumuco, today's Phnom Penh, they heartened each other by recalling that they "were old soldiers, with experience in the Low Countries, France, Africa, and England, in addition to these parts of the West . . . the Philippines" (éramos soldados viejos que en Flandes, Francia, África e Inglaterra y en estas partes del poniente . . . las islas Filipinas), according to the testimony of one of the participants.[81] Their movement, as we have seen, was crucial to structure some of the major routes and networks of imperial power, including those uniting Spain with the Americas, Portugal with its eastern colonies, Italy with the Netherlands, and Mexico with the Philippines. The Habsburg courts, the African and Italian presidios, the migrating military camps of Europe's battlefields, the Asian and American colonial garrisons, and the metropolis of the returning soldier were some of the physical and social spaces in which soldiers had a key role as cultural agents.[82] These soldiers were not only producers of epic, lyric, and *relaciones* but also consumers of the same kind of products; they were not only the makers but also the partakers of an intense literary circulation and exchange. The vast network of spaces articulated around the political and military institutions of early modern European empires facilitated the wide and rapid circulation of literary works in the context of a never-ending and worldwide imperial contest; it also provided an institutional ground for the formation of military publics. "The increased mobility of things themselves," it has been argued, "created public life in early modern culture."[83] The practices that allowed for the global mobility of imperial armies—travel, march, sea voyage, deployment, encampment—turned soldiers into crucial actors in the global circulation of textual materials during the period.

Some scholars have argued that the rise of the news market in early modern Europe was closely related to military conflict, particularly the Habsburg-Valois wars of the first half of the sixteenth century and the Mediterranean confrontation with the Ottomans.[84] Soldiers were indeed key agents in the production, dissemination, and consumption of news and ballads, in the form of pliegos de cordel, or broadsheets, from the very first days of the military and the printing revolutions. The *Coplas noevamente fechas de la guerra y presa de Fuente Rabía y de Salvia tierra y Monleón* (Barcelona: Carles Amorós, ca. 1525) were composed by Juan del Rincón, a "soldier who was in all of the said war" (soldado que se halló en toda la dicha guerra) of Navarre in the 1510s. Some *Coplas de la presa de Túnez* are said to have been "made by a soldier" (fechas por un soldado), who wrote in traditional octosyllabic verse about the 1535 imperial conquest of the North African city. Hernando Colón's bibliographies also tell us about another anonymous "soldier who says in verse that the king of France is the cause of the Emperor's wars" (soldado que dice en coplas ser el rey de Francia causa de la guerra que tiene el Emperador), also lost today.

Some romances and other forms of traditional octosyllabic verse were composed about the landmark battle of Pavia, sometimes based on the imperial commanders' reports from the battlefield, such as the *Coplas nuevamente hechas al caso acaescido en Italia en la batalla de Pavía*, "which can be sung to the melody of Condes Claros" (las cuales se pueden cantar al tono de Condes Claros).[85] The conquest of Granada, the never-ending Wars of Italy, the struggle with the Ottomans for the control of the Mediterranean, and even the New World battles of the empire were all sung far and wide in the traditional form of *romances* and *coplas* and distributed in print through the ephemeral, disposable materiality of the *pliego suelto*.

Early in 1551, Joannes Steelsius printed *Romance de la conquista de la ciudad de África en Berbería* in Antwerp, which had been written during the Habsburg reconquest of the Tunisian city of Mahdia (also known as Africa) in September 1550. The ballad, "sent by a soldier who participated in the conquest to a friend of him who resides in Italy" (enviado por un soldado que se halló en la conquista a otro amigo suyo que reside en Italia), attests to the agile circulation of poetry through the complex political and social geography of the imperial spaces of war, from North Africa to Italy and from Italy to Antwerp.[86] Sometimes this geography of exchange, which is coextensive with the physical and institutional spaces of the Habsburg military machine, is nonetheless surprisingly dynamic and efficient. Baltasar del Hierro, a veteran from the same Mahdia campaign serving in Milan in 1560, published a sonnet about the Portuguese viceroy Constantino de Bragança's military success in India in 1559. In a little over a year, the war news had traveled from Goa to Lombardy, presumably carried by Portuguese soldiers, had been transformed into a sonnet by an infantryman garrisoned in Milan, and had reached the popular Sevillian printing workshop of Sebastián Trujillo. The propagation of news and poetry, of oral and printed texts on the matters of war, is one of the main pillars of an increasingly transnational soldiers' republic of letters. The constitution of a public around the matters of war also reinforced a sense of corporate identity and proud solidarity among soldiers who were serving far away from each other, an identity that oftentimes was at odds with the aims and methods of empire administrators. As we will see, the global reach of the Habsburg military corporation generated solidarities and fraternizations—"that familiar headache of military administrators" in Hale's words—between soldiers and civilians of different nations, different religious allegiances, and even different sides of the conflict.[87]

Literacy rates, I argued earlier, seem to have been higher in the army than in other social spaces and professional groups, allowing for the articulation of relatively large publics. Bernardino de Escalante took for granted that many infantrymen, to whom he addressed his *Diálogos del Arte militar* (1583), would be able to read his book. "I decided to write these military dialogues," he says, "so that the fresh, unexperienced recruits can quickly become expert soldiers by reading them" (me determiné a hacer estos diálogos militares . . . para que los soldados bisoños, leyéndolos, se hagan pláticos en breve tiempo).[88] Being a priest and a commissary of the Holy Office of the Inquisition at the time he wrote his treatise, Escalante made sure to point out that he had been "raised in war since childhood," once again grounding his discursive authority in his own military experience. It was natural for military writers to assume that their works would circulate fluidly and rapidly among the spaces of war, and he envisioned his treatise helping soldiers in "the provinces of Peru, New Spain, the Philippines and other islands of that ocean." Furthermore, just as *bisoños* were expected to be trained in the arts of war by the *pláticos*, it seems that training in letters was also part of the process of military socialization. Escalante offers his work as only a provisional contribution to the art of war "until some of you can write with more propriety about this art, since you practice it so courageously" (hasta que algunos de vuestras mercedes escriban con más propriedad esta arte pues la ejercitan con tanto valor). If we believe Escalante, the ability to read and write seems to have been widespread among those "illustrious gentlemen" (muy ilustres señores)—a common form of soldierly respectful address, regardless of social background—"of the Spanish infantry that serve in the presidios of the kingdoms and estates of king Philip, our lord" (de la infantería española que asiste de presidio en los reinos y estados del rey Felipe nuestro señor).[89] Escalante was not particularly self-delusional: a Jesuit criticizing the newly founded Reales Estudios de San Isidro (1629) claimed that what was taught in the Chair of Fortifications in one year "would be read amply by a soldier from Flanders in three months."[90] Books must have been as familiar a presence on the front line as in the college classroom.

Texts, as Escalante suggests and we know well, also traveled easily between the Old World and the New thanks to a large extent to the conquistadores and settlers who ventured to cross the Atlantic.

The circulation and consumption of books, particularly those of chivalry, among the Spanish conquistadores is a well-known story since Irving Leonard's classic study, although his idealizing view of this phenomenon has been rightly criticized.[91] Books also circulated among garrisoned or retired soldiers in the Indies. In his will, the Chilean veteran Melchor Xufré del Águila declared that he owned "about eighty bound books" (como ochenta cuerpos de libros), most of which we should assume came from Spain. The retired soldier also stated that he left "a ream of paper" (una resma de papel) and three more books at Lieutenant Andrés de Góngora's house, which he was supposed to sell as part of a debt settlement.[92] According to Bernal Díaz, moreover, the conquistadores of Mexico carried in their memories *romances viejos*—old narrative ballads of octosyllabic verse that rhymed assonantically—that were frequently sung during the conquest wars and to a certain extent shaped their interpretations of New World events. In turn, the heroic feats of the respected commander Hernán Cortés gave way to the composition of new ballads that were transmitted orally and crossed the Atlantic back to the metropolis.[93]

The spaces generated by global armed conflict and imperial expansion during the early modern period also allowed for the cross-cultural dissemination of all kinds of literary products and genres, far beyond ballads, relaciones, or sonnets. With the occasion of Philip IV's ascension to the throne in 1621, the *cabildo*—municipal council—of Manila decided to organize a theater festival to bring a glorious end to the city's celebrations. Despite the fact that Manila had a university and a large number of active lettered clerics, the cabildo appointed the soldiers of the San Felipe garrison to carry out every aspect of the performances. According to Diego de Rueda y Mendoza, one of the soldiers who participated in this theatrical event, the cabildo found "among the soldiers of this garrison some skilled in this matter [of theater] to whom it commissioned three [plays]. Some of them being men of good taste, and others witty, funny, and talented musicians, they took them in charge, and designed the stage, dramaturgy, and costumes" (habiendo hallado entre los soldados de este campo algunos práticos en esta facultad les encargaron tres; que unos como hombres de buen gusto y otros de donaire y gracejo y diestros músicos las tomaron a su cargo y fueron dispuniendo de su traza, invenciones y vestuario).[94] Soldiers of Spanish, Portuguese, and Italian origin were present among the attendants to the performances, along with a highly heterogeneous audience of Tagalog, Chinese,

Mexican, and Japanese civilians who lived in Manila, one of the most diverse cities of the early modern world. Similarly, Rueda y Mendoza was invited to a Chinese wedding in Manila where he described "a comedy in the Chinese style" (una comedia . . . a usanza de China) that was performed over lunch.[95] Miguel de Loarca, another soldier serving in the Philippines like Diego de Rueda, also described a Chinese performance in his *Relación del viaje que hecimos a la China*. Being received by a local governor in southern China, the soldiers and priests in the Spanish legation were the privileged audience to "a play, and the *entremeses* lasted for the whole meal, and there were singers and vihuela players" (una comedia, que duraron todos los entremeses toda la comida, hubo cantores, músicos de vihuela de arco).[96] By virtue of their wandering, multicultural, and socially heterogeneous nature, the armies of the monarchy of Spain were spaces of cultural encounter as much as they were the frightening carriers of extreme violence that they were and are known to be. The production, circulation, and reception of the body of literature on the matters of war were intricately related to the progressive formation and increasing institutionalization of these spaces and with the social practices and discourses that constituted them.

The spaces of war were not structured sites of assembly but unstable, moving, and heterogeneous spaces of cultural production and exchange. Lettered soldiers are bound together not only for their interest in the matters of war as producers but also as consumers and agents of exchange of literary materials. The circulation of texts discussing "las cosas de guerra" among its practitioners is crucial to understanding the soldiers' republic of letters but also the society of soldiers at large. One of the main arguments of this book is that soldierly literature, both manuscript and printed texts about the matters of war, was not only *distributed in* the already existing structures of social intercourse enabled by the global military machine but also *constitutive of* them, being a crucial factor in the articulation of the society of soldiers. The literary sociability enabled by the circulation and consumption of these multiple forms of writing, moreover, contributed to a great extent to the development of a collective identity for the common soldiery.

Whereas many writing soldiers explicitly addressed their works to "those who know how to fight" (los que saben pelear), thus articulating a public of fellow comrades-at-arms, all kinds of textual products were distributed and consumed in the soldiers' republic of letters, and

not only those produced by insiders.[97] The complexity of the soldiers'
literary practices is illustrated by an episode from the Sack of Rome
in 1527.

The prestigious Italian humanist Paolo Giovio, perhaps one of the
most renowned historians of the time in the intellectual milieus of
Renaissance Europe, had set out to write a monumental history of
his own present time. His *Historiarum sui temporis tomus primus*
(Rome: Laurentii Torrentini, 1550) started with a series of "epito-
mes" that summarized books 5–10, covering the years from 1498
to 1512, and 19–24, which covered the decade from 1517 to 1527.
The original books seem to have been dramatically disfigured under
unclear circumstances, since Giovio's elucidation of these lacunae was
contradictory and changed over time.[98] First, the humanist explained
that he had hidden the manuscripts in the crypt of a church, but they
nonetheless fell into the hands of the furious sackers. Two Spanish
captains, named Herrera and Antonio Gamboa, are said to have kept
those written on vellum and bound, while disdainfully discarding
everything written on paper. The former would eventually be ran-
somed by the humanist, imprisoned with Pope Clement VII in the
Castle of Sant'Angelo; the latter was used by the soldiers as toilet
paper (*dissipati in foedos usos*).[99] According to a second version of the
events, the manuscripts were recovered from the troop "with the aid
of certain famous generals who understood their import for their own
fame."[100] And one of Giovio's Spanish translators gave yet another,
similar account of the kidnaping of the humanist's manuscripts. The
slight variation, nonetheless, is significant, since in this case the protagonists are not two Spanish captains but the collectivity of the soldierly mass: "The soldiers came across these papers and tore some of
them apart. Once peace was reestablished thanks to the pope's commands, together with Giovio's begging and money, they returned the
books to him, although damaged and incomplete" (Viniendo estas
escrituras en manos de soldados, rompieron y hicieron pedazos algunas dellas. De apaciguadas las cosas, con mandamientos del Papa, con
ruegos y dineros del Jovio, volvieron los libros a su poder, aunque en
algunas partes faltos y rasgados).[101]

While it might seem that Spanish soldiers acted in that manner
out of sheer ignorance and barbarism, the opposite is quite possible.
The sections seized or selectively destroyed by the Spanish soldiers
were those dedicated to narrating the Italian wars between France
and Spain in the first decades of the century, when the reputation of

the Spanish armies' effectiveness and ruthlessness rose exponentially in Italy and beyond. Giovio, generally a rather committed supporter of the imperial cause and the official apologist for some of its most famous commanders in Italy, was not always flattering to the imperial victors of Pavia in 1525, the same soldiers that only two years later sacked the Holy City and subdued the pope, and thus was harshly criticized by some for his occasional hostility to the Spaniards.[102] Had they known this, the furious soldiers of the imperial army might not have liked what Giovio was writing about them. Were that the case, whether they ripped them apart out of rage or used them "in foedos usos" because they were otherwise useless, the gesture remains meaningful. And like the German soldiers' defacing of Raphael's paintings or the burning of books in the Holy City during the same episode, it would indicate a fluid, but tense, relation with Renaissance high culture on the part of the plebeian army[103]—meanwhile, some other Spanish soldiers harassed the pope, who had taken refuge in the castle of Sant'Angelo, by shouting out adapted versions of traditional songs and a satirically glossed Pater Noster.[104]

The story, in any of its versions, shows a highly complex relationship between literacy, orality, consumption, and soldierly agency. Soldiers were willing to intervene violently in the public pláticas on war through the seizure of uncomfortable historiographical works about their ethos and action. Through vehement erasure, they were rewriting the discursive representation of their own military life and public identity. Whether some enlightened generals confronted the soldierly mass to recover the papers for their own sake or some captains and anonymous soldiers partially kidnaped the material, the anecdote provides an extreme example of Michel de Certeau's observations about the nature of cultural consumption and his warning that "the elite . . . always assumes that the public is moulded by the products imposed on it. . . . This misunderstanding assumes that 'assimilating' necessarily means 'becoming similar to' what one absorbs, and not 'making something similar' to what one is, making it one's own, appropriating or re-appropriating it."[105] Even if it was just an act of radical carnivalization and Bakhtinian degradation of the humanist's writings through the workings of "the lower stratum of the body," the gesture is still meaningful.[106]

The anecdote powerfully recalls the moment in Castiglione's discussion of the theme of arms and letters when one of his chatting courtiers playfully but brutally asserts the ultimately self-evident superiority of arms over letters. "If you think the contrary," the Count tells Bembo, "wait until you hear of a contest in which the man who defends the cause of arms is allowed to use them, just as those who defend the cause of letters make use of letters in their defense; for if each one uses his own weapons, you will see that the men of letters will lose."[107] In the episode just recounted, the soldiers' quite literal appropriation of Giovio's account of their action forces us to explore how the circulation of written matter, whether in print, manuscript, or oral form, contributed to the organization of a very peculiar discursive community. Although humanists and soldiers had occasion to interact and, like many other Renaissance historians, Giovio had often relied on the oral accounts of soldiers and captains for his ambitious historiographical enterprise, the story requires us to wonder how a mass of furious soldiers could have found out what a learned humanist was writing about them.[108] It makes us wonder whether a group of Spanish soldiers could have accessed Giovio's elegant humanistic Latin. Thus the "Giovio affair" suggests the necessity of taking into account the stories, opinions, and ideas that were disseminated orally in the republic of lettered soldiers and that interacted richly, as this anecdote shows, with the written culture of Renaissance Europe.

PUBLIC OPINION AND ORAL CULTURE

According to a soldier fighting in Chile in the 1640s, war had become debatable ("se ha hecho openable").[109] Indeed, war and the people who waged it were at the center of early modern forms of publicity and political discussion since the first moments of the military revolution. Massimo Rospocher has shown, in a series of important essays, the richness of the popular public sphere in the cities of Renaissance Italy.[110] The business of war was, not surprisingly, the main object of public discussion all throughout the peninsula, whether in the papers being written, printed, sold, bought, and sung in the streets of Venice or in Pasquino's anonymous posts loudly echoing the public voices of Rome. Popular poetry provided a language of political communication that circulated widely, though ephemerally, through a diversity of discursive practices, from mouth to mouth, to manuscript or print reproduction and dissemination. "Nowadays everybody discusses war" (hor tutto'l mondo di guerra raggiona), said an anonymous popular poet in 1509 Venice.[111]

Spanish sources confirm Rospocher's emphasis on the matter of war as the main topic of early modern popular opinion and public discourse. The account of the battle of Pavia by common soldier Oznaya makes reference to Pasquino's facetious coverage of the Wars of Italy. "The imperial army," writes Oznaya, "was ignored to the point that a paper appeared one morning on Maese Pasquino: 'Whoever knows anything about the Emperor's camp, which got lost in the mountains of Genoa a few days ago, please reveal it and he will be rewarded'" (Era tan poco el caso que del ejército cesáreo se hacía, que en este tiempo amanesció puesta una cédula en el Pasquino de Roma deste tenor: "Quien quiera que supiese del campo del emperador, el cual se perdió entre las montañas de la ribera de Génova pocos días ha, véngalo manifestando y darle han buen hallazgo"). A few days later, after a successful military campaign for the imperial camp, Pasquino mockingly announced that the imperial army had finally appeared.[112] High-ranking Spanish officials in Italy also showed an acute interest in street rumors related to the matters of war. Charles V's ambassador in Rome, Luis de Ávila y Zúñiga, wrote in December 1539 to Francisco de los Cobos, the emperor's secretary, that he was surprised by the fact that Pasquino could only produce positive gossip about one of the most prestigious imperial generals in the Wars of Italy, Alfonso de Ávalos (1502–46), Marquis of Vasto.[113] Pasquino, the Roman machine of popular rumor and political opinion, had been interested in the business of war ever since the battered statue was unearthed from the underground of Renaissance Rome.

Pasquino's ways traveled easily to the New World. After the conquest of Tenochtitlán, the soldiers and their captains engaged in disputes over the division of the spoils, and consequently disruptive rumors (*murmuración*) emerged about Cortés's justice toward his subordinates. Although Bernal Díaz does not go as far as other soldiers in accusing the captain of keeping the gold treasure for himself, he records the episode: "While Cortés was in Coyoacán lodging in some palaces that had their walls plastered and white-washed on which it was easy to write with charcoal and other inks, numerous rather malicious sentences (*motes*) appeared [on them] every morning, some written in prose and others in verse, in the way of pasquinades" (Y como Cortés estaba en Coyoacán y posaba en unos palacios que tenía blanqueadas y encaladas las paredes, donde buenamente se podía escribir en ellas con carbones y con otras tintas, amanecía cada mañana escritos muchos motes, algunos en prosa y otros en metros, algo maliciosos, a manera de mase-pasquines).[114] Bernal readily summarizes some of these *coplas*—or traditional

Spanish octosyllabic stanzas rhyming in consonant—but refuses to reproduce them because most of them contained "words that cannot be put in this story" (palabras que no son para poner en esta relación). First Cortés took pride in answering the accusations "by good rhymes much to the point" (por buenos consonantes y muy a propósito) since the captain "was something of a poet himself" (era algo poeta). When the *coplas* became too impudent, Cortés famously wrote "a blank wall is the paper of fools" (pared blanca, papel de necios), to which the restless soldiers replied: "and of wise men and of truths and His Majesty will soon know it" (aun de sabios y verdades, y Su Majestad lo sabrá muy presto). Cortés ended up threatening the satirists with serious punishment.[115]

Ballad singing and writing were pervasive in the soldiers' everyday practices in the New World and contributed to the rapid circulation of military news. Among Pizarro's men, one Saravia used satirical circumstantial *coplas* in his correspondence with conquistador Pascual de Andagoya. The improvisational skills and malicious use of traditional ballads and songs by the caustic Francisco de Carvajal—a feared old veteran soldier and field marshal of Gonzalo Pizarro during Peru's civil wars in the late 1540s—were proverbial. Lope de Aguirre's seemingly demential rebellion gave way to the composition of new songs usually recorded in writing by other soldiers, such as Gonzalo de Zúñiga.[116]

In the wildly rich narrative world of Juan de Castellanos's *Elegías de varones ilustres*, a voluminous epic history mostly on the conquest of New Granada, the author praises his longtime friend and veteran Lorenzo Martín, a commoner like the author himself, as an accomplished poet in the old Castilian style. Famous for his "gracias y facecias," Castellanos tells us, Martín intends to cheer up the melancholic survivors of starvation during an expedition to the New Granadan northwest by reciting a "stream of improvised *redondillas*" (torrents / de coplas redondillas repentinas), of which Castellanos reproduces only six that someone copied for him. Martín's oral stanzas poke fun at some of his famished comrades, one of whom has just devoured with delight a tallow candle. Their clothes have grown large at the same rate that their bodies shrank; the stumbling movement of the undernourished is likened to a *gambeta* dance; their napes are all peels (*hollejos*); and their empty bowels happily sing *villancicos*, a form of Castilian popular verse. Martín resorts to the eschatological humor so dear to Renaissance culture, popular or otherwise, to laugh at some comrades who cannot stop farting after sustaining themselves with only leaves of the *bihao* plant for two weeks. The sacrifice of the conquering soldier, which in most instances bestows honor and legitimacy upon the bodies and voices of the empire's agents, is carnivalized here with a Rabelaisian degrading imagery of popular and oral stock.[117]

The soldiers' republic of letters, its peculiar publicity, was built upon a complex interaction between the spoken and the written word. The production, circulation, and consumption of soldierly writing should not be dissociated from the many forms of oral speech that constituted everyday military sociability in the spaces of war. A rich, tumultuous oral culture, constantly intersecting with its written forms, emerges when we look at the sources. Bragging, cursing, arguing, joking, gossiping, conversing, and even "speaking soldier" (hablar a lo soldado), among other oral practices that shaped their public identity, are crucial for understanding not only the social lives of the common men-at-arms but also their literary and political culture.[118] Francisco de Quevedo referred to the soldiers' jargon as "lengua soldada" in *La vida del Buscón* and the petitioning soldier who accompanies Pablos on his way to Segovia considered cursing and swearing the very substance of the soldier's profession. Informal conversation about recent battles, or about ancient warfare for that matter, arose in every corner of their makeshift encampments. Epistles exchanged among fellow soldiers deployed on different fronts finish conversations that started in the same trench. Ballads created or improvised after the heat of the battle are sent to friends or to potential printers, who in turn distribute them as widely circulated pliegos de cordel. Traveling bisoños disseminate political rumor from the court, while the returning veteran brings the latest military news from the battlefield to the streets of Seville or Madrid. Collective criticism of the commanders' strategy by their subordinates could start in the camarade's shared tent and end up reaching the streets of Milan in the form of a satirical pamphlet. "The fluid, transitional nature of communication in the sixteenth century" between the written and the spoken word also applied to the discursive practices of the soldiers' republic of letters.[119]

Throughout his military career as infantry captain and castellan of Capua, Marcos de Isaba wrote a series of "papers," as he called them, that were collected with the goal of "getting the military back to the good order and discipline it used to have" (la Milicia torne a la buena diciplina que solía tener) and published in 1594 under the title *Cuerpo enfermo de la milicia española*.[120] To open his examination of the history of warfare and empire, Isaba refers to the frequent discussions that took place orally in the social spaces of the professional soldiery: "In their everyday conversations, those soldiers who are somewhat curious wonder about what was the origin of ancient soldiering, who first went out to conquer, and where were arms invented for the first time" (En plática se trata cada día entre gente de guerra un poco curiosa, sobre el principio de la milicia antigua, por saber quiénes y cuáles y dónde fueron los primeros que salieron a conquistar y dónde fue la primera invención de las armas).[121] The discursive formation of "the matters of war" is thus constituted not only by the texts written by fighting and witnessing soldiers but also by their everyday, informal, oral communicative practices. More important, the tools and technologies of their professional trade are not isolated from the history and politics of empire in Isaba's discourse. For Isaba, accustomed to the long sieges and bloody battles of the Italian Wars, the wars of the past were occasional, short, and usually clement with the vanquished. Eventually, however, "kingdoms and senates and empires with many provinces were formed, and they invented many kinds of weapons," including "gunpowder and artillery, arquebuses, muskets, mines, fire trumpets, bombards and many other instruments" (después formándose reinos y senados e imperios de tantas provincias como hay en él, inventaron otros muchos géneros de armas . . . pólvora y artillería, arcabuces, mosquetes, minas, morteretes, trompas de fuego y tanto género de instrumentos) that made wars longer, more cruel, and unjust.[122] For this and other soldiers who engaged in the professional *pláticas* of their trade, military technology and imperial expansion were inextricably linked. Equally familiar with the material realities of war and with the political and practical reason derived from years of service in different imperial fronts, the soldiers of the republic placed the politics and history of warfare at the center of their verbal exchanges. The technicalities of the business of war were inextricably linked to the political history of empire, to its legitimacy and its limits.

Military speech, whether in writing or in oral form, proved time and again to be dangerous for the political elites of the empire. Military authorities were thus always concerned about the vitality of the soldiers' verbal practices and repeatedly tried to curtail the proliferation of words about the matters of war. Open criticism of the decisions, strategies, and general policies of the military high command and the imperial political authorities was frequent both in the civil public sphere and in the soldiers' conversations. In many cases, this criticism was tolerated and channeled through certain genres, institutions, and practices that helped temper and integrate them in official discourse. But more often than not, soldierly *pláticas* were rowdy and untamable. The soldiers' public sphere was a tumultuous and noisy space for the exchange of war news, satire, panegyric, and rumor, where consent and dissent were negotiated between the military and civilian authorities and the soldierly mass.

Let us pause for a moment at a soldierly exchange that shows the complex interaction between private and public, oral and written communication, and of tolerated and intolerable talk in the soldierly republic of letters. In 1568, Jerónimo de Arbolanche and Sancho de Londoño corresponded about Charles V's imperial defeat in Metz against the French in 1552—public discussion about military matters could last for years after the campaigns had ended. At Metz, an imperial army of 55,000 led by Charles V tried to recover the city, garrisoned with 5,800 French soldiers after Henri II occupied it in the summer of 1552. The siege lasted from October of that year to January 1553, ending in a calamitous defeat for the emperor that left many dead mostly from cold, hunger, and disease. As we will see, the high number of casualties and the abandonment of those who were sick and wounded in the fields seem to have generated a heated debate among the troops.[123]

Jerónimo de Arbolanche was very likely a commoner from Tudela, Navarre, known in literary history as the author of the long and now forgotten antiquarian poem *Las Abidas*, which deals with the mythical prehistoric past of Spain. What has remained unknown even to his biographers is that he was also a soldier serving in the Sicilian tercio of Alba's army and that he was mobilized in the 1567 long march to the Netherlands by the Spanish road.[124] Sancho de Londoño, a minor nobleman from La Rioja, has always been considered by military historians as one of the finest soldiers and officers of the sixteenth century, a counselor to the 3rd Duke of Alba, Fernando Álvarez de Toledo, and the general (*maestre de campo*) of the Lombardy tercio. His poetic activities, however, have remained completely unknown to cultural historians.[125] The poetic exchange of these two "íntimo[s] amigo[s]"—as Londoño himself refers to their relationship—is exemplary of the production and circulation of public opinion about

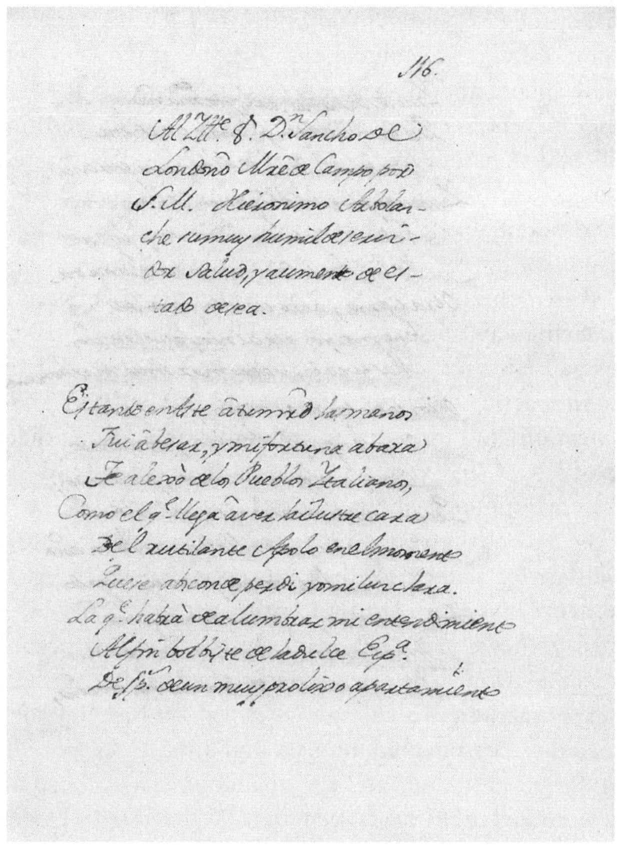

Figure 3. *Poesías del Maestre de Campo don Sancho de Londoño.* BNE, Mss/21738, 116r.

military and political matters in the social spaces of professional warfare.[126] Jerónimo de Arbolanche's epistle is in Italian tercets, written from Brussels with the usual bitter tone of war lyric, and offers a vivid depiction of the hasty daily life of a common soldier walking the Spanish road:

> ¡Cuán miserable es la vida del soldado!
> Estaba el tercio en Malta ahora ha un año
> y está en Brabante ya muy sosegado.
> Todos nosotros, si yo no me engaño,
> temíamos salir de Lombardía
> para emprender camino tan estraño.[127]

(How miserable is the soldier's life! One year ago, I was in the Malta
tercio and now we are in Brabant, peacefully. If I am not deceived, we
were all scared of leaving Lombardy to walk this unfamiliar road.)

In his epistle, Arbolanche tries to convince Londoño to write a poem
about the epic feats of their general and the latter's patron, the great
Duke of Alba.[128] What captures the commander's attention in Arbolanche's letter, however, is a passing reference to the French city of
Metz on the army's way to Brabant, a fleeting mention that would
prompt Londoño to offer a response several times longer than his
friend's motivating epistle:

Que a Mez no vimos, quizá porque pena
no nos causase ver su ancha campaña
de blancos huesos de españoles llena.[129]

(We did not see Metz, perhaps to avoid the grief of seeing its wide
surrounding countryside whitened by Spanish bones.)

With his hyperbolic metonymy about the Spanish bones covering the
field, Arbolanche is obviously referring to the high number of casualties at Metz. More than fifteen years after the siege, the place was still
marked in the memory of the soldiers by the carnage of 1552, and a
soldier serving in the Sicilian tercio and walking the Spanish road on
their way to Flanders could not help mentioning it in a letter to a more
veteran soldier who would walk the same road in a different contingent a few weeks later.

In his reply, Londoño recounts the details of the military campaign
of Metz from the perspective of a captain in charge of a company of
arquebusiers, reserving for himself a leading role in every strategic
development, praising Alba, and making veiled references to other
officers he considers responsible for the defeat because they did not
follow his advice. Yet for the veteran commander, the main intent of
his letter is to "uproot such an error" (desarraigar tan mal concepto)
about the number of victims by contrasting the army's muster rolls
and the number of fallen soldiers of his own company with those
circulating in informal soldierly *pláticas*, which he intends to prove
false. Londoño points out, by the end of his epistle, that "the talk was
started" (se ha la plática movido) by "so many bad poems" (tantas trovas mal trovadas) that it is difficult to set the count straight in the public's perception of the events.[130] Participating soldiers and witnesses
generated a substantial body of discourse and opinion that circulated
publicly, mostly in verse, and that Londoño aims at disavowing in

the soldierly public sphere.[131] Oral and written pláticas fed each other in a fluid interaction that oftentimes confronts the official narrative about specific military events or about the nature and limits of war and empire in general. As if he did not want to contribute to the noise of the soldierly public opinion, he instructs his friend Arbolanche to destroy his own poetic letters: "Once read, sir, I beg you to tear them apart" (Que leídas las rompáis, señor, os pido).[132] Londoño signed his letter "in Liexa, without Mars and without Apollo / . . . lacking everything that we long for, / this year of sixty eight, / except for reading and writing" (quedo en Liexa sin Marte y sin Apolo / . . . sin cuanto, en fin, por bien se procura / este año de sesenta y ocho quedo / excepto la lección y la escriptura).[133] The reproduction of the soldierly republic of letters, favored by the military otium of peacetime, herein remains assured, and the complex interplay between oral and written modes of textual production and exchange, a determining feature of the soldiers' literary culture, is clearly in evidence.

Class tensions within the army, a constant source of pláticas about the matters of war, may have also been at play in the public discussions and soldierly *trovas* about what happened in Metz and in Arbolanche and Londoño's private exchange about it. According to the famous French surgeon Ambroise Paré, present at the siege of Metz, the Duke of Alba "declared to the Emperor that the souldiers dyed dayly, yet, more than the number of two hundred, and that there was but little hope to enter into the Citty." The emperor then asked whether his men dying under the walls of the sieged city "were gentlemen of remarke or quality," to which Alba replied that "they were all poore souldiers." Charles V's reply was quite crude: "Then, sayd he, it makes no matter if they dye, comparing them to caterpillers and grashoppers, which eate the buddes of the earth. And if they were of any fashion, they would not bee in the campe for twelve shillings the month."[134] The anecdote may very well be false, particularly considering that Paré spoke from the other side of the front line, but it does remind us that class and rank indeed structured the production, distribution, and consumption of soldierly pláticas. And it confirms the existence of different memories about military events, of competing—many times irreconcilable—views and values about war and soldiering.

Whether or not the emperor ever uttered such harsh words, common soldiers had many reasons to share their discontent about the military and political superiors who governed their republic. The everyday conversations described by Isaba, Arbolanche, and Londoño could easily be transformed into illicit forms of speech that could go far beyond the limits when criticizing royal policies. It was precisely Sancho de Londoño who made the first systematic effort to discipline speech within the soldiers' republic. His widely read military treatise, *Discurso sobre la forma de reducir la disciplina militar a meyor y antiguo estado*, which would be repeatedly copied, imitated, and extracted during the last decades of the sixteenth century, was requested by and dedicated to the Duke of Alba in 1568, and it included a well-known set of military ordinances that give us a glimpse of the soldiers' daily life while in camp, marching, or in battle.[135] Interestingly, many of these dispositions regulating a wide range of soldierly everyday practices, most notably drinking, whoring, and gambling, were driven by the authorities' concern about the limits of legitimate speech in the spaces of war and were aimed at controlling what soldiers could and could not say. One of the often-mentioned liberties of soldierly life was the possibility of engaging in legal gambling. Illegal gambling, however, was forbidden because "it provokes curses, blasphemies, and swearing" (reniegos, blasfemias y juramentos), and military commanders and treatise writers agreed that "no soldier shall blaspheme or curse" (ningún soldado reniegue ni blasfeme).[136] Blasphemy, not a minor fault in civil society as it could be charged and punished by the Inquisition, was more tolerated among soldiers, for whom swearing was just one more component of their public personae, a form of *bizarría*, according to Bernardo de Vargas Machuca, a soldier in the Americas.[137]

Bizarría was mix of dash, proud daring, arrogant gallantry, and military discipline, all publicly displayed in a combination of gestural demeanor, verbal manners, and dressing habits—a certain bodily *hexis*, that is, a "pattern of postures that is both individual and systematic [social], because linked to a whole system of techniques involving the body and tools, and charged with a host of social meanings and values."[138] It defined a whole behavioral pattern that was ultimately the essence of the soldierly habitus of the new war. Veteran colonial soldier Santiago de Tesillo warned Chilean *bisoños* against their hurry to become *pláticos* and *bizarros*, "since they think that one becomes a soldier just by enrolling; the drum sounds, they sign their names, loosen their cloaks, change the way they walk, they dally and threaten, and they think that is all they need to be soldiers" (pues piensan que no hay más que entrar a ser soldados y serlo desde luego.

Suena la caja, concurren, asientan plaza, sueltan la capa y mudan el paso, galantean y desgarran, sin presumir por necesaria otra circunstancia).[139] The authorities' concern, however, was not only about the soldiers' morality and devotion. There is a thin line between *bizarro* blasphemy and swearing, and the kind of "scandalous words" that, according to Londoño's warning, "may cause tumult and mutiny" (palabras escandalosas de las cuales puede causarse tumulto o motín). Anyone uttering them or covering up a brother-in-arms who does so was to be punished with immediate death.[140] Similarly, the main reason for banning heavy drinking does not seem to lie in moral concerns about the soldiers' temperance or in doubts about its effects on their professional performance in camp and battle. Rather, intemperate drinking was again prosecuted because too much wine "turns men into beasts and with its heat they dare to say certain words that provoke mutinies, and new sects and opinions" (vienen los hombres a convertirse en fieras y con el calor osan decir palabras bastantes a motines y a nuevas sectas y opiniones).[141]

All these mandates regarding the most basic aspects of soldierly daily life are aimed at disciplining speech by regulating what could and could not be spoken. Londoño's public ordinances, like his private correspondence, suggest the existence of a rich—and dangerous— public culture in the republic of soldiers, one that often intersected with the civilian spaces of political communication and that threatened the most basic structures of imperial armies. Military authorities had every interest in trying to effectively curb potentially subversive talk and the circulation of unsettling news, opinions, and ideas in the discursive community of the *plático* soldiers. The most explicit of Londoño's regulations to control the serious threat posed by the informal constitution of popular spheres of soldierly public opinion orders that "there shall not be secret gatherings or public coteries, because that is where mutinies are formed and they conjecture about what has been discussed in secret by the military command, from which many times the enemy is warned and the defenders of posts are discouraged" (que no haya juntas secretas ni corrillos públicos, porque en los tales se fabrican los motines y se trata por conjecturas de cuanto pasa en los consejos secretos, de que procede avisar a los enemigos para que se aperciban y muchas veces desaniman a los que tienen cargos de defender fortalezas).[142]

In 1590, the conquistador Bernardo de Vargas Machuca, like a New World Londoño, wrote his *Milicia indiana*, a military treatise intended to describe the different modes of colonial warfare and to discipline the soldiers of the American conquest wars accordingly. For Vargas Machuca, the ideal soldier should never be "gossipy and restless" (revoltoso ni chismoso), "vices that most of the time engender mutiny" (destos vicios las más veces se suele engendrar un motín). Again, the informal institution of the *camarada*, which both Londoño and Vargas Machuca explicitly encouraged in their treatises, seems to have given coverage to political gossip and soldierly public opinion. The good soldier, according to Vargas Machuca, "should not save the face of even his own comrade if he sees him going against the king" (a la misma camarada no debe guardar la cara si viere que va contra el rey).[143] For Pedro de Valdivia, the (failed) conquistador of Chile, "pláticas" had an intrinsically negative, subversive sense. Pressed to rebel against his king by some conspirers in Peru, he was forced to respond "to those who moved these talks" (a los que me movían estas pláticas)."[144] "Mutiny" is etymologically related to the verb *to move*, and *pláticas*, in this context, can only mean subversive talk.

The same practices that were institutionalized and encouraged by military authorities in order to foster and strengthen the soldierly ethos and military morale could easily transform themselves into illicit forms of organization. Camaradas could turn into "secret reunions" (juntas secretas) and "public gatherings" (corrillos públicos).[145] These social spaces constituted by the circulation of political and military opinions, by conversations about their trade, also allowed for the production and dissemination of dangerous *pláticas*. While it provided the basis for the esprit de corps that military administrators and strategists valued so highly, oral and written culture in the soldiers' republic also contributed to a great extent to the articulation of resistance and to the constitution of a collective identity for the soldierly mass that was oftentimes at odds with the aims and methods of the administrators of imperial war. And soldierly unrest could easily travel back home to threaten even the most sacred institutions of early modern Spain. In 1579, *alférez* don Fernando Díaz, a veteran of Flanders, and Juan de Minaya Maldonado started a conversation about "whether it was easy or not to kill a king" while strolling through the streets of Ledesma, in Salamanca. Someone must have overheard the conversation and reported them to the authorities: "Don Fernando said that he had just come from the court, complaining about not being given the post he expected by his majesty the king, whom he wanted to kill although he did not know how" (Dijo don Fernando que venía de la corte quejoso de su majestad e que le deseaba matar e que no sabía cómo lo hacer porque no le había proveído con cargo a su gusto para la guerra).[146]

As we have discussed, the written and the spoken word interacted in a complex regime of publicity that was constitutive of the society of soldiers. The republic of curious soldiers, or any republic for that matter, was hardly a harmonious one. The class tensions that inhered the spaces of war could eventually generate conflict and subversive attempts, particularly from the subaltern sectors of that society. One of Sancho de Londoño's most detailed dispositions was meant to keep track of the soldiers' handwriting in order to control the proliferating practice of mutiny:

> Otrosí por excusar los motines y los medios que se usan para move-llos y cuajallos, se debe mandar que todos los Capitanes cuando reci-bieren los soldados, entiendan si saben escrebir y hagan que los que los [sic] supieren, escriban sus nombres y los de sus padres, madres y tierras en un libro que cada furrier tenga para tal efecto, con lo cual en gran parte se excusará el poner de los carteles, pues pocos saben disimular tan bien su letra que en algo no conforme y se pueda co-noscer, teniendo cómo poder cotejarla, que pocos en tales casos se osan fiar de otros.[147]

> (In order to avoid mutinies and the means they use to organize them successfully, all captains must inquire if the soldiers they enlist know how to write; and those who do, must write their names and the names of their fathers, mothers and homelands in a book kept by the quartermasters. With this we will avoid the hanging of posters, since very few know how to dissimulate their handwriting to the point of becoming unrecognizable, and we will be able to collate it, since in these cases they never trust anyone else to write them.)

Both the practice of the mutiny *cartel* or poster and the authorities' effort to suppress it insist upon the spread of literacy within the army: there were enough literate infantry soldiers to force military authori-ties to keep track of them in the quartermasters' (*furrieres*) books. Writing was a valuable skill for the captains and other officers who were in charge of administering and disciplining an infantry com-pany but also for rank-and-file, potentially mutinous soldiers. It was instrumental, as we have seen, in the organization of imperial armies, a crucial technology to sustain the structures upon which the defense and expansion of empire relied. But as Londoño knew all too well, writing also allowed for the organization of the social and political resistance previously, and simultaneously, articulated in the soldiers' oral practices.

Londoño's regulation tellingly speaks to the complex relation between the discursive practices, written and oral, and the political culture of the soldiers. But more important, it stands as an illuminating metaphor of the power of writing in relation to the practices of imperial war, showing that literacy enabled subversion. However conventional in the rhetoric of dedications and preliminary poems, the contiguity of the pen and the sword was potentially dangerous. Just as literate soldiers could help start a mutiny and disturb imperial practice on the field, they could also tell and read stories that voiced some of the exploitative conditions under which they worked or challenge the basic tenets and goals of imperial practice and discourse.

The Truth About War

ROLDÁN AND THE KING OF FRANCE

In one of the most spectacular military events of the century, Charles V's imperial troops famously captured the French king Francis I at the battle of Pavia in February 1525. Juan de Oznaya, a common infantryman who participated in this and other campaigns of the Wars of Italy (1494–1559), recounted in 1544 how some rank-and-file Spanish soldiers had the chance, while they marched after the battle, to chat with the most powerful monarch in Christian Europe:[1]

> En esto llegó un soldado español arcabucero, llamado Roldán, y bien se le podía llamar por su esfuerzo. Traía dos pelotas de plata y una de oro de su arcabuz, en la mano; y llegado al rey, le dice: "Señor, Vuestra Alteza sepa que ayer cuando supe que la batalla se había de dar, yo hice seis pelotas de plata para vuestros Mosiores, y la de oro para vos. De las de plata, las cuatro yo creo que fueron bien empleadas, porque no las eché sino para sayo de brocado o carmesí. Otras muchas de plomo he tirado por ahí a gente común; musiores no topé más, por esto me sobraron dos de las suyas. La de oro véisla aquí y agradecedme la buena voluntad, que deseaba daros la más honrosa muerte que a príncipe se ha dado, pero pues no quiso Dios que en la batalla os viese, tomalda para ayuda a vuestro rescate, que ocho ducados pesa; una onza tiene." El rey tendió la mano y la tomó, y le dijo que le agradescía el deseo que había tenido y más la obra que en darle la pelota hacía.[2]

> (And then there arrived a Spanish soldier, an arquebusier named Roldán, a truly fitting name for such a valiant man. He came to the king carrying in his hand two bullets made of silver and one of

gold, and he told him: "Lord, your highness should know that when I found out yesterday that the battle would take place today, I cast six silver bullets for your noble vassals and one of gold for yourself. I believe I made good use of four out of six silver bullets, for I fired them into gilded brocade and crimson shirts. I fired off many others, made of lead, towards the common people, because I could not come across more noblemen, and thus I have two left. But this gold one right here (you should thank my goodwill) I saved to ensure you the most honorable death that a prince has ever received. God did not want me to see you during the battle, so here you go, have it and count it as my contribution to your ransom, for it is one ounce, worth eight ducats!" The king took it in his hand and retorted that he was grateful for his thoughtfulness, but even more than that he appreciated receiving the bullet in that fashion.)

When collated with other available sources, Oznaya's seems like a remarkably rich and reliable historical account of the watershed imperial victory at Pavia. The factual accuracy of his war story about his comrade Roldán, however, is harder to assess—if not completely off. It resembles too closely the structure of the facetiae and apothegms so dear to learned humanists and popular audiences alike during the Renaissance. But it also resonates with many war stories that, orally or in writing, circulated in the soldiers' republic of letters. For modern readers, it may seem hard to believe that a soldier would spend over two months' worth of salary in making a gold bullet, but the rituals of early modern warfare and the codes of soldierly gallantry or *bizarría* could potentially explain the soldier's liberal, cavalier attitude. Regardless of the actual factuality of the episode, however, Oznaya would probably agree with his modern counterpart, the Vietnam veteran and fiction writer Tim O'Brien: "I had to make up a few things, but listen, it's still true."[3]

Indeed, Oznaya's apothegmatic anecdote reveals many of the truths about modern warfare with which Renaissance authors had to come to terms. Roldán's actions and sayings distill a mix of respect and contempt for his betters—no other than the king of France and his most noble vassals—that is characteristic of the popular soldierly ethos in early modern Europe. The use of a distinctly oral register and a somewhat debased idiom of vassalage to blatantly address his superiors is peculiar to the linguistic behavior of the plático soldiers, as was the playful quipping about the rather serious matter of killing and dying in battle. The commoner's pride in having slaughtered a bunch of noblemen not in single chivalric combat but with his arquebus, the most plebeian of weapons, is indicative of the shocking effects that the military revolution had on previous beliefs, attitudes, and practices of warfare. The truth about war was that in Pavia, on February 25, 1525, a plebeian Spanish rank-and-file soldier could have shot down the king of France—whether the bullet was made of gold or lead, whether Oznaya's story happened as he recounted it or otherwise. Eight ducats, two months of the arquebusier's salary: that was the price of the king's life for Roldán, and that was Roldán's insolent contribution to his ransom. The truth about war was that the new military technologies and tactics had forever altered the social logics of warfare and of its representation.

Roldán is a somewhat unlikely name for a Spaniard of the time in any of its variants, but it must have surely been a common nickname for soldiers, either seriously extolling military attributes or ironically mocking excessive bravado. Whether real or fictional, the name of this particular character reveals the extent to which the *matière de France*, as contained in both Spanish *romances*, or ballads, and Italian *romanzi*, or narrative chivalric poems, had penetrated the spaces of the early modern soldiery. Yet Oznaya's war story also strongly emphasizes the distance between Roland, the medieval paladin unfailingly loyal to the king of the Franks, and Roldán, the Spanish plebeian arquebusier trying to kill him—and arrogantly giving him some change for his ransom. The narrative and ideological order of epic, the most time-enduring discursive frame to narrate warfare, has been definitely and radically transformed.

Roldán, the Spanish arquebusier, also contrasts sharply with the most famous reincarnation of his namesake in the days of the battle of Pavia. Cantos 9 and 11 of Ariosto's 1532 edition of *Orlando furioso* fictionalized the revolting effects that gunpowder had for the chivalric imagination of European aristocracy. Cimosco, king of Frisia, used against Count Orlando a "strange new weapon."[4] The arquebus is in Ariosto's fiction a hellish invention of some northern, aggressive tyrant, and it will take Orlando himself to throw it into the ocean, so that no one could ever recover it: "that never more a cavalier may be / advantaged by your aid, nor evil gain." A legendary necromancer, however, would retrieve "the infernal machine" with a spell. The arquebus, which stands, metonymically, for the radical transformation of warfare in the first moments of the military revolution, is alien to the referential universe of *romanzo* fiction. The genre can only rationalize it by tracing a mythical genealogy that vaguely refers to the historical invention. But the moral condemnation of gunpowder as the destroyer of individual valor and chivalric heroism had deep social implications. The fraudulent weapon of lowly cowards, the arquebus was associated with the plebeianization and massification of the early modern army, and thus it shook the ground of the nobility's most powerful legitimations as the exclusive practitioners of the noble art of war. As it happened in Pavia, the "brutta invenzïon" had indeed revolutionized the social logics of warfare: "How many lords, alas! How many more / among the bravest of our cavaliers / have died and still must perish in this war / by which you brought the world to bitter tears / and Italy left stricken to the core?" (Per te son giti et anderan sotterra / tanti signori e cavallieri tanti / prima che sia finita questa guerra / che'l mondo, ma più Italia, ha messo in pianti).[5] The resistance against the gunpowder revolution in the aristocratic imagination of the age can be found everywhere outside Ariosto's fiction. In 1536, for instance, one nobleman from Valencia challenged a peer to a duel, accusing his rival of having schemed "to have some lowly people shoot their arquebuses," and was utterly outraged for "those things do not belong among gentlemen" (concertar de tirar arcabuces por medio de bellacos . . . tales cosas no han de caber en caballeros).[6]

When rewriting his poem for his 1532 edition, when Ariosto added to the princeps (1516) the series of episodes on Olimpia that contained the story about Cimosco's arquebus, the poet might have indeed been reacting to the shock of Pavia, as condensed in Oznaya's anecdote about Roldán. The battle of Pavia has long been considered a turning point in the military, political, and even social history of early modern Europe, the climax of the Italian Wars.[7] The engagement represented, at the military level, the ultimate triumph of a professional army based on the massive use of infantry companies of pikemen and arquebusiers over a fighting force still relying too much on the heavy cavalry of men-at-arms for which the French were famous. From a political point of view, the young and ambitious Charles of Habsburg achieved a crucial victory over his main continental rival, a victory that would break with the Italian—and thus European—hegemony of the Valois. Finally, Pavia would be remembered during the sixteenth century for having dramatically changed values and beliefs about the social consequences and meaning of warfare. Contemporary witnesses and modern historians often noted how plebeian infantrymen like Roldán, making good use of the gunpowder revolution, had slaughtered the crème of the French nobility. An army of Roldanes overpowered and killed the old Orlandos. When in the battle of Pavia gunpowder weapons became "the arbiter of battles and sieges," many longstanding assumptions on war were shattered.[8]

Many of Ariosto's contemporaries and successors reacted in a similar fashion to the social (and national) dangers of gunpowder and firearms. Sebastián de Covarrubias devoted four long columns and more than two pages to the *arcabuz* entry in his dictionary *Tesoro de la lengua castellana*, quoting extensively from *Orlando furioso*.[9] A religious man of letters, Covarrubias apologized for "not having followed the career of arms, but of spirit" (porque no he seguido la milicia . . . heme criado en la espiritual) and thus for the potential inaccuracies of a layman's definition.[10] His humanistic, antiquarian impulse does not prevent him from giving firearms a mythical origin that would go back to the medieval fantastic chivalric world as imagined by Renaissance poetic fiction but that would find continuity in Iberian history: "The first time that firearms were used in Spain was in the siege of Algeciras in the year of 1344, when king Alfonso XI conquered it from the Moors, who fired into our people from the fortress" (La primera vez que en España se usaron los tiros de pólvora con pelotas de hierro fue en el cerco de Algezira, cuando el rey don Alonso el Onceno la ganó de los moros, año de mil y trecientos y cuarenta y cuatro, que los de dentro tiraban a los nuestros).[11] If for Ariosto, gunpowder weapons were a hellish invention from the barbaric north that was ravaging the flowers of Italian civilization in the days of the "horrendous wars," for Covarrubias they had their origin in Spain's Muslim, equally barbaric south. The lexicographer adds ethnic overtones to the class markers of the staple technology of the military revolution, contributing to its moral and social dismissal, while grudgingly acknowledging the weapon's supremacy in Europe's military battlefields. The word *arcabuz*, he says, is composed of "the Greek *archos*, princeps" and "*buso* or cannon, for this is the prince and lord of all weapons and there is none that can compare to it" (por ser este *buso*, o cañón, príncipe y señor de toda cualquiera arma y que no hay ninguna que se le pueda comparar).[12]

Soldiers like Roldán and his princely plebeian weapon would indeed rule over the wars of early modernity, as well as their literary representations. The arquebusiers who killed throngs of noblemen in Pavia significantly altered aristocratic conceptions of warfare and made a durable impact on the cultural memory of this class and their intellectuals. The gun, as Michael Murrin rightly pointed out, "posed a problem for the writers of romance," but the popular soldiery of

Spain's army enthusiastically embraced it, in their professional practice and in the stories they told themselves.[13] In the 1560s, a group of Spanish soldiers not dissimilar from Oznaya or Roldán set out to write in verse the wars of the monarchy of Spain. And they did so in a particularly innovative form of epic poetry that emerged in Spain in the second half of the sixteenth century. By focusing on the place that Italy and the wars that ravaged it in the first half of the sixteenth century had in the literary culture of the plático soldiers, I will discuss contrasting kinds of heroic discourse that made different claims about the nature, the goals, the ethics, and the social logics of warfare. I will also attempt to explore the social distribution of different heroic traditions within the army and the emergence of new epic forms that better fit the concerns and aspirations of the popular soldiery.

THE ROMANCE OF ITALY

The impact that the Wars of Italy had on the cultural production of both Italy and Spain can hardly be overemphasized. Italy was in every sense the alpha and omega of the soldiers' lives, the desired destination for fresh Castilian recruits, the object of longing for Flanders' veterans, the center, if there was one, of the military machinery and the political imagination of imperial Spain. The Italian experience determined the soldiers' linguistic practices, models of heroism, international relations of friendship, solidarity, and patronage, their desires and aspirations. Garcilaso, the father of all soldier-poets in Renaissance Spain, yearned for Naples, "once full of leisure and love" (de ocio y d'amor antiguamente llena), while traveling the roads and inns of France.[14] Cervantes's nostalgia, or desire, for Italy glimmers between the lines of *El licenciado Vidriera*, and for its main character, soldier Tomás Rodaja, Italy stands for pleasure, freedom, opportunity, and bounty.[15] Pedro de Valdivia, a veteran of the Italian Wars, persisted in the use of Italianisms and Italian proverbial idioms well after he became the first European settler of Chile in the remotest frontier of the empire.[16]

The glittering pleasures of Italy would eventually become a problem for military administrators. According to the Duke of Parma, a commander in the army of Flanders, "a Spanish soldier who had never breathed the air of Italy served better in the Netherlands than two who had, because they never lost the desire to return."[17] More important, Italy is the crucial crossroads in the itineraries of soldierly literary culture. It was the academy and university of the soldiers' republic of letters. Naples, Rome, and Milan were at least as important nodes as Madrid, Valencia, and Seville in the cultural networks of the writing soldiers. The Spanish garrisons of Italian cities and towns became spaces of cultural production, distribution, and consumption. Italian linguistic and literary practices, it has long been recognized, shaped to a large extent Spanish Golden Age culture; yet more important for the argument developed here, soldiers were among the key agents of this cultural exchange and cross-fertilization.[18]

The two peninsulas had long been politically connected on the upper side of their respective societies. By the early sixteenth century, Aragonese aristocratic families had intermarried with their Italian counterparts since the times of Alfons el Magnànim, and some Castilian lineages established solid alliances with Roman, Lombard, Genoese, or Neapolitan patricians. Aragonese and Castilian kings accompanied their aggressive military policies with strategic patronage and local alliances. The Iberian elites in charge of administering the Habsburg "soft" or informal empire in Italy were often fluent in Italian and Spanish or Catalan, if not fully bicultural. The Spanish courtier and veteran general Luis de Ávila y Zúñiga was at ease going back and forth between Italian and Spanish. He oftentimes code-switched between the two languages in his witty, facetious correspondence with Spanish officials, such as the emperor's secretary Gonzalo Pérez or Italian writers such as Aretino. In a letter sent from Rome to Charles V, on November 20, 1539, he studiously apologized for changing to Italian, purportedly without noticing: "I have turned to Italian, which I speak like Spanish. I promise your majesty that I am struck by myself, and if I wanted, the whole letter would be in Italian" (Yo he tornado a la lengua italiana, que la hablo como español. Yo prometo a V. M. que me espanto de mí mismo y que si quisiera, que toda esta fuera en italiano).[19]

At the center of the literary culture developed in this transnational republic of letters were two modes of heroic writing that succeeded among the most diverse groups of readers but particularly among these military and courtly elites: Spanish books of chivalry and Italian *romanzo*. With the Spanish came chivalric fiction, which developed and rose exponentially as a genre during the very same years of the Wars of Italy and the military revolution. The Italians enjoyed *Amadís*'s bright tales of chivalry just as much as the Spanish avidly consumed and mimicked Orlando's feats of arms and love.[20] One of the outstanding heroes of the military revolution, the victor of Pavia, the Marquis of Pescara, Fernando de Avalos, had grown up in late fifteenth-century Naples reading books of chivalry.[21] Questioned by one of his Italian interlocutors in his *Diálogo de la lengua*, Juan de Valdés acknowledged a quasi-Quixotic passion for books of chivalry: "For ten years, the best of my life, that I spent in palaces and courts, I did nothing more virtuous than reading these lies, which I enjoyed so much that I would devour my own hands after them. So note how spoiled my taste was, that if I took a book of those translated from Latin into our vernacular and written by true historians, or so considered, I would never be able to finish it" (Diez años, los mejores de mi vida, que gasté en palacios y cortes, no me empleé en ejercicio más virtuoso que en leer estas mentiras, en las cuales tomaba tanto sabor que me comía las manos tras ellas. Y mirad qué cosa es tener el gusto estragado, que si tomaba en la mano un libro de los romanzados en latín que son de historiadores verdaderos, o a lo menos que son tenidos por tales, no podía acabar comigo de leerlos).[22] Romance was indeed associated with the spaces of political and social power, the palaces and courts in the memory of the Italianized Valdés. Although we know that they did not completely prevent a book from reaching popular audiences, the material elaboration and the high prices of romances of chivalry must have certainly limited their potential publics. According to Daniel Eisenberg, "the romances of chivalry are clearly the most expensive Spanish literary works" in the well-supplied library of Renaissance collector Hernando Colón in the first decades of the sixteenth century.[23]

The tales of Italian *romanzo* and Spanish books of chivalry became ingrained in the literary culture of these elites to the point that the two heroic traditions seem to have merged into one at some point—as they were one century later in the mind of Alonso Quijano.[24] The materiality of Italian chivalric poems and that of Spanish prose romance usually shows that both genres were meant to compete for the same readers. And a quick look at the transnational circulation of these books confirms that the two literary traditions were closer than we usually think. The first French translation of *Orlando furioso*, published in Lyon in 1543, is explicitly said to compete in the market with the French translation of *Amadís*.[25] In the same year, Bernardo Tasso, Torquato's father, decided to translate the Spanish best seller *Amadís de Gaula* in Italian verse at the request of Ávila y Zúñiga and Francisco de Toledo—a member of the Alba family and the future viceroy of Peru.[26] Just as Bernardo translated the prose of *Amadís* in Ariosto's ottava rima, the Spanish Vázquez de Contreras, years later, converted the stanzas of *Orlando furioso* into Spanish chivalric prose.[27] In the cultural world of the two peninsular aristocratic and military elites there existed a tight connection between Italian romanzo and Spanish chivalric fiction.

The story of the first Spanish translation of Ariosto's *Orlando furioso* confirms that the highest layers of European aristocracy were involved in the promotion and patronage of these genres. In 1549, Prince Philip of Spain arrived in Antwerp, accompanied by most of the Spanish nobility and a few Italian potentates, after a glorious journey—or *felicíssimo viaje*, as it was referred to in Spanish—throughout the European territories of the Habsburg composite monarchy. The voyage from Barcelona to Genoa, from Milan to Trento, from Augsburg to Brussels, was intended to introduce Prince Philip to the vassals and allies of the Austrian house in Europe in order to secure the loyalty of the social and political elites of those territories. When it arrived in the Habsburg Netherlands, Prince Philip's itinerant court joined the retinue of his father, Charles V, in an atmosphere of political euphoria after the emperor's triumph in Mühlberg and the recent death of Francis I of France in 1547. Just two weeks before Philip's select entourage of the *felicíssimo viaje* entered Antwerp on September 11, 1549, the prosperous local printer Martinus Nutius, active in the city from 1540 to 1558, had published *Orlando furioso traduzido en Romance Castellano*, which would become one of the most frequently and successfully reprinted Spanish books of the sixteenth century. A member of a dispossessed hidalgo family from Navarre, the translator, Jerónimo Jiménez de Urrea, pursued a lifelong military career, mostly in Italy and Germany, which earned him the post of infantry captain and eventually a habit of the Order of Santiago. After the victory at Mühlberg and in the days of the *felicíssimo viaje*, his military service must have granted him some kind of access to the courtly circles of Emperor Charles and Prince Philip, since it seems that Urrea personally offered the latter a copy of his *Furioso traduzido*.[28] The book must have aroused much enjoyment from the courtly and aristocratic circles of the prince's entourage. "Dear reader," says the printer in one of the preliminary texts, "the main cause that has moved us to print the *Orlando furioso in Castilian* has been . . . the dearness and want of these books in the present kingdoms; to this we should add the requests of our friends and noble gentlemen from

Spain and other nations, which we decided to heed first because they were fair, and also because they have helped us with the correction of the book" (Amigo letor, la principal causa que nos ha movido a imprimir el *Orlando furioso en Romance Castellano* ha sido . . . la carestía y falta que hay destos libros en estos reinos. Hase allegado a esto las rogarías de nuestros amigos y señores españoles y otras naciones las cuales hemos querido obedecer por parecernos justas, como por la ayuda que nos han dado en la correción del libro).[29]

The immediate market for Urrea's *Orlando traduzido* is indeed the cream of the European high nobility, which gathered around Prince Philip in his continental tour of 1549, in the context of one of the most magnificent chivalric celebrations of Renaissance Europe in Mary of Hungary's palace at Binche, in the Southern Netherlands. The courtly festivals that took place there in the summer and fall of that year were informed by the literary tales of *Amadís* and *Orlando*.[30] A jamboree of banquets, theatrical performances, dances, and, above all, elaborate jousts and "adventures" was designed in order to entertain those who still liked to think of themselves as belonging to the warrior class. In a world made of damsels, islands, enchantments, giants, and flamboyantly named knights, a cohort of grandees and titled aristocrats reproduced in the rituals of the court society the literary models provided by romance fiction, whether in verse or in prose. Romance fiction was actively used, collectively, in the elaboration of a transnational courtly sociability. Individually, reading or hearing chivalric tales was part of the "aristocratic *bildung*" of many noble houses and courts.[31]

Castiglione's *Book of the Courtier* has always been invoked in discussions of aristocratic education and noble sociability. From the very beginning in Castiglione's handbook, Count Lodovico di Canossa asserts that "the principal and true profession of the Courtier must be that of arms."[32] These *arms*, however, have little to do with the dramatic transformations of warfare that were taking place just outside the walls of the Duke of Urbino's palace and other such Renaissance courts. When Castiglione writes that the courtier, "born of a noble and genteel family," should "know how to handle every kind of weapon, both on foot and on horse" but "be especially acquainted with those arms that are ordinarily used among gentlemen," he is referring to the different modalities of courtly tournament and joust, as well as the aristocratic practice of duel. The courtier's fighting skills have nothing to do with the real practice of warfare but with the ritualized sociability of courtly chivalry. Castiglione's courtier, rather than a perfect soldier, must be "a perfect horseman in every kind of saddle," an accomplished jouster, a virtuoso of stick throwing, bull-fighting, *juegos de cañas*, hunting, and ball game.[33]

It has rarely been noted that the social model of the courtier, as far as arms are concerned, is precisely built against that of the soldier.[34] "We do not wish him," said Count Lodovico, "to make a show of being so fierce that he is forever swaggering in his speech, declaring that he has wedded his cuirass, and glowering with such dour looks."[35] And indeed what follows this passage is a courtier's joke about a coarse soldier who, not being conversant with the codes of the palace's sociability, arrogantly rejects a lady's offer to dance.[36] Castiglione, moreover, despises even what constitutes the very definition of modern soldiering, that is, serving in war in exchange for a salary. "The true stimulus to great and daring deeds in war," he says, "is glory, and whosoever is moved thereto for gain or any other motive, apart from the fact that he never does anything good, deserves to be called not a gentleman, but a base merchant."[37] As opposed to the knight's, a soldier's identity is inextricably linked to money; it is constituted by it from the very etymology of the word *soldado*.[38] The opposition between the professional soldier and the amateur knight could not be stated more clearly. The court and the battlefield will generate not only two different patterns of social behavior but also two distinct, and many times opposed, literary cultures.

Renaissance courtly sociability has indeed been described as a "shelter against the universal calamity of the Wars of Italy . . . a space aristocratically separated from the real world."[39] Romance's representations of combat were utterly anachronistic to actual fighting men, fit to be reproduced in the palace by a group of high-born jousters but far from the realities of Italy's battlefields. Of course, the ritual mimicking of war in courtly practice remained an enjoyable theatrical recreation for the knights of the palace and played an important role in court society; but it could no longer be justified as a mirror, let alone training, for actual military practice. "The cult of the emblazoned individual heavy cavalryman" and the "glamorized choreography" of the celebrations at Binche and elsewhere were at odds with the newly massive, plebeian, and quite bloody character of Renaissance warfare.[40] And in the eyes of many, the disconnect between the practice and the representation of warfare in the world of the high nobility ended up destabilizing their social legitimacy, traditionally based in the profession of arms and the defense of society. The tales of *Orlando* and *Amadís* seem to have been more appropriate for those "more keen to courtesy than to war" (di cortesia più che di guerre amico), as the author of the former would eloquently put it.[41]

In fact, the representational traditions of romance fiction in prose and verse clearly privileged the image of the "medieval centaur," the relevance of an aristocratic corps of heavy cavalry whose role on the battlefields of Europe was decreasing at the same rate that the output figures of *Orlandos* and *Amadises* printed in Venice or Seville swelled.[42] This literature legitimized the social preeminence of the *bellatores* against the emerging social logics of new warfare practices and discourses. The rise of the court nobility was accompanied by a proportional decline in the aristocracy's traditional military function. The social and cultural practices of the noblemen that constituted the ideal audiences for Ariosto's romance in the Habsburg world ultimately veiled the crucial developments that historians have associated with the military revolution, such as the generalization of gunpowder and siege artillery, the new infantry formations of pikemen, and the improvement of military engineering and fortification. More important, the substitution of massive infantry squadrons for a select and aristocratic corps of heavy cavalry as the backbone of the army entailed somehow a democratization of military activity, which was now accessible to plebeians and low hidalgos.[43] This is not to say that the high nobility completely abandoned its traditional military function or that cavalry totally disappeared from European armies, but the centrality of both was substantially displaced after some of the Renaissance battles that transformed warfare, from Ravenna (1512) to Bicocca (1524) or Pavia (1525).[44] By the time Urrea translated the *Furioso* for the enjoyment of Prince Philip's noble entourage in 1549, the protagonists of European battles were not the "men-at-arms" (gens d'armes, gendarmerie) who jousted in Binche but the plebeian infantrymen who fought in Italy and Germany in large, disciplined armies based on the pike and the arquebus. The individual effort of the chivalric ethos had been replaced by the soldier's obedience and professionalism, together with the technical knowledge and strategic skill of meritorious officers.

The aristocratic rules of individual fighting, the prominence of the horse in knightly culture, the honor codes that had been outmoded by the new culture of warfare, the fantastic fictionality of imagined wars as opposed to those the soldiers experienced distinctly—none of these aspects could provide an undisputed model for the literary culture and social practice of the soldierly mass. Soldiers appropriated some elements of the language, the rhetoric, the narrative patterns, and the names of the chivalric traditions. They may well try to imitate and participate in the noble practice of joust on one occasion and openly mock it as ridiculous or anachronistic in another. Strategic sameness as well as strategic difference would guide the practices and discourses of the common soldier in relation to those of their social superiors. Soldierly culture is shaped after and in confrontation and competition with aristocratic literary forms.

Indeed, Italian linguistic and cultural competence was taken for granted not only among the commanding elites but also among many of the rank and file. As early as 1517, the lack of Italian skills of Juan Gozález and Pero Pardo, the laughable *bisoños* mocked for being "raised in the court of the plow" (crïados / en corte de los arados) and for not being "fluent in the Italian language" (no son enseñados / en la lengua italïana), was the main source of amusement for the presumably bilingual audience of Torres Naharro's *Comedia soldadesca*.[45] The Captain, Guzmán, Manrique, and Mendoza, veterans who served in the armies of the feared Cesare Borgia, Pope Alexander's son, or under the command of Gonzalo Fernández de Córdoba, the Great Captain, all are fluent in Italian. Popular readers certainly appropriated and enjoyed the stories of chivalric literature, and common soldiers were, as a matter of fact, familiar with the sagas of *Orlando* and his progeny.[46] Yet however attracted the common soldiery of early modern Europe was to the chivalric tales of *Amadís* and, above all, *Orlando*, the rank and file's exposure to and active appropriation of these literary traditions were rarely exempt of tension.

In his military memoir about Mediterranean soldiering and captivity, Jerónimo de Pasamonte quotes a full stanza of *Orlando furioso*, but he does so in the context of a narrative coincidence that he deems miraculous and that shows the author's fictional elaboration of this episode in an otherwise highly verisimilar narrative regime. While relaxing on the grass by the Fountain of Caño Dorado, in Madrid's Prado de San Jerónimo, on a pleasant Sunday afternoon, Pasamonte claims to have sung "with no little flair" (con no poca gracia) the first stanza of *Orlando furioso*'s canto 23 ("Studisi ognun giovare altrui; che rade"), which is a warning for readers to do all the good they can to others, for any damage they inflict will unexpectedly be reciprocated. An old acquaintance of his times of captivity, who had once betrayed him, overheard the Italian song and inquired, approvingly, about Pasamonte's linguistic and musical skills. The soldier retorted gallantly with a mix of Spanish and Italian—"Caro me costa"—and explained to the traitor how he had acquired these skills while spending "many years in captivity among Italians" (muchos años captivo entre italianos). The persuasive fictionality and emplotment devices of romance serve in Pasamonte's text to emphasize the exceptional nature of a conventional anagnorisis.[47]

Similarly, Alonso de Contreras's autobiography contains one mention of the chivalric tales of *Orlando furioso*. While serving in the galleys of Malta, Contreras participated in a sally to the coasts of Barbary in order to fight off some of the corsairs who had recently attacked the positions of the Order in the island. During this expedition, they briefly docked in Lampedusa, which "they say . . . is enchanted and that it was in this island where Ruggero and Bradamante fought against each other, which I think is just a fable" (dicen está encantada y que en esta isla fue donde se dieron la batalla el rey Rugero y Bradamonte, para mí fábula).[48] The hearsay that Contreras puts down in writing in his autobiography makes clear that Ariosto's fiction figured prominently in the daily pláticas of the Spanish popular soldiery, to the extent that it shaped the ways they made sense of the physical spaces of war with which they were most familiar. Yet at the same time, it shows that the value of these tales, their legitimacy as literary models to recount the experience of serving soldiers eager to tell the truth about war, was always in dispute. If romance textuality impregnates military writing and even the soldiers' daily lives, it frequently shows up in their tales in an ironic fashion, or in an open negation, that reveals the tensions involved in its regime of fictionality.

A GUNPOWDER POETICS

The epic poem can only refer to the sixteenth-century military figure through occultation or allusion.

(Le poème épique ne peut entretenir avec la figure militaire du XVIe siècle qu'un rapport fait d'escamotage et d'allusion.)

—FRÉDÉRIQUE VERRIER, *Les armes de Minerve*

The fight for Italy transformed not only the art of war and the forms of government, as Guicciardini famously proclaimed, but also "the very modalities of narrating war."[49] Thus Matteo Maria Boiardo, Count of Scandiano, dropped his pen sometime in September 1494. For eighteen years the poet had been writing his *Orlando innamorato* in the Este's Ferrarese palace. Suddenly, when the barbarian armies of Charles VIII of France crossed the Alps and invaded Italy, his light tales of love and chivalry somehow stopped making sense. "While I sing," says Boiardo, "I see all Italy in flame and fire by these French." The fire of the first artillery train in history obliterates the burning love of Fiordespina's tale, now "vain," which the narrator promises his readers to take up again soon.[50] The poet died, however, shortly after giving up his massive poetic and narrative enterprise, in December of the same year. For the writers of *romanzi*, Charles VIII's descent in Italy must have been traumatic.[51] It is as if the ravages of real war, the increasingly destructive technologies and tactics of the military revolution, could find no place in Boiardo's bright, chivalric world of love and arms. Moreover, the most powerful monarchy of Christendom, which in the fictional world of the Carolingian narrative cycles defended European Christianity against the barbarian Saracens, turned into the invading barbarian king destroying the soil of ancient Rome.

Though Charles VIII's stunning onslaught in 1494 made Boiardo drop his pen, it did not silence the writers of the popular pamphlets that reported, in the same metrical form, *true* stories about the Wars of Italy.[52] For Massimo Rospocher, the poems published in cheap print or performed by street singers about the Wars of Italy, known as *guerre in ottava rima*, contrasted in important ways with the tradition of the chivalric poem as it was practiced by Boiardo or Ariosto, which had initially shared the frame, language, and structure of their popular counterparts.[53] First, this corpus of verse was crucial in "the emergence of contemporaneity," a new perception of current events that linked the military and political realms in the media of public communication, successfully capturing "the dramatic urgency of the present."[54] The wide distribution of these texts allowed the audience to contrast their own experience of the facts with those poetized in the popular pamphlets. This genre created a new relationship between the written matter of war and its readers and listeners. A sense of novelty, moreover, pervaded the typographical and rhetorical strategies of these popular prints. An emphatic rhetoric of truth versus the shining, elaborate fiction of the *romanzi* became a feature of the genre, and a gory realism shaped the referential world of the guerre in ottava rima that was incompatible with the courtly idealization of warfare in chivalric discourse. Some soldiers, moreover, were involved in the production and distribution, both orally and in print, of these songs. Ercole Cinzio Rinuccini, for instance, wrote several poems on the wars he personally fought, while storyteller Eustachi Celebrino claimed to have written *La presa di Roma* after the prose eyewitness account of a captain who participated in the sack of 1527.[55]

The traditions of *romanzi* and the *guerre in ottava rima* run parallel, competing with and feeding each other. Most scholars of Spanish epic have rightly emphasized the weight that the former carried in the development of the genre in the Iberian peninsula and elsewhere.[56] I would like to suggest, however, that the guerre in ottava rima, a tradition of popular print and war writing quite distinct from chivalric fiction, might have played as significant a role as the romanzo tradition in the emergence of Iberian epic in the middle years of the sixteenth century. The ephemeral products of popular print, these war stories circulated widely and could be found anywhere, from the urban centers of Italy to the strongholds and galleys of the Mediterranean war stage where Italian and Spanish soldiers always mingled. The impact of this textual tradition of popular origin on the literary culture of the Habsburg soldiery may have important consequences for our understanding of epic as a genre and of war writing in general.

What I will call, following Michael Murrin's argument, gunpowder epic, shared a number of key textual elements with the *guerre in ottava rima*.[57] First, a rhetoric of factual precision often punctuates the narrative with specific dates and times, provides the number of combatants, and records the names of commanders and common soldiers alike.[58] Second, the enthusiastic embracement of the technologies and ethos of the military revolution, as I have already mentioned, oftentimes pits itself against the aristocratic rejection of the lowly forms of new warfare.[59] Third, the urgency of the present, in Rospocher's felicitous formulation, leads soldiers to confront those who "today sing about ancient things and leave in oblivion the new ones" just to avoid the pain of telling them (molti cantono ognhor le cose antiche / e lasson preterir l'altere e nove / per seguir l'otio e per fugire fatiche).[60] Finally, and more important, an explicit rejection of romance's regime of fictionality is at the root of many war songs. "I will not sing of Orlando or Ruggiero," says one of these poems, "but of the true subject" (suggetto vero) of the war of Parma in 1551.[61] In the same vein, a widely distributed compilation of war stories from the 1510s opened with a negative to celebrate Orlando, Rinaldo, or Morgante, opting instead to recount just "the events that happened on Italian soil."[62]

Drawing from this tradition, the Spanish soldiers picked up the pen exactly where Boiardo dropped it. Scores of common soldiers, an army of military poets, set out to recount the contemporary wars of the empire in a poetic idiom that sharply contrasted with the fictional registers of chivalric romance. None of these authors lost his grip on his pen in the face of the new, more brutal and diabolic realities of warfare. In lieu of conjuring away or vaguely alluding to this reality, as Verrier claimed in the lines quoted earlier, the new epic poets embraced it as a worthy, novel, enticing, and profitable literary matter. They claimed, insistently and with passion, to tell the truth about war, and that truth entailed "a set of military values that contrasted with the chivalric code."[63]

Both Ariosto's *Orlando* and Urrea's translation are absolutely crucial to understanding Spanish Renaissance epic. They functioned as a rhetorical, narrative, and linguistic archive that nurtured the war stories soldiers liked to tell themselves and others. But their multiple and complex relations to romance fiction were often underwritten by an oppositional logic. Michael Murrin made a crucial point when he asserted that "critics so far have not recognized or acknowledged that the two genres [epic and romance] present different kinds of war. The warrior in romance usually fights on horseback, while in classical epic Achilles and Aeneas chase their enemies about the field on foot. Romance thus fits the old cavalry battles of the Middle Ages, while classical epic better accommodates the new styles of infantry fighting adopted by the English, Swiss, and Spanish."[64] The epics that began to be published in mid-sixteenth-century Spain indeed constituted themselves as the enunciation of this sociocultural difference, as a gesture of both emulation and rejection of the chivalric cultural models that would continue to shape most of the courtly and literary practices of the early modern nobility.

Most likely a commoner and a soldier in his younger days, Jerónimo Sempere was a modest shopkeeper in his native Valencia by the time he published his *Carolea* (Valencia: Joan de los Arcos, 1560), an epic about the military deeds of Emperor Charles.[65] Sempere's two-part, nineteen-canto epic in octaves is one of the first long narrative poems to deal with the contemporary wars of the Spanish empire.

The first part of his *Carolea* is devoted to the "hard-fought war that happened in Italy between the Spaniards and the French until the battle of Pavia" (la reñida guerra que pasó en Italia entre españoles y franceses hasta la batalla de Pavía). It recounts, he continues in the opening "Argumento," "the skirmishes, the marches, and the battles of that war, and the capture of cities and fortresses, and it describes the foundations and the sites of many towns in Italy" (cuenta los rencuentros que hubo en ella en muchas jornadas y diversas ocasiones, y las presas de ciudades y fortalezas. Y descríbense las fundaciones y sitios de muchos pueblos de Italia, y otras partes).[66] In sharp contrast with the elusive referentiality of romance representations of war, the novelty of Italian poliorcetics and the operationality of the new war constitute the object of Sempere's poetic chronicle of the Wars of Italy in the 1520s.

Carolea's first part, as rich in Virgilian reminiscences as it is in historical detail, culminates in the emblematic battle of Pavia, where the French gendarmerie, Francis I's corps of aristocratic heavy cavalrymen, was crushed, according to Paolo Giovio—and our Roldán— "with good shots of arquebus" (con buenos disparos de arcabuz).[67] By narrating war with the brutal technical precision that became characteristic of soldierly discourse, Sempere celebrates what Ariosto and Boiardo had condemned. Firearms, which allowed foot soldiers to fight the hitherto invincible heavy cavalry of the French army, brought about a new social dynamic to the representation of warfare. In Sempere's rendering of the battle, as in Oznaya's, Spanish arquebusiers, whether anonymous or flaunting rather plebeian names, kill ranks of famous French knights, some of whom belong to the most illustrious lineages of French nobility: "Ranks of arquebusiers destroy the French knights, gallant skill! With bursts of gunfire, they killed scores of enemies" (Deshacen a los Gallos caballeros / con mangas de arcabuces, bella maña: / con darles ruciadas de pelotas / mataban de enemigos muchas flotas).[68]

Sempere depicts the gendarmerie's lavish display of aristocratic fashion—Roldán's "golden brocades and crimson shirts"—as a lack of adaptability to the new realities of war and as poor strategic judgment. For it is the material culture and the ethos of the old aristocratic warfare, which the rank and file mock as more fit for jousting than for real fighting, that allow both Roldán and Sempere's arquebusiers to identify and exterminate the flower of French nobility. "Brocade," "rich arms," and "golden harnesses" are of little use against the disciplined rank-and-file arquebusiers of the imperial army.[69] The luxury of courtly war games is at odds with the harsh realities of the battlefield. Francis I goes to war, according to Sempere, as he would to one of Binche's tournaments, which is what facilitates his capture by Spanish soldiers by revealing the presence of the king.[70] The poet barely hides his enthusiasm for the plebeianization of new warfare. Sempere concludes his narration of Pavia by enumerating the ranks of titled nobility and the dozens of *mussiores* or noblemen that the Spanish infantrymen sent to fill the ranks of Death—"muy rica fue la muerte de Señores." Soldierly writing oftentimes becomes a quite literal version of class warfare.[71]

In 1561, the experienced soldier Baltasar del Hierro published in Granada his *Libro y primera parte de los victoriosos hechos del muy valeroso caballero Don Álvaro de Baçán*.[72] In spite of the title, which echoes with chivalric paratextuality, Hierro's epic stanzas concerned the most recent military events of the empire and purported to be a factual account of the Marquis of Santa Cruz's naval Mediterranean and Atlantic campaigns against Algerian and French privateering, in which the author participated. Hierro explicitly delimits the object of his epic poem as a highly professionalized version of warfare: "the clashes, skirmishes, and battles, the many sieges and the many squadrons and ranks of arquebusiers" (los grandes recuentros, escaramuzas o batallas y diferentes sitios de tierras [y] diferentes los escuadrones y mangas que se hacen).[73] Bazán was a highly respected general among sixteenth-century Spanish soldiery, and thus he is unequivocally celebrated in a poem that bears his name in its title. But the heroes in Hierro's poem are also his comrades-in-arms, the plático soldiers he fought alongside, those who "have seen a great number of towers, walls, casemates, ravelins, moats and ditches, artillery plots in bridges and walls; and they understand the blows of the trumpet and the playing of the drums as if they spoke to them" (han visto gran número de torreones caballeros, murallas, casasmatas, revellines, fosos y contrafosos, entradas o salidas de puentes, con sus traveses; y entienden como si les hablasen las palotadas de las cajas, o los retumbos de las trompetas).[74] The representation of warfare becomes almost conflated with the representation of military discipline and the soldierly esprit de corps. War is understood as the professional business of a group of fellows-in-arms who derive their discursive legitimacy from their technical expertise. The works of Sempere and Hierro are arguably the first narrative poems in octaves in Spanish that addressed the new realities of contemporary warfare, with that urgency of the present foregrounded by the guerre in ottava rima.

The consolidation of gunpowder epic came with the publication of Alonso de Ercilla's first part of *La Araucana* in 1569. In his prologue, Ercilla claimed that his poem was "a true history about the matter of war" (una historia verdadera y de cosas de guerra) that memorialized soldiers who would otherwise remain "in perpetual oblivion" (en perpetuo silencio).[75] Furthermore, the opening lines of Ercilla's extremely popular epic are a general indictment of the romanzo's referential universe: "I do not sing of ladies, love, or the courtesies of enamored knights" (No las damas, no amor, no gentilezas / de caballeros canto enamorados).[76] Although the parallels with Boiardo's and Ariosto's chivalric propositions, which Ercilla counters almost word by word, have long been noted, its close connections with the tradition of the popular war narratives known as *guerre in ottava rima* have never been pointed out.[77] Moreover, Ercilla's epic, as has often been noted, downplays the role of the individual hero in favor of a collective protagonist. It is significant that Ercilla deprived García Hurtado de Mendoza, Francisco de Villagrá, and even Pedro Valdivia of the traditional narrative centrality granted by epic, or colonial chronicles, to the military leader. The heroes of *La Araucana* are either the Spanish arquebusiers and pikemen, "gente de arcabuz y de la pica," or their like-minded enemies, the Araucanian "plático soldiers" on the other side of the battlefield.[78] In contrast with traditional epic protagonists, heroes in Ercilla's narrative are always accompanied by a populous cohort of comrades-in-arms of both American—as Indian allies or "indios amigos"—and European origin. With the characteristic pride of the professional soldier, Ercilla represents himself "amid weapons and rough terrain, immersed in a thousand hard-fought combats" (en medio de las armas y aspereza / sumido en mil forzadas ocasiones), engaging the enemy, or dismounting his horse to fight shoulder to shoulder in the same "ranks and files" (mangas e hileras) as his Spanish and indigenous comrades.[79]

After Ercilla many other soldierly texts reproduced the trope of the true war story that excludes or opposes the fictions of love and chivalric adventures. One of Ercilla's numerous poetic descendants in Chile, Hernando Álvarez de Toledo's *Purén indómito*, insisted on differentiating his true military narrative about the endless Arauco War from the "vain fictions" and "feigned poetic fables" (ficciones vanas; fábulas poéticas compuestas) of chivalric referentiality by dwelling on the concrete materiality of indigenous weaponry, as eyewitnessed by the author: the catalogue of native weapons that follows that proposition becomes a metonymy for the truth of the soldierly narrative.[80] Regardless of its actual factual values, the rhetorical production of truth will be a key feature of soldierly epic, the *true* poetry of war. Lacking any other source of enunciative legitimacy—such as solid erudition, reliable patronage, poetic genius, moral integrity, or religious prerogative—common soldiers resorted to an elaborate language of truth based on their professional skill and their testimonial presence in the events they recounted.

After these first poems of the 1560s and the 1570s, and especially after Ercilla's widely read poem was first issued, it can be said that the gunpowder epic had succeeded. A number of texts published in the second half of the sixteenth century attest to the consolidation of the new epic genre as the discourse of Spain's plático soldiers who aspired to see their role as the true defenders of the monarchy recognized and rewarded against the courtly nobility and their cultural models. Particularly during the 1580s, several professional soldiers belonging to the plebeian and low hidalgo layers of peninsular societies wrote a series of epic poems in octaves, on different fronts of the empire, that recounted the military victories of Philip II's reign with the increasingly confident voice of their victorious armies and of a progressively consolidated social group.

In *La Maltea*, published in Valencia by Joan Navarro in 1582, Hipólito Sans narrated the unsuccessful Turkish assault on Malta in 1565. The war narrative of this Valencian hidalgo who participated in the defense pauses to describe the new Italian-style fortifications of the Maltese strongholds, the siege tactics of the Turkish artillery and janissary infantry, and the complex maneuvers of the supporting fleet.[81] The poem, reproducing the antifictional rhetoric that we have already explored, refused to sing the "lies, fictions, love fables, and strange adventures" (mentiras y ficciones, / fábulas de amor y la extrañeza / de aquellas aventuras), offering instead a harsh narration of every single military event, small and big, in a war starring arquebusiers and engineers.[82] Spanish *soldados viejos* who have served in Italy for decades, knights of Saint John from every *lengua* or nation in Europe, imperial infantrymen from Germany, and Turkish renegades, among others, participate in a successful defense that boosted Christian confidence and received a significant amount of public attention. References to religious struggle, however, or to the crusade as an interpretive model of Mediterranean warfare are surprisingly scarce in the poem. The battle is mostly depicted in technical terms as a struggle between two disciplined, professional, multinational armies.

The son of a dyer (*tintorero*) from Córdoba, Juan Rufo would eventually become the singer of Don John of Austria's most famous military deeds. He participated in the local administration of the Alpujarras war against the Morisco uprising of 1567 and then joined the companies that manned the fleet of the Holy League on their way to Lepanto. Both military campaigns were the object of his gunpowder epic, *La Austríada*, which benefited from the privileged perspective of an *entretenido* soldier with access to Don John's entourage, an appointment to which his undeniable wit, as shown in his *Las seiscientas apotegmas* (Toledo: Pedro Rodríguez, 1596), may have very well contributed.[83] The poem was issued in three consecutive editions in the years 1584, 1585, and 1586 by very important Castilian printers (Madrid: Alonso Gómez, Toledo: Juan Rodríguez, and Alcalá: Juan Gracián, respectively), a considerable success for a work of poetry during the period. Under direct patronage of the emperor's illegitimate son, "protector of soldiers" (amparo que fue de soldados), Rufo somehow became his official poet.[84] Thanks to a petition the poet addressed to the Council of War in 1591, we know that a close collaboration between the commanding hero of the epic and the humble poet may have taken place. Don John himself seems to have sponsored or even commissioned the poem in the immediate aftermath of Lepanto, and Rufo intended to add a second part singing the prince's deeds in Flanders based on *relaciones* personally written and sent by the general to the epic poet.[85] Rufo's case shows that the military elites of the empire, particularly those more committed to a professional and meritocratic model of military organization, may have sanctioned the success of one of the central discursive models of the imperial soldiery: gunpowder epic.[86]

In Flanders we find examples of equally successful military epics written by the empire's proud infantrymen in the midst of the "fire and flame" of modern warfare. Miguel Giner was an arquebusier from Aragon who wrote *El sitio y toma de Anvers*, a highly personal, testimonial poem about his fight in the conquest of Antwerp during the series of successful military campaigns led by Alejandro Farnesio between 1584 and 1585.[87] The poem was first "printed in Zaragoza in 1587 and reprinted in Milan the same year by Pacífico Poncio," as we read in the colophon of the latter, the Milanese edition. This brief text in six cantos, printed in the portable octavo format of most, if not all, gunpowder epics, must have circulated rapidly. In 1588 the poem was printed again, for the third time in two years, and less than three after the events narrated took place, in Antwerp by Christopher Plantin.[88] The editorial history of the poem follows the trajectories of the Spanish road, from Zaragoza to Milan and from Milan to Antwerp, which was traveled by thousands of Iberian and Italian soldiers after the rebellion broke out in the Low Countries. The military networks of the Habsburg military corporation are at the root of Giner's accomplishment and prove to be an excellent distributor of literary and printed matter among a potentially massive audience of soldiers.[89] The practices, structures, and discourses of the professionalized armies of the Habsburgs seem to have provided common soldiers with opportunities for promotion. In January 1599, Miguel Giner was already a captain and he was granted an *ayuda de costa* of 100 ducats by the Council of Aragon.[90]

All of the poems just listed share similar mechanisms for the construction of the soldier's enunciative authority, the thorough thematization of the practices and spaces of modern warfare, the same bibliographical materiality based on a cheap octavo format that allowed for low production costs and for greater transportability, the same patterns of production and attribution of value.[91] To a certain extent these poems entail a victory of the discourse of the common soldiery, of the poets of the new war, vis-à-vis the increasingly delegitimized fictionality of romance. Soldierly writing was able to intervene in the social and political dynamics of war and the army, supporting a system based on merit, seniority, and skill. Gunpowder epic becomes the discourse of the military class, of a brotherhood of comrades-in-arms that was oftentimes defined by its opposition to the aristocracy and their social and cultural practices. Infantry soldiers, and not aristocratic knights, write, star in, and consume these epics.

THE DEEDS OF THE COMMON MEN

It is not only that Ariosto's *Orlando* and Rodríguez de Montalvo's *Amadís*, and particularly their representations of warfare, had little to do with what soldiers experienced on the battlefield. More important, they were wrong about something more fundamental: these authors lied about the protagonists of their stories, about the *true* heroes of military action. The catalogues of historical noblemen and noblewomen that Boiardo and Ariosto included in their poems had perhaps a lot in common with their fictional counterparts but little to do with the scores of poor men, as Bernal Díaz put it, that constituted the bulk of Renaissance armies. Many instances of soldierly discourse aim explicitly at correcting what they perceived as an unfair distribution of glory in the stories that circulated between the court and the battlefield. The heroes of imperial expansion, whether they agreed or not about the extent of its glories, were *them*, the common soldiers that romance fictionality utterly obliterated. The question should not be whether their stories are true or false, or what is fictional and what historical in the soldiers' tales. Neither should we be concerned about stressing the factual accuracy of the lines that explicitly claim to be historically accurate. What interests me instead is that the soldiers' rejection of romance forms of fictionality is inflected by class tensions. Fictionality, in the discourse about war, had to do, mainly, with one fundamental *fiction*: the idea that the medieval *bellatores*, the members of a class whose privileges were based upon their military role, still were in charge of the defense of society as a whole.

Jerónimo de Urrea, the author of the best-selling translation of *Orlando furioso* I discussed earlier, poses very vividly the terms of this opposition between the new epos and the social and discursive spaces privileged by romanzo. Between 1568 and 1570 Urrea wrote an epic poem that can be counted among the gunpowder epics briefly described earlier. The *Vitorioso Carlos Quinto* relates in detail the emperor's campaigns against the Protestant princes of Germany in 1546–47, in which Captain Urrea himself led an infantry company while he presumably put the finishing touches on his *Furioso traduzido*.[92] The poem is written in "endecasílabo blanco," or blank verse. In one of the two manuscripts in which the text has been preserved, the poem is preceded by a prologue in Italian terza rima where Urrea reflects on the truth regime of the poem, quite different from that of his successful translation of Ariosto's masterpiece. Urrea explicitly refrains from singing the "courtly finesses of love" (finezas cortesanas y de amores) associated both with romance fiction and with the courtly sociability of European aristocracy. In this prologue, the poet addresses his own writing, warning his book about potential critics that are clearly identified:

> Ten por satisfación, ten por consuelo
> que la causa por que estos te aborrecen
> no es por que te los dejas en el suelo,

que ellos conocen bien que no merecen
tener su nombre en la inmortal memoria,
pues ellos se lo borran y escurecen.

Su invidia es ver aclarecer la gloria
de quien ellos mal quieren, sea cualquiera,
y sus obras lustran eterna historia.

No miran cuánto más error te fuera
los hechos encubrir de hombres famosos,
que tan bien han corrido su carrera,

que fingir vanos cuentos fabulosos
para loar aquellos que ni en obra
ni palabra los vieron valerosos.

Destos en quien la invidia tanto sobra,
que así los ha olvidado el fiero Marte,
más que de otros ternás siempre zozobra.[93]

(Be satisfied and consoled: the reason why these loathe you is not
because you bring them to the ground; because they know well that
their names do not deserve to be immortalized, for they themselves
erase and obscure them. They envy the shining glory in those they
dislike, those whose deeds glitter in an eternal history. They do not
see how much worse it would be for you to silence the feats of famous
men, who have so well run their courses, and to make up vain, lying
tales in order to praise those who have never been valiant, either in
words or actions. These envious men, whom Mars has forgotten, will
always give you trouble more than anyone else.)

Urrea explicitly rejects the textual models of heroism based on the
"vain, lying tales" that fictitiously celebrated those who have been forgotten by Mars, whom he now renounces to sing. This Urrea sharply
contrasts with the translator of Ariosto who in 1549 had manipu-
lated the *Furioso*'s original text to celebrate the courtly nobility of
Habsburg Spain by adding several catalogues of Spanish ladies and
gentlemen from the highest aristocratic families in order to meet the
expectations of his immediate audience.[94] He no longer seems willing to praise those who do not deserve it by honoring that part of the
nobility who had manifestly relinquished their traditional military
duties and responsibilities. The vast majority of the lords who accompanied Philip on his Italian and North European voyage in 1549 and
whom we have seen as the core of the *Furioso traduzido*'s initial audience, did not participate in the wars of Germany narrated in Urrea's
new epic poem, and therefore they did not deserve the epic praise of

a soldier who did not see them fighting by the banks of the river Elbe. In the late 1560s Urrea begins his epic poem by making explicit the tensions between two models of heroic storytelling and the tensions between two clearly distinct social groups, taking sides with those who intended to tell the truth about war. The loyalties generated by the military corporation, the professional militia of the plático soldiers, seem to have outweighed other forms of social association and allegiance, such as clientelism or patronage networks, or even class solidarity.[95]

Urrea's gesture reveals itself to be even more significant if we compare it with the writing of the strictly contemporaneous Luis Zapata. Zapata published his *Carlo famoso*, a long, comprehensive epic about Charles V's military campaigns, in 1566 (Valencia: Joan Mey). He had started to write it, however, in 1552, only a couple of years after his return to Spain from the splendorous chivalric festival of the *felicíssimo viaje*, where he had a leading role in the courtly celebrations of the cream of European aristocracy.[96] The poem has usually been considered together with Urrea's and Sempere's texts as a subset of the characteristically Spanish historical epics dealing with the feats of emperor Charles V—frequently grouped as *caroleidas*—and linked to the emblematic model of the genre, Ercilla's *La Araucana*. As I have argued elsewhere, however, Zapata's *Carlo famoso* is better understood as a meticulous rewriting of Ariosto's *Orlando furioso*, closer to the representational traditions of chivalric romance than to the poetics of gunpowder epic.[97] *Carlo famoso* is indeed a mirror for jousters, poets, lovers, and courtiers. It is a summa, a compendium, and a synthesis of Renaissance chivalric culture, showcasing the fictional adventures of a few aristocratic Spanish families who are also intended as the privileged readership of the poem.

Quite strangely for a mid-sixteenth-century Iberian bookman, someone at Joan Mey's workshop attached a printer's prologue to Zapata's prefatory materials in order to explain some important editorial decisions and to make anxious remarks about the legitimacy and authority of the poem's *res gestae*.[98] Zapata's fictionalization of Charles V's historical matter was so intense that the printer decided to mark typographically the most novelistic passages with asterisks by the opening and closing stanzas of the episode, an equally uncommon editorial practice for the period. "I place this signal *," he says, "next to the beginning and the end of each fiction, so that, though they can be easily noticed, those who have their wits blinded by envy, can touch them with their hands" (Va puesta en cada fictión esta señal * en la margen donde comienza y acaba para que aunque de suyo se vían, los ciegos o de ingenio o de envidia, las toquen así con la mano).[99] Mey's omnipresent asterisks materially segregate "the fictions and fables" (las fictiones y fábulas) from those episodes where the poet is said to adhere to "the truth of history" (la verdad de la historia).[100] And as can be seen in Figure 4, the typographical marks could be attached to a passage in which the poet fictionalized the participation of a few young noblemen in the defense of Rhodes in 1522.

This typographical device, albeit rare in Iberian editorial practice, had been previously used at Joan Mey's workshop. In the 1555 translation of Boiardo's *Orlando innamorato*, by the Valencian gentleman soldier Francisco Garrido de Villena, the stars had been used to mark passages that the translator inserted in praise of the house of Borja, in a fashion similar to what Urrea had done, without warning his reader, in his 1549 *Furioso traduzido*.[101] Again, this bibliographical antecedent at the same workshop helps explain what is going on with Zapata's book. The typographical intervention on *Carlo famoso*'s chivalric passages attempts to domesticate a matter that Mey and his employees perceived, perhaps, as too heterogeneous and fantastic for a product that otherwise claimed to be historically accurate and pertaining to no one other than the emperor himself. But it also emphasizes and highlights those passages where the aristocratic families that star in the fictional adventures of chivalric romance are featured, as if to facilitate a selective appropriation of the printed matter by those potential readers.

Furthermore, in Zapata's *Carlo famoso*, Mey delegates the defense of the poem's fictional feats to those for whom they have been imagined in the first place: "Let those princes and gentlemen in whose name these fictions have been composed defend the poem, for they [these fictions] have been plotted to celebrate them [the knights], which means that in case those gentlemen had the opportunity to perform the great feats that these fictions contain, they would do it" (Defiendan[las] aquellos Príncipes y caballeros en cuyo nombre se han hecho estas fictiones por celebrarlos, como dando a entender que aquellos de quien se fingen grandes hazañas y hechos famosos hicieran lo mismo si les viniera el caso).[102] This is a surprising acknowledgment of the purely fictional nature of the military feats of the princes and knights who had been oblivious to their Martian responsibilities. The heroic narrative tradition of Ariostean

Año de M.D.XXIII.   CANTO

Lo diffuadio, diziendo: En efto ueo
  Señores, yo, y ueo mil inconuinientes,
  Bien que à fu Mageftad y à fu deffeo
  Queriamos eftar todos obedientes:
  La breuedad del tiempo, aquel arreo
  Que cumple, y la fazon fon differentes,
  Que armada fe hara en tan poca pieça
  En que auenture el mundo fu cabeça?

Pues fi en armar fe tarda lo qu'es dado,
  Si hauia fu Mageftad de yr en perfona,
  Quiça quando ya à Rhodas fea llegado,
  Sera como el focorro de Efcalona:
  Y q̃ haya antes la tierra el Turco entrado,
  Que la flota falga aun de Barcelona,
  Sera bien pues un Rey tan foberano
  Que ua à un cafo tã graue, uaya en uano?

Mas profupongo, aun que à tiempo arribe,
  Lo que impoßible es, qu'en tanto fea,
  Segun lo que de Rhodas hoy fe efcriue,
  Que la cofa fe trata y fe menea:
  En un mes, es poßible que fe abiue
  Tanta armada, armas, gente à la pelea,
  Qu'efte contra el exercito guerrero
  Qu'en un año ha juntado el Turco fiero?

Y concedo efto, aunque toda uia
  En tan poco fe pueda juntar gente,
  Que alla à la multitud Barbareria
  Del gran Turco tan prefto haga frente:
  Aca hafe de dexar Fuenterrabia
  Que tiene el Rey de Francia injuftamente?
  Y aun haura mas defpues: à nadie es bueno
  Perder lo fuyo, por ganar lo ageno.

Aqueftas y otras cofas añadiendo,
  Reduxo el Real Confejo aquefte intento,
  Que un Capitan famofo à Rhodas yendo,
  A Efpaña Carlo fe quedaffe atento:
  Y le diffuadio à el qu'eftaua ardiendo
  En juuenil ardor, tal penfamiento:
  Torno à replicar Carlo, mas fue en uano,
  Se remitio al confejo en fin mas fano.

Hallandofe à efta conclufion prefente
  El muy buen Prior don Diego de Toledo,
  Hijo del Duque de Alua, el que ualiente
  Se hauia moftrado affaz fobre Toledo,
  Del tronco del qual claro y excelente
  Tambien yo de una rama afirme puedo:
  Ant'el Emperador en efte inftante
  Parefcio con gentil y alto femblante.

Y le fuplica que para efta emprefa
  Le dieffe facultad luego y licencia,
  Que Prior de fant Iuan el fiendo, le pefa
  Que fu religion paffe tal uiolencia:
  Y qu'el fino pudieffe, en una artefa
  Paffaria luego el mar con diligencia,
  Mas que con fu fauor y con fu armada
  Dexaria en breue à Rhodas defcercada.

Aßi lo dezia el, que aun no fabia
  De los hados do uan los penfamientos,
  Y fus palabras como el las dezia
  Se las lleuauan por demas los uientos:
  Fue otorgado al Prior lo que pedia,
  Se partio de la Corte en dos momentos:
  Tras el figuio para eftos trances fieros
  Muy mucha juuentud de caualleros.

* Con el fue don Enrrique de Toledo,
  Y el de Guzmã, à quiẽ el Prior mucho ama,
  Y el muy claro don Diego de Azeuedo,
  Y Garcilaffo muy digno de fama:
  De aquefte refplandefcera, fi puedo,
  Muy mucho en efte mi papel la llama,
  Y don Hernando fue à aquefta jornada
  Señor de la pequeña Horcajada.

Don Pedro de Toledo, y el Clauero
  Su hermano, qu'era un hõbre de grã maña,
  Y grande arte, y Bofcan que fue el primero
  Qu'efte uerfo Thofcano truxo à Efpaña: *
  Con gran gentio y con tanto cauallero
  El Prior de fant Iuan fale à efta hazaña.
  El Emperador, que yr la gente mira
  Donde el quifiera andar, gime y fofpira.

Figure 4. Luis Zapata, *Carlo famoso* (Valencia: Joan Mey, 1566), 67v. HSA.

romanzo is based on the fabulation of chivalric adventures for the aristocrats who did not fight in real wars. Moreover, Mey's discussion of the poem's referential system insists on the class-inflected conception of romance fictionality, on the close connection—in the mind of a printer familiar with the tradition—between the discourse of Italian *romanzo* and the sociability and identity of aristocratic elites. This is why the poets of gunpowder epic insistently characterized chivalric writing as false, illegitimate tales about war. It was not the fictionality of those "poetic" episodes that adorned their true tales about war that they attacked. Chivalric fiction just praised the wrong heroes at the expense of the true ones.

One last example will eloquently show the class ethos of gunpowder epic. In 1591 some Habsburg units of the army of Flanders under the command of Alexander Farnese, Duke of Parma, descended into France in order to break the siege that Henry IV and his English and Dutch supporters had laid to the forces of the Catholic League in the city of Rouen. Emanuel Antunes, a Portuguese soldier serving in the army and a participant in the campaign, wrote about it, on the battlefield, an epic poem in ottava rima. *Primera parte de la baxada de los españoles de Francia en Normandía* was first printed in the very city of Rouen by George l'Oyselet in 1593, barely a year after the end of the campaign.[103] Antunes's proposition, in Ercillian idiom, rejects the "inventions and tangled lies" (invenciones y marañas) of romance fiction in order to record the true feats of his comrades-in-arms.[104] A gunpowder epic in every sense, the poem recounts the Spanish victory by focusing on the deeds of one company of soldiers led by his brother, captain Simão Antunes, who would eventually become maestre de campo in the army of Flanders. While depicting himself, his biological brother, and his brothers-in-arms as proud and disciplined soldiers, a critique emerges in the text, somewhat apologetically but consistently. "It is reason that obliges me to write this at least, or I will explode" (La propria razón es quien me oblige / a que escriba solo esto o a que reviente), he warns the reader: "The soldier, if he deserves it, should be first appointed captain, rather than the gentleman who has never served in war, however noble and refined" (Al soldado le toca ser primero / capitán si lo tiene merescido, / que al más noble y pintado caballero).[105]

That military posts should be given to experienced soldiers and not to favored aristocrats was a commonplace in the early modern discourse about warfare. But Antunes goes a little further when, in a similar vein, the poet repeatedly complains that commanders, not soldiers, unjustly get all the credit for hard-won military victories ("al que el gobierno lleva y no al soldado"). In contrast with common soldiers, who remain always poor and unrewarded, military leaders see "their estates, their riches, and their honor" augmented by successful military campaigns. While unable to reward them materially, Antunes is nonetheless determined to restore at least the glory to whom he considers the true heroes of the war, his comrades-in-arms: "I want to give the glory to the soldiers, for they themselves won it fighting" (A los soldados dar la gloria quiero / pues ellos la ganaron peleando).[106] It is thus no wonder that, like the other authors of gunpowder epic that I discussed earlier, Antunes invokes his fellow soldiers as the privileged readership of his poem: "I will not summon those enamored to read my cantos . . . but only soldiers I will call, turning my verses into war drums" (No llamo a leer mi canto enamorados / . . . mas solamente llamo a los soldados, / haciendo de mis versos atambores).[107]

Class solidarity and mutual support in the society of soldiers may help partially explain the collective ethos of gunpowder epic and its oppositional logic in relation to the aristocratic inertias of civil and military government. In 1596, soldier and writer Juan Rufo—himself an author of this kind of poem, as we have seen—depicted himself discussing with some comrades the strong feelings of brotherhood and friendship that normally bind soldiers:

> Tratábase de cuán estragadas y respectivas amistades son las de los cortesanos y cuán verdaderas y en su punto se hallan entre los que profesan la guerra. Para lo cual dijo [Rufo] que había cuatro causas: la una, el renacer en los peligros y quedar entre los partícipes dellos un virtuoso principio de hermandad; la otra, porque cada uno, como testigo del valor de sus compañeros, los ama y estima por él; la tercera, porque cada soldado es recíprocamente padrino y ahijado del otro; y la última, porque los que han sufrido los trabajos y peligros militares, sólo con verse después se dan alegres parabienes.[108]

> (They were discussing how corrupted and self-interested was friendship among courtiers and how true and perfect it was among those who professed war. To this he [Rufo] said that there were four reasons: first, because among those who overcome many dangers there remains a virtuous principle of fraternity; second, because each one is a witness to the valor of his comrades, which makes him love and esteem them; third, because all soldiers are godfathers and godsons to each other; and lastly, because for those who have suffered military travails and dangers, surviving is enough reason to congratulate each other.)

For those who lead "that kind of life which is always neighbored by death" (aquella vida, que tan cerca tiene la muerte), as Cervantes warned the readers of *El licenciado Vidriera*, witnessing and remembering through writing was one of the most solid forms of military friendship that bound together the soldiers' republic.[109]

The soldiers of the Habsburg armies strived to write their own stories. If the military revolution had allowed commoner and low hidalgo recruits, socialized and professionalized in the Habsburg military machine, to exploit the monarchy's imperial voracity as a means of public recognition and social promotion, they always did so in open confrontation with their superiors. The matter of the gunpowder epic is indeed the feats of the "soldados pláticos," its collective protagonists, and most poems record the names not only of worthy military leaders but also those of the plebeian mass of infantrymen.[110] All of the poems discussed thus far explicitly claim to restitute the glory of military action to those who deserve it, to take it back from the courtly princes and gentlemen whom Mars had forgotten. Horace delimited the object of epic with remarkable clarity: "res gestae regumque ducumque tristia bella."[111] Gunpowder epic addressed the "sorrows of war," and it certainly recounted "the deeds of kings and captains," but it also recorded the actions of foot soldiers, the deeds of the common men of war.

According to the humanist Pedro de Navarra, the historian who praises those who do not deserve it should be called "poet of fictions rather than historian of truths" (mejor . . . poeta de ficciones que historiador de verdades).[112] The relative success of the gunpowder epic in restoring the glory to the real heroes of war, however, would eventually threaten the very raison d'être of soldierly writing, namely its claim to tell the truth about war. A serious reservation about the new representational regime based on eyewitness accounts emerged when some authors perceived that the proliferation of war narratives, whether in prose or in verse, threatened the very possibility of narrating war with any measure of historical accuracy and reliability. According to Pedro de Navarra,

> La causa porque se hallan pocas verdades en algunas crónicas es por ser escritas por relación ajena y no por vista propria. . . . Así como hace poca o ninguna fe el testigo que habla de oída, así es indigno de ser creído el historiador que escribe por lo que otros le informan. Y para que veas la razón que hay para esto, toma ciento que se hayan hallado en un sermón y verás que cada uno te contará de diferente manera. Y toma mil que se hayan hallado en una batalla y no hallarás cuatro que sean conformes en lo que dicen que pasó.[113]

> (The reason why in many chronicles we find little truth is because they are based on the testimony of others rather than on one's own eye-witnessing. . . . Just as the witness who declares what he has heard deserves no credit, we should not believe the historian who writes based on what others have told him. And so that you see that this is right, take a hundred people who have been to a sermon and you will see that each one will recollect it differently. And take one thousand who have been to a battle and you will not find four that agreed about what happened.)

There is a crucial paradox inherent in Navarra's reasoning. He first tries to establish a contrast, based on legal practice, between first- and secondhand testimonies as the legitimate basis for truthful history writing; but in the last sentence he ends up conflating testimonial and hearsay evidence. How can eyewitnessing be accepted as an indispensable condition for the truthfulness of a historical account, as he claims in the first part of the paragraph, if one thousand witnesses can provide as many different versions of the same battle? Eyewitnessing both grants and disperses the authority of a war narrative. The accounts of fighting and writing soldiers would never offer a monoglossic, unitary narrative of war but a multiple, conflicted, heteroglossic one. In the campaign of 1634 during the war of Arauco, Santiago de Tesillo confirms in practice Navarra's theory: "I wanted to write truthfully about the success of this campaign, not having been present to it . . . I received two letters from the two leaders, Maese de Campo and the Sergeant Major, with narrations of the events so different that they could not agree even in the substance of it all" (El suceso de esta campaña he deseado escribir sin perjuicio y con acierto, no habiéndome hallado en ella . . . tuve cartas de los dos cabos, Maese de Campo y Sargento Mayor, con relaciones del suceso tan disconformes en la sustancia que no se pudieron ajustar).[114]

The soldiers' republic of letters was becoming unruly, and writing about war would indeed get out of hand. The new forms of epic articulated by these curious soldiers who reclaimed their military glory were also well suited to voice either disillusioned or openly critical views of imperial and military policies. Moreover, as we will soon see, the same literary forms that served to celebrate victory would be used to narrate defeat, captivity, and survival from the one thousand perspectives of the curious soldiers. The truth about war was indeed rather painful for those who claimed to tell true stories about war.

Rebellion, Captivity, and Survival

MUTINOUS VERSE

With his usual clarity and insight, Braudel, in his opening remarks to the section titled "Forms of War" in his *The Mediterranean and the Mediterranean World in the Age of Philip II*, establishes the grounds for a social and cultural history of warfare that overcomes both the heroic ideological overtones of old military history and the contemporary reticence to acknowledge the centrality of war in the everyday life of the early modern world:[1]

> War is not simply the antithesis of civilization. Historians refer constantly to war without really knowing or seeking to know its true nature—or natures. . . . We talk about it because we have to: it has never ceased to trouble the lives of men. Chroniclers give it first place in their narratives; contemporary observers are addicted to discussion of the responsibilities for and consequences of the wars they have witnessed. While I am determined not to exaggerate the importance of battle history, I cannot allow myself to neglect the history of warfare, a powerful and persistent undercurrent of human life. . . . War punctuated the year with its rhythms, opening and closing the gates of time. Even when the fighting was over, it exerted a hidden pressure, surviving under ground.[2]

The present chapter takes Braudel's reflection as the point of departure for an examination of soldierly writing in a Mediterranean ravaged by the wars between the Ottoman Turks and the Spanish Habsburgs. In keeping with the spirit of Braudel's proposal, I will largely sidestep some of the most symbolic battles, such as Lepanto

(1571), focusing instead on two moments of crisis and defeat for the Spanish side. The fight for the small Tunisian town of Mahdia (known in the Christian world as Africa, Ifriquiya, or Afrodisio) in the early 1550s and the Ottoman conquest of the Spanish strongholds of Tunis and La Goleta in 1574, though understudied, are indeed among those historical events "opening and closing the gates of time"—in Braudel's veiled Virgilian reference to Janus's "iron Gates of War"—that punctuated the undercurrents of human life in the Middle Sea.[3] I will follow the lives and writings of two veteran Spanish soldiers who participated in these events and wrote about them from the perspective of the rank and file. Frequently treated by some of their superiors as disposable human resources, they suffered hardship, deprivation, defeat, and captivity. I will analyze the poetic writings of two survivors who, against what is expected from "those who do not write," took up the pen to claim the right to speak for themselves about their lives and aspirations.[4] Rather than an epic of empire, the texts these common soldiers wrote constitute an epic of survival and authorship, of rebellious soldierly pride and subaltern camaraderie that did not necessarily advance the aims of the military and political machine that employed them.

Habsburg ventures in North Africa were indeed as tentative and precarious as any other expansionist enterprise of imperial Spain. War and soldiering in the extremely complex and heterogeneous social space of North African presidios challenged the national and religious loyalties of those in service. According to John Hale, "War offered experiences and camaraderies that during its long inactions broke the spell of national identity."[5] Furthermore, the role of war-waging in state-building, long held to be instrumental, has been seriously reconsidered.[6] Similarly, though war and empire appear to be naturally and mutually constitutive, war being the most obvious mechanism of imperial domination, representations of empire and representations of war as embodied in the discourse of soldierly writing could at times collide in strange ways. The professional practices of the soldiery, together with the cultural practices that articulated and distributed their self-representations, constituted a military sociability with its own dynamics, many times opposed to the political logic of imperial power.

In the spring of 1550, Dragut Reis, the commander of the Ottoman fleet in the Mediterranean, took over the small Tunisian town of

Mahdia. The captain, who had been Barbarossa's lieutenant, planned to use the town as a new operational base to harass the shores of southern Italy. The Habsburg authorities in Sicily and Naples, however, perceived it not only as a new platform for privateering activities but also as a larger threat for the Hafsid kingdom of Tunisia, which as a loosely controlled Spanish vassal might now fall into the hands of the Turks. Action, therefore, was resolutely taken. In the summer of the same year, an imperial army was organized under the command of Juan de Vega, Charles V's viceroy in Sicily, with the help of Andrea Doria's Genoese galleys and García de Toledo's Neapolitan fleet. After a three-month siege by Spanish and Italian soldiers, the town was successfully conquered. Dragut managed to elude capture and the imperial troops set out to rebuild the fortress of Mahdia for the establishment of a new North African presidio.[7]

This military success over the Turks, which was to be compared, somewhat pompously, to Charles V's conquest of Tunis in 1535, generated a heated debate about the possibility of a new expansionist policy in North Africa. The discussion, however, was short-lived. The practical difficulties of managing and supplying a Tunisian stronghold, the constant Franco-Turkish threat, and the unexpected mutiny of the soldiers against their military superiors would turn Mahdia into a costly failure. Four years after the conquest, the imperial authorities decided to abandon the town of Africa and the garrison was taken back to Sicily.

All of the events related to this historical episode—the siege, the conquest, the mutiny, and the dismantling of Africa—were witnessed by Baltasar del Hierro. Though little is known about this plebeian soldier and his imperial wanderings, some recoverable bits of his life story deserve to be recounted. Most likely a native of Seville, Baltasar del Hierro served in the campaign of Africa from the beginning of the siege to the destruction of the fortress. This means that before the summer of 1550 he was already serving in one of the Italian *tercios viejos*, the elite regiments of Lombardy, Sicily, Naples, and Sardinia that formed part of Spain's multinational infantry force, the units that were first sent to the Tunisian coast in 1550. Once the citadel of Africa was abandoned in 1554, he must have returned to Italy to participate in the imperial campaign against the French-backed republic of Siena, as did the rest of Africa's garrison.[8] He took part in the Marquis of Santa Cruz's Atlantic and Mediterranean naval campaigns against Algerian and French privateering in the late 1550s; in 1560, he was serving in the castle of Milan under the Duke of Sessa's governorship. We also know that he was in Barcelona in 1563 and that two years later in April 1565, according to the House of Trade's register of passengers, he traveled to the New World as "criado de Francisco de Bahamón," recently appointed governor of Puerto Rico.[9]

The travels of this common soldier thus took him from Seville to Naples, from Sicily to Tunisia, from the galleys of Santa Cruz to the castle of Milan, and from the streets of Barcelona to the New World, situating him as a privileged witness and narrator of many important events. In the course of his military career, Baltasar del Hierro wrote *Destruición de África* (Seville: Sebastián Trujillo, 1560) and *Libro y primera parte de los victoriosos hechos del muy valeroso caballero Don Álvaro de Bazán* (Granada: René Rabut, 1561), two gunpowder epics about the Mediterranean wars in which he participated.[10] Accompanying both works, he also printed one narrative *romance* and several lyric pieces. While in Barcelona, he wrote and printed *Triunfos y grandes recebimientos de la insigne ciudad de Barcelona a la venida del famosísimo Felipe rey de las Españas* (Barcelona: Jaime Cortey, 1564), a descriptive account of the celebratory reception of Philip II by the Catalan city.[11] Hierro's previously unknown oeuvre attests to the intense literary practices in which the common soldiers of early modern imperial armies engaged, in a context of global travel and continued cultural contact. Hierro's war narratives also provide us with the unique view of an insider to the social spaces and the practices of early modern warfare, as well as a privileged standpoint from which to look at the "forgotten frontier" of the Habsburg Mediterranean world in the central years of the sixteenth century.[12]

Baltasar del Hierro's *Destruición de África* is a three-canto epic poem in ottava rima that tells an intriguing Mediterranean tale of imperial war, frontier politics, espionage, and soldierly rebellion. The title page of Hierro's poem advertises the author as "a soldier in the castle of Milan." Together with Jerónimo Sempere's *Carolea*—also printed in 1560 in Valencia—Hierro's epic is the first narrative poem to deal with the contemporary history of the empire, the first of the series of soldierly testimonial poems about the "matters of war" mentioned in the previous chapter. It was written and circulated in the very same social and physical spaces that it painstakingly describes, and it was printed in Seville by Sebastián Trujillo, whose workshop specialized in vernacular popular literature such as ballads, broadsheets or *pliegos de cordel*, and entertainment literature in general.[13]

In contrast with the traditional image of Renaissance epic poetry as the highest of genres, the most learned and aristocratic kind of literature, the *Destruición de África* was written by a rank-and-file soldier of presumably quite modest upbringing and education. Furthermore, Trujillo's humble product shows that the material elaboration of these new epics in print, and perhaps their social distribution, had more in common with popular literature and with the materiality of *pliegos de cordel* than with the aristocratic or humanistic circles and markets we generally associate with Renaissance epic. Indeed, Trujillo fashioned the small octavo volume of Hierro's poem as a "newly and beautifully composed story" (agora nuevamente por muy gentil estilo compuesta), in the commercial language of pamphlets and broadsheets produced in abundance in the Atlantic capital. That only one copy of the poem has survived is arguably due to its wide circulation and the ephemerality of popular print products.

Trujillo's imprint includes, in fact, Hierro's "Romance de la tomada de África," printed as an attachment to the main epic. Despite its title, the ballad resolves the conquest in a couple of lines, focusing instead on what soldier Toral y Valdés called "la codicia de la acción," the impatient lust for action of the waiting infantrymen:[14]

> Con muy gran regocijo
> toda la gente esperaba:
> la de dentro espera salto,
> la de fuera se le daba.
> Todos estaban muy quietos
> que nadie no boqueaba,
> el cuerpo por la trinchera
> descubierto se mostraba
> De cualquier infante nuestro
> que de nada recelaba,
> cada cual el pie izquierdo
> del derecho aventajaba
> y su hierro de la pica,
> que con la mano apretaba,
> esperando ser primero
> con atención escuchaba
> cuándo la señal se hiciese.[15]

(All soldiers waited with great joy: those inside [the fortress], to be assaulted, and those outside, to attack. Everyone stood still, no one opened their mouths; the bodies of our fearless infantrymen stuck out from the trench, their left foot ahead as they grabbed their iron pikes,

Figure 5. Baltasar del Hierro, *Destruición de África* (Seville: Sebastián Trujillo, 1560). © Real Academia de la Historia.

everyone waiting to be the first, listening closely to hear the signal to attack.)

Many soldierly ballads graphically depicted all sorts of combat operations in Homeric and Virgilian tones, from the large-scale military maneuvers to individual engagements, from the war cries of soldiers under artillery fire to the crushing of limbs and heads in the fury of battle.[16] Hierro's song, however, avoids the war music of traditional epic in favor of the tense intimacy and contained anxiety of those who await the thrill of combat. This rewriting of war from the ranks, which somehow reveals "the face of battle," is characteristic of Hierro's poetry and other texts by the *pláticos*.[17]

In his main text in octaves, Hierro again refuses to sing the conquest of Mahdia in which he himself participated, opting to instead recount what happened afterward, during the four years that the presidio was held under imperial sovereignty between 1550 and 1554. This surprising decision eventually destabilizes the rhetorical structure of the entire poem, since the garrison's daily life in Mahdia, as we will see, lacked the obvious epic dimension of its conquest. Yet the novelty of Hierro's referent authorizes the very act of utterance: "Since others have already written about the siege / I write about what happened after it was conquered" (Porque del cerco ya otros han escripto / escribo desde que fue ya ganada), says Hierro to justify his decision.[18] The "others" are the historians of all kinds who had in fact taken on the events of Mahdia and produced a large corpus of historiographical literature. A series of chronicles in Latin and the vernacular, widely circulating *relaciones*, and Italian *songs* and *guerre in ottava rima* attest to the relevance of the event in the political imagination of early modern Europe.[19] Hierro's familiarity with one or more of these texts before publishing his poem speaks to the intense circulation of print matter throughout the Italian and North African spaces of war in which he spent the 1550s. The institutional networks of early modern European armies, as we have seen, facilitated such distribution of a specialized discourse on contemporary war throughout the frontiers of imperial Spain.

The first canto of the *Destruición de África* deals with the first two years of the occupation of Mahdia, from the conquest in 1550 to the rebellion of the garrison in 1552. The stronghold is led by Hernando de Vega, Juan's son, a "young but wise gentleman" (mancebito / en seso es de edad bien acabada) whom Hierro considers a brother-in-arms and whose command is narrated in the poem with the technical detail characteristic of soldierly writing.[20] Along with the six infantry companies charged with the defense of the North African frontier, we find "all kinds of people," including the army's accountant (*contador*), the vivandiers or independent suppliers (*mercadantes*), the military engineers (*ingenieros*), the foremen (*sobrestantes*), and the six hundred pioneers (*gastadores*), all of them the officials and professionals who made early modern imperial warfare possible.[21] In contrast with the representational conventions of Spanish books of chivalry and Italian *romanzi*, which adhered to medieval chivalric modes of aristocratic warfare, the financial and logistical complexity of the new practices and institutions derived from the military revolution is an integral part of the referential universe of this and other gunpowder epics. What we might have expected to be the bombastic story of a crusading holy war against the Islamic infidel becomes a down-to-earth epic narrative that does not spare any detail regarding the tasks carried out to repair the ramparts, the herding of flocks of sheep, or the pruning of the surrounding olive groves by the troops.[22] For a readership accustomed to the heroic grandeur of chivalric war, this material would hardly have been epic.

Soon in Hierro's poem, however, we find the usual scenes of combat. To replace Hernando de Vega, Charles V appoints the nobleman Sancho de Leyva as the new governor of Mahdia. Whereas Hernando de Vega had envisioned a strictly defensive policy for the presidio, aiming at peaceful relations with the neighboring towns and sheikhs, Leyva initiates an aggressive campaign of raids against the surrounding villages that refuse to pledge obedience to the new authorities.[23] As in other North African presidios, the ravaging of Mahdia's environs generates a profitable border economy (based mostly on the slave trade) as well as a local political logic of its own, far different from the court's grand strategies. Furthermore, this tension between the two imperial administrators over the frontier's role and the politics of space will have an important role in Hierro's narrative.

As an arquebusier, Baltasar del Hierro proudly narrates in the first person the small skirmishes of this dirty war of plundering and punishment against neighboring towns and lords, such as the "small village" of Capulla or the "Sheik of Vakalta (al-Bikalita)."[24] He tells us: "Four hundred of us set out, well armed / ready and eager to fight" (Partimos cuatrocientos bien armados/ oh cuán deseosos ya de pelear), which reproduces, as in the accompanying ballad, the characteristic soldierly ethos and rhetoric of the experienced fighters of Habsburg Renaissance armies.[25] After the battle, the distribution of the loot of slaves and cattle helps strengthen the social bonds within the troop: "Everything was there so bountifully allocated / that all the people rejoiced" (Allí se repartió tan largamente / que bien contenta fue toda la gente).[26] As a professional soldier, Hierro pays special attention to the material and technical dimensions of the enemy's equipment and weapons. He observes that the enemy foot soldiers are armed with *barragán* y *lanzuela* (small shield and short pike), flanked by the *escopeteros*, or arquebusiers, and that they lack the *adarga*, the traditional leather long shield of the Iberian Reconquista wars, which is "not used by anyone in that country" (nadie en aquel país usa el adarga).[27] These displays of specialized knowledge about the author's military profession, as we have seen with other soldierly texts, delimit a discursive object for the new heroic writing and a public of fellow professional soldiers.

Because of the pervasiveness of its classical models, the language of epic poetry has always been characterized as elevated, learned, Latinizing, and sublime, as expected for the highest and most elegant of all poetic forms of the Renaissance. A conversational orality, however, informs Hierro's unabashed poetic idiom, characterized by features like rhyming diminutives in *-ito* or a distinctly oral and popular lexicon, such as *letijo* for *litigio* ("alteration"), or *Sarças*, presumably soldierly jargon for *Saracens*, a feature that his poem shares with other epics and with other forms of military speech.[28] In addition, the *Destruición de África* is also full of inside jokes that are linked to the material world of the soldiers and based on their professional practice and jargon. Hierro's epic stanzas, for instance, deridingly compare a sword blow to the enemy's head with the shearing of sheep, or the effects of a shot to the face with red sealing wax.[29]

The first canto ends by anticipating the public that Baltasar del Hierro expects for his poem, a gesture that confirms the crucial role that reading and writing had in the creation of a distinct sociability in the physical spaces of early modern warfare. Don Sancho de Leyva organizes a small maritime expedition to capture a corsair who is interrupting the fort's supply line from Sicily. The narration of this event—a victorious naval battle—might well fit the generic patterns of epic. The *Destruición de África*, however, offers no such small-scale Actium or Lepanto.[30] Hierro's competence as a professional soldier and his presence in the events recounted determine the limits of the narratable matter, and he explicitly omits the episode: "I was not present at that campaign / because I am no good at sea combat" (Testigo yo no fui de tal jornada / y es porque por la mar no valgo nada).[31] The same criteria, moreover, appear to regulate the reception of the book, according to the author's projection: "I will not write about the fleet / that sailed in chase of corsairs; / let those who know how to fight / recall what a naval clash looks like" (De la flota no escribo que por mar / en busca navegaba de Epirotas / estimen los que saben pelear / qué puede ser rencuentro de dos flotas).[32] Hierro addresses his text to a public of fellow soldiers and comrades, "those who know how to fight." Again, the epic's rhetorical emphasis on the veracity of its referent is linked to the construction of a soldierly identity based on shared military experiences in the social spaces of war.

The second canto of the *Destruición de África* narrates the garrison's mutiny against the imperial authorities during the governorship of Sancho de Leyva, establishing an extremely problematic heroic referent for its narrative stanzas. The story of an uprising against imperial authority and the ensuing period of soldierly self-government by a group of mutinous soldiers should be difficult to accommodate in the genre that has been thought to embody the very discourse of empire as no other mode of writing.[33] Hierro's, nevertheless, is one of the first accounts of an early modern mutiny told from the inside. Furthermore, the rich documentation produced by the rebellious soldiers, Hierro's comrades, in their negotiations with the imperial authorities, now stored at the Archivo General de Simancas, constitutes a unique source of historical information about the mutiny, one that Braudel nonetheless considered "mysterious."[34] But when juxtaposed with the *Destruición de África*, written in the immediate aftermath of the events it recounts, this archive also provides us with invaluable insights into early modern military culture and into the discursive strategies of soldierly self-representation in the Mediterranean world.

Hierro's rationale for the Mahdia rebellion coincides with the documentation produced by both the imperial administration and the rebel soldiers—both identify the delays in paying the troops—"por apenas dos pagas"—and the soldiers' dissatisfaction with their captain general, Sancho de Leyva, as the immediate causes.[35] The soldiers' grievances about Leyva were common motives for mutiny in the early modern period. According to the governor himself, "They complain about me, and they do not want me as their governor because they say I hold their pay and I raise the price of supplies above their cost in Sicily" (Se quejan de mí y no me quieren por gobernador porque dicen les tengo sus pagas . . . y les hago dar los bastimentos en mayores precios que valen en Sicilia).[36] In taking up the mutiny, the narrator abandons the first person that characterized his narration in the first canto, along with his self-portrait as an active arquebusier in the presidio. He initially dissociates himself from the rebels, an overwhelming majority of the garrison according to Leyva's own version of the events in a letter to Juan de Vega. According to Hierro, his mutinied comrades, whom he calls "comuneros encendidos" ("enraged rebels," after the Castilian revolt of 1520), would have "betrayed [their masters] / for greed of money" (traición, que se tenía / pensada por cobdicia de dinero).[37] However, Hierro's construction of a clear stance against the mutineers of 1552—natural for a soldier serving in Milan at the time he published his poem in 1560—is immediately undermined by his depiction of the violent expulsion of Leyva, who runs away in a panic, along with his aristocratic entourage of *entretenidos*, as all of them "fled to the mountains . . . and hid in wells / such was their dread" (corriendo se amontaban . . . se metían / en pozos, por el miedo que tenían).[38]

This is not the only time that Hierro's voice betrays derision toward the military superiors he is supposedly endorsing against his mutinied colleagues. When Leyva tries to go ashore from his refuge in a galley in order to negotiate with the rebels, he is received with cannon shots from the citadel. Again, the poem mocks the hurry with which the captain desists from his attempt: "The round iron so chivvied him along / that he lifted anchor, so as not to sink" (Que tal priesa le da el hierro redondo / que el áncora levó, por no ir al fondo).[39] Despite Hierro's efforts to distance himself from the mutineers, the scornful rendering of Leyva's flight echoes the claims made by "Los Soldados de África," as the mutineers signed, collectively, their correspondence with imperial authorities. "We are determined in brotherhood," the soldiers of Africa wrote to their former general, Juan de Vega, "not to admit Don Sancho as our superior in this land. We would all rather die, since we cannot trust a man who plots against his own people and when everything is disturbed flees like a coward" (Estamos conjurados de no admitir más por superior al señor Don Sancho ni recebille en la tierra; antes morir todos por ello, porque se puede fiar muy poco de un hombre que en su mesmo pueblo anda tramando sediciones y alborotos y después de revuelto pone los pies en huida).[40]

Indeed, after this last mention of his escape, Leyva vanishes from the poem. Hierro devotes a couple of stanzas to the restructuring of power in the now self-governed stronghold. The soldiers vote on a *consistorio*—the designated executive body of a mutinied garrison, including the offices of *electo, canciller,* and *barrachel.*[41] Then, and despite the violent rupture with the legitimate authority over the presidio, Hierro's epic narrative continues as if nothing had really happened. Moreover, it appears that the self-managed garrison is now more effective at supplying and defending the citadel than it had ever been. Luis de Mármol Carvajal, who was far from sympathetic with the rebels in his account of the events in his *Descripción general de*

África, had to acknowledge that "in the ways of government and the administration of justice they were very well ruled by Aponte" (en la manera del gobierno, y en administrar justicia eran muy bien gobernados por Aponte), the democratically elected leader of the mutineers.[42] Hierro's attitude toward the military actions undertaken by the rebel soldiers is equally enthusiastic. In the expeditions against Tabulbah, Moconi, and Monastir, his fellow arquebusiers "did not fail in the cruel fight . . . Goths in valor and strength" (al crudo pelear faltó ninguno . . . en el valor y fuerza de los godos).[43] Indeed, the canto ends with a complex verdict on the feats of arms performed during the mutiny that problematizes both Hierro's previous assertions about the rebellion and the heroic status of his epic matter: "Whether what they did is memorable / and deserves merit and eternal glory / I will leave for someone wiser to judge / since I do not know what I write" (Si lo que estos hicieron memorable / de eterna gloria, mérito concibe/ déjolo a juicio más notable / que el mío, que no entiende lo que escribe).[44]

It is impossible to ascertain which side took Hierro during the mutiny, despite his later self-fashioning as a soldier loyal to the imperial authorities. But we do know that he remained in the fortress for the long months that it lasted and was not among those who fled or were expelled as loyalists. Moreover, according to John Hale, "nothing so fused a sense of solidarity among soldiers off the battlefield as mutiny," and it seems safe to assume that he was one of the mutineers.[45] Thus, for this new form of heroic writing, mutiny becomes a perfectly epic matter. In Hierro's narrative of Mediterranean war, the practices and the social spaces of the *soldados pláticos*, as well as their professional and moral codes, generate a discourse of belonging and pride that prevails over the condemnation of the mutiny in the previous canto. The *Destruición de África* makes very clear the fact that epic writing was about soldiering more than it was about the victorious battles of generals or the imperial designs of kings.

The third canto narrates how the garrison, despite its successful administration during the eleven months of the mutiny, was dismantled by a combination of imperial intelligence and increasing discontent among the mutinied soldierly mass. According to the documentation produced by their leaders, the soldiers of Africa not only negotiated on their own with the Muslim king of Kairouan but were also willing to surrender the town and the garrison to the king of France, "or any nation," "although," they wrote to Juan de Vega, "we would be sorry to act against our nation" (aunque nos pesara hacer cosa contra nuestra nación).[46] Despite the seriousness of the potential betrayal, what triggered the new pro-imperial loyalist movement within the garrison was the rumor that the leaders of the mutiny, weary from the hardships of frontier life, planned to leave Africa without the soldiers' consent, breaking the collective, radically democratic agreement of the soldierly body.[47] This new rebellion is based on the same experiences and practices that had enabled the success of the first mutiny, but the instability of loyalties and the local logic of the remote presidio have made political allegiances difficult to pin down:

> Por una calle asoma gente armada,
> por otra viene ya arcabucería,
> está la ciudad tan alborotada,
> quel que enemigos tiene, no salía;
> quien dice ¡viva el Rey! le es demandada
> palabra de qué Rey o cuál decía,
> que declare hablando sin magaña:
> diga el Emperador o Rey de España.)[48]

> (On one street people in arms show up, another is filled with arquebusiers; the town agitates in riot; those who have enemies hide out, and when someone says "long live the king!" he is asked to clarify, with no duplicity, which king he is referring to, and to say loudly "the Emperor" or "the King of Spain.")

The protagonist of the new loyalist movement is "a soldier that in the presidio / had always been well regarded" (que en la frontera / había sido siempre acreditado), who drew together the companies of Mahdia to fight and imprison the leadership they themselves had previously elected.[49] Hierro's poem celebrates the arrival of the envoy sent by the viceroy Juan de Vega from Sicily to appease the garrison and meet the demands that caused the mutiny in the first place. Again, the *Destruición de África* strikingly resembles the discourse found in some documents collectively signed by the soldiers of Mahdia in celebrating the arrival of Juan Ossorio de Quiñones: "We accept him willingly and lovingly, because in addition to being known by many of us who are here, we know that he is a soldier [sabemos que es soldado], which is what we desired most and what we thought to be more fitting to our purpose."[50] The soldierly esprit de corps based on the shared experiences and the social bonds generated on the frontiers of the empire override any other discourse of social affiliation. What reunites a soldierly mass that had been fractured by its confrontation with the imperial authority and then with the very leaders of the mutiny itself are the strong links of professional solidarity generated by their coexistence in the social spaces of war, a solidarity that texts such as the *Destruición de África* served to articulate discursively and to disseminate among the fighting soldiers. Other forms of social ascription and public identity available in this remote *frontera*, such as that of the Christian versus the Muslim faith or that of national belonging, remain subordinated to the proud defense of the soldiers' prerogatives and their pragmatic political culture.

This idea is confirmed by the surprising conclusion of the poem. After the successful restoration of imperial authority, the garrison receives the new governor sent by Charles V, the famous Renaissance writer Hernando de Acuña.[51] A poet and an infantry captain from a young age, Acuña (1520–80) had already played an important role in Northern Italian and German campaigns of the 1540s, particularly in the pacification of soldierly mutinies in Lombardy and the Piedmont during the same period. After appeasing the rebellion, Acuña was instructed to demolish the fortress of Africa before leaving the town. And the poem closes with an indefinite, inconclusive identification of the sixteenth-century Tunisian town of Mahdia with ancient Carthage, a vague intertextual move that echoes an equally indirect allusion earlier in the text:

> Ya se le acaba el hilo de la vida
> de la ciudad antigua que Africanos
> fundaron en el mundo, tan temida
> en tiempo que reinaron los Romanos.
> Acábase, mas no de ser tenida
> de contino entre Sarças y Christianos;
> acábanse los cabos de quemar
> fenecen las murallas con volar.[52]

> (Now the thread of life is cut of that ancient city that Africans
> founded in the world, when it was so feared by the Romans. It comes
> to an end, but not the continuous fight between Moors and Chris-
> tians. As the fuses burn to the end, the walls of the city perish with
> the blast.)

Carthage had been hinted at, just as vaguely, in the dedication of the *Destruición de África* to a local Andalusian nobleman, Alvar López de Herrera, in which Hierro had characterized Mahdia as "a city as feared as it was renowned in ancient times" (ciudad en sus tiempos tan temida como nombrada) without making explicit reference to the

Punic capital that is also the oblique allusion at the end of the poem.[53] The title of Hierro's poem had itself promised an unmistakably imperial epic, since it echoed the victorious *destruction* of Carthage by the Roman republic in the second century B.C. In 1560, moreover, *Africa* referred not only to the small fortified town of Mahdia but also to the continental dimension of the Islamic enemy. Its annihilation, however, does not consist of the reenactment of a sweeping imperial triumph over a new Carthage, over a new Africa. The title of Hierro's poem refers instead only to the leveling of the stronghold by the same Habsburg imperial authorities that had invested a vast array of human, financial, and political resources in its conquest and defense.

The poem's last stanza also makes clear that the destruction of Mahdia does not imply the end of the struggle between "Sarças y Christianos" for North Africa. There seems to be no true victor in Hierro's narrative. Indeed, the *Destruición de África* appears to be unable or unwilling to impose a clearly legible imperial order upon the events its author witnessed in the small Mediterranean town of Mahdia. Hierro refuses to sing the story of its conquest and offers, instead, the story of its self-destruction, which ends up emphasizing the failure of the whole enterprise and showing the gap between soldierly epic discourse and the Habsburgs' imperial projects in North Africa. There are no promises about the conquest of Jerusalem, no prophecies about the ultimate triumph of Christianity. The grand Mediterranean designs of the Habsburg political elites are often at odds not only with the resistance posed by a seemingly infinite frontier and a multiple enemy—be it neighboring dwellers and kingdoms, Ottoman soldiers, or French pirates—but also with the practical reality of the spaces of war and the society of soldiers. Hierro's inconclusive narrative about matters of war, directed to "those who know how to fight," clearly contributes to the constitution of a social identity based on the professional practice of war, like other instances of Renaissance soldierly epic. But it also reveals the instability of the social, political, and cultural allegiances of those soldiers who, despite being the assumed agents of the empire, were often willing to rebel against imperial authorities or to negotiate with the most irreconcilable enemies of the monarchy to defend themselves, their honor, and their prerogatives.

THE EPIC OF AUTHORSHIP

Hierro's refusal to give a legible closure to his poem may appear clumsily odd to Virgilian humanists or to imperial officials. But the realities of Mediterranean warfare, as lived by soldiers, were indeed far messier than imagined by the imperial designs of Madrid's councilors of war or Sicilian viceroys. The sea, soldiers must have thought, was ruled by the whimsical sway of a reckless and disorderly Fortune. The inconclusive alternation of victory and defeat, the seemingly endless cycle of fighting between *sarças* and *cristianos*, must have felt chaotic and purely contingent for the soldiers on the field and on the galley.[54]

Even after an *ordering* event of extraordinary symbolic and discursive dimensions such as Lepanto (October 7, 1571), the soldiers' lives, in Braudelian idiom, continued to be punctuated by the rhythms, openings, and closings of warfare. Indeed, historians like the Ottomanist Andrew Hess reframed the debate around the historical transcendence of Lepanto by calling our attention not to 1571 but rather to 1574—with the Habsburgs' loss of Tunis and La Goleta—as the actual turning point that stabilized the imperial equilibrium in the early modern Mediterranean and consolidated the Turkish hegemony in the Maghreb.[55] Since Charles V famously conquered Tunis and fortified La Goleta in 1535, both had been considered crucial enclaves for the safety of Naples and Sicily, as well as for confronting the Turkish advances in North Africa and the western Mediterranean. In 1569, an internal conspiracy favored an attack by the Ottoman forces in Algiers, which then recovered Tunis for Selim II. Don John of Austria conquered the city again in 1573, returning it to its previous status as a pseudo-protectorate of the Spanish monarchy, and ordered the construction of the Nova Arx before the city of Tunis, intended to support La Goleta in defense of the territory. In the summer of 1574, Selim II launched a new, ambitious onslaught in the western Mediterranean in order to recover the initiative temporarily lost at Lepanto. La Goleta and Tunis fell after eight weeks of intense siege and bloody fighting.[56]

Sharply contrasting with the glamorous publicity of Lepanto, which in barely three months had produced 190 publications, broadcasting throughout Christendom the most resonant victory of the century, very few printed accounts of the apparently more consequential events of 1574 have survived, perhaps only two.[57] Significantly, however, it is possible to reconstruct a rich corpus of manuscript writings,

Figure 6. Tunis and La Goleta. Georg Braun, *Civitates Orbis Terrarum* (1633, first edition 1575), fol. 58v. University of Chicago, Special Collections.

in prose and verse, produced by the handful of soldiers who escaped death. The violence of the combat, the long period of captivity that followed the defeat for the very few survivors, and the loss of a strategically important territory remained for a long time in the cultural memory of the Spanish side of the conflict. The symbolic and discursive dimensions of defeat in the Mediterranean, however, have received significantly less scholarly attention than spectacular victories such as Lepanto.[58] In this section I will show that when dealing with defeat, captivity, and survival, soldierly writing gave way to a very different reflection on the nature of Mediterranean conflict, the aspiration and the limits of the monarchy of Spain, and the exacting human costs of imperial policy.

Cervantes himself, in *Don Quixote*'s interpolated tale about the captive Ruy Pérez de Viedma, invites us to explore the cultural consequences of 1574.[59] The captain devotes twice as much space to narrating the loss of Tunis and La Goleta as he does to the victory of Lepanto, at which he was captured and enslaved. In order to avoid tarnishing the mythical narrative of Lepanto, the captive considered the loss of La Goleta "a special grace and mercy that heaven conferred on Spain" (particular gracia y merced que el cielo hizo a España), alleging that the benefits did not compensate for the costs of its possession.[60] Another Cervantine—and historical—character, the soldier Jerónimo de Pasamonte, was among the survivors of La Goleta in 1574 who wrote an autobiographical account about the long period of his captivity.[61] The manuscript miscellany that Pascual de Gayangos published as *Memorias del cautivo de la Goleta* and that he arbitrarily attributed to Pedro de Aguilar, companion of Pérez de Viedma in Algiers according to Cervantes's fiction, contains the heterogeneous verse of at least one more surviving soldier of La Goleta.[62] Jerónimo de Torres y Aguilera, for his part, wrote an interesting chronicle of the Levant and Barbary covering the years between 1570 and 1574 after being captured in the same presidio, as he himself recounts.[63] Other soldiers, such as the Italian Bartholomeo Ruffino (for whose account of the Christian defeat Cervantes wrote a couple of panegyric sonnets), officers Juan de Zanoguera and Gabrio Serbelloni, and numerous anonymous infantrymen wrote manuscript *relaciones*.[64] The abundance of testimonies allows us not only to reconstruct the events with painstaking detail and complexity but also to establish biographical and discursive connections among the many fighting and writing soldiers who, after the fall of the legendary fortress, occupied part of their melancholic idleness in captivity by registering their actions and thoughts in often shocking prose and verse.

Moreover, many of these texts show interesting continuities and tensions between epic and autobiography as two privileged modes of war storytelling, soldierly self-representation, and subject production. This is certainly the case in Cervantes's captive tale, in Jerónimo de Pasamonte's memoir, and in the poetic diary of Gayangos's anonymous captive, which intriguingly combines, in the same text, heroic stanzas and autobiographical lyric. Scholars of autobiographical writing have often emphasized its generic instability and hybridity, yet on the other hand, when pointing out its limits as a generic category vis-à-vis other literary forms, Paul de Man opposed it precisely to epic as a solidly consolidated and legitimate model of generic codification.[65] Thus, if we understand them as full-fledged generic categories, epic and autobiography could not be more dissimilar from each other. Epic is usually understood as a poetic narrative of heroic nature about war or travel that oftentimes provides the discursive foundation of a collectivity, the multiplicity of its theoretical and historical formulations notwithstanding. Autobiography, in contrast, has been defined as a "retrospective prose narrative that a real person writes about her own existence, emphasizing her individual life," and it is normally associated with ideals of autonomy, authenticity, and transcendence.[66] Classical epic, for example, would be linked to the representation of an absolute past, inaccessible, according to Bakhtin, in which the hero is "a fully finished and completed being," identical to himself from the beginning to the end of the narration.[67] On the contrary, autobiography is often considered as an intrinsically modern genre, constitutive of modern subjectivities precisely through the introspective and analytical gaze of an individual who narrates, as Lejeune would put it, "the history of his personality."[68]

The forms of narrative poetry that emerged in sixteenth-century Spain, however, produced a peculiar generic form that linked, in a tense relation, the two modes of textual production that we have come to call epic and autobiography. As we saw in the previous chapter, the soldiers who started to write epic poems in the second half of the century, imitating classical and Italian models—and competing with both—purported to offer truly reliable accounts of the multiple wars of the empire from the participating witness's point of view— far, therefore, from Bakhtin's absolute past and from the distanced, monological enunciation of the classical epic voice. Thus the technical expertise of the soldier, together with the authority of the eyewitness, replaced the cultural capital of the professional writer as the main foundation for legitimate enunciation. The enunciative structure of this new form of epic therefore became significantly closer to certain forms of autobiographical discourse, such as the memoir or the diary.[69]

The object of these epic narratives was not, however, the individual lives of the soldiers. If we resort provisionally to the traditional narratological categories with which Lejeune describes autobiographical enunciation, the soldiers were the authors and narrators of their stories but were not their protagonists as individuals. Epic has to do with the discursive constitution of the social identity of the professional soldiery, as we have seen, which usually contributes to the subsumption of the narrator's presence in the mass of the infantry troop. The protagonist, therefore, is collective, rarely individual. What happens, then, when the soldier poses not only as the author and narrator of

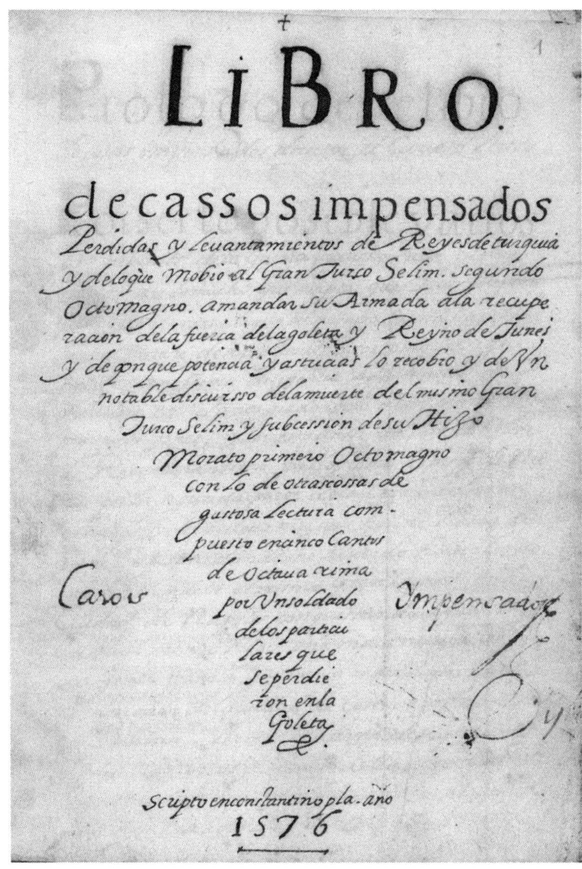

Figure 7. *Libro de cassos impensados* (1575), fol. 1r.
Real Biblioteca, Madrid. © Patrimonio Nacional.

his epic but also as its main character? How does this narrative gesture affect the discursive formation of the matters of war? To what extent does the implicitly or explicitly autobiographical codification of soldierly writing reinforce or problematize the epic narration that is largely constitutive of the soldiers' social identity and their discursive community?

The *Libro de cassos impensados* (Book of unexpected events) was "written in Constantinople in the year of 1576" by "one private soldier of those lost at La Goleta" and who survived the Ottoman siege and conquest of the stronghold in 1574.[70] An intensely autobiographical prologue in prose provides more details about the conditions under which this story of Mediterranean war and confinement was written, conditions that determine the enunciation of the epic matter from the very beginning:

> Como soldado algo curioso y particular de veinte y cinco años de servicio regio en [la] misma Goleta, puedo bien afirmar que todo el tiempo de cuarenta y tres días que estuvo cercada de turcos, e yo dentro della combatiendo cada hora con los mismos turcos por todos recuentros y rebatos y asaltos, de vista de ojo vi y noté lo que pasó dentro y fuera de la misma Goleta. Y que de lo que no pude alcanzar a ver, me informé de algunos de los setenta y tres soldados que, malheridos y cautivos de turcos como yo, escaparon con la vida. Y lo mismo después desto en Constantinopla, tanto de pláticas de turcos renegados como de cristianos de todas lenguas que habitaban allí y de otras personas que se hallaron sobre la armada turquesca en lo desta conquista que, preguntándoles yo, supieron cumplidamente informarme de lo del particular desta jornada en Constantinopla.[71]

> (As a somewhat curious private soldier with twenty-five years of royal service in the said Goleta, I can assure that in every battle, skirmish, and assault, I have been fighting all the time against the Turks during the forty-three days that the fortress was under siege, and that I saw with my own eyes and noted everything that happened inside and outside of the said Goleta, and that what I was not able to see I gathered from some of the seventy-three fellow soldiers who survived, although seriously wounded, and were enslaved by the Turks just like me; and also, from conversation with Turkish and Christian renegades of all the languages who lived there [in Constantinople], and from other people who were in the Turkish navy in this conquest.)

A foot soldier of obscure origin, despite his claims to be a *particular*, the seemingly anonymous author had been serving in La Goleta for twenty-five years, according to his own testimony, when the Ottoman army laid siege to the citadel.[72] The author's self-representation as a participant, on the one hand, and as a surviving captive who had access to the complex informational economy of Constantinople's bagnios, on the other, constitutes the main source of authority and legitimacy for his historical and poetic narrative. Toward the end of the poem, in the characteristic gesture of soldierly writing that we have seen, linking the enunciation to the material conditions of military life and *otium*, the author claims to have composed his text in five cantos of ottava rima "during the little time I was not rowing" (en los ratos que me dio lugar el remo).[73]

In the same prologue, the anonymous soldier makes explicit the two reasons that motivated him to write about some of these events: "First," he says, "so that with this curious occupation I can release the great burden of unbearable thoughts brought to my mind by slavery" (Por con tan curiosa ocupación, vacar de la grande carga de pensamientos que acarrea la intolerable esclavitud).[74] Recent excellent studies by María Antonia Garcés, Lisa Voigt, and Ana María Rodríguez-Rodríguez have noted how the experience of captivity triggered the practice of writing in many different contexts of the sixteenth-century Hispanic world.[75] But the almost therapeutic necessity of "vacar los pensamientos" of slavery and loneliness is unequivocally linked to the space of public debate that followed the defeat. The author also writes his poem—and this is his second reason—"so that I can erase from the public's memory the many opinions, conversations, and debates about this loss" (para con ello mismo apartar de la memoria del vulgo lo de las muchas porfías y debates que sobre lo desta pérdida se han platicado y platican).[76] Political and military responsibility for the loss of La Goleta had indeed been harshly disputed in the royal courts and throughout the spaces of war in both Italy and Spain, as shown by the assertive opinions of Cervantes's captive captain in chapter 39 of the first *Quixote*.[77] One of the accusations that circulated in those conversations or *pláticas* was that the soldiers of La Goleta were not courageous enough and had surrendered the stronghold without fighting it to the end. In a straightforward defense of his comrades' honor, the author does not hesitate to blame the fatal strategic mistakes of the military commanders in charge of the fortresses and, indirectly, the political irresponsibility of the monarchy's higher officials. La Goleta fell, according to the author, because of "the ill government of the superiors" (por mal gobierno de superiores) and, more specifically, because of the priority given to the Nova Arx, the unfinished new citadel in front of Tunis, over La Goleta, where the author himself fought during the siege.[78] The continuous and confrontational critique of the strategy followed by the Spanish commanders, intertwined with the battle narrative, unavoidably intensifies the authorial presence in the epic.[79] In this sort of autobiographical epic, the private and public dimensions of soldierly discourse seem to be equally important for the constitution of the subject as an author.

In addition to discussing the conditions and purpose of his writing practice, the pragmatics of the text, his poem carefully delimits

its inventive matter (*inventio*), the content of his cantos and stanzas. Following the conventions of soldierly epic, the proposition (*propositio*) at the beginning of the first canto reproduces the anti-Ariostean and anticourtly rhetoric popularized by Ercilla and others, dismissing romanzo fictionality and exalting the heroic deeds of his fellow soldiers in the defense of La Goleta:

> No cantaré de amor, no de aficiones,
> no damas, no aventuras imperfetas,
> no de galanes bravos invenciones,
> no motes de personas mal discretas;
> mas cantaré un valor de corazones
> de hispanos vueltos contra mahometas,
> con ruina y destruición de fuertes muros
> que al vulgo vi tener por muy seguros.[80]

> (I will not sing of love and affection, nor of ladies and faulty adventures, not fictions of gallant gentlemen, nor courtly mottos of thoughtless people; but I will sing of the valiant hearts of Spaniards facing Mohammedans, with the ruin and destruction of strong walls that the public always thought very safe.)

As in Hierro's military epic, the destruction sung in this new Mediterranean poem, far from a sweeping victory over the enemy, is indeed the defeat of the author's side, the loss and leveling of La Goleta. The heroic and valorous defense by the Spaniards, nonetheless, still deserves epic praise. The "second prologue in ottava rima, addressed to the curious reader" (degundo prólogo por octava rima, direto al mismo curioso lector), however, which precedes the stanza just quoted, offers a very different and utterly unconventional proposition that somehow subverts the logic of the epic *inventio* as we typically find it:

> Ansí canto una historia relatando
> de cautiverios, pérdidas y daños
> que halla en Constantinopla, a Dios clamando,
> hecho esclavo a Turquía y sus engaños,
> la libertad perdida lamentando;
> de cómo la perdí, versos estraños
> me puse a componer de nueva historia,
> porque en perpetuo siglo haya memoria.[81]

> (Thus I sing a story of captivity, loss, and ruin; for I find myself in Constantinople, praying to God, enslaved to Turkey and its deceits, lamenting my lost freedom. I set out to compose a new history of how I lost it, in strange verse, so that it can be perpetually remembered.)

The story that the poem tells, the heroic resistance of La Goleta's soldiers, appears subordinated to the autobiographical narration of a subject who laments the loss of his hard-won freedom. Epic glory precedes, as we will see, the author's fall into the total abjection of slavery. The "new story" that the author means to leave to posterity in his *Libro de cassos impensados* is not that of the successful Mediterranean crusade of a Christian empire, as suggested earlier, but rather one of "captivity, loss, and ruin" focalized on the author as a slave of the Turks.

The first two cantos of the poem recount, with the customary thoroughness of soldierly epic, the stubborn but ultimately unsuccessful resistance of the garrison of La Goleta against an overwhelming Ottoman army after the arrival of Sinán Baxá's fleet to the North African coastline.[82] The digging of the trenches around the fortress, the battering of La Goleta's walls, and the skirmishes of arquebusiers are all narrated, as in Baltasar del Hierro's poem, with the technical realism of a professional speaking about his trade and with the vividness of someone who saw the battle for La Goleta "with his own eyes," from the inside of the stronghold. The presence of the self in the war narrative is even more prominent here than in other Renaissance epics and the author asserts his own protagonism in several moments of the combat. "I myself witnessed the raising of the bastion" (alzando un gran bestión yo fui testigo), he says, from one of the west ramparts where he was fighting.[83] A few stanzas later, in an emphatic first person he registers the fight of a common foreman of *gastadores*, or pioneers, to defend another part of the fort: "Antón Sánchez, sobrestante . . . / yo le vi en Santiago muy delante." This enunciative rhetoric based on the first person and the punctuation of the narrative with the scrupulous record of the exact dates of major and minor military events often make the stanzas of the *Libro de cassos impensados* seem like a war diary in verse.[84]

The volume of this authorial voice gets louder as the war narrative ends in defeat. Toward the end of the second canto the discourse turns upon itself to question, conventionally, the suitability of the heroic register for the story the soldier tells: "In which style shall I write it?" (¿Con qué estilo sabré yo componerlo?)[85] By the beginning of canto 3, once the defeat is completed and the survivors have been enslaved, the poetic voice suddenly modulates to the lyric lament for lost freedom and enacts a rupture with the previous epic intonation: "May my saddened voice burst the sky / may a sad veil cover my soul / since I lost the free self that I had. / Let my eyes be fountains night and day / since my freedom is stolen by this enemy" (Rompa mi triste voz el ronco cielo . . . cubra de hoy más mi alma un triste velo / pues perdí el libre ser que poseía / sean mis ojos fuentes noche y día / pues mi libertad lleva este enemigo).[86] Heroic discourse can account for the resistance of La Goleta but not for its fall and the subsequent imprisonment of its surviving defenders. When the epic discourse collapses in the face of defeat, the soldierly voice turns to increasingly lyric and autobiographical registers. The fall of La Goleta is equated with the loss of the self— "el libre ser"—that speaks it. The poetic voice addresses a personified stronghold with the following apostrophe: "I will weep for you Goleta, famous fortress / since your loss and mine force me to do so" (Llorarete, Goleta insigne fuerza, / pues tu pérdida y mía a ello me fuerza).[87]

Jonathan Culler and Paul de Man have emphasized the relevance of apostrophe as a crucial rhetorical device to understand both lyric and autobiography. The prosopopoeia, the elegiac appeal to a personified La Goleta, is dragged on into the following stanzas, not so much as an intensified signifier of passion but rather as a device through which "the poet makes himself a poetic presence through an image of voice," as Culler pointed out:[88]

> ¿Adónde estás, diré, Goleta insigne?
> Aunque ya sin señales ni blasones,
> pues no hay en vos cristiano que se incline
> a rezar, ni que en vos haga oraciones
> vuestro eterno nombre, del cual vine
> a morir entre turcos babilones.
> ¿Dónde está vuestra victoria tan constante,
> dónde está el temido fuerte tan triunfante?
>
> No quiero más llorar, que todo es lloro
> cuanto en esta tragedia triste escribo,
> pues solo aquí prosigo aquel tesoro
> de la Goleta y solo en esto estribo;
> porque siendo yo esclavo agora de un moro
> no cabe en mí contento aunque esté vivo;
> mas ya que estoy subjeto a tristes hados
> ¡Llorad sin descansar, ojos cansados![89]

(Where are you, I say, illustrious Goleta? Already without blazons or flags, since no longer Christians kneel down on you to pray, nor does your eternal name motivate invocations, from which I came to die among Babylonian Turks. Where are your repeated victories, where the feared, triumphant stronghold?

> I want to weep no more, for everything is weeping in this tragedy
> that I write, and that treasure of La Goleta I preserve here [in these
> writings], and I myself depend on this. Because I am now the slave of
> a Moor, I find no consolation in being alive; but since I am subject to
> this sad fate, weep without rest, my tired eyes!)

The epic promise of the proposition—"cantaré un valor de corazones /
de hispanos vueltos contra mahometas"—has explicitly turned into a
tragedy. After first questioning the validity of the heroic referent, and
then, to further complicate the generic stability of this autobiographical epic—or epic tragedy—a lyric subtext erupts in a new apostrophe
as an "act of radical interiorization and solipsism."[90] "¡Llorad sin descansar, ojos cansados!" reproduces a line from a widely copied poem
in ottava rima that has been attributed to, among others, Francisco
de Figueroa and is ultimately evocative of Garcilasian echoes, particularly Salicio's famous refrain in the First Eclogue ("Salid sin duelo,
lágrimas, corriendo").[91] The lyric burst interrupts the narrativity of
epic and reinforces the authorial presence in a genre whose grandeur
would seem to largely depend upon the enunciative distance with the
military events being narrated. The substitution of "temporality of
discourse" for "referential temporality," of *discourse* for *story* in their
narratological sense, contributes to privileging the moment of enunciation over that of the epic action. The fall of La Goleta as narrated
in the epic is overshadowed by the image of the author writing in captivity: "escribo [. . .] siendo yo esclavo agora de un moro." Exactly at
the point that the epic narrative ends we find a chain of prosopopoe-
ias that, together with the reference to the conditions of enunciation,
reinforces the lyric, autobiographical, and, more important, authorial
dimensions of soldierly discourse.

Cantos 4 and 5 contain the captive's memoir, including personal
accounts of the course of the Turkish fleet through the Mediterranean, the return to Constantinople, and the death of Selim II and
ascension of Murad III. Once in the Turkish capital, the lament for
the loss of his freedom is woven into a description of the city and the
political intrigues at the Ottoman court.[92] This is followed by a long
description of the Safavid Sha's embassy to the new Sultan codified as
a *triunfo*, an essentially ekphrastic discourse depicting the entrance of
a high authority and his entourage into a city. This was a genre that
Spanish soldiers also practiced extensively, and Baltasar del Hierro,
as I mentioned, wrote and published a piece with these characteristics
in 1564. But in the case of the *Libro de cassos impensados*, instead

of the ekphrastic rhetoric, we find a first-person account of the narrator's tour through the streets of Constantinople.[93] A story about a group of Christian galley slaves who rebelled against their masters in Alexandria and fled with the ship closes the fifth and last canto, a feat that also features in the memoirs of the author's comrade Jerónimo de Pasamonte.[94] What unifies this heterogeneous matter, which deserves more attention than can be devoted to it here, is not the voice of the fighting soldier but the voice of the Christian slave. After the narrator has pointed out the responsibilities of his superiors in the military defeat, legitimate enunciation is now sustained by the necessity of "emptying the thoughts" (vacar los pensamientos) of the captive's memory. More important, however, the author of this generically unstable poetic narrative will ultimately ground the authority of his voice in an insistent elaboration of the relevance of his "act of authorship," as I will immediately show.[95]

In the concluding section of the fifth canto, the author offers his poem to "the soldierly reader" (el letor de la milicia).[96] As usual, the text appeals to a privileged readership to further authorize his narration of the events, asking the same reader for "fraternal amendment" in case of factual inaccuracies.[97] The enslaved survivors of La Goleta and the captives of Constantinople are the ultimate readers of the *Libro de cassos impensados*, according to its own projection, and their testimony the ultimate guarantee of the truth of the eyewitness's discourse. It is in this context that the author reveals his name for the first time. The poem I have been referring to as anonymous—since neither the title page nor any of the two prologues contained any information about the author's name—is actually signed. The author's name, we are told in the last few lines of the poem, is "concealed and fearful" (escondido y temeroso), in some octaves from the first canto: "For the first letters you will find it / in the beginning of this tragic history, / where I recorded my name. / It goes in seventeen lines shrunken / like I am myself [shrunken]" (Por las primeras letras va descrito / en el trágico asento de la historia / do mi nombre al principio hago memoria. / Va en diez y siete versos encogido / como yo lo estoy).[98] And indeed, it is in the first few stanzas of the first canto that we find the author's name constructed with the initial letters of seventeen acrostic verses: ALONSO DE SALAMANCA.

It is simply not possible to ascertain whether or not the hand who wrote this manuscript is Alonso de Salamanca's. But at first, the acrostic device may seem old-fashioned or naïve for the reader of

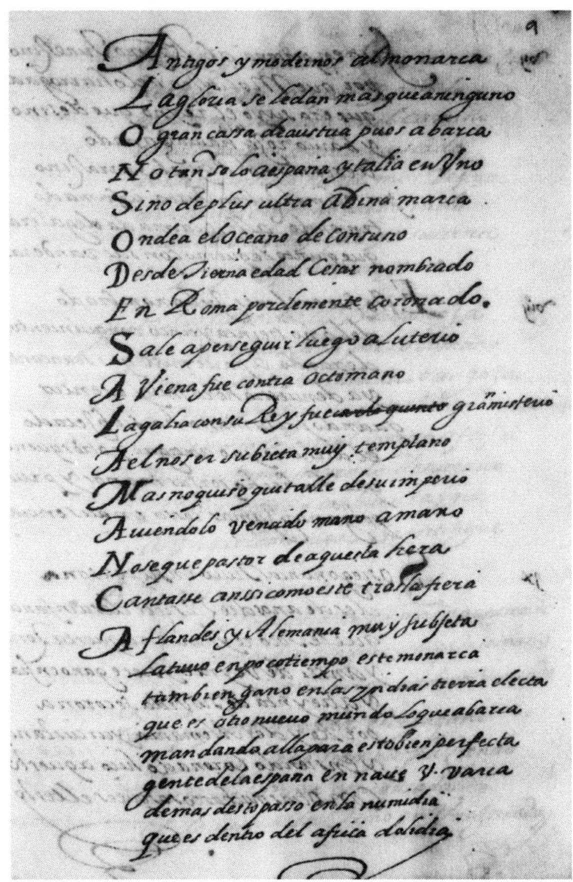

Figure 8. Alonso de Salamanca, *Libro de cassos impensados* (1575), fol. 9r. Real Biblioteca, Madrid. © Patrimonio Nacional.

this particular copy: the materiality of writing forces the reader to come across an emphatically rendered ALONSO DE SALAMANCA in the first canto, making unnecessary the recourse to the explanatory lines at the end of the poem just quoted. Yet what would have happened in other manuscript copies of the text had the acrostic initials of these seventeen lines not been thus highlighted? What if the text had reached the print stage—as the ultimate purpose of this particular copy seems to have been, if we look at the graphic signs closing the blank space of the page in Figure 8? The material mechanisms of textual reproduction in Renaissance Spain would have definitely altered the author's play with the proper name in ways that were not under his control. In any case, the manuscript lacks the paratextual elements that frequently organize authorship in early modern Spanish books, whether printed or manuscript, since there is no dedicatee, no patron, no institutional support, no locatable social space, no *don*, lord of, bachelor in, secretary of. On the other hand, we find no reference to Alonso de Salamanca in other eyewitness versions of the same events authored by his comrades-in-arms such as those by Torres y Aguilera, Bartholomeo Ruffino, and Juan de Zanoguera. His name, finally, is nowhere to be found on the list of captives in Constantinople that a Christian spy drafted in those very same years, although this list makes clear that there were "other soldiers of whom we did not know the names or who they were."[99]

The apparently conventional hide-and-seek play with the proper name poses a significant tension between two interpretive possibilities.[100] On the one hand, it could be read as a symptom of the insecurities about authorship sometimes found in writers of commoner origin. The poet does not seem to be fully determined or sufficiently self-assured to follow the usual mechanisms of attribution and signature, of inscribing his proper name in the work, opting instead to weave it into the texture of the epic stanzas. As in the autobiographies produced by early modern European artisans analyzed by James Amelang, soldiers experienced reading, authorship, and writing itself very differently from other social groups characterized by greater familiarity with lettered practices.[101] The soldiers' experience was marked by doubt, reflexivity, and an acute awareness of their marginality as authors, an awareness that usually manifests itself as a poignant *excusatio* that goes far beyond its purely rhetorical, conventional value. In Hierro's dedication to the local nobleman Alvar López de Herrera in the *Destruición de África*, for instance, the soldier refers to himself as a "little ant" (pequeña hormiga) not fit "to even crawl to the boots" (llegar solo al zapato) of his addressee and of other poets, in a distinctly oral and colloquial idiom that completely outdoes the rhetorical conventions of *captatio benevolentiae*.[102] It is the gesture of the outsider, of the intruder into the republic of letters.

On the other hand, no matter how *hidden* and how *fearful*, the acrostic device is in the end a way of structurally and materially highlighting his proper name. He forces the reader to uncover it and to go back and forth through the pages of his work. Salamanca's tense play with the proper name needs to be understood in relation to what Amelang has described as "the assumption of the act of self-authorship by persons who according to normal social expectations would never have any reason or ability to do so."[103] The anxiety of the amateur writer, of the professional soldier, is in conflict with "the deepest impulses underlying autobiography: an insistence on bearing witness, on leaving to self and others a convincing testimony of experience, and on regarding such testimony as an avenue to a new, if not wholly assumed, identity, that of *author*," as Amelang has also remarked elsewhere.[104] Only a few years after Salamanca finished his text, Sebastián de Covarrubias defined *authors* as "those who write books and title them with their names; and a book without author is badly received, since no one can defend it or account for it" (los que escriben libros y los intitulan con sus nombres, y libro sin autor es mal recibido porque no ay quien dé razón dél ni le defienda).[105] "So that [my reader] can correct me," Alonso de Salamanca says, "I will note my name as I bid farewell" (Para que pueda corregirme / mi nombre aquí le apunto al despedirme), thus signing a poetic memoir that would otherwise remain anonymous.[106]

It is this sense of the autobiographical that I am interested in emphasizing here. For Lejeune, "not only is the system of the author a formal condition, it is in a certain way the fundamental message that the autobiographical genre conveys," while for Paul de Man—despite his critique of Lejeune—the autobiographical moment "makes explicit the wider claim to authorship that takes place whenever a text is stated to be by someone and assumed to be understandable to the extent that this is the case."[107] Authorship and discursive authority are not a given for most common writing soldiers, hence the tense and hesitant voice of the outsider who ventures to participate in the public *pláticas* of the republic of letters. The claim to authorship favors the emergence of the vital, experiential elements—first-person combat, concrete references to slavery, or the eyewitness description of the captive's life in the Ottoman capital—that produce what de Man called "the illusion of reference."[108] The rhetoric of autobiography and the rhetoric of authorship are, thus, intimately related.

The clearest emergence of the author's voice, signaled by the anxious appearance of the proper name in the acrostic, also makes visible a fracture in the discourse of empire. And this rupture is again determined by the tension between epic and autobiography as generic modes for the representation of warfare and in the discursive production of soldierly identity. Instead of inserting the acrostic in the *propositio* or the *invocatio*, perhaps more fitting places to organize the enunciation of the text, the letters of the author's name are embedded in the very beginning of the epic *narratio* and right before starting his story of Tunis. These first *narrative* stanzas begin by sketching a geopolitical history of the Habsburg monarchy in the first half of the sixteenth century: Charles V's imperial coronation, his fight against Protestantism in central Europe, the partial conquest of Italy and of the "New World of the Indies," and, especially, the ongoing conflict with the Ottomans, Alonso de Salamanca's vanquishers and captors.[109] Salamanca's claim to authorship/authority is structurally and metrically embedded in a textual cartography of the emperor's world, but the reader can only *read* this moment after having heard the autobiographical voice of the defeated soldier and the suffering captive, who points to the acrostic in the last stanzas of the text, a voice that promises to write no more heroic stories of empire but new cantos "dealing with slavery, the uttermost evil," as he says in the last lines of the poem.[110] "I did not come out of this war unscathed" (no fue sin daño mío esta contienda), says Salamanca in a transitioning moment of the narrative.[111] Truthful—as he claims—autobiographical writing, the eyewitness narration of both unsuccessful fighting and of his experience of captivity, cannot but undermine the epic writing of the empire by showing its weaknesses and its consequences.

In a passing reference to his classic "What Is an Author?" Foucault wondered "at what point we began to recount the lives of authors rather than of heroes."[112] The question, while posed in a different context, seems particularly relevant for the case I have just examined. What is remarkable about this new form of epic poetry, and particularly about the *Libro de cassos impensados*, is that by virtue of the peculiar discursive economy developed by the soldiers of imperial Spain, these texts tell the story of both heroes and authors. The triumph, so to speak, of the author is parallel to the defeat of the hero. It would seem that we began to recount the lives of the authors at the very moment it was no longer possible to recount the lives of the heroes.

"We must locate the space left empty by the author's disappearance, follow the distribution of gaps and breaches, and watch for the openings this disappearance uncovers," wrote Foucault at a moment when "the death of the author" had become an old literary and critical commonplace.[113] Perhaps we should invert the logic of this program of research in the case of popular and soldierly writing, and we should attempt to locate the spaces where the author *appears* where he or she is least expected in early modern texts, in the form of a shy plebeian signature or in the form of a self-referential, autobiographical rhetoric that destabilizes the literary codes of epic. Enrique García-Santo Tomás has called our attention to the relevance of autobiography in the "depiction of the darker side of the soldierly experience."[114] The discursive articulation of defeat helps us question imperialist narratives that have determined, whether we are aware of it or not, critical practice on the Spanish Golden Age. The complex generic codification of these soldierly texts attests to some insecurities about soldierly identity, the imperial enterprise, and the discursive constitution of the self. It is hard to deny that texts such as those written by Hierro and Salamanca aim at celebrating the heroism of their comrades-at-arms in Africa or La Goleta, forced to fight against an overwhelmingly stronger enemy and abandoned to their luck by their own military superiors. But these texts also tell us a lot about the epic efforts of those who do not write to become authors, the authors of their own social and discursive identities, and who do write to make their small voices audible in the public *pláticas* dominated by those military and political superiors who, ultimately because of "bad government," condemned them to a life of "captivity, hardship, and loss."

LIFE AFTER WAR

Some twenty years after Alonso de Salamanca wrote his epic memoir in captivity, many seventeenth-century soldiers started to write autobiographies in prose, soldiers like Alonso de Contreras, Jerónimo de Pasamonte, Miguel Castro, and Catalina de Erauso.[115] As I will discuss, these were fully autobiographical narratives, retrospective recollections of the self that tried to impose some unity and meaning onto usually plotless lives of personal and collective struggle and material deprivation. Far from the heroic idiom of many sixteenth-century epic poems, they turned to a picaresque mode that has always troubled conservative military and cultural historians because it entails somehow a second, more radical proletarianization of the army.[116] Interestingly, all of these texts remained unpublished in their time. Whereas soldierly epic poems such as Juan Rufo's *La Austríada* and Alonso de Ercilla's *La Araucana* were successfully reprinted during the sixteenth century, autobiographies written by soldiers remained almost entirely in obscure manuscripts until the nineteenth or twentieth century. An author such as Alonso de Salamanca might help us understand this change from printed military epic to manuscript picaresque autobiography as the main generic modes articulating soldierly identity in early modern Spain. The *Libro de cassos impensados* seems to be somehow halfway between these two literary cultures.

While we have no conclusive evidence about whether he tried to publish his poem—although some material features of the manuscript may suggest that he did, as noted earlier—we do know that Salamanca continued to write about the matters of war during and after his captivity and that he did strive to publish a text of very different characteristics. For many surviving veteran soldiers, life after war was very much about the attainment of recognition through an afterlife in print. The will not only to write down their lines on the front but to leave a mark in the memory of their societies through the publicity of print entailed, somehow, a second survival.

The scant documentation about Alonso de Salamanca stored in Spanish archives allows us to reconstruct the story of his life after he put an end to his autobiographical epic in 1577.[117] After serving in North Africa for over twenty-five years, he remained in captivity for fifteen more. His wife and children, also captured in the battle of La Goleta, suffered the same fate. With his meager savings and a significant amount of money borrowed from some of his fellows-in-arms who, just like him, were enslaved in Constantinople's bagnios, Salamanca was able to purchase the freedom he had so poignantly longed for in his *Libro de cassos impensados*. If the social bonds among La Goleta's defeated soldiers were only strengthened by the long period of captivity in the hands of the Turks, the dense networks of merchants, friars, and soldiers in the early modern Mediterranean must have helped him reach Sicily at some point in 1589.[118] In Trapani, only 160 miles from La Goleta, his professional experience and the symbolic capital of ex-captives in the eyes of their military superiors gained him the post of master of artillery, a trade he declares to have exercised for most of his professional life.

Later in 1589 we find him in the streets of Madrid, weary and poor, petitioning the king for his old salaries in order to pay off "part of the 500 ducats that I owe for the ransom of my two maiden daughters who cannot marry because they lost their dowries in La Goleta, where I also lost myself with them" (alguna cantidad de los 500 ducados que debo del rescate de dos hijas doncellas que tengo por casar a causa de haber perdido sus dotes en la Goleta, donde me perdí yo con ellas).[119] The language of the petition resonates with the lyric laments of Salamanca's autobiographical epic. The Council responded favorably at least on this occasion and paid him the monthly salary accrued during his period of captivity: "The Council [of War] finds that it is fair to pay this poor man what the crown owes him and, if it pleases your majesty, to provide him with some help to fix his need, which is urgent" (Al Consejo paresce que es cosa justa que a este pobre hombre se le pague lo que se le debe y que, siendo vuestra majestad servido, se le podría dar aquí alguna parte con que pudiese remediar su necesidad que debe ser grande).[120]

The money was not, however, the only order of business Alonso de Salamanca brought from Sicily to Madrid. Together with his letters of recommendation, *cédulas*, *cartas de poder*, and other papers, he presented to the Council the *Libro del servicio de artillería, compusiciones de pólvora y de fuegos artificiales*, "a book he has composed to teach artillery."[121] He solicited a license to print 1,200 copies of it, because "once the book is published, it will be the greatest service that any master of this profession has ever done to the king, since with no other master than this book's rules and figures, any artilleryman, whether in the Indies or in the other province where the language is understood, will be able to learn" (después de hecho y estampado el libro no parecerá que maestro alguno desta profesión pasado ni presente haya hecho a su rey y señor servicio tan importante como el sinificado, pues con solo el libro sin otro maestro, tanto por provincias de Indias como por las demás que se entienda bien la lengua . . . se podrán enseñar artilleros).[122] This request was followed by the customary administrative labyrinth that returning soldiers had to navigate in order to attain their aims. The Council granted a *privilegio* for twenty years and some money to support the publication of the book, after requiring the author "to reduce it to a briefer style" (le reduzga a más breve estilo) and better handwriting. Although Salamanca reviewed his piece diligently in order to accommodate the demands of the Council, the *Libro del servicio de artillería* would never be published. The story of why and how this may have happened sheds light on the ambitions and limits of the literate soldiery during the early modern period.

His treatise on artillery was reviewed by several people, most illustrious among them Juan de Herrera, Philip II's famous mathematician and architect, and an ex-combatant himself, who evaluated Salamanca's writings positively and encouraged publication. The rhetorically hesitant but courageous voice of the *Libro de cassos impensados* seems to grow increasingly confident. "If it is true," he says, "that most military books touch on this matter [of artillery], and in particular one about *The Perfect Captain* that has just come out, it is also certain they were not written by a serving master, and thus they draw everything from not-very-well understood sources and from a Tuscan book on geometry and mathematical proportion, which is a science misunderstood by most artillerymen" (Si bien en los más libros militares se trata algo desto, y más en particular por uno del *Perfecto capitán* que de presente ha salido, es cosa cierta que no hay en ellos razón de maestro que haya servido artillería, por do se conoce que lo que declaran ha sido sacado de papeles mal entendidos y de un libro de lengua toscana fundada en zumetría [*sic*] y matemática proporción, que es ciencia mal entendida de los más artilleros).[123] Salamanca is referring, first, to don Diego de Álava y Viamont's *El perfecto capitán instruido en la disciplina militar y la nueva ciencia de la artillería*, published in Madrid by Pedro Madrigal in the first months of 1590, just a few weeks before Salamanca sent his *memorial* to the Council of War, and, second, to the influential Italian mathematician Niccolò Tartaglia, one of the founders of Renaissance ballistics.[124] Following a logic similar to the discursive authorization of soldierly literary writing, Salamanca pits his "experience and perfect knowledge of how to put it in practice" (espiriencias y en saber perfectamente obrallas) together with "rule and compass, weight and measure" (con regla y compás, peso y medida) against the rhetorical "compositions of mere words" (compusiciones de palabras).[125] He puts forth his knowledge not only of Italian and Spanish artillery—having traveled throughout Castile examining castles and cannons for a year—but also of Ottoman technologies and practices. If processed on time in 1589, Salamanca's could have been the first treatise on artillery written by a soldier to see the light of print in Spanish.[126]

After careful review, some officials at the Council of War still thought Salamanca's manuscript should be "sent to Ferrufino."[127] Julián Ferrufino had just arrived in Madrid in 1589 to teach mathematics and ballistics in Philip II's newly founded school of artillery and became a respected scholar in Castile's community of military humanists.[128] Julián's son, Julio César Ferrufino (or Firrufino), inherited the post at his father's death, together with all of his papers. It is likely that the copy of Salamanca's unpublished manuscript sent to his father by the Council of War ended up in the hands of the son after

Salamanca's probable death in the last years of the century. In 1626, Julio César Ferrufino published a *Plático manual y breve compendio de artillería* (Madrid: Viuda de Alonso Martín), an artillery handbook that he says he composed "after having seen everything that I laid my hands on about this matter [of artillery], and after having taught it many times as a professor" (después de haber visto todo lo que ha llegado a mis manos de esta materia y de haberla tratado larga y difusamente como catedrático de ella).[129] It does not seem unreasonable to assume that Salamanca's forty years of military experience, as decanted in his manuscript, may be found, at least partially, in Ferrufino's pedagogical imprint.

This story shows, again, the centrality of writing and reading in the society of soldiers. It tells us about the circulation of manuscript and print materials among veterans, ex-captives, imperial officials, and scholars, in spaces ranging from the bagnios of Constantinople, to the presidios of Sicily, to the streets of Madrid. But it also summarizes some of the problems soldiers faced in their struggle for public recognition. Their aspirations to publicity through authorship and print were not exempt from ambiguities. Unlike Baltasar del Hierro, who was able to publish three works during his lifetime, Alonso de Salamanca never saw his *shrunken, fearful* name printed on a sheet of paper. Hierro's success could have arguably been the result of his insertion into the structures of patronage through his remote connection with two noblemen, one of them the renowned writer and courtier Luis Zapata.[130] Salamanca, in contrast, had to ask the Council of War for the name of a potential patron to address his treatise, "a noble person who, in service of your Majesty could take charge of this book and print the 1,200 copies that I promised for these kingdoms and the Indies" (alguna persona particular que para servicio de vuestra majestad tome el libro y con él imprima los mil y docientos que yo prometí imprimir para estos reinos y los de las Indias).[131] Back in Madrid, after forty years away from Spain, he had no access to the institutional arrangements or to the social networks that facilitated publication and organized authorship in the early modern republic of letters. His "pilgrimage to patronage," whether aristocratic or state sponsored, was ultimately unsuccessful.[132]

In *The Letters of the Republic*, Michael Warner argues that "the cultural meaning of printedness can easily remain invisible."[133] Questioning the ultimately deterministic nature of some of the most influential arguments about the history of print that considered the technology as "a nonsymbolic form of material reality," Warner emphasizes the mutual, reciprocal determination between the technological developments of print and the broad, value-laden cultural transformations with which it is usually associated, such as the democratization of knowledge, the spread of literacy, and the constitution of the public sphere.[134] What Warner calls the "metapolitics of speech" regulated access to public discourse and was "the basis for deciding who speaks, to whom, with what constraints, and with what legitimacy."[135] For many of the soldiers who wrote about war, print publicity was indeed loaded with cultural and symbolic values: it endowed their writings, their *pláticas*, with the authority of those who were legitimately able to speak and write. Alonso de Salamanca's truncated attempt to publish a book that condensed forty years of military life and professional experience, his last act as staunch survivor, tells us a lot about the meaning of publication for the curious soldiers of the Habsburg armies but also about the obstacles they faced in their pursuit of public recognition through print.

In the opposite corner of the empire, a fellow soldier fighting in an infamous war that had dragged on for too long made some reflections on the issues discussed in this chapter. Santiago de Tesillo, who was raised to the rank of general (*maestre de campo*) in the Arauco War, wrote his *Epítome chileno, ideas contra la paz* (Lima: Jorge López de Herrera, [1648]) in order to defend a more aggressive military policy against the Mapuche confederation that challenged Spanish hegemony in Chile. But he printed it, according to one of his approvers, because "credit and reputation [are] safeguarded by the immortal life of print" (el crédito y la opinión, resguardos de inmortal vida en la estampa), even though this yearning should be considered a self-delusional "engaño hermoso." The same censor asserts that the soldiers of Chile, who will be the focus of the next chapter, are "oprimidos en las prensas del olvido," oppressed in the (printing) press of oblivion.[136] The paradoxical, and even oxymoronic, formulation of these ideas points to the same ambiguities we have seen in Hierro's and Salamanca's attitudes toward their textual production, their authorial claims, and the publicity of print. Writing could bestow credit upon the forgotten soldiers of imperial Spain and establish their favorable reputation, against the neglect of their superiors or of the nation at large. It could serve to remember and pay tribute to fallen comrades, or it could memorialize mutinied soldiers. It could help broken soldiers have an afterlife in the shared space of public discourse. Writing, and particularly *publishing*, was indeed yet another strategy of survival for a group of individuals accustomed to "live dying," to eschew the repeated onslaughts of death, hunger, poverty, and slavery. But printing, the light of the public sphere, could equally work, oppressively, against the soldiers' aspirations, as a space that belonged to the lettered men of the court personally sanctioned by the king, as a system of exclusion and containment. Writing and printing were indeed "technologies of power" mediated by class, rank, and status that could either advance or curtail the social aspirations of the soldiers.[137]

CHAPTER 4

New World War

Reino feroz, Chile indomable,
de la cruda Belona casa fuerte
y duro campo de batalla esquiva;
castillo de la Parca inexorable,
infierno de la Furia vengativa,
trono de Marte, silla de la muerte.

(Fierce kingdom, indomitable Chile,
Bastion of cruel Bellona
Harsh, elusive battlefield
Parca's unyielding castle,
Hell of the vengeful Furies
Throne of Mars, seat of Death.)

—DIEGO DE HOJEDA

INDIAN MILITIA

The connections between the two longest and bloodiest conflicts faced by what was arguably the war-weariest state in early modern Europe did not go unnoticed to observers. In 1674, Jesuit Diego de Rosales, writing the general history of Chile, felicitously subtitled his work *Flandes indiano*:

> Los españoles que por tierra han descubierto y poblado este Reino
> de Chile, han tenido bien en qué ejercitar su valor, hallando en él
> un Flandes indiano, una sangrienta guerra, una valiente oposición
> y osada resistencia en los naturales desta tierra, que desde el año de
> 1545 hasta este de 1674 han sustentado la guerra contra el poder
> español, contra tantos Gobernadores valerosos y ejercitados capitanes
> de Flandes, por espacio de ciento y veinte y nueve años.[1]

> (The Spaniards who have discovered and settled the lands of this
> kingdom of Chile, have had many occasions to exercise their valor,
> finding in this Indian Flanders a bloody war, a valiant opposition,
> and a daring resistance among the naturals of the land, who from
> the year of 1545 to this of 1674 have waged war against the Spanish

> power and against so many worthy governors and experienced captains of Flanders for 129 years.)

Rosales's powerful analogy linked in a common structure of meaning the two wars that imperial Spain would never manage to win against allegedly weaker enemies. A metaphorical chiasmus of remarkable productivity, as we will see, *Flandes indiano* evokes both historical and symbolic connections that would end up conflating the European and American discourses on warfare and questioning the discourse of colonial difference that had been constructed by some early conquistadores. In Chile, the military and political success of the Mapuche stood as an exception to much of the historical experience accumulated by the Spaniards in the conquest wars of the New World. But the reasons why Chile was different from the rest of the countries on the continent lay precisely in the striking similarities that participants in the war observed with their own—European and Spanish—military practices, values, and institutions. A massive volume of discourse was produced on the Arauco War, mostly by fighting soldiers, in order to understand and ultimately overcome the political and military challenge that the Mapuche confederation posed to the once almighty Spanish empire.

In the following pages I will explore how the New World experience of colonial warfare eventually modified the military practices and literary self-representations of Spain's soldiery as they had been developed in European and Mediterranean theaters of war. I will also explore the narrative articulation of victory and defeat in an outstanding corpus of sixteenth- and seventeenth-century letters, pamphlets, poems, military treatises, and chronicles about the Chilean war, most notably among them Alonso de Ercilla's *La Araucana*. When considered together, these texts give us a shocking picture of the distribution of power and hegemony in the Chilean frontier. They convey a sense of radical contingency and chaos on the Spanish side of the conflict, an almost always retreating empire constantly challenged by the sometimes expansive Mapuche. And when brought back to Europe, these new representations of warfare revealed, once again, the tensions between the participant's narration of war and the legitimation of the empire.

"As all things differ according to their causes, it is thought that wars as well should have different modes and practices, as diverse as the lands, the peoples, the spirits, and the arms with which they fight according to their invention" (Siendo así que todas las cosas difieren conforme sus causas, de creer es, las guerras también tendrán diferente modo y prática cuanto fueren diferentes las tierras, las gentes, los ánimos y las armas con que pelearen a su invención).[2] For veteran soldier Bernardo Vargas Machuca, the Spaniards had shown no less inventiveness than the Amerindians in the ways they adapted their military practice to the needs of the new territories and the realities of conquest. New World warfare thus required "new discourse and new practices, setting aside those of Italy for the most part" (nuevo discurso y nueva prática, dejando la de Italia en mucha parte).[3] His *Milicia y descripción de las Indias*, published in 1599, was written to account for these differences and to systematize the innovations of this new "school of warfare." Vargas Machuca has been vividly characterized as "a short-tempered and arrogant Renaissance pragmatist" and his book as both "the first manual of guerrilla warfare ever published" and "the first known manual of anti-guerrilla, or counterinsurgency, warfare."[4] The *Milicia Indiana* is indeed a brutal handbook of conquest war that incorporates a whole set of largely original tactics, concepts, and practices into the new war of the European military revolution.[5]

Born to a petty hidalgo family from Simancas, in Old Castile, Vargas Machuca spent eight to ten years in Italy after having fought, at a very early age, in the war of Alpujarras against the Morisco uprising (1569–72). Once in the Indies, since 1578, he fought English pirates, resistant maroons, and indigenous insurgents, soldiering in New Spain, Peru, Tierra Firme, and New Granada. In this kingdom he married twice, in both cases to daughters of the encomendero elite, but none of these quite successful unions sufficed to appease the restless conquistador. Never entitled to an encomienda himself, Vargas Machuca spent the last years of his life serving in minor government offices, as *alcalde mayor* and paymaster of the Portobelo fortresses, rarely receiving his due salary, and as governor of the Margarita Island, no fancy destination for the ambitious soldier. He died poor in Madrid in 1622.[6]

Vargas Machuca wrote his *Milicia y descripción de las Indias* upon his return to Madrid in 1596, where he spent over three years among the many *pretendiente* veterans that flooded the empire's capital in pursuit of the king's rewards for their service. This largely explains the bitter, accusing tone of the treatise, which is built on the begging rhetoric of conquistadores' *probanzas de mérito* and which reproduces the complaints of other veteran conquistadores such as Bernal Díaz's regarding the crown's abandonment of its soldiers and conquerors. While in Madrid, Vargas Machuca tried everything: *alguacil mayor* or chief bailiff of Santa Fe de Bogotá, captain general of the Philippines, governor of the regions of Santa Marta and Riohacha, and, more significant for our purposes, captain general of Chile.[7] He could indeed call himself a *baquiano* soldier, an expert Indian fighter with the differential knowledge required to deal with the harsh realities of New World warfare. Nevertheless, he secured none of those posts and he was denied a habit of Santiago. The life and writings of this hopeless hidalgo, a latecomer to the conquests that enriched and elevated so many of his kind, are a perfect example of the military culture that plático soldiers developed in the New World.

Vargas Machuca's peculiar art of war, like a New World Machiavelli, is indeed a thorough "art of conquering" (arte de conquistar) that systematizes "the new arms of warfare in the Indies" (las nuevas armas de la indiana guerra), in the words of two different writers who contributed preliminary poems to the book.[8] Soldiering in Italy is, therefore, fundamentally different from the Indian militia (the way of fighting in America), says Vargas Machuca, experienced in both. First and foremost, albeit no less honorable than their European peers, American soldiers do not earn their salary from the king's treasury, but from the captain's purse. "In the Indian militia," says Vargas Machuca, "the prince has no expenses" (en la milicia indiana el príncipe no hace gasto).[9] One New World soldier is paid "more than ten in Italy" (a un soldado en Indias se le da más que a diez en Italia), but fifty soldiers in New Granada do as much as two hundred in Italy.[10] This crucial difference, which is at the core of the soldier's identity and social role, does not free colonial militiamen from the strict military discipline that Vargas Machuca aims at systematizing. Furthermore, however counterintuitive it may seem, this difference makes the soldiers in the Indies serve the crown and the captain more loyally than do their Italian counterparts, because the former "could quit any time, since they are not obliged by the king's salary" (en su mano está el dejar de hacerlo [servir al rey], pues por ello no tira sueldo).[11] The structure of command in the Indian militia also differs significantly from that of the European armies, since sergeants, ensigns, or corporals are only formal offices of little practical consequence in the Indies, where the caudillo has power over life and death: "He governs, punishes, mediates, distributes, and commands his troop in every aspect, and above all pays them" (Él gobierna, castiga y compone y media, reparte su gente sargenteándola).[12] Warfare in the Indies was far less homogeneous than in the Europe of the military revolution, since arms and tactics "are adapted to the fury and arms of the Indians" (las acomodan a la furia y arma del indio) and as the different lands and peoples require.[13] Whereas commanders in Europe need basic engineering skills to deal with "fortifications of castles, mines and countermines" (fortificaciones de castillos, minas o contraminas), in the Indies they just need to build bridges to wade across vast rivers.[14] In Italy, the recruit's age does not matter, but soldiering in the Indies is so physically taxing that they cannot grow as old as they do in Europe.[15] In the New World, conquistadores have to be expert botanists, trackers, and craftsmen, whereas these skills would not be expected even from the most veteran of Spanish Old World tercios. *Pláticos* become *baquianos* in the New World, just as *bisoños* would be called *chapetones*, both terms being interchangeable in the military discourse on the American conquest.[16]

The discontinuity between the European military revolution and warfare in the Indies has been emphasized by modern historians of colonial America, as well as by the main participants in such events. The respective chronologies of the early conquests and of the Italian Wars only partially overlap. The first imperial wars in the New World predate some of the most long-lasting events and transformative developments of the military revolution, whereas the initial conquests of Mexico and Peru run parallel to the most important European battles of the period. Some historians of colonial America have argued that the "arms of the conquest" were archaic and old-fashioned, tending to associate them with the tactics and material culture of the war of Granada rather than with the Wars of Italy or Flanders. In any case the technologies, practices, and tactics of the conquest responded to diverse temporalities and were, as everywhere else, flexible and eclectic. It is true, for instance, that horses and cavalry acquired a new relevance on American soil that contrasted with their diminishing relative importance on Italian battlefields. Furthermore, military and colonial historians have frequently—though not so convincingly—downplayed the relevance of gunpowder.[17]

The same discontinuities that have been observed regarding strategy, technology, and material culture have been noted with regard to the men of the conquest. Bernardino de Escalante, a contemporary of Vargas Machuca with wide-ranging European military experience but none in the Americas, noted that the Spanish soldiers in general, but particularly those who went to serve in the Indies, were in "want of all military discipline" (*faltos de toda diciplina militar*). The captains of these particularly clueless *bisoños* were no better, according to Escalante: "The officers of the troops sent to the provinces of Peru, New Spain, the Philippines and other islands of that ocean have never soldiered and they have not seen armies battling in their whole lives" (*Los oficiales de la gente de guerra que se lleva a las provincias del Perú y Nueva España y a las Filipinas y otras islas de aquel mar no han militado ni visto jamás campear ejércitos*).[18] There are important exceptions to Escalante's remark. Pizarro's father fought under the command of the Great Captain in the Wars of Italy, and it has been suggested that Francisco himself had Italian experience. Cabeza de Vaca soldiered in Italy, fighting in Ravenna in 1512, and in Spain, against the Comunero revolt in 1521.[19] But in general, only a few of the early conquistadores had previous military experience in Europe when they embarked on the American enterprises.

In his authoritative portrayal of "the men of Cajamarca," Lockhart showed that the vast majority of Pizarro's *soldiers* had no military experience in Europe, although many of them were already veterans of the *milicia indiana*. Only 3 or 4 of Pizarro's 168 men identified themselves as veteran soldiers from the Old World's wars. In Jiménez de Quesada's initial conquest of New Granada, where Vargas Machuca spent most of his life, only 8 out of 115 had engaged in combat in Italy, the Iberian peninsula, or the Mediterranean.[20] Similarly, few among the men of Cortés had European military experience before joining the 1519–21 campaigns during the conquest of Mexico. Veterans Andrés de la Tovilla, "good with the pike," and Benito "Tamborino," the drummer, must have certainly been picturesque characters among Cortés's troops.[21] In his portrayal of "the typical conquistador," Matthew Restall concluded that "he would not in any sense be a soldier in the armies of the king of Spain," an army that he counts among his "seven myths of the Spanish conquest."[22]

Both Lockhart and Restall are right in pointing out the significant differences between the European formal armies and the informal companies of the conquest. Lack of formal training and uniform, unsteady salary, flexible command structures, and private enterprise in financing and managing the conduct of war, however, were as much characteristics of early modern European armies as they were of the marauding bands of conquerors in the New World. Spanish recruits sent to Italy, or *bisoños*, were as inexperienced as some of Cortés's or Pizarro's *chapetón* soldiers. Lockhart's and Restall's analyses, however, corroborate that European experience was an asset in American territory: the *soldados viejos* with experience in the Italian, Mediterranean, or northern European fronts of the Habsburg empire, albeit few, often had prominent roles in the early conquest wars.

Every conquistador with some experience would certainly agree that New World warfare was substantially different from that of the Old World. The pride of baquianos, as opposed to both chapetones in America and Spaniards back in Europe, together with the self-aggrandizing discourse of conquistadores such as Cortés, Bernal, and Jiménez de Quesada, was based precisely on the differential know-how that they could provide the crown and the imperial authorities. This difference was constitutive of their public identities and their discursive practices before the crown and among their compatriots on either side of the Atlantic. Both sixteenth-century observers and today's scholars seem to agree that the men, the material culture, and the practices of warfare were substantially different in the New and the Old worlds.

It is against this background that we should understand the conquistadores' shock after their arrival in Chile, where the accustomed patterns of previous conquests seemed to fail time and again. The experience of war in one of the most remote frontiers of the Habsburg monarchy forced the same men to come to terms with a disturbing similarity that suddenly challenged the discourse of difference on American warfare. The Indian militia, as practiced in Chile, required the men of Cajamarca and beyond to fight an enemy that looked too much like a European army. Soldiering in Chile, Vargas Machuca would have said, was not that different from soldiering in Italy. The American experience of war on the southernmost edge of the empire effectively shattered some of the most defining self-representations of the Spanish imperial soldiery, which had been consistently elaborated on the European and Mediterranean fronts of the empire and refashioned in the American context. The Chilean question generated a massive amount of discourse not only on colonial warfare but also, eventually, on the limits of imperial practice and discourse and on the presumed cultural hierarchies that had previously shaped the colonial encounter.[23]

As a result of the trajectories and geographies of the conquest that led to Chile, most of the first Europeans who set foot in the territory had previous experience in the warfare of the New World. The expedition led by Diego de Almagro in 1535 was comprised partly of the "men of Cajamarca," who would infamously return to Cuzco in 1537 as "los rotos de Chile"—the broken soldiers of Chile—after their encounter with the Mapuche armies. In contrast with the vast majority of imperial campaigns in the New World, the next Chilean expedition was led by a plático from Italy and counted among its members a few of his kind. Pedro de Valdivia was arguably one of the most veteran soldiers among the conquistadores in the New World. "I served Your Majesty in Italy, as I was obliged, in conquering the State of Milan and imprisoning the king of France in the times of Próspero Colonna and the Marquis of Pescara" (Haber servido a V. M., como era obligado, en Italia en el adquerir el estado de Milán y prisión del Rey de Francia, en tiempo del Próspero Colona y del Marqués de Pescara), he said in his most detailed service report to the king, where he also remarked on his service in the Low Countries.[24] His European experience provided him with an expertise that was very much appreciated in the Indies, where unseasoned bisoños abounded according to Escalante, but also, no less importantly, with a crucial symbolic capital that allowed veterans to lead with authority. Once in America, he took part in the conquest of Venezuela and in the campaigns against Manco Inca Yupanqui's resistance, when Pizarro, "knowing my desire and my experience in the matters of war" (conociendo mi deseo y experiencia en las cosas de guerra), chose him maestre de campo general.[25] Finally, he was instrumental in the imperial victory over Gonzalo Pizarro's rebellion during Peru's civil wars.

Writing from Concepción to Emperor Charles in 1550, after crossing the Bío Bío that demarcated the Arauco region, Valdivia reports how he found some Indian battalions who fought "in such a way that, I swear to my faith, in the thirty years that I have served Your Majesty in combat against many different nations, I have never seen people fighting in battle with such determination as these Indians did against us" (de tal manera, que prometo a mi fe, que ha treinta años que sirvo a V.M., y he peleado contra muchas naciones y nunca tal tesón de gente he visto jamás en el pelear, como estos indios tuvieron contra nosotros).[26] The charges of the Spanish cavalry were repeatedly repealed by the discipline of the Mapuche army, and only after hours of intense combat did the Spanish infantry finally force the Araucanians to retreat.[27] Just as in Europe the efficiency of mounted knights had largely decreased after the tactical and technological rearrangements of the military revolution, and against the new currency cavalry gained in American conquest wars, it failed this time, according to Valdivia, precisely because the Mapuche armies fought like their European counterparts: "They defended themselves very bravely," says Valdivia, "fighting in perfect battle formation, like the Germans" (cerrados en escuadrón, como tudescos).[28]

The comparison was anything but fortuitous. Writing from Florence in 1521, while Valdivia fought in Lombardy, Machiavelli compared the Macedonian phalanx and the Roman legion to the battalions of Swiss and German pikemen. "The present mode of arming," says Machiavelli, "was discovered by the German peoples," who "were poor and wanted to live freely."[29] Valdivia compares the Araucanians to those Machiavelli identified as the pioneers of the military revolution. The Spanish armies that later became exemplary for Machiavelli in their imitation of the Germans, in turn, will have to relearn the lessons of Seminara, Ravenna, or Pavia in order to face the Germans of the New World. If "all that is good in the present military depends on the example of those peoples who," like the Germans, "are altogether jealous of their states" and "maintain themselves lords and honored," the Mapuche fighters are represented from the very first contact as American masters of the most sophisticated European arts of warfare.[30]

Valdivia was not the only veteran startled by the similarities of indigenous warfare to their own, in contrast with the constitutive differences signaled by Vargas Machuca and others. "When they come to war," said veteran soldier and chronicler Jerónimo de Vivar following Valdivia's reasoning, "they come in squadrons in such a good discipline and order that it seems to me that if they had learned to wage war with the Romans they would not come in a better order" (Vienen en sus escuadrones por buena orden y concierto, que me parece a mí que, aunque tuviesen acostumbrado la guerra con los romanos, no vinieran con tan buena orden).[31] In addition to their efficiency in open field combat, the Araucanians mastered the other, equally defining dimension of the Renaissance military revolution. Called by some of the German masters *der kleine Krieg*, petty war "was thus as much the staple of early modern warfare in many parts of Europe as pitched battles and protracted sieges . . . guerrilla was as important as guerra."[32] "It seems to me," continues Vivar, "that in the sleights they use in war and their way of fighting they are like the Spaniards when they were conquered by the Romans, and so they are as excellent as we are in Spain" (Me parece a mí en los ardiles que tienen en la guerra y orden y manera de pelear, ser españoles cuando eran conquistados de los romanos. Y así están en los grados y altura de nuestra España).[33] The Chilean Indians resemble not only the Roman imperial armies but also the Numantines, the ancient *Spaniards*—in Golden Age antiquarian discourse—who heroically resisted the Roman empire. Vivar establishes a chiasmatic comparison that will end up being equally troubling for the discourse on the Arauco War.

The Chilean exception stubbornly problematized the discourse of colonial difference, of a specifically *Indian* militia, as tentatively systematized by Vargas Machuca in his American art of war. In Chile, after the partial or total failure of several conquest attempts, soldiers in what would arguably be the first standing army of the continent were paid by the crown. Strict European models were invoked and implemented in order to save the army from the barbarization of the Spanish Indian militia. Many of the soldiers and commanders fighting in Chile after the second general uprising of 1598 were veterans from Europe. Indigenous soldiers in Chile were fierce, disciplined, honorable, and successful, as opposed to the general picture painted by the New Granadan Vargas Machuca.

These practices and representations had a crucial impact on colonial discourse in general and they forced curious soldiers back in Europe to reformulate some of the basic tenets of their public identity and discursive practice. The soldierly texts that I have commented on thus far exemplify some of the complexity and subtlety that imperial warfare acquired in colonial Chile after the first Araucanian rebellion led by Caupolicán and Lautaro in 1553, which would leave an indelible mark on the cultural memory of early modern Spain thanks to the pen of the most famous of Chile's European soldiers, Alonso de Ercilla. A dispossessed member of the Basque hidalguía who became a soldier and adopted the ways of the *pláticos* in the colonial spaces of war, Ercilla created one of the most memorable pieces of military literature of early modern Spain. *La Araucana* is one of the earliest and most influential attempts at understanding the failure of empire in the southernmost edge of America, and it contributed like no other text to the production of the Chilean exception. The poem's interpretive complexity partially stems from the same tensions and surprises that we have seen in Valdivia's and Vivar's writings and thus should be read within this discursive and social context. Valdivia's offspring, the soldiers who fought, read, and wrote in and about Chile had indeed to deal with the "most infamous land of the Indies" (la tierra más mal infamada de cuantas hay en las Indias).[34]

THE WAR INSIDE OUT

> Y si a alguno le pareciere que me muestro algo inclinado a la parte de los araucanos, tratando sus cosas y valentías más estendidamente de lo que para bárbaros se requiere, si queremos mirar su crianza, costumbres, modos de guerra y ejercicio della, veremos que muchos no les han hecho ventaja, y que son pocos los que con tan gran constancia y firmeza han defendido su tierra contra tan fieros enemigos como son los españoles.[35]

> (And if it seems to some that I show myself somewhat inclined toward the side of the Araucanians, treating their affairs and deeds more extensively than is required for barbarians, we might look at their upbringing, their customs, their methods and exercises of warfare, and we should see that many have not surpassed them and that few are those who with such constancy and firmness have defended their land against such fierce enemies as are the Spaniards.)

Ercilla's apologetic tone in defending his praise of the Araucanian people in the prologue to the first installment of his poem suggests that for the author, or even for his first readers, his indigenous inclinations could have been problematic. The poet responds to this anticipated criticism by offering a detailed poetic ethnography of the barbarian enemy, an extended discussion of their military practices and institutions throughout the poem that would justify his legitimate admiration. Ercilla's narration of Chile's Indian militia, however, will go far beyond the epic conventional praise of the worthy enemy who is defeated by an even worthier hero. In the discourse of early colonial Chile, as founded by Ercilla's wildly popular poem, there is a consistent conflation of the representations of the indigenous warriors and some of the most defining self-representations of the Spanish imperial soldiery. The soldiers of the Habsburg armies in both the Old World and the New would confront in southern Chile an enemy that was disturbingly similar to themselves. By challenging the construction of colonial difference, furthermore, this discourse of identity between the Spaniards and the Araucanians would eventually allow for a troubling reversal of the imperial hierarchies of colonizer and colonized.

Some of Ercilla's readers have emphasized *La Araucana*'s ethnographic drive, but fewer have noted that the main object of this ethnographic observation is specifically a repertoire of "the customs and modes of war of the natives" (las costumbres y modos de guerra de los naturales).[36] In the first canto, Ercilla exposes in detail the military institutions and practices of the Mapuche, including the leading role of the sixteen caciques of the *Estado* (State) who are entrusted with the teaching (*dotrinar*) of the matters of war (*las cosas de guerra*) down the structures of command. Officers are exclusively elected for "their arm's virtue and excellence" (la virtud de su brazo y la excelencia) rather than by their social standing, lineage, or wealth (*calidad, herencia, hacienda*). Soldiers are meticulously trained in their weapons of choice and in military discipline, as they are taught to form in those solid, but tactically flexible, squadrons that made such a vivid impression on the European veterans of the conquest. Finally, Ercilla devotes some attention to Mapuche military technology and engineering, describing war devices and fortifications with the sophisticated technical vocabularies of Italian poliorcetics.[37]

Moreover, it is not only their military virtue, institutions, and practices that bring the Araucanians close to the Spanish warriors they face. The bodies of Mapuche soldiers, far from the exoticizing gaze of much colonial discourse, are also read and represented through the social codes and vocabularies of European pláticos. Araucanian soldiers in Lautaro's squadron rushed to fight the Spanish contingent in the site of Andalicán "in an agile and graceful march, / more gallant than brave Germans, / dashingly parading back and forth" (con muestra airosa y contoneo/ más bizarros que bravos alemanes/ haciendo aquí y allí gentil paseo).[38] Bizarría came to characterize not only the bodily hexis of German lansquenets and Swiss pikemen but also the public image of Spanish soldiers after the Renaissance military revolution, as we have seen. The same behavior characterizes the Mapuche army, when they return victorious to the Arauco valley as "bárbaros bizarros," or Lautaro's talk with Marcos Veaz at the Spanish fort, where the Araucanian hero gallantly threatens the defeated Spaniards, leaning on his bloody pike as a Virgilian, Antarctic lansquenet.[39] When displayed in the New World, the vocabularies of professional warfare contributed to conflate the representation of the other and some of the most defining self-representations of the imperial soldiery.

The multiple stories of *La Araucana* function as a practical and varied sampler of the brief but comprehensive military ethnography displayed in the first canto, an art of war that turns out to be put into practice by American soldiers quite similar to their European counterparts. The Araucanians become "soldados pláticos"—as Ercilla calls them throughout the poem—of a kind very similar to that of Valdivia, Vivar, Ercilla, and the rest of the Spanish soldiers in Chile.[40] When Caupolicán is captured incognito, some Spaniards recognize him despite the fact that he looks like a rank-and-file, plebeian, low-salaried soldier ("incógnito soldado / de baja estofa y sueldo moderado").[41] It is precisely the inaccuracy of the terms—we know that the Mapuche had no system of retributed military service—that reveals Ercilla's conflation of his Spanish comrades-in-arms and his enemy's captain. All of them are *soldiers*. The social world and discursive practices of the pláticos, when transplanted to the Indies, engendered representations of the enemy that unsettled the hierarchies and the othering tropes constructed elsewhere in imperial discourse.

This reversal of the imperial gaze regarding the matters of war has implications of great consequence, since political subjection follows defeat on the battlefield. It will thus be worth revisiting some of the multiple moments when Ercilla displays the European vocabularies of political power to rationalize Araucanian supremacy. In addition to the Roman military virtue of their soldiers, and the Numantine valor of their resistance, Ercilla's heroes are also donned with the prudence, daring, and shrewdness of Renaissance politicians, which adds to the protean identity of the Mapuche in Ercilla's poem. When discussing the etymology of the polity's very name, Ercilla establishes a Venetian analogy that would be crucial throughout the rest of the poem. *Arauco* comes to be the name of the state by a semantic extension of Peteguelén's valley, just as the "free nation" (pueblo libertado) of Venice gives name to the rest of the *signoria*'s territories.[42] *Señoría*, indeed, is repeatedly used, together with *senate*, *state*, and *republic* (senado, estado, república), to refer to the Mapuche confederation; and the Araucanian rebellion in Ercilla's story always aims at restoring "the force of our repressed old laws of freedom" (nuestras viejas leyes oprimidas / sean en su libre fuerza restauradas), in Caupolicán's words.[43] Ercilla's discussion of the political constitutions and practices of the Estado del Arauco is built on republican discourse, likely of Machiavellian origin. Venice's seemingly boundless ability for political survival in the tumultuous context of Renaissance Italy, under *fortuna*'s realm of pure contingency and swayed by the Aragonese, the French, and the Castilians, provided a trope and a vocabulary to approach the political practice and institutions of Chile's "free, independent, indomitable people" (gente libertada, esenta, indómita) of Ercilla's poem.[44] Venice stands as the emblem of political success not only in maintaining its ancient liberties but also in keeping up with a prudently ambitious policy of imperial expansion based on a sophisticated and innovative inquiry into the modern matters of war.[45] The virtue of the military order is strictly linked in Machiavelli to the virtue of the republican constitution and to civic life. The Arauco State is, for Ercilla, a perfect republic of soldiers. And the Spanish knew all too well, like the Florentines, that the only way to conquer a people used to living in freedom was their total destruction, "because when it rebels, it will always be able to appeal to the spirit of freedom [libertà] and its ancient institutions [ordini antichi], which are never forgotten, despite the passage of time and any benefits bestowed by the new ruler."[46]

The second installment of the poem continues some of the themes of the 1569 first canto. In the exordium to canto 25, which narrates the landmark Spanish victory of Millarapué, Ercilla poses the problem in very precise terms:

Cosa es digna de ser considerada
y no pasar por ella fácilmente
que gente tan ignota y desviada
de la frecuencia y trato de otra gente,
de inavegables golfos rodeada,
alcance lo que así difícilmente
alcanzaron por curso de la guerra
los más famosos hombres de la tierra.

Dejen de encarecer los escritores
a los que el arte militar hallaron,
ni más celebren ya a los inventores
que el duro acero y el metal forjaron,
pues los últimos indios moradores
de araucano estado así alcanzaron
el orden de la guerra y diciplina,
que podemos tomar dellos dotrina.

¿Quién les mostró a formar los escuadrones,
representar en orden la batalla,
levantar caballeros y bastiones,
hacer defensas, fosos y muralla,
trincheas, nuevos reparos, invenciones
y cuanto en uso militar se halla,
que todo es un bastante y claro indicio
del valor desta gente y ejercicio?[47]

(It is certainly worth pausing to carefully consider that these people, so remote and isolated from communication with any other people, surrounded by unnavigable oceans, have come to know by the practice of warfare as much as the most famous men on earth.

Let the writers not praise those who invented the military art, let them celebrate no longer those who invented steel and forged metal, since the farthest Indian inhabitants of the Araucanian state so perfected the discipline and order of warfare that we can learn from them.

Who taught them how to form squadrons, to present battle in order, to raise towers and bastions, to build defenses, moats, walls, trenches, fortifications, war machines, and everything that is found in military practice—since this is a clear enough sign of the valor and training of these people?)

In these stanzas, Ercilla goes well beyond the genre's conventions, turning the epic praise for the enemy, encoded with the vocabularies of the new European war, into an outright acknowledgment of Spanish inferiority. Soldier Alonso de Góngora Marmolejo, writing in 1575 after having read Ercilla's first part of *La Araucana*, insisted on some of his ideas: "Many will be pleased to hear that at the end of the world these naked, disarmed, and barbarian people are so bellicose, astute, and daring in the defense of their land" (Muchos se holgarán de saber en el cabo del mundo gente desnuda, bárbara y sin armas sea tan belicosa, ardidosa y arriscada por la defensión de su tierra).[48] Alonso de Ovalle, who dismissed Ercilla's "hyperboles and exaggerations of poetic art" (hipérboles y encarecimientos propios del arte poético) while praising the general historical accuracy of the poem, would quote these stanzas in full just to judge them as an understatement of Araucanian valor: "It does not suffice to entirely understand what these people are" (No basta para hacer entero juicio de lo que es esta gente).[49] The Araucanian state, surrounded by oceans and far away from any plausible contact with the *civilization* of war derived from the European military revolution, has been able to reach the same degree of excellence in the conduct of warfare as the masters of Renaissance military treatises and the experienced generals of the Wars of Italy—or Flanders. The rhetorical questions of the last quoted stanza challenge the military superiority of the Spanish of Pavía, or even of San Quentin and Lepanto, which feature prominently in cantos 17, 18, and 24 of the poem.[50]

In order to fully appreciate the radicalness of Ercilla's poetic ethnography and the ramifications of his epic excess, it is useful to turn to the most standard formulation of imperial discourse's rationale and justification of conquest. Sixteenth-century Spanish jurist Juan Ginés de Sepúlveda's defense of the wars against the peoples and polities of America compared warfare practices, institutions, and values of Europeans and Amerindians in order to argue for the superior rationality of the former.[51] In a conventional historical narrative, Sepúlveda surveyed the innate military virtue and *fortitudo* of Spain's fighters as proof of their undeniable superiority. The feats and virtues of the Great Captain and Emperor Charles, their campaigns in Italy, Africa, and Germany, and the valor of the "Spanish legions" are not comparable to those of the American "little men" (homunculos illos; hombrecillos).[52] Sepúlveda's brief history of Spain's ancient and modern landmark campaigns was published in 1544, the same year Valdivia first crossed the border into Arauco territory on the southernmost edge of the new continent just to find warriors very similar to those he had fought against and along with in Milan and Naples or in Belgium and France. Those warriors also made veteran Jerónimo de Vivar, campaigning with Valdivia, wonder whether they looked like Roman "legions" or rather like the Spanish Numantines who resisted them. *La Araucana* is in fact a magnificent poetic spectacle of the *fortitudo* of Araucanian *legiones*. Ercilla's reconceptualization of indigenous warfare and military culture entails a radical inversion of the cultural and political hierarchies of colonial discourse. The Spaniards should mirror the indigenous military *doctrine* if they aspire to win a war that both in 1557, the historical time of Ercilla's narrative, and in 1578, when these lines were first read in print, was irremediably heading toward defeat. The Chilean war experiences of the plático soldiers, those to whom Sepúlveda dedicated his first *Democrates*, destroyed in practice the theoretical superiority of the Spaniards. Ercilla's representation of the Araucanian plático soldiers calls into question some of the basic tenets of colonialist discourse.

Colonial representation is always structured through hierarchical difference. "The essence of Sepúlveda's position," says Rolena Adorno, "is not the characterization of the Indians as such, but rather, in the hierarchical relationship that emerges from their encounter with other (superior) peoples."[53] Similarly, Mary Gaylord considered Sepúlveda's Aristotelian argument as one of the most defining identity tropes to understanding early modern Spanish self-fashioning. What she called "the mastery model of identity" was based on a dissimilarity that always entailed hierarchy and domination, the basis of "a system that values some parts and persons over others, and claims for its distinctions the status of the natural order." If writing is the most efficient way to control the system of differences, Ercilla's poem constitutes one of the most significant "retropings of identity," first through the production of similarity and then through the inversion of hierarchies. Ercilla will become, indeed, a "master of metaphor, controller and arbiter of relations and hierarchies, differences and substitutions" through the reversal of the "positional superiority" of the European *optimates* over the indigenous *homunculos*.[54]

As the war progresses, the conflation and ultimate inversion of the colonial positionality would only make things worse for the Spanish attackers. The efficacy and sophistication of the institutions and practices of indigenous warfare, as we saw in the previous section, sufficed to problematize some of the more stable discourses of European superiority. Yet it is also remarkable that in the representations and practices of warfare in the Arauco the Mapuche came, by virtue of their imitative skills, to look like Spanish soldiers more than the Spanish soldiers did themselves. The Spaniards did actually "learn from the teachings" of Araucanian military practice and doctrine. Conquistadores adopted indigenous technologies and customs such as the Chilean version of the *escaupil*, a light armor made of pressed cotton, Araucanian fortification, and dietary habits that better suited them for war in southern Chile.[55] Even someone like Vargas Machuca seemed willing to acknowledge that "the natives of those lands have invented so many war stratagems, as we said, that they have taught us some we now use, which are necessary to counter them" (son tantas las invenciones de guerra de que usan los naturales de aquellas partes, como ya queda dicho, que nos han enseñado algunas de que usamos y son necesarias para contraminalles).[56] But the Araucanian were far more effective in their surprisingly expeditious and efficient appropriation of European military practices, a fact that has often been noted by historians of the conquest of Chile and that accounted to a significant extent for the success of the Araucanian rebellion.[57]

The Araucanians successfully imitated and improved the use of horses in battle, and *La Araucana* narrates numerous episodes where Indian cavalry successfully competes with Spanish horsemen.[58] Furthermore, the Mapuche improved their pikes through the fruitful appropriation of European technologies and materials, as well as their fortification techniques.[59] Eventually they would also adopt the use of firearms, a move that would further complicate the identity effects of soldierly discourse and gunpowder culture in the Chilean context. Already in the seventeenth century, Santiago de Tesillo summarized as follows the adaptive skills of Araucanian soldiers and concluded, with Vivar, that "they have become excellent soldiers through the practice of arms in the course of this war; they ride horses and handle weapons with swiftness and dexterity . . . and this, I think they do it better than us" (hanse hecho estos indios con el curso de las armas y largo ejercicio de la guerra, excelentes soldados; ejercítanse a caballo y manejan las armas con desenfado y destreza . . . y por este lado juzgo que nos hacen grandes ventajas).[60]

Instances of indigenous appropriation of Spanish practices, objects, and technologies can be found in all the three parts of *La Araucana* and in many of the stories it recounts. However, it will be worth pausing for a moment at one particularly celebrated and compelling episode of Ercilla's narrative that fictionalizes the process of cultural mimesis. After the first successes of the Araucanian rebellion, including the execution of Valdivia and the sack of Concepción, the caciques gather in "the Great Senate" in order to discuss the course of action against the Spanish invader, still far from being completely defeated. A triumphant Caupolicán appears before his army and his fellow citizens in the following fashion:[61]

> Llevaba el General aquel vestido
> con que Valdivia ante él fue presentado:
> era de verde y púrpura tejido,
> con rica plata y oro recamado,
> un peto fuerte, en buena guerra habido,
> de fina pasta y temple relevado,
> la celada de claro y limpio acero,
> y un mundo de esmeralda por cimero.
>
> Todos los capitanes señalados
> a la española usanza se vestían;
> la gente del común y los soldados
> se visten del despojo que traían;
> calzas, jubones, cueros desgarrados,
> en gran estima y precio se tenían;
> por inútil y bajo se juzgaba
> el que español despojo no llevaba.[62]

(The general donned that dress that Valdivia was wearing when he came to him: woven in purple and green, richly embroidered with gold and silver, a strong breastplate won in good war, well forged in a fine alloy and bas-relieved, the helmet made of bright steel, all crowned by a crest of emerald.

Every important captain was dressed in the Spanish fashion; the common people and the soldiers also clad themselves in battle spoils: breeches, doublets, and torn leather were held in high esteem, and he was thought lowly and useless who had no Spanish spoil.)

Many testimonies of the Arauco War, as it often happens in Ercilla's poetic rendering, certify the currency of this practice among the historical Mapuche, regardless of the relevance of the classical mediation in Ercilla's text.[63] In 1606, in the attack on Boroa during the second Mapuche general uprising, Diego de Rosales described how "three thousand selected foot soldiers and six hundred cavalrymen marched flashing bright steel armors, crests, ribbons, and fine full dresses that had been sacked from the cities of Imperial, Valdivia, and Villarrica, and many wore surplices and priestly habits to deceive the Spaniards into believing that they were not Indians or just to mock them and to show off the spoils" (tres mil infantes escogidos y seiscientos de a caballo, marcharon con grande lustre de armas de acero, penachos, bandas y vestidos de gala de las muchas que habían saqueado en las ciudades de la Imperial, Valdivia y la Villarrica, y muchos iban vestidos con sobrepellices, hábitos de clérigo y vestiduras sacerdotales para engañar a los españoles y que entendiesen que no eran indios o por mofar de ellos y hacer gala de los despojos).[64] Similarly in a later passage, where Ercilla recounts how the young Araucanian athletes compete over some weapons captured from the Spanish enemy, the poet is echoing not only Virgilian and Homeric models but also the actual practices of material appropriation by the Araucanians, which played a crucial role in their military and political success against imperial Spain, and which surprised their incapable enemies. By the time Escobar edited the papers of Captain Mariño de Lobera, another curious soldier who told the story of the wars he fought in Chile, Caupolicán had reached an almost legendary dimension, as he was seen "riding a white horse in a maroon cloak, as a very imposing Spaniard in command and attire . . . with the aspect and the ability of the most expert captain of Naples or Flanders" (en un caballo blanco y con una capa de grana, como si fuera un español muy autorizado así en su traje como en el mandar . . . con la expedición y traza que pudiera hacerlo el capitán más diestro de Nápoles o Flandes).[65]

Barbara Fuchs has convincingly argued that the representation of deliberate *cultural mimesis* problematizes the construction of colonial difference. "The very distinctions on which imperial ideology depends," she says, "are trumped by the production of simulacra, facsimiles, or counterfeits within the text of colonial culture. Ideology pirated or ventriloquized becomes surprisingly vulnerable—instead of reproducing it, purposeful mimesis undermines imperial claims to originary authority." The increasingly effective imitation and appropriation of techniques, practices, and tactics that had constituted the core of the public identity of the Spanish soldiery, the grounding of their discursive legitimacy, is not a process of imperial acculturation—real or fictional—but rather one of resistant hybridity and threatening mimesis, as the deliberate representation and performance of sameness that calls into question the original.[66] Deliberate *assimilation* to the Spaniards, in this sense, despite having the identity effect that made Vivar or Ercilla compare the Mapuche to valiant Numantines or imperial Romans, to German and Spanish plático soldiers, is an obvious form of resistance. To get *Hispanicized*, we could say, paraphrasing Homi Bhabha, is for the Araucanians an emphatic way of not being Spaniards.[67]

But it is not only what we may call *symbolic* resistance in the act of mocking them that is at stake; it is also the effective cannibalization of objects, practices, and technologies of the conquistador in order to reverse the course of history. The Araucanians, dressed as conquistadores with the spoils of Valdivia's army, threaten not only to repel the Spaniards from southern Chile but also to wipe them out completely, presumably from the Viceroyalty of Peru and ultimately from Spain. Caupolicán, donned with Valdivia's arms and clothes, gives his most aggressive and imperialist speech about the war of Arauco to the senate of the victorious republic: "I will easily invade Spain / and subject the invincible emperor Carlos to Araucanian dominion" (Entrar la España pienso fácilmente / y al gran Emperador, invicto Carlo / al dominio araucano sujetarlo).[68] The episode powerfully recalls the world turned upside down that Alonso de Ovalle later described in his *Histórica relación del reino de Chile*:

> Vestíanse los indios de las vestiduras de los españoles en señal de triunfo, con lo que en una hora se volvió toda aquella república lo de dentro afuera, los españoles vestidos de indios y los indios vestidos de españoles; éstos, sujetos y esclavos, obedeciendo a los indios como a sus señores y los indios mandando como amos y dueños. . . . De las ciudades no hicieron caso sino para abrasarlas y consumirlas . . . sin que se vea hoy en ellas sino solamente las lastimosas ruinas de lo que fueron.[69]

> (The Indians wore the Spaniards' clothing in sign of victory, which
> in just one hour turned that republic inside out, the Spaniards
> dressed like Indians and the Indians like Spaniards; the latter subject
> and enslaved by their Indian lords, and the former ruling over the
> Spaniards as their owners. . . . The cities were burned and leveled
> down . . . being today just pitiful ruins of what they were.)

The war turned "inside out"—"lo de dentro afuera"—that Ercilla and
his fellows-in-arms narrated also entailed a turning upside down of
the discursive structures of colonial domination. The representational
conflation of Europeans and Indians that we saw in the preceding
pages has been pushed to the extent of representing the Araucanians
as a powerful, expanding empire, which goes hand in hand with the
emergence of a more radical discourse signaling the barbarization of
the Spaniards in Chile in several sources. The American experience
unsettled in practice, from the very beginning of the Chilean wars,
the technological and cultural hierarchies of the colonial encounter
naturalized by the discourse of Spanish military superiority. Moreover, the straightforward acknowledgment of the Spanish inferiority
would also entail a new distribution of power and its representations.

VICTORS AND VANQUISHED

Caupolicán's threat has rarely been taken seriously. Some modern
readers of Ercilla have tended to frame Caupolicán's imperial design
as a joking hyperbole that emphasizes the barbarian, uninformed
character of the Araucanians or, at best, their punishable hubris. The
episode has been read as an example of the "fictive transculturation"
that contributes to the humanizing representation of the indigenous
other but always integrated into a taming European imaginary.[70] It
has also been suggested that it parodies the expansionist rhetoric of
the Spaniards themselves, showing the emptiness of the imperial project as a whole.[71] Most of these readings rightly emphasize Ercilla's
ambiguity and the complexities of the ideological allegiances of the
poem, but all of them regard Caupolicán's speech, like other instances
of Araucanian expansive aggressiveness, not as a real threat to expel
or conquer the Spaniards but as the rhetorical excess of the commander's conventional epic speech. I would like to suggest that this is
far from clear in the poem's emplotment of victory and defeat, in its
distribution of the narrative roles attributed to the main contenders
as winners or losers. But more important, when we situate the poem

in the larger discursive context of the Arauco War, it becomes more evident that for Ercilla's contemporaries and his later readers, empire was indeed reversible.

In *Epic and Empire*, Quint has delineated "a political genealogy" of the epic tradition going back to Virgil's *Aeneid* and Lucan's *Pharsalia*.[72] The imitation of these two foundational texts, also distinctively associated with epic and romance as two opposed modes of textual production, would imply intrinsically opposed ideological values: "To the victors belongs epic, with its linear teleology; to the losers belongs romance, with its random or circular wandering."[73] *La Araucana* is, in Quint's reading, one of the finest examples of the "epic of the defeated" in the Lucanian tradition, where the turn to romance contributes to the formal and political resistance to Virgil's hegemonic "epic of the victors." Furthermore, the argument of *Epic and Empire* is intimately related to an older interpretive split among Ercilla's readers, a divide between those who read the poem as pro-Spanish and those who read it as pro-indigenous.[74] It is difficult to summarize briefly the richness and nuance of this scholarly discussion. There is, however, some common ground between those who read the poem as a Virgilian epic of empire and those who read it as a more subtle or more radical questioning and undermining of the imperial enterprise the author was supposed to uphold.[75] There seems to be no doubt that, whatever stance the poet Ercilla took regarding the Arauco War, his Spanish fellows-in-arms are the ultimate imperial victors and the Araucanians are the losers. The anti-imperialist reading assumes that the victorious Spaniard Alonso de Ercilla has an active sympathy for the legitimate resistance of the losers, the Araucanians, and offers a strong moral condemnation of Spain's imperial policies. I would like to argue, however, that by accepting this we are already, inadvertently, falling into the trap of a teleological politics of interpretation, somehow falling victim ourselves, to borrow Quint's formulation, to the "epic victors' single-minded story of history"—or imperial historiography—even if we situate Ercilla's *La Araucana* on the pro-indigenous side of the debate.[76] In colonial Chile, certainly more than elsewhere in the Americas, victory and defeat were never final and very often difficult to assess.[77]

La Araucana distributes the *narrative* roles of victors and vanquished from its very first lines. The epic proposition, as complex and ambivalent as the rest of the poem, purports to sing the feats and valor of the Spaniards, who "placed yokes of bondage / on the neck of untamed Arauco" (a la cerviz de Arauco no domada / pusieron duro yugo por la espada). A logical, literal reading of these lines is impossible, since Arauco cannot be simultaneously untamed (*no domada*) and subject to bondage. No reader, to be sure, would have trouble understanding that Arauco's neck was untamed *until* the Spaniards tamed it, or that "no domada" is actually a litotes emphasizing the *untamable* character of the poem's antagonist but not literally *untamed* in the resultative sense of the past participle. The problem arises, however, when immediately after the text insists that this antagonist "obeys no king" (a ningún rey obedecen). Poetic license does not suffice to avoid contradiction here. King Philip, who is immediately addressed in the next stanza as the dedicatee of Ercilla's poem, does not rule over the Mapuche. Moreover, Spanish syntax in the last lines of the second stanza is fundamentally ambiguous, complicating things even further. The deeds sung "más los españoles engrandecen," where "los españoles" could be the subject or the object of "engrandecer," to elevate, to magnify. It is naturally assumed that the Spaniards are ennobled by their victory over a truly courageous enemy; but syntax allows for the exact opposite reading, in which the Araucanians would be elevated by the valor of their defeated enemy. This propositional passage formulates the founding tension upon which the poem is based. Ercilla purports to write the epic of the Spanish victors even though the harsh reality of the Arauco War tells everyone otherwise. This paradoxical point of departure for the discourse on the wars of Chile is confirmed by Pedro de Oña's competing rewriting of the campaigns poetized by Ercilla.[78] In his *Arauco domado* (1595), Oña says: "I decided to give [my poem] the title of *Tamed Arauco*, although it is true that now, for our faults, it is not" (Acordé dalle título de *Arauco domado* aunque sea verdad que agora, por culpas nuestras, no lo esté).[79]

Indeed, the first part of *La Araucana* recounts decisive Mapuche victories and the consequent miseries of the Spanish side, the former always having the military initiative and narrative prevalence over the latter. The Spaniards have been defeated in Tucapel, in Andalicán, in Concepción, and the remaining Spanish fighters and settlers have retreated to the north to take refuge in Santiago.[80] One time after another the narrative voice reconvenes to bring the vanquished Spaniards back to the reader's attention after having followed for too long "the fortunate side" (el bando afortunado) of the victorious Araucanians. Enunciation is thematized, in a typically Ariostean move, in order to redirect the story.[81] Epic storytelling is always with the winning side.[82] When the narrator assesses the main storyline of the first *Araucana*, he can only conclude that the Araucanians have subdued the Spaniards, who can only "surrender and submit" (se rinden y someten) to their empire.[83]

In part 2 of the poem this distribution of power, this narrative structure, is naturalized. The Spaniards attack the arrogant victors with more valor than is granted to the vanquished: "con mayor valor que de vencidos / al vencedor soberbio acometían."[84] Even in the battle of Millarapué, moreover, it is a sudden twist of Fortune between cantos 25 and 26 that allows for a precarious Spanish victory, a twist that the text presents as totally unexpected: "The vanquished now turned victors" (Quedaron vencedores los vencidos), says Ercilla in a characteristic instance that shows the actual position from which he was writing his poem.[85] But not even this sudden reversal of fortune for the Spaniards will grant them ultimate victory. In Galbarino's prophetic curse, the fierce defense of republican *libertas* anticipated by Machiavelli ("We can be dead, but not vanquished, / nor our free spirits oppressed" Muertos podremos ser, mas no vencidos / ni los ánimos libres oprimidos), is accompanied by a vow to extend the "Araucanian monarchy," in a significant discursive gesture that gives imperial currency, *monarquía*, to the estate of Arauco.[86] The poem refers to the military force of the Araucanian army in different moments of the three parts as *potencia* and *pujanza*, precise political concepts linked to power, reputation, and hegemony, through the dissuading force of sheer imperial military power.

By the end of the third installment of the poem, the Spaniards capture Caupolicán, the Mapuche leader who killed Valdivia, after the battle of Cañete, perhaps the first significant Spanish victory. It could be argued that with his capture and execution, the poem ended with a reversal of the upside-down world of the Chilean wars described by Alonso de Ovalle and poetized by Ercilla. But the poem does something quite different. Caupolicán announces that his death by impalement, however cruel and exemplary, would not put an end to the Mapuche offensive. In fact, he promises "that there will be a thousand Caupolicanos" (habrá otros mil Caupolicanos) to lead Arauco to their final victory. In the stanzas that follow, the poem confirms that the brutal punishment could only infuriate the Araucanians "with a vicious thirst for vengeance" (con sed rabiosa de venganza) and move them to new war.[87] Far from putting an end to the rebellion and to the narrative matter of the poem, the renewed furor that inflames Tuca-pel, Rengo, Lincoya, Purén, and other familiar heroes would require the poet "a larger book" to recount. Colocolo, the wise Mapuche leader of the first cantos, summons a junta that reproduces, in a never-ending cycle of attack and counterattack, the political gathering that gave rise to the rebellion in the first place.[88] As Quint eloquently puts it, "The poem has simply begun anew."[89]

In the fashion of other war writing, Ercilla meant his front lines to be read by those "keen to the matters of war" (aficionados a las cosas de guerra), by those comrades who fought alongside him in the remote frontier and who would not allow him to lie. We know now that the poem indeed circulated not only in the learned social spaces and the courtly aristocratic circles that have been often assumed as its natu-ral milieus but also among the common fighting men of the Spanish monarchy, in a soldierly republic of letters with a solid transatlantic dimension. Different editions of the poem, always printed in Euro-pean presses, circulated widely in colonial Latin America. In 1583, bookseller Juan Jiménez del Río from Lima ordered fourteen copies of *La Araucana*. In 1591, merchant Francisco Butrón bought four cop-ies, presumably of the newly complete three-canto edition. After the general uprising of 1598, the matter of Arauco must have gained new currency for the citizens and soldiers of the viceroyalty. Booksellers Antonio Fernández de Acosta in 1601 and Miguel Méndez in 1606 bought, respectively, eighteen and seven copies of Ercilla's poem.[90] And Melchor Xufré del Águila, resident of Santiago, experienced sol-dier, and the writer of a chronicle about the Chilean wars, repeatedly declined to narrate events recounted in Ercilla's poem, assuming that his reader "will have already read it / being as it is known to every-one" (entiendo ya lo habréis leído / como cosa de todos tan sabida).[91]

The movement of soldiers and settlers between the viceregal capi-tal and the Chilean frontline was constant, primarily because of the extremely high death toll of the Arauco War. According to a pam-phlet published in Lima in 1647, 20,000 Habsburg soldiers had died fighting the Araucanians, and 212,000 ducats of the king's treasury in viceroyal Peru had been spent every year to fund this army.[92] In 1664, a veteran with thirty years of experience gave an even higher figure: 29,000 Spaniards and 60,000 indios amigos died fighting the Araucanians.[93] Diego de Rosales, yet another chronicler of Chile, asserts that the war killed 44,000 Spanish soldiers between 1603 and 1674, "a great number for the Indies, where there are so few of them" (gran número para las Indias, donde hay tan pocos), and cost 39 million pesos.[94] When compared with the population figures provided by cosmographer Juan López de Velasco in 1575, which counted 1,380 heads of household for the whole kingdom of Chile, the number of casualties is staggering.[95]

Thus it is worth wondering how *La Araucana*'s plot of victory and defeat was to be read by those residing in the southern regions of the Viceroyalty of Peru and by the Europeans fighting in the fields of Arauco during the sixteenth and seventeenth centuries. It seems to me that Caupolicán's or Galbarino's warnings would not be read as rhetorical excess or ironic parodies by the colonists who were forced to hastily abandon the seven cities south of the Bío Bío river in 1598, or by the surviving broken soldiers of the destroyed forts of Tucapel, Penco, and Boroa, or by the thousands of soldiers who were recruited in the main cities of the Viceroyalty of Peru to serve in the battlefields of Chile, few of whom ever made it back.[96] The same would be true of the citizens of Lima whose tax money helped pay for the *real situado*, an unprecedented ad hoc budget established to fund the first permanent, stable state army in American territory on the basis that the Chilean war was a real threat.[97]

What the massive textual production on the Arauco War, to a large extent produced by soldiers in the field, gives us is a shocking picture of the distribution of power and hegemony in the Chilean frontier, a sense of radical contingency and political and military chaos on the Spanish side of the conflict, an almost always retreating empire constantly challenged by the—sometimes expansive—Araucanian *Estado*. After the third general uprising of 1598—there would be a fourth one in 1655—the precariousness of the conquest and colonization of Chile became more apparent than ever before. We, the modern readers of Ercilla, have even forgotten that during the first half of the seventeenth century a stalemate was considered a victory by the Spaniards and that the strategy adopted by the military authorities and designed by the Flanders veteran Alonso de Ribera was called "defensive war."[98] A number of soldiers produced texts that took as their point of departure the repeated defeat of the Spanish at the hands of the Mapuche, aiming at restoring or repairing what had been lost. González de Nájera, another veteran of Flanders fighting in Arauco, wrote the *Desengaño y reparo de la guerra de Chile*, which aimed at recovering the military initiative. For his comrade Francisco Núñez de Pineda y Bascuñán, who fought the Araucanians before being "happily" enslaved by them in the late seventeenth century, the war had been irremediably lost long before.[99] And Santiago de Tesillo, another veteran soldier of Chile, wrote two different pieces trying to turn the course of a war that had infused the rebel with "so much arrogance and haughtiness" (altivez y arrogancia) that they "judged themselves the owners [dueño] of the battlefield and the land," and they "assigned among them our people and our cities as their war spoils" (juzgábase este rebelde dueño de la campaña y de toda la tierra; repartir entre los suyos la gente y las haciendas de nuestras ciudades como si ya las tuvieran por despojo de sus victorias).[100] From the war-weary frontier presidios of southern Chile, the sordid reality of constant warfare would have made any kind of triumphalist discourse sound hollow.

The testimonies of anxiety, impotence, and fear are innumerable during these years, and they seem to have flooded the streets of major Spanish colonial capitals with frightening reports from the battlefield, which rarely came with good news for the Spaniards.[101] Lima's popular print in the seventeenth century provides countless examples of uncertainty about the ultimate fate of the Arauco War, alarming colonial society with "lastimosas relaciones," or pitiful accounts, coming from the south.[102] Commander in the field Francisco de Quiñones had no doubt when he wrote to the king at the turn of the seventeenth century that the Araucanians were capable of "the destruction of the kingdom, driving out the Spaniards by the force of their arms, an incredible feat for barbarians" (la destrucción del reino . . . echándolos [a los españoles] dél a fuerza de brazos, hazaña increíble de bárbaros).[103] An anonymous *Relación* printed in 1631 tells how the indigenous captives taken in a battle that surprisingly ended in victory for the Spaniards related to their captors "how all in the land have determined and take for granted that they will take over the kingdom with this rebellion, they will kill the Spaniards, and give the ports to the Dutch and other corsairs with the intention that Spaniards could never recover them" (cómo generalmente en toda la tierra tenían asentado por trato y cosa cierta el acabar con los españoles y apoderarse con esta gran junta de todo el reino, y entregar los puertos de él a los holandeses y otros cosarios con disinio que los españoles no pudiesen volver a recuperallos).[104] Replicating the language of Ercilla's troubled proposition, another anonymous *relación* published also in Lima in 1642 stated that "the never tamed and inveterate Araucanian lifted his head and rebelled, throwing off the yoke barely

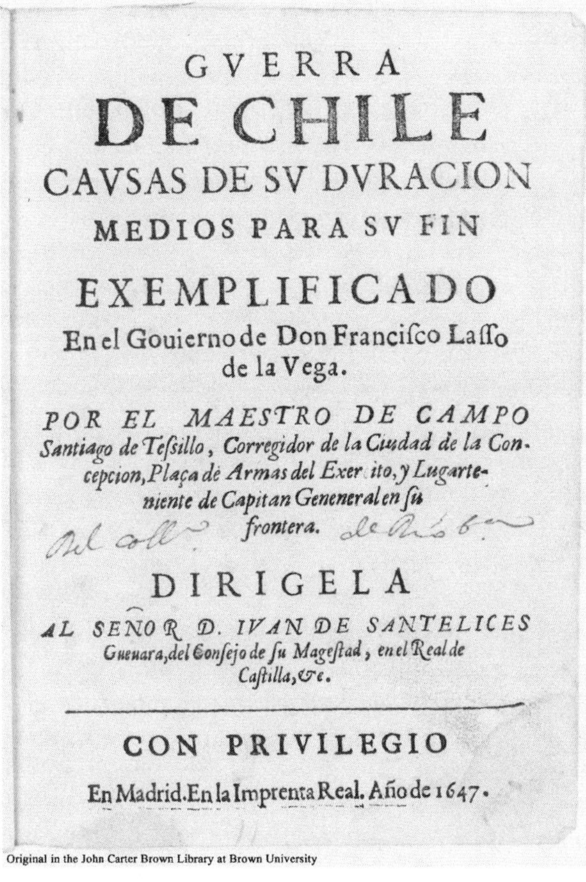

Figure 9. Title page of Santiago de Tesillo, *Guerra de Chile, causas de su duración, medios para su fin* (Madrid: Imprenta Real, 1647). Courtesy of the John Carter Brown Library, Brown University.

put on him by the Spaniard" (levantó la cerviz el nunca domado y mal sufrido araucano y sacudiendo el yugo que apenas le había puesto el español se volvió contra él).[105]

In the manner of Ercilla's poem, the names of the Araucanian fighters—Quepuante, Lientur, Butapichón—are recorded in the news sheets published in the printing houses of Lima, which must have had a frightening effect among the population, since these were popular heroes and feared enemies.[106] Miguel de Aguirre, in another pamphlet published in 1647, bitterly acknowledged that in "these wars that have lasted for a hundred years, with no rest, and having so many valiant captains and soldiers from Europe attempted to finish them, the Spaniards have lost rather than won" (han porfiado tanto las guerras que han durado sin cesar cerca de cien años y habiendo venido valerosos capitanes y soldados de la Europa a fenecerlas, antes han perdido que ganado los españoles). Since 1612, he confirms, there is "so little hope of restoring what has been lost and to advance in the conquest, that the war has become purely defensive" (poca esperanza de restaurarlas y adelantarse en las conquistas en lo por venir, se redujo toda la guerra a defensiva).[107]

Many of us might have been persuaded by the somehow *romantic* (romance) appeal of resistance. We might have naturalized a metanarrative based on a generalization of the pattern of conquest, resistance, pacification, and colonization derived from the historical development of the imperial process in other regions of the New World. If we are to recover the contingency of any historical process, of any imperial discourse, it would be healthy to revise our politics of interpretation regarding Ercilla's poem. What *La Araucana* showed, like much of the soldierly discourse on Arauco, is that the story could have ended differently. Caupolicán's aggressiveness, the arrogance and indomitability of the Mapuche in the eyes of the Spaniards, their increasingly confident, audacious, and eventually expansive attitudes, as depicted in the discourse of this New World war, show that "the fate of indigenous cultures was not necessarily an irreversible slide toward dispossession, depopulation, and cultural declension . . . almost diametrically opposite trajectories were possible."[108]

Soldiers, from Arauco and elsewhere, knew all too well that sheer force could and did change the course of history. Ercilla's Araucanian hero Tucapel had a point when he confronted his senior, the more conservative Peteguelén, who was in favor of a defensive strategy against the Spaniards: "Fortune is in the strength of your arms" (La fortuna es la fuerza de los brazos).[109] The virtuous captain, said Vargas Machuca, "grabs fortune by her hand" (tiene la fortuna por la mano).[110] It was the necessity, for the first time, of accounting for the defeat of the empire that generated the massive amount of discourse on the Arauco War to which *La Araucana* belongs. And this discourse effected a reversal of the trope of the miles gloriosus and of the omnipotent Spanish soldiers and the empire's war machine as a mark of national identity in Europe, turning all of them into "los rotos de Chile." The experience of the Chilean frontier challenged and destabilized not only the discursive construction of colonial difference but also the hegemonic gaze of a group of Europeans that, perhaps for the first time in American territory, looked at the empire as a reversible process, with the eyes of those who, being used to writing the epic of the victors, now had to construct for themselves an epic of the defeated.

Madrid, summer 1599. It is not difficult to picture Captain Vargas Machuca in the streets of the imperial metropolis, among the other petitioning soldiers who rambled around the palace's vicinity, engaging in the popular market of political news run, to a large extent, by veteran soldiers like himself. His *Milicia indiana* is fresh off the press of Pedro Madrigal, the same printing house that issued, a decade earlier, the first complete edition of *La Araucana*. Whether back in the Indies or while in Madrid, there is no doubt that Vargas Machuca, like many other indiano soldiers, read Ercilla's stanzas. And they seem to have made a lasting impression on him. The stories and episodes of the Chilean *Iliad*, which sometimes were at odds with Vargas Machuca's thinking on colonial warfare, remained a powerful subtext that occasionally—*exceptionally*—surfaces in the *Milicia indiana* to haunt and complicate the veteran's overall argument.

In his treatise on New World warfare, Vargas Machuca depicts the Indian soldiers against whom he spent his life fighting as savage but meek fighters "with no virtue altogether" (sin género de virtud). This turns out to be, again, utterly contradicted by Ercilla's Araucanians, "the most famous of all people in the Indies" (los indios más famosos de todas las Indias)—as he grudgingly acknowledges in the same paragraph.[111] In accordance with his naked pragmatism that might have motivated the censors' amendments to his text, Vargas Machuca unabashedly acknowledges that the pursuit of wealth is the single most important motivation for the conquest: "For it the soldier labors" and because of wealth "we have seen and will see many victories and great conquests and discoveries" (Por ella el soldado trabaja . . . por ella habemos visto y veremos muchas victorias y grandes conquistas y descubrimientos).[112] And yet again, Ercilla stood on Vargas Machuca's ways. "Because of [Spanish] greed they [the Indians] have been obliged many times to rebel, killing a great number of people, emptying the villages, and waging war for many years" (Por su causa han sido obligados [los indios] muchas veces a alzarse, matando gran número de gente, despoblando muchos pueblos y sustentando la guerra largos años), said Vargas Machuca, following closely Ercilla's reelaboration of Virgil's *auri sacra fames* in the episode of Valdivia's death.[113] Hunger for gold, asserts Vargas Machuca, built an empire; hunger for gold, reminds Ercilla, could destroy it.

Yet it is one specific story in *La Araucana* that Vargas Machuca will remember time and again in his soldierly writings. When insisting on his portrayal of Amerindians in general as "leaderless and disorderly people, with neither a sense of merit nor valor," the Chilean exception emerges immediately to remind him of "that Araucano mentioned by Alonso de Ercilla who, before and after having his hands cut off by us Spaniards, promised great harm . . . as it so happened" (aquel valeroso araucano de quien cuenta don Alonso de Ercilla que antes y después de cortadas las manos por nuestros españoles prometía grandes daños . . . como así sucedió).[114] Galbarino's serious threatening while waving his mutilated arms at the Spanish, as memorably narrated by Ercilla in an impressive rehearsal of the conventional epic curse, stood against Vargas Machuca's usual eagerness for brutal repressive tactics.[115] In Chile, iron-fist military policies were utterly ineffective.

Although printed in 1599, his *Milicia indiana* was likely finished in 1597. Shortly after his *Milicia indiana* came off the press in 1599, however, and while Vargas Machuca was still petitioning in court, Madrid learned about the new conflict in the farthest frontier of the empire, perhaps through some of those "pitiful accounts" coming from Chile via Lima. To Madrid arrived the news of the Araucanian rebellion of 1598 during which Governor Martín García de Loyola had been famously killed by the Mapuche and the Spaniards expelled from southern Chile. On August 31 of the same year, Captain Vargas Machuca wrote with his own hand *Discurso de guerra para la pacificación y allanamiento de los indios del Reino de Chile*, a companion, to be sure, to his application for the post of captain general of Chile.[116] If the veteran soldier had a hard time coming to terms with the Araucanian exception to the general *baquiano* rules of his *Milicia indiana*, Galbarino's mutilation and his epic curse still haunt the memory of the staunch soldier a few years after he wrote his handbook. The kind of punishment applied to Galbarino, he says in his new piece of impulsive war theory, "multiplies their courage and their willingness to die in battle" (multiplica el coraje de morir peleando), just as Ercilla had said in verse. Those who are not outright killed "remain preachers urging revenge, and it is well-known that the lack of their hands' strength multiplies their tongue's" (quedan hechos unos predicadores persuadiendo a la venganza y es cosa natural y conocida que al que le falta la fuerza en las manos se le multiplica en la lengua).[117] The shadow of the brave Araucanian, his epic curse, looms large in the memory of the veteran soldier and reader Vargas Machuca.

But the baquiano soldier goes further: "Severing Galbarino's hands gave rise to this rebellion, which has caused the damages that last until today" (Por cortar las manos a Galvarino se levantó aquesta gente haciendo los daños que hasta hoy duran).[118] This new reading of Ercilla's story is remarkable. It is not clear to what events Vargas Machuca is referring with "this rebellion," whether the original, 1553 uprising narrated by Ercilla or the recent, 1598 one he had just heard about. But to be sure, it was not Galbarino's mutilation that started either of them, and we know that this historical Mapuche warrior only gained momentum in Ercilla and in other texts on Arauco after Valdivia's death, during García Hurtado de Mendoza's expedition. His reading of the episode is a fulfillment in the real world of Ercilla's poetic prophecy. Galbarino's long shadow seems to drag over the third part of Ercilla's poem, bypassing the provisional battle of Cañete and the impalement of Caupolicán as signs, however fragile, of a potential resolution to the war favorable to the Spaniards. His military *arbitrio* makes clear that Galbarino's curse persists, as wonderfully misread by Vargas Machuca, as the origin and the ultimate fate of the war of Arauco.

FLANDES INDIANO

There were as many things Flemish about Arauco as there were Chilean about the Netherlands. As Diego de Rosales pointed out, the American conflict did indeed require the participation of veteran soldiers and commanders of the Netherlandish "school of Alba" such as Alonso de Ribera and Alonso García de Ramón, who in the first two decades of the seventeenth century were appointed to completely overhaul the military strategy and face the Araucanian rebellion of 1598.[119] Throngs of common soldiers followed the commanders, some of them presumably carrying copies of Flemish editions of Ercilla's poem. However, the power of Rosales's chiasmatic metaphor—Flandes indiano—does not lie exclusively in the transatlantic trajectories of specific servicemen but rather in the way it links the multiple wars of empire, large and small, American and European, in a common structure of meaning, in a narrative of defeat that, as we have seen, was already plotted into the octaves of *La Araucana*.

What follows is an attempt to unravel the historical and symbolic continuities entangled in Rosales's analogy by tracing it back to Europe. The soldiers of both sides of the Eighty Years' War seem to have read *La Araucana* as avidly as their colonial counterparts, and they reworked it amid the trenches of Europe's most important battlefield. Rosales's metaphor, which had crucial consequences for the cultural understanding of the two conflicts and the limits they imposed on imperial practice and discourse more broadly, has frequently been understood unidirectionally, following a colonial geographical logic. The Arauco War would thus be a war of Flanders in miniature, a New World conflict that mimics, however worthily, the true wars of Europe. Even if colonial writers used the analogy to call attention to and dignify a conflict that they considered as serious as its European counterpart, I will show that the symbolic productivity of the analogy works both ways, profoundly affecting, *Americanizing*, so to speak, the practices and representations of warfare back in the Old World.

Twenty years after King Philip toured the region in 1549, Ercilla among his splendorous entourage of courtiers, scores of Spaniards and Italians arrived again in the populous cities of the Low Countries. These visitors, however, were of a very different kind from those knights, the cream of European high nobility, who styled themselves as Amadís or Orlando in the most glaring chivalric celebrations the region would ever see. In the winter of 1567–68 it was the soldiers of the Italian *tercios viejos* commanded by the Duke of Alba who flooded the streets and squares of the Netherlands' capitals and inflamed a region that would remain at war for eighty years. In the second *Araucana*, Belona urges Ercilla to behold the "large army mobilized" (grueso ejército movido) and the "black, thick smoke and cloud of dust" (el negro humo espeso y polvoreda) that covered the "frontier of Flanders" (el confín de Flandes) on the eve of the 1559 battle of San Quentin. The goddess of war would also foretell, in the characteristic idiom of Araucanian patriots, that the outcome of the war against those rebellious kingdoms "will remain uncertain for a long time" (durarán gran término dudosas).[120]

Esteban de Garibay, who wrote one of the early biographies of his friend and Basque compatriot Ercilla, relates in his autobiography how he arrived in Antwerp with the intention to print his *Compendio historial* in the world's capital of the book industry, only to find Plantino's workshop too busy with Arias Montano's *Biblia políglota*, one of the most astonishing printing projects of the era. In his *Discurso de mi vida*, a rich collection of anecdotes and stories, Garibay paints a vivid picture of the bustling activity of Antwerp's printing industry around the Kammerstraat, the booksellers' street, where he settled. He recounts the comings and goings of all sorts of written matter through artisans' workshops, taverns, marketplaces, horse stables, and the humanists' study rooms.[121] War in the economic engine of northern Europe, a truly global commercial entrepôt, did not stop this tumultuous exchange and circulation of printed matter. Quite the contrary, it seems to have encouraged the production, importation, sale, and consumption of books. Among the many references he makes to this intense bibliographical activity, Garibay tells how a copy of the first *Araucana* arrived in Flanders in 1571:

> Estando yo este año en Bruselas, pueblo del ducado de Brabante, como un correo llevase allá un cuerpo de ella [*La Araucana*], fue recibida con tal aprobación y estimación entre los cortesanos y gente de milicia allí residentes dados a la poesía, que unos le igualaban con Ariosto y otros le concedían mayor lugar que a él.[122]

> (When I was this year in Brussels, a town in the duchy of Brabant, a mailman brought a copy [of *La Araucana*], and it was so well accepted and esteemed among courtiers and soldiers keen to poetry that resided there, that some paired it with Ariosto, while others considered it superior.)

As I argued previously, it was precisely the institutional structures of early modern imperial war that allowed for the quick arrival of this copy of Pierre Cossin's small octavo, printed in Madrid barely two years earlier. The typographical traditions of gunpowder epic and the distribution channels enabled by the logistic networks of early modern armies facilitated the consumption of these products in the socially heterogeneous spaces of war. Garibay's phrasing, moreover, allows for two equally valid interpretations of the publics of *La Araucana* at this particular moment. The most apparent one would give us a picture of undifferentiated reception, with individuals in a heterogeneous group of courtiers and soldiers mingling with each other and arguing over the literary merits of both poems. But Golden Age Spanish syntax also allows us to understand *La Araucana*'s competition with *Orlando furioso* as a more clear-cut dispute between *unos* and *otros*, reading literally the distributive structure of the sentence. The courtiers (*unos*) would have seen in *La Araucana* a worthy competitor for their favorite literary text, Ariosto's *Orlando furioso*, whereas the soldiers (*otros*) would have seen in Ercilla's book an even greater poetic achievement. Ercilla's proposition, rejecting the love fictions of courtly knights and embracing only true feats of arms, could have had a historical correlate in the actual reading publics of gunpowder epic and Italian *romanzo*. The same oppositional logics of the curious *plático* soldiers versus "los olvidados de Marte" could have been in place in the literary disputes of the Netherlandish cities set on fire by "the Spanish fury."

However exciting, the mailman's lonely copy of *La Araucana* could hardly satisfy the demands of courtiers and men of war who seem to have found it at least as enjoyable as the Renaissance icon of literary pleasure. Coinciding with the years of Garibay's account, the Habsburg authorities ordered a large-scale military operation in an attempt to put down the Dutch rebellion. Between the spring and summer of 1572, the Duke of Alba mobilized thousands of soldiers to be brought to the Netherlands through the Spanish road. At its peak under the duke's command, the army of Flanders had around 67,000 soldiers on the payroll, and even in peacetime their number never went below 13,000 enlisted men. This was arguably one of the most populous republics of soldiers ever seen in Renaissance Europe, and the workshops of Antwerp and Brussels rushed to provide print material for a potentially very large readership.

In 1575, *La Araucana*'s first part was reprinted in Antwerp by Pedro Bellero, in a typically Flemish twelvemo. In 1586 Bellero insisted on the same format when printing once again the *Primera, y Segunda Parte de la Araucana* and in 1597 he issued another edition of the complete, tripartite poem. Practically all of its twenty-five editions between 1569 and 1632 were made in octavo or smaller formats, following the typographical standards of humble gunpowder epics such as Joan de los Arcos's *Carolea* or Sebastián Trujillo's prints of Hierro's poems that have already been discussed. This particular materiality facilitated the global transportability of soldierly works, lowered their production costs, and differentiated them from the quartos and folios of the romance heroic tradition. In his *Histórica relación del reino de Chile*, Alonso de Ovalle commented on the rich editorial history of *La Araucana* and its availability in the international book market well into the seventeenth century: "Although more than fifty years have passed since first printed in Spain, Flanders, and other parts, bookshops are replete with copies [of *La Araucana*], for care is taken that it is regularly reprinted so that there is no want of them, which is a true sign of how well accepted it has been" (Con haber más de cincuenta años que se dio a la estampa en España, en Flandes y otras partes, están las librerías llenas de ellos, por el cuidado que hay de restamparle para que no falten, que es buena señal de cuán acepto ha sido).[123]

José Toribio Medina, an expert on the textual tradition and editorial history of *La Araucana*, had already pointed out that the series of Antwerpian reprints must be linked to the demand created by the crowds of Iberian and Italian soldiers, never entirely satisfied with the copies sent from Madrid and other cities: "It was this demand . . . that moved Bellero to publish this edition, which was thought, thanks to its small format, for those Spanish soldiers who enjoyed the reading of their compatriot's poetry, perhaps comrade of old, could carry it in their pockets and take delight during the times of idleness in their camps."[124] Medina had good reason to imagine, if creatively, this scene of reading on the battlefield. When approving the publication of the 1597 edition, the Dominican friar Mateo de Ovando extolled the poem's "heroic feats of arms," which "not only the noblemen, soldiers, and captains, but also the Christian philosophers and poets should imitate" (los heroicos hechos en armas . . . no sólo caballeros, soldados y capitanes, pero también filósofos cristianos y poetas, tienen bien qué imitar y admirarse).[125] For Ovando, directly involved in the spaces and practices of northern European warfare, the military uses of Ercilla's gunpowder epic were evident. In a preliminary poem to the epic of his comrade-in-arms Emanuel Antunes, *Primera parte de la baxada de los españoles de Francia en Normandía*, lieutenant Alonso Coronel de Olivera confirms the extent of Ercilla's popularity among the soldiers of the army of Flanders: "Of Arauco sings frightening deeds / Don Alonso, famous in this land" (De Arauco canta hechos muy terribles, / Don Alonso, el famoso en este suelo), says the soldier. Universally famous in the soldiers' republic of letters, Ercilla will remain an inescapable model for war writing back in the rebellious provinces of the Netherlands.[126]

The wide availability of *La Araucana* in the Flemish context was supported by the masses of mobilized soldiers in the region and by Antwerp's access to global markets and exchange networks. The soldiers of Chile became exemplary for those fighting in the Netherlands. Paradoxically, however, *La Araucana*'s visibility and availability in the context of the Eighty Years' War allowed for dangerous readings and heterodox appropriations. Just as soldiers crossed enemy lines to change sides continuously, both in Chile and the Netherlands, so did books.

In 1619, the *Historiale beschrijvinghe der goudtrijcke landen in Chile ende Arauco, ende andere provincien in Chili ghelegen*, an abridgment in Dutch prose of Ercilla's poem, appeared in Rotterdam, translated by Isaac Janszonius and printed by J. v. Waesberghe. It was surely based on Antwerp's complete edition of 1597, and it replicated the typographical codes of political print and pamphleteering of the Dutch revolt. For the Dutch, who launched three expeditions to southern Chile to establish commercial and military alliances with the rebel Mapuche in their common fight against the Spanish Habsburgs, *La Araucana* was a useful source of information. But more important, it provided a symbolic "American analogy" for their own fight for freedom, a metaphor through which the United Provinces imagined their struggle against Habsburg domination in terms similar to those of Amerindians fighting the Spanish conquest, as Benjamin Schmidt has argued.[127] Not only is the American analogy relevant for our understanding of Dutch geographical imagination about the New World, but it also conditions the political practice and the discursive construction of the republic's identity. The fight of the indomitable Chileans was ultimately their own, and this rhetorical gesture reverses Diego de Rosales's "Flandes indiano" to transform the Netherlands into a kind of Flemish Arauco for the Spaniards. A seemingly local and remote conflict was suddenly linked into the entangled, worldwide dimensions of imperial warfare and discourse.

Dutch navigator Olivier van Noort reported in the early 1600s about the general uprising of 1598, praising in characteristically Ercillian idiom, the "valiant warriors" of Chile and their "glorious victories," while Antwerpian geographer Joannes de Laet wrote in 1630 that "the native of this land will not suffer the foreign Spaniards and will not bear the yoke of Spain." In the last of the three Dutch expeditions to contact the expanding state of Arauco, commander Elias Herckmans extolled the Mapuche's warlike virtue and their love for a free motherland in front of an army of 1,200 Araucanian warriors, while reminding his audience "that the Netherlanders had likewise engaged the Spanish for nearly eighty years to maintain their freedom." And in 1671 Arnoldus Montanus's *America* highlighted the "war-like Araucanians" when describing Chile.[128] The prominent place that the Mapuche occupied in Dutch political imagination and actual practice is crucially shaped by Ercilla's text and its discursive progeny.

In the prologue to his work, translator Isaac Janszonius pointed out that the Spaniards of Chile have no control over the "free country" of Arauco, clearly distinguishing between the two polities— Chile and Arauco, that is. After having abridged in prose Ercilla's verse narration of the wars between them, the translator added an epilogue to point out a crucial fault in an otherwise ethnographically accurate work. Ercilla, says Janszonius, carefully avoids narrating how "the mentioned Indians chased the Spanish out of their provinces" and how the Araucanians "now live in freedom under the government of their own princes and caciques, which the author, being a Spaniard, in my opinion deliberately left aside not to diminish the honor attained in the preceding wars."[129] The translator's reading of *La Araucana* confirms that the distribution of power in the Chilean frontier, as the Dutch perceived it, could allow for unexpected and potentially surprising developments. *La Araucana* deserts the Spanish trenches, just as its author had done poetically, to fight for the enemy in the chaos of the Eighty Years' War. "For traveling texts such as *La Araucana*," says Barbara Fuchs, "reception—and in particular translation—may productively complicate our expectations of a given genre's ideological allegiances."[130]

Let us turn our attention to another example of Ercilla's circulation in the Flemish republic of soldiers. Cristóbal Rodríguez Alva was a professional soldier who fought in both Italy and the Netherlands. In 1594, in Turin, he finished an epic poem in ottava rima titled *La inquieta Flandes*.[131] The poem, which remained in manuscript form and was never published, narrated in twenty-six detailed cantos the events of the war in the Netherlands from 1585 to 1590, when Rodríguez Alva saw action under the command of his dedicatee, maestre de campo Alonso de Idiáquez. Although we know nothing about the author's biographical background, he seems to have been well connected with some important leaders of the army of Flanders: a good number of high-ranking commanding officers provided commendatory pieces for his promising epic. The wealth of preliminary poems included in the volume, moreover, speaks to the intensity of literary practices in the spaces of war and gives us important insight about the distinct networks of patronage that structured the soldiers' republic of letters.

Rodríguez Alva was one of those soldiers who eagerly read, in the midst of the toughest war in Europe, Ercilla's verses about the Indian Flanders. Never mentioned explicitly, *La Araucana* remains a powerful, yet problematic, model for Rodríguez Alva's epic of Flanders. External, material devices of the volume, such as the "Explanation of some questions that this book may raise" (Declaración de algunas dudas que puede haber en este libro) and the "Table of this book's contents" (Tabla de lo contenido en este libro), were undoubtedly inspired by *La Araucana*.[132] Reflexive exordia to most of its cantos, the asyndetic accumulations of verbs and nouns to eloquently narrate combat, the characters of the magician Gociano, modeled after Fitón, or Charlota, after Tegualda, are just a few of many textual and structural elements, as well as specific fictional episodes in *La Araucana*, that *La inquieta Flandes* deliberately replicates. The first canto of the poem, in which Rodríguez Alva describes the landscape, economy, political organization, and customs of the "Belgians," is also based on Ercilla's ethnography of the Mapuche. The strong intertextual relationship between *La inquieta Flandes* and *La Araucana* suggests, however, that Ercilla's poem might have unsettled the expectations of some of his comrades-in-arms. Particularly revealing is the way in which the opening lines of *La inquieta Flandes* mimic *La Araucana*'s proposition:

> No las bárbaras armas, ni los hechos
> canto de algunas bárbaras naciones,
> ni de cobardes ánimos y pechos
> las frágiles y vanas pretensiones;
> ni tampoco sucesos contrahechos
> de algunas fabulosas invenciones,
> ni menos del amor, aunque gustosos,
> la variedad de casos amorosos.
>
> Mas el valor, proezas, gallardía,
> altas impresas y efectos altos
> de los varones que la España envía
> contra las belgas gentes de fe faltos.[133]

(Not the barbarian weapons, nor the feats of some barbarian nations I sing; neither the coward hearts and spirits, nor the weak and vain pretensions; neither the fake stories of some fabulous inventions, nor the variety of love's affairs, however pleasing.

But rather the valor, deeds, gallantry, high endeavors, and achievements of those men that Spain sends against the infidel Belgian people.)

By 1594 Ercilla is a completely consolidated model for the writing
of epic poetry. On the one hand, the veracity of the narrative and its
popular, anti-court soldierly ethos are points of departure for Rodríguez Alva. On the other, however, Rodríguez Alva's imitation of
Ercilla's negative *propositio* shows that for a soldier fighting in Flanders during the peak of *La Araucana*'s popularity, the object (*res*) of
Ercilla's epic song and rhetorical praise, the heroes of the Virgilian
cano, had indeed been the "barbarian nations" of Chile. For Rodríguez Alva, *La Araucana*'s main characters are not "those valiant
Spaniards" (aquellos españoles esforzados) but rather, as modern critics have often suggested, those "people who obey no king" (gentes
que a ningún rey obedecen) of Ercilla's proposition. If the Chilean
war was to be figured as a hellish "Indian Flanders," Rodríguez Alva
seems anxious to restore "Flanders" to Europe, to dissociate the matter and the stakes of his poem from those of Ercilla, to defend Europe,
so to speak, from Ercilla's barbarians.[134]

The power of *La Araucana*'s textuality and fictional world, however, were hard to dismiss with a voluntarist epic proposition. In
canto 8 of *La inquieta Flandes*, which narrates the battle of Bommel
in 1585–86, an enemy vessel approaches the island that the Spanish
troops are defending from the Dutch navy. The noise of the intense
shooting does not mitigate "the echo of a thundering voice" (el eco de
una voz así tronando) of an enemy Dutch soldier that resembles too
closely Galbarino's anti-Spanish curse in which he denounced, waving his mutilated hands to the Araucanian senate, the evangelizing
goals of the conquest as hypocritical rhetoric barely covering their
greedy appetite for gold:

> Decís que os mueve el religioso culto
> y que queréis sembrar vuestra doctrina,
> tomar venganza del causado insulto,
> que aquí, decís, se ha hecho en su ruina;
> aqueso todo es hablar a bulto,
> que ya en lo exterior se determina:
> que debajo de especie y buen ejemplo
> lo que robáis primero es lo del templo.
>
> El celo que tenéis es la cudicia,
> en solo el interés ponéis los ojos
> y contra de derecho y de justicia
> causais en el país cien mil enojos.
> Sois insolentes, llenos de malicia,
> quitáis a las doncellas los despojos,

> sois hinchados, soberbios y profanos,
> indómitos, crueles y tiranos.[135]

(You say that religion motivates you, and that you want to sow your doctrine and take revenge of the insult that here, you say, has caused your ruin; this is talking nonsense, because it can be seen, behind the exterior appearance of exemplarity, that the first thing you rob is the church's riches.

The devotion you have is greed, you only look after your own interest and against law and justice, you cause a hundred thousand wrongs in this land. You are insolent, full of malice; you take the maidens' spoils; you are arrogant, full of wind, and profane, indomitable, cruel, and tyrannical.)

A critical voice, not dissimilar from that of several characters in *La Araucana*, emerges to dispute the true motives of Spanish imperial war in northern Europe. One of the most characteristic and successful of Ercilla's epithets for the Araucanians, *indómitos*, is repeatedly applied to the Spaniards in different moments of the poem, problematizing the distinction precariously made in its proposition. A Spanish soldier tries to respond to the anonymous Dutch voice but is silenced by "a cloud of cannon shots" (un ñublo de cañones antepuesto).[136] In his rehearsal of the epic curse, Rodríguez Alva's reading and rewriting of *La Araucana* shows the radical and transformative power of the discourse on Chile regarding the empire's goals, means, and limits. The Spanish barbarian is now the indomitable, resisting agent in a new reversal of the historical and narrative roles of the victor and the vanquished. Barbara Fuchs pointed to "the incommensurability of epic convention and the American experience" as one of the sources of ambivalence in Ercilla's complex poem, but Rodríguez Alva's imitation of *La Araucana* seems to suggest that Ercilla's ambivalent but powerful refashioning of the genre has made all epics American and that the epic curse has somehow become the curse of Spanish imperial epic and soldierly writing.[137]

The proliferation of soldiers' stories, whether in the Old or the New World, was not necessarily good news for Spain's national and imperial elites. The multiplicity of stories written by servicemen seems to have troubled—or cursed—imperial discourse and practice instead of reinforcing them. In his *Compendio historial del descubrimiento, conquista, y guerra del reino de Chile* of 1631, Melchor Xufré del Águila complained of there being too many diverging opinions on the war of Chile, too many stories told by men "grown old and tired by that war" (cansados / y envejecidos en aquella guerra).[138]

Figure 10. Title page of Melchor Xufré del Águila, *Compendio historial del descubrimiento, conquista, y guerra del reyno de Chile* (Lima: Francisco Gómez Pastrana, 1630). Courtesy of the John Carter Brown Library, Brown University.

His comrade-in-arms Santiago de Tesillo went much further to assert in his *Guerra de Chile* not only that there were too many writing soldiers in the army of Arauco but that they were largely responsible for the Spanish defeat in Chile:

> Alguno habrá discurrido muchas veces que le ha sucedido a esta guerra de Chile lo mismo que le acontece a un animalejo que comúnmente llamamos ciempiés. A este le hace torpe la abundancia dellos y apenas da paso adelante por tener tantos. Así han regido siempre los movimientos desta guerra, no solo las espadas, sino las plumas

de muchos, que escribiendo cartapacios y pareceres distintos y
encontrados, han seguido estilos tan sin efeto que parece sin duda
haber embarazado el fin que se pretende y las resoluciones únicas
que se pudieran haber tomado en tiempos menos fatigados que los
presentes.[139]

(Someone will have thought many times that what happened in this
war of Chile is what usually happens to that verminous creature that
we usually call centipede. Its many feet make it clumsy, and he can
barely move a step forward, for he has so many. This is how this war
has been governed, where not only the commanding swords but also
the pens were many, which wrote contradictory verdicts and followed
useless methods; it undoubtedly seems that the pursued goal has been
trampled, impeding a single solution that could have worked in a time
less weary than ours.)

Incapable military leadership is equated with disorderly writing—too
many swords, too many words. Tesillo intriguingly argues that it has
been the plurality of soldierly voices that has made the empire fail
in Chile. We do not need to agree with the veteran's argument to
see the point that soldierly writing, whatever its declared aims, often
trampled rather than advanced the goals and expectations of empire.
The unruly multiplication of the polyphonic, small voices of the common soldiery of the army of Chile, to which Xufré and Tesillo paradoxically contribute with their own texts, questions the discursive
viability of the empire. The proliferation of soldierly writing turned
out again to be dangerous. The troops of the Spanish army of Chile
are not the perfectly formed squadrons of the good militia, whether
Indian or European, but a clumsy centipede of soldier-poets with as
many pens as swords.

CHAPTER 5

Home from War

Abre tus brazos [patria] y recoge en ellos
los que vuelven confusos, no rendidos.

(Open your arms [motherland] and embrace
Those who return confused, not surrendered.)

—MIGUEL DE CERVANTES

THE BALLAD OF THE BROKEN SOLDIER

Nowadays, the brave and wandering soldiers all seem to be Petrarchs and Dantes.

—PIETRO ARETINO

No parece sino que en cada español soldado de la conquista hubiera encarnado un coplero.

(It just seems that every Spanish soldier of the conquest was a balladeer.)

—RICARDO PALMA

Repeated Spanish defeats in Chile and the Netherlands loomed large not only in the political imagination and military practice of the ruling elites but also in the everyday lives of common people and in the cultural production of the period. The astonishingly large number of veterans from these two wars returned home to publicly show the wreckage of their broken bodies, which were easily assimilated to the ruins of empire.[1] The trope had been there since Almagro's men, as we have seen, returned to Peru as "los rotos de Chile," after his failed first incursion in Mapuche territory. *Rotos*, or *estropeados*, meant defeated, poor, ragged, mutilated, and mad, depending on the context.[2] Melchor Xufré del Águila, the veteran fighter of the wearisome Arauco War, declared that the name of *soldier* fit him poorly because most of his multiple fractures and injuries had never been properly *soldered*: "Con impropiedad mucha del nombre de soldado, pues si bien una pierna cuyo tobillo vi a su rodilla junto, estaba sana, otras mil quiebras graves no soldadas me retiraron de la continua guerra deste Reino de Chile."[3] Through his revealing pun, which plays on the homophony of both words in Spanish, Xufré del Águila dissociated the word *soldado* from its etymological origin in salaried professionalization (*sueldo*) and linked it to the language of the *broken* veterans (*roto, soldar*) who, "poor and unrewarded," lamented retrospectively the course of their lives. Even the very name of their kind and profession, which was once carried with pride, could derive into a tragic irony that points to the disjunctures that, both literally and metaphorically, were characteristic of soldierly life. The language of bodily suffering, of an anatomy permanently under the threat of wound and fracture, hunger and disease, pervades the everyday *pláticas* and literary discourse of the monarchy's servants.[4]

The disjunction of the body, which finds in the lyric its most versatile form of expression, is usually linked to geographical displacement. Soldiering is depicted as a continuous movement that decenters the subject, that uproots a self previously grounded in a familial network, a local *patria*, a marriage. Wandering constituted the very essence of soldiering. Seemingly aimless traveling, guided by the whim of Fortune, is usually linked to a different kind of disjuncture, that of the broken bodies of mutilated veterans. Góngora, who never served in war, captured this connection wittily in one of the ballads in which he mocked the ways of one discharged *bravo*, "soldado por cien mil partes, / y rompido por las mismas," where *partes* refers both to parts of the body and to regions of the world, and *soldado* plays on the same pun exploited by Xufré.[5] Years later Estebanillo González would also play on the homonym when, "realizing that because of being a soldier I was more soldered than an old pot" (viéndome que por causa de ser soldado estaba con más soldaduras que una caldera vieja), he decided to desert the military.[6]

Many soldiers bitterly cursed the deceiving paths of glory that they had been forced or persuaded to take, condemning themselves to a life of extreme deprivation for predictably negligible rewards. Writing soldiers spent much of their time of service longing for home and complaining—silently or publicly—about the harshness and absurdity of their profession. Like the uncoordinated hundred feet of the clumsy centipede in Tesillo's revealing analogy, the Spanish armies often disbanded in attrition, mutiny, and desertion. But when they did return from the front, bringing back home the scars and stories of their time of service, their passage from the soldiers' republic to civilian society was anything but smooth. The proliferating voices of the defeated soldiers and returning veterans readily abandoned the epic mode—however unique—for lyric and autobiographical forms. I do not intend my narrative to mimic the rise-and-fall narrative of decadence: the loud protest of the exploited soldier, we have seen, was there from the beginning, and the conflict between the state and its soldiers was constitutive of their writing practices and their republic of letters. But the encounter of the stories brought back from the soldiers' republic of letters with the spheres of popular public opinion and protest and with the picaresque underworld of Spanish urban centers did indeed pose a new threat to an empire besieged by foes and friends alike.

This closing chapter gathers many of the narrative threads that have been woven into my own war story. It spans, chronologically, from the 1560s to the 1650s (but with a focus on the seventeenth century) and it travels, geographically, from the battlefields of the Low Countries to the streets of Madrid whether as the object of longing or as the actual space of homecoming. It presents several scenes of return, several alternatives for the war-weary soldier who abandoned, in very different ways, military life. These are the stories of the deserters, the rebels, the retirees, the veteran pícaros and criminals, the disobedient, and the unreturned. Here are some of the stories soldiers wrote while trying to find their way back home—if they ever did.

Winter is cold in the Netherlands. Relentless rain, dearth of coal, or the frigid touch of a breastplate must have made it all the more difficult to endure for a soldier used to the more temperate and dry weather of Spain. The problem was not a minor one. Some mutineers of the army of Flanders demanded from the Duke of Alba in 1574 that "His Excellency should not keep the soldiers more than six months in the field unless there is great necessity on account of the great sufferings caused by frosts and the cold which have caused many soldiers to die, frozen to death on the open road or keeping watch in the trenches."[7] In one of Francisco de Aldana's less Platonic images, the soldier describes how his spit instantly freezes before reaching the floor of the trench.[8] Cold, moreover, was tightly linked to the imagery of the broken soldier in its more literal instantiations: "the cold and ice were so great" during a Flemish campaign in the winter of

1619, says common soldier Toral y Valdés, "that many soldiers lost arms and legs to the frost" (los fríos y hielos fueron tan grandes que a muchos soldados cortaron los brazos y piernas, de helados).[9]

Winter was awaiting the first contingents of Spanish soldiers that, in the summer of 1567, occupied the Netherlands in an attempt to suppress the first revolt of some provinces. It must have been between November 1567 and March 1568 that an anonymous soldier, stationed in Antwerp's citadel since the previous summer, wrote his particularly cold epistle to an unidentified correspondent back in Spain. The "Letter that a soldier sent from the fort of Antwerp" (Carta que un soldado envió del castillo de Amberes) is first recorded in a manuscript collection of poetry bought by bookseller Juan de Escobedo in 1568 and was reworked repeatedly, presumably by other soldiers, before 1586.[10] In yet another version of the late sixteenth century, this poem was indeed titled "Stanzas of a penniless soldier in the winter" (Redondillas de un soldado que no tenía blanca en invierno).[11]

Remarkable in many ways, this anonymous text starts as a gloss of a famous couplet, originally by Garci Sánchez de Badajoz (1460–1525), that had somehow become a standard, quintessential lyrical lament, glossed ad infinitum by sixteenth-century poets:

> Salgan las palabras mías
> sangrientas del corazón,
> entonadas de aquel son
> que cantaba Jeremías
> en el monte de Sión.

> (I shall let my words out of my heart in blood, sung to that melody of Jeremiah in the Mount of Zion.)

The original biblical allusions in the love song of a courtly poet are recontextualized in the soldierly ballad, and the crying voice now laments the impossibility of buying coal in the wintry Netherlands. The song of Jeremiah, which stood as the emblematic origin of lyric weeping, is now sung to a very different rhythm, that of the shivering teeth caused by the freezing temperatures and the "melody of my own pain":

> Salgan las palabras mías
> sangrientas del corazón,
> manifiesten la pasión
> del triste que en estos días
> no alcanza para carbón.

> Salgan con estas heladas
> muy teritanto de frío
> sienes, muelas y quijadas,
> porque vayan asondadas
> al tono del dolor mío.

> (I shall let my words out of my heart in blood; let them show the suffering of the poor one who these days cannot even afford to buy coal. Let also my temples, teeth, and jaws come out frozen, so that they are tuned to the melody of my own pain.)

Triste, the nominalized adjective referring to the soldier, is not only used in its literal meaning of "sad," a crucial epithet in the discourse of Renaissance love poetry. *Triste* was indeed a synonym of poor and broken, linking the melancholy of the mourning lyric voice to the material deprivation of the common, physically mistreated soldier—in the most lyric moment of his autobiographical epic, captive Alonso de Salamanca had exclaimed: "Rompa mi triste voz el ronco cielo." Gaspar Correia, in his chronicle of Portuguese India, defends the figure of the "sad soldier who starves to death for not getting his due pay" (*triste* soldado que morre à fome porque lhe não pagam), while Vargas Machuca assures that "no soldier [in the Indies] is so poor that he cannot afford a horse and a saddle, a blanket to sleep, and something to eat" (no hay soldado por *triste* que sea que no tenga y alcance caballo y silla, un vestido y una frazada en qué dormir y quién le dé de comer). In his defiant letter to one of his enemies, the mad soldier, Lope de Aguirre, referred to the bodies of his rebel comrades as "tristes cuerpos," since "they have more patches than a pilgrim's cloak" (estos *tristes* cuerpos, que están con más costurones que ropas de romero).[12] The soldiers' sorrow, departing from the conventions of love lyric, has to do with their chronic poverty and their wounded body. The affects of Petrarchist discourse are transformed in military lyric to voice the bodily suffering of common soldiers.[13] Domingo de Toral y Valdés, exhausted in the middle of the Persian desert, collapses in tears only when his body fails to hold him up any longer. Tears, the outer manifestation of a spiritual damage, rather than being "the sweet grievances of his soul" (las sabrosas quejas de su alma) of different lyric traditions, are linked to corporeal pain in many of the soldiers' self-representations.[14]

Remarkably, the author intertwines lines from popular narrative ballads, or *romances viejos*, into the verses of the protesting guard, turning the poem into a witty collage of famous songs that comment on the hardships of military life. Some of these lines, which confirm the relevance of this literary genre in the soldiers' republic of letters, would have been in everyone's memory in the second half of the sixteenth century.[15] In 1445, popular ballads (*romances y cantares*) were regarded by a noble writer such as the Marquis of Santillana as "the lowest form of poetry . . . only enjoyed by people of servile and lowly condition" (estos romances y cantares de que las gentes de baxa y servil condición se alegran).[16] Although there is enough evidence to contest the restricted social distribution of romances as characterized by Santillana, ballads did indeed circulate widely among peasants, artisans, and, of course, soldiers. They show the extent to which the rich orality of popular culture was ingrained in the soldiers' reading and writing practices.

The soldier asserts to know by heart (*de coro*) "Paseábase el rey moro," a song in which the penultimate Nazari king of Granada, Muley Abu-l Hassan, bitterly weeps for the loss of Alhama in 1482. The wife of the penniless soldier is referred to as "la bella malmaridada," the first line of one of the most famous ballads of the sixteenth century originally dealing with adultery and honor killing. The historical and fictional heroes of the *romancero* that populate the text, such as Don Rodrigo, the dueling *cavallero zamorano*, the king Don Fernando, Roland, and Lancelot, rarely encourage the singer in "Salgan las palabras mías" with their exemplary martial virtue. They rather serve, in the author's debased vision, to remind the soldier of his misery. The mythical world of chivalry sharply contrasts with the material world of the soldier that only possesses his ragged clothes— "everything I have I bring on me" (cuanto poseo / lo traigo conmigo a cuestas)—and cannot even afford a piece of bread. The lines of another well-known *romance* in the mouth of his wife—"it is time, my lord, it is time to leave this place" (tiempo es el caballero / tiempo es de irnos de aquí)—serve to remind the weeping soldier that it may be about time to desert his post in Antwerp's citadel. Yet it is again the cold outside that dissuades the couple from leaving the citadel for the freezing roads. The poor infantryman resorts to the solidarity of the republic of soldiers and requests a loan from his comrades to cover food expenses, but the bitter conclusion leaves little room for any kind of military heroics: "sorrowful and miserable is the life of that one who needs someone else" (negra vida y duelos tiene / quien a otro ha menester).[17]

Some soldiers obtained licenses to return home during the winter in order to make petitions to the Council of War or to visit family.

But those who made it back through temporary or permanent discharge did not fare much better than the deserters or the starved men in service. At home, hunger, cold, and disease awaited the returning veterans who tried to get the back pay they were owed or to request a military office as a reward for their services. The miseries of the petitioning soldier are shown in "A letter that a soldier gave to king Philip" (Una carta que un soldado dio al rey don Felipe. De requesta), written most likely before 1586.[18] Weary of the secretaries and councillors he had to deal with in order to request rewards or back pay, this anonymous veteran from Flanders, an "old, poor, and broken" soldier, addresses his protests directly to the king. The poem is divided in two parts, a series of *quintillas* and a *romance* that is sung "por Nápoles y Gaeta / camino de la Goleta," and it reproduces the material structure of the *memorial*, or petition, the main form of interlocution between soldiers and the state, whereby they briefly reported their years of service, the campaigns, and their commanders to the Council of War. The "Carta," which starts with the conventional address form "Católica Majestad," includes a *sobrescripto* ("address") at the end of the poem that mimics the brief label on the outer side of the folded document that was used to indicate the addressee and summarize the content:[19]

> Anda, vete, memorial
> a la Majestad del rey
> y en llegando a su bondad
> dirásle con humildad:
> Señor, miserere mei.

> (Go, letter, to the Majesty of the king, and once you arrive to His Kindness, you will humbly say: "Lord, have mercy on me.")

The line from Psalm 51 in Vulgate Latin condenses the attitude of the pleading soldier who pits himself against the lettered officials that stand between him and the king's grace. The *secretaries* kill the soldiers with their pens more efficiently than do the French with their swords, says the anonymous author. To the soldiers' enthusiastic battle cries—"cierra, cierra" and "marche el escuadrón"—the king's officials retort "no ha lugar" and "no hay dispusición," the conventional formulae for the denial of a failed request. In the *romance*, a Dantesque army of broken soldiers (*mancos y heridos*) and dead men being eaten by dogs invokes a roster of respected commanders of the meritocratic army of Flanders—Londoño, Sande, Bracamonte, Julián

Romero, and so forth—to defend them from those who have killed soldiering (*la milicia*). The soldiers lay dead in a geography mapped with the real names of the *letrados*, or administrative officials, responsible for the soldiers' misery: the "valley of [Diego de] Vargas," "the field of [Clemente] Gaytán [de Vargas]," and "the forests of [Francisco de] Eraso," all secretaries of Philip II in the 1570s.[20] The king intercedes for the soldier at the end of the poem, instituting military hospitals to tend to the wounded, a longtime request of Spanish veterans.[21] But the antagonistic drive of this poem against the bureaucratic elites of the empire, like other forms of soldierly discourse, is not fully resolved by the king's benevolence. The text points out the *broken* logic of the relationship between the state and its veterans, which will reverberate in many other soldierly texts:

> Que pasar tanta pobreza
> quien ha perdido la sangre
> por servir a Vuestra Alteza
> no es caso de gentileza
> dexalle morir de hambre.
>
> (Because to leave in poverty those who have served Your Highness
> with their blood, and let them starve to death does not seem very
> gentle.)

In a similar vein, the anonymous ballad "Mirando estaba el retrato" situates the returning soldier, "a poor old soldier" (un pobre soldado viejo), in front of Philip III's portrait.[22] When he arrives in Madrid, the ex-combatant has lost his right leg and his left eye to musket shots received in the Low Countries. To the bodily ruin of the crippled soldier, retirement only adds extreme poverty, to the point of turning discharged veterans into urban beggars:

> Pidiendo andamos limosna,
> santo rey, por vuestros reinos,
> los que por defensa suya
> estamos en carne y huesos.
>
> (Those who got injured, naked, and starved in the defense of your
> kingdoms wander around them begging.)

The situation back home was surprisingly similar to what they had left in Flanders, where "starving and naked soldiers go begging from door to door," and "their misery and abandonment" is such that "scores of them die, and none from wounds" (muertos de hambre, en carnes vivas y pidiendo de puerta en puerta . . . hase llegado a lo sumo su miseria y desnudez . . . han muerto infinitos y ninguno de herida).[23] The poem and the official correspondence from the war share the language and tropes of extreme material deprivation. The broken soldier bursts into tears in front of the pictorial representation of his king, whom he encourages to wear his arms and lead his soldiers as his forebears had done. Both the "Carta que un soldado dio al rey don Felipe" and "Mirando estaba el retrato" fictionalize the soldiers' desire for unmediated access to their king without the burdensome administrative operations of the letrados that rule the Council of War and deny their petitions. If in the "Carta" the tension was clearly unresolved, in "Mirando" the soldier's epic call to arms is brutally satirized when in response he is imprisoned by an urban patrol; and lament turns into protest:

> Llegó en esto un alguacil
> y echóle mano, diciendo
> que por vagamundo y pobre
> le mandaban echar preso.

> (Then came the constable and arrested him, saying that he was a poor vagabond.)

The ballads of the broken soldiers produced and circulated on the battlefields of Flanders and in the streets of Madrid combined a variety of textual resources. Biblical imagery and language, some Petrarchean elaborations, the oral and printed traditions of the Spanish *romancero*, the practice of the gloss, and the formal and material conventions of the soldierly *memorial* contribute to articulate the multiple experiences of war. These texts offer a vivid portrait of both the soldier's longing for home amid the hardships of military life, whether on the battlefield or in the winter quarters, and the return of disenfranchised veterans. By publicizing the soldiers' bodily deprivation and suffering, they contrast sharply with the writings of other servicemen in the Low Countries, such as the series of epigrams or blazons to the commanders of the army of Flanders written during the same years by the petty nobleman and soldier Diego Ximénez de Ayllón.[24]

In 1605, Cervantes wrote that "those who have been rewarded, and survived, can be counted in three digits" (se podrán contar los premiados vivos con tres letras de guarismo).[25] And in the same year, the soldier and poet Andrés Rey de Artieda published a sonnet by his comrade Antonio Vázquez that starkly described the lives of their peers and foreshadowed an even grimmer future for them:

Cruzar caminos, enfadar naciones,
mudar de camas, vinos diferentes,
aires fríos, templados y calientes,
costumbres varias, varias opiniones.

Desquijalar serpientes y leones
(que es domar unas gentes y otras gentes),
rompiendo siempre por inconvinientes
y siempre esclavo de las sinrazones.

Os darán diez escudos de ventaja,
pagados por la mano de un verdugo,
enemigo mortal del trato humano.

Ya largos años, cuando al cielo plugo,
que veáis parte dellos en la mano,
serán para comprar una mortaja.[26]

(Walking roads, troubling nations, changing beds; different wines,
cold, mild, and hot winds, various customs and opinions. Skin-
ning snakes and lions (that is, to tame one and other people), always
storming through troubles and always a slave to injustice. They will
pay you ten extra escudos, handed by a hangman, a mortal enemy of
humankind. And then, when many years later, God willing, you get
to touch them, they will only buy you a shroud.)

By summarizing a century of soldierly experience, Vázquez's superb
sonnet poignantly shows how the extreme proletarianization of the
army generated discourses of resistance among the common soldiery.
Going far beyond the language of travails and sacrifice that permeates
soldiers' writings, Vázquez questions their very raison d'être and the
most basic legitimations of waging war in early modern Europe. The
soldiers' salary was handed out by accountants and paymasters, but
it ultimately came from the king's treasury. It is thus quite disturbing
for the unfamiliar reader to hear a serving veteran referring to them
as bloodthirsty executioners and "mortal enemies of humankind."
The first tercet reveals the macabre and irrational nature of modern
state violence. The more efficient a killer a soldier is, the more he will
get paid ("escudos de ventaja"). And yet the king's paltry pay, if it
arrives at all, will only buy you a miserable shroud.

Furthermore, by referring to himself and his comrades as "esclavos de las sinrazones," Vázquez reproduces a self-representation of
the rank and file that conflates the image of the soldier, allegedly the
human backbone of imperial expansion, with that of the slave, its most
conspicuous victim. "It is not right that [crippled soldiers] be treated

the way blacks are treated who are emancipated and freed when they are old and can no longer serve, and are thrown out of the house and called free men, making them slaves to hunger from which only death can liberate them" (Porque no es bien que se haga con ellos lo que suelen hacer los que ahorran y dan libertad a sus negros cuando ya son viejos y no pueden servir, y echándolos de casa con título de libres los hacen esclavos de la hambre), said Don Quixote to the boy who goes to war in chapter 24 of the second part of Cervantes's novel.[27] The parallelism reveals the stark abasement of the military profession throughout the sixteenth century, but it also discloses the constitutive social tensions of military discourse—Cervantes, the veteran, knew what he was talking about. The trope of the soldier as the empire's slave seemed appropriate to emphatically protest the barely tolerable levels of bodily violence, material deprivation, social marginalization, and personal disenfranchisement endured by soldiers.

Renaissance military culture inflected and enriched, in ways that we are only beginning to explore, one defining discourse of modern subjectivity—lyric poetry—and contributed to its transformation into a capacious and multifaceted genre to talk about the self. The lament of the captive, the new forms of affect of the married soldier and the camp prostitute, the comradeship of blood brothers or even the affection of the same-sex lover all deserve further study. Yet it is the grievances of the hungry infantryman or the mutilated/traumatized— *broken*—veteran that interest me most here. The lyric persona of the grumbling soldier entailed above all a harsh critique of the military policies of the empire. If epic was a (problematic) celebration of the heroism of comrades-in-arms, the professionalism and efficiency of their practice, the esprit de corps of the proletarians of warfare, lyric and autobiographical modes of writing would clearly engage with the "the darker side of soldierly life." The ballads of the broken soldiers and their autobiographical accounts had an enormous subversive potential not only on the frontline but, moreover, back home. By publicly and emphatically showing the miserable lives of heroes, rather than exhorting the sacrifice of loyal servants, they encouraged mutiny, desertion, resistance to recruitment, and even criminal alternatives for basic survival.

VETERANS AND THE UNDERWORLD

Very much like Tomás Rodaja—*El licenciado Vidriera*—Vicente de la Roca (or de la Rosa) was "the son of a poor farmer" (hijo de un pobre labrador).[28] Toward the end of the first part of *Don Quixote*, and after twelve years of military service, mostly in Italy, Vicente returns to his hometown in La Mancha dressed as a colorful *papagayo* (parrot), wearing the glaring outfit that was the prerogative and the pride of plático soldiers. The veteran exposes not only his clothes, which he skillfully combines to impress the skeptical villagers, but also his body to public scrutiny by showing off his war scars (real or fake) in the village square. As we have seen, the exposure of the injured body, whether in writing or in flesh and bones, is a privileged mode of relation between the veteran and his society or the state: bodily deprivation, disease, wounds, and hunger contributed to legitimize the voice of the returning and petitioning veteran. Playing the role of the *soldado fanfarrón* or boasting soldier of the miles gloriosus tradition, he immediately catches the attention of the townsfolk, whose responses range from admiration to incredulity when listening to his war stories. Sitting in the town's public square, "he would keep us all openmouthed with suspense as he recounted great deeds to us" (nos tenía a todos con la boca abierta, pendientes de las hazañas que nos iba contando), says Eugenio, the rich youth turned goatherd who recounts the story to Don Quixote and his party. "There was no land anywhere in the world that he had not seen, and no battle in which he had not fought; he had killed as many Moors as live in Morocco and Tunis and had engaged in more single combats than Gante and Luna, Diego García de Paredes and another thousand men he named" (No había tierra en todo el orbe que no hubiese visto, ni batalla donde no se hubiese hallado; había muerto más moros que tiene Marruecos y Túnez, y entrado en más singulares desafíos, según él decía, que Gante y Luna, Diego García de Paredes y otros mil que nombraba). In his interaction with his former neighbors, Vicente displays the socially defiant ways of the *pláticos'* ethos: "With unparalleled arrogance, he would address his equals, even those who knew him, as *vos*, saying that his father was his fighting arm, his lineage his deeds, and as a soldier he owed nothing to no man, not even the king" (Con una no vista arrogancia llamaba de vos a sus iguales y a los mismos que le conocían, y decía que su padre era su brazo, su linaje sus obras, y que, debajo de ser soldado, al mismo rey no debía nada).

In Cervantes's story, the veteran's homecoming attracts as much attention and admiration as suspicion and mistrust. The ultimate threat to the social order of the community, however, is linked to his literary and performative abilities. The brave soldier was a poet and a guitar player, an improvisational jongleur: "For each trivial event in the village he would compose a ballad at least a league and a half long" (De cada niñería que pasaba en el pueblo componía un romance de legua y media de escritura). Here is how Leandra, the beautiful daughter of a rich and honorable landowner coveted by many in town, eventually falls victim to the ways of the boisterous, bizarro soldier, "enchanted by his ballads, for he made twenty copies of each one he composed" (encantáronla sus romances, que de cada uno que componía daba veinte traslados). The girl admits to secretly leaving town with Vicente, carrying some of her father's riches, to start a new life together in Naples, "the richest and most joyous city in the world"—again the romance of Italy. After the townsmen find Leandra robbed and abandoned by Vicente, who fled with her money and jewels, her father locks her up in a convent and her suitors turn the village's surroundings into a "pastoral Arcadia" where they spend their lives "singing the praises of Leandra or reviling her" (cantando juntos alabanzas o vituperios de la hermosa Leandra).

Though it does not seem to have elicited much commentary from scholars, the pastoral framework of Cervantes's soldierly tale is partially shaped by its most canonical intertext. In Virgil's *Eclogue* 1, Meliboeus complains to his senior, Tityrus, that a godless, barbarian soldier (*impius*; *barbarus*) will take over his lands as a result of Augustan confiscations, condemning him to a life of exile.[29] The similarities between both texts make the connection almost inescapable; the disparities, however, are also relevant.[30] Virgil's pastoral series opens with Meliboeus's pledge to sing no longer after his eviction (*carmina nulla canam*), a significant gesture for a genre where singing was the thematic focus since Theocritus. In contrast, the village's rich youths turn into weeping poet-goatherds only after a guileful soldier, their lesser, has seduced Leandra, the object of their desire. In Virgil's eclogue discharged soldiers threaten to shatter the pastoral world when they receive part of it as a reward for their service in war, whereas in Cervantes's story Arcadia only emerges when the unrewarded veteran comes back to unlawfully take his share. It is the peaceful peasant community of the village—"though small, one of the richest" (aunque pequeña, es de las más ricas)—that is threatened by the irruption of war in the form of a veteran and his ballads. But here the proverbial conflict between soldiers and peasants is posed in class terms: the soldier "who owed nothing to no man" returns to seek retaliation from the farmer who was "very well respected" (muy honrado). Through Leandra and his landowning father, Vicente purges resentment and takes revenge on a community that he himself had had to leave for the army because for the son of a poor peasant, unlike for his richer neighbors, that seems to have been the only option.[31]

The meanings of bucolic poetry have always been conditioned by Arcadia's antithesis—the filthy chaos of war. Conversely, as Paul Fussell has brilliantly shown, pastoral fantasies about a return to a peacefully Arcadian home will often inform the poetry of war.[32] In this instance, the poor farmer's son uses his war stories and ballads to defeat the mellifluous courting and the pastoral singing of the fake shepherds—to add to the villagers' derision, Quixotesque, comical violence eventually dissolves the pastoral scene when a carnivalesque fight breaks out on the dining table between the knight and Eugenio, who has his nose flattened by a loaf of bread turned sword.[33] Moreover, the story entails some reflection about the nature and stakes of lyric poetry in the Spanish Golden Age. Vicente's guitar beats Anselmo's rebec, which stand as metonymies of two modes of lyric singing, the popular *romance* versus the learned tradition of pastoral poetry, although disguised in a truly rural instrument, with its elaborate urban appreciation of *rusticitas*—the canon later likens the goatherd to a courtier.[34] The guiles of the shrewd broken soldier as exemplified particularly by his ballads, the story seems to suggest, run over the pastoral naiveté of his rich neighbors.

Vicente de la Roca exemplifies the two most important roles attributed to returning soldiers by the literature of the period: as boastful criminals and persuasive raconteurs. In order to explore these roles, however, we have to move away from the mock pastoral world of Vicente's village and immerse ourselves in the loud and rowdy streets of turn-of-the-century Madrid, the empire's capital of both roguery and storytelling. Since the late 1580s ranks of returning veterans had occupied every corner of the imperial metropolis, petitioning for old salaries, military offices, and pensions or just trying to survive once their source of income was extinct. Francisco de Quevedo, writing at the same time as Cervantes, provided in his *Vida del buscón* a literary image of Vicente's urban counterpart. Like the soldier in Cervantes's story, the lieutenant Mellado ("damaged") that the *pícaro* finds right after the "rhymester sexton" (sacristán coplero) exposes his injured body to a group of skeptical travel companions, who wonder whether the scars are pike wounds or hemorrhoids, gunshots or chilblains. Mellado, a broken soldier and a suspicious braggart, is on his way out of Madrid after unsuccessfully soliciting a post of infantry captain:

> Es [la corte, Madrid] pueblo para gente ruin. Más quiero, ¡voto a Cristo!, estar en un sitio, la nieve a la cinta, hecho un reloj, comiendo madera, que sufriendo las supercherías que se hacen a un hombre de bien. Y en llegando a ese lugarcito del diablo, nos remiten a la sopa y al coche de los pobres de San Felipe, donde cada día, en corrillos, se hace Consejo de Estado y Guerra en pie y desabrigada. Y en vida nos hacen soldados en pena por los cimenterios; y, si pedimos entreten-imiento, nos envían a la comedia, y, si ventajas, a los jugadores. Y, con esto, comidos de piojos y güéspedas, nos volvemos a este pelo a rogar a los moros y herejes con nuestros cuerpos.[35]

> ([Madrid] is a town for vile people. I would rather, for God's sake!, be in a siege, with the snow all the way up to my belt, fully armed, and eating wood, than suffering the injustices that a good man has to endure there. When we arrive at that hellish place, they send us to the soup kitchen of the poor in San Felipe, where every day, those cote-ries gather and hold a Council of State or War standing in the open. When we are alive, they make us soldiers drag ourselves to the cem-eteries like lost souls. And if we ask for *entretenimiento*, they send us to the theater; and if *ventajas* to the gambling house. And in this mis-erable way, eaten by lice and inn hostesses, we beg to get again closer to Moors and heretics.)

In a fascinating study, Javier Castro-Ibaseta shows that Mellado's his-torical counterparts, despite his arrogant dismissiveness, were instru-mental in the constitution of the *mentidero*, a crucial social, cultural, and political institution in Baroque Madrid.[36] The majority of veter-ans who flooded the streets of Madrid and crowded the desks of war councillors were driven, like the urban poor and the pícaros with whom they mingled, by "the basic business of foraging for a living."[37] In an attempt to alleviate the burden of this new army of poor men on the local and the court's administrative bodies, many of them were sent by the municipal authorities to the soup kitchen in the Augustin-ian convent of San Felipe, in the Puerta del Sol. The surroundings of the convent, particularly the stairs, the atrium, and the caves under-neath, eventually became known as the "mentidero de los soldados" or "mentidero de San Felipe," a physical and social space of popular opinion, political rumor, literary exchange, and news distribution that connected the town and the court, the veteran and the state, the literate and the illiterate, the noble and the plebeian. Material deprivation had been the main theme of the broken soldiers' ballads and will soon be a driving leitmotif of the autobiographical narrative modes that some soldiers embrace in the early seventeenth century. Furthermore, hunger and literary enunciation were tightly connected in the Spanish case at least since *Lazarillo de Tormes* pioneered the picaresque genre. Strange though it might appear, moreover, the soldiers' hunger is also crucially related to the historical development of Spain's public opinion and, as Castro-Ibaseta has shown, to the political dynamics of the town, the court, the Spanish kingdoms, and the Catholic Monarchy.

Soldiers had long been the bearers of political and military talk. From the first years of the sixteenth century, as we have seen, soldiers participated enthusiastically in the circulation of news and ballads (*relaciones* and *romances*) and had a crucial role in the unruly, boisterous market of popular print. The cycles of deployment, travel, combat, and discharge allowed soldiers to move fluidly between the republic of soldiers and the society at large, carrying news and stories about the current events of the empire, from the epic exemplarity of victory to the discouraging laments of the defeated. Yet the role of soldiers as public storytellers and Mercuries, or news carriers, though old, gained momentum when an unusual number of them gathered in the streets of Madrid between 1585 and 1608.[38] Castro-Ibaseta shows the correlation between this surge in the number of soldiers petitioning the Council of War in this period and the first articulations of the mentidero, which was consolidated in the 1610s, most likely due to a new invasion of ex-combatants after the signing of the Twelve Years' Truce with the United Provinces in 1609. Soldiers joined and transformed the already existing illegal street marketplaces (*baratillos*) and the spaces of popular rumor and opinion (*corrillos*) into a discursive machine that intensified the circulation of oral and printed news, gossip, political criticism, ballads, and satires, dramatically affecting Spain's early modern political culture and imperial policies. While pursuing offices and claiming overdue pay in the palace's surroundings, soldiers had partial access to the court's outskirts and limited interlocution with the king's councils and other bodies of decision making. Storytelling, and the practices of literary production and distribution developed in the soldiers' republic of letters, from public performance to multiple hand copying, situated ex-combatants at "the center of Madrid's popular publicity."[39] The protean verbal regime of the soldiers' republic of letters—the voices, rumors, conversations, and poems, the multiple registers of political opinion and political communication that I described in Chapter 1—found in the mentidero a place for growth and proliferation.

Vicente de la Roca and Lieutenant Mellado were not purely fictional creatures with no connection to historical reality. In fact, we can now recognize some of the names of these storytelling returning veterans among the mostly anonymous soldierly mass. As we have seen, in late 1589, Alonso de Salamanca arrived in Madrid after a lifetime of war and captivity to represent his poverty before the Council of War. In 1590 Miguel de Cervantes related to the Council of Indies his twenty-two years of service, "particularly in Lepanto, where he was injured many times and lost his hand from a gunshot" (particularmente en la Batalla Naval, donde le dieron muchas heridas, de las cuales perdió una mano de un arcabuzazo), hoping for a "post in the Indies" (un oficio en las Indias) that he was denied; he petitioned again in 1594, only to end up in Seville's jail.[40] In May 1591, Andrés Rey de Artieda was in Madrid soliciting an *ayuda de costa* and declaring himself to be "in urgent necessity" and to "lack any way of subsistence" (la urgente necesidad y falta de medios que padece)—his oldest son had also died in Philip II's service.[41] Years after his first deployment, poet Juan Rufo also found himself in Madrid in the early 1590s, "poor and naked" (pobre y en pelota), according to his own colorful version.[42] Around 1595, Bernardo de Vargas Machuca arrived in the metropolis to petition, repeatedly and with little success, every military and government office he knew of, and the rhetoric of the poor conquistador pervades every line of the military treatise he was writing in those very days, *Milicia Indiana*. In 1600, Alonso de Contreras was also back in Madrid to petition the Council of War and to visit his mother, after sixteen years away, dressed "very gallantly, soldier's style" (muy galán, a lo soldado); and in a second return, he would provide one of the most vivid narrative descriptions of the veterans' activities along Madrid's streets and in the palace's corridors.[43] Around 1596 it was Juan Rufo who asserted that Madrid "did not have the shape of a town, but of a billeted army made of various nations" (no tenía forma de lugar, sino de ejército de varias naciones, alojado en campaña); the analogy, intended to point metaphorically to the city's chaotic diversity, could hardly occult its literal value.[44]

There were indeed throngs of writing soldiers, whose biographical and authorial careers must have been similar to those of these now familiar names. The spaces of popular publicity and soldierly activity associated with the mentidero increased exponentially the numbers of these little-known military writers in the seventeenth century. In 1615, Manríquez Sarmiento, "lieutenant of a company," signed an account in verse of a recent minor naval victory against the Turks, and in 1640, Francisco Cortes "translated in verse" a letter sent by a sergeant that summarized the military developments of the year in the Wars of Italy and the Netherlands.[45] Common soldier Diego Suárez Montañés authored a series of *pliegos de coplas* between 1605 and 1607,[46] and soldier Francisco de Segura, who rose to the rank of lieutenant (alférez) and *entretenido* in the court of Aragon's viceroy in Zaragoza, was an active composer of popular poetry, as well as a collector and editor of ballads at the turn of the seventeenth century.[47] The variety of media through which texts were distributed—in oral, manuscript, and printed form, in ephemeral broadsheets and in the cheap romanceros produced in Antwerp or Valencia—had a multiplying effect on their circulation and public impact.

Romances and *relaciones de sucesos* were indeed so pervasive in the republic of letters—the soldiers' or otherwise—that at some point they were a constitutive feature of the soldier's social identity and public image. After meeting Lieutenant Mellado in Quevedo's picaresque narrative, Pablos temporarily comes across another soldier named Magazo, who is mocked as a stereotypical miles gloriosus, the "arrogant, ambitious, and boasting soldier" (milite superbo, ambitioso, vantatore) that Italian comedian Francesco Andreini popularized in Italy as Capitano Spavento.[48] Magazo "had been captain in a play and fought with Moors in a dance" (había sido capitán en una comedia y combatido con moros en una danza). In the way of world-traveling soldiers, Magazo "told those of Flanders that he had been in China, and those of China, that he had been in Flanders" (a los de Flandes decía que había estado en la China; y a los de la China, en Flandes). Moreover, "he named turks, galleons, and captains; all of which he had read about in some *coplas* that were circulating" (nombraba turcos, galeones y capitanes; todos los que había leído en unas coplas que andaban desto).[49] As Cervantes's narrator seemed to be suggesting for Vicente de la Roca, talking war replaces war waging. The circulation of news and ballads allows anyone to become conversant with the matters of war; one can become *plático* just by reading or hearing about it. A few years later, the *Diablo Cojuelo* will assure that from the soldiers' mentidero, "news comes out before events happen" (salen las nuevas primero que los sucesos).[50] The mentidero, as Castro-Ibaseta has largely shown, was mainly a *literary* institution, a discursive regime defined by the suspicious yet fascinating poetic excess associated with soldierly culture.

There is a very fine line between the overdone bravado of the boasting soldier and the rodomontades (*fieros*) of the criminal petty lords (*valentones*) of the urban underworld. There may also be an unexplored relation between the changing regime of truth associated with soldierly narratives and the increasingly debauched perception of soldiers as active or potential criminals among the civilian public. To be sure, this perception had never been positive; but the image of those soldiers who pledged to tell the truth about war by writing on the battlefield, by sticking to the plainness and accuracy of their professional languages, and by appealing to a public of fellow soldiers in order to sanction the value and truthfulness of their tales progressively degraded. The depiction of soldiers as untrustworthy storytellers is hard to dissociate from their characterization as lying crooks. The rich connotative resonance of the very term *mentidero*, etymologically and morphologically linked to *mentir* ("to lie"), would immediately invoke a space of both illegitimate speech and criminal roguery. Looking retrospectively, therefore, the disputes over the truth about war, about the referential value of the soldiers' writing, were indeed a struggle about their very social identity and their place in the republic.

Not unlike the literary and social practices of the soldiers' republic of letters that I have discussed thus far, the activities of the *mentidero* were indeed perceived as dangerous by the local and imperial authorities. From 1585 onward, the Sala de Alcaldes, one of Madrid's main bodies of local government in charge of public safety, repeatedly attempted to suppress the "gatherings of vile people" (cierta junta de gente ruin), as Covarrubias defined the *corrillos* that harbored all kinds of illegal activity, in addition to illegitimate political talk. Some of the measures implemented particularly targeted Madrid's wandering soldiers.[51] *Corrillos* also abounded in the army, and the language used by military authorities to forbid them is the same as that of civilian authorities. Military commanders, moreover, banned soldiers from frequenting "public taverns or inns to eat, unless they are marching" (taberna o bodegón público a comer, si no fuere de camino), which was meant not only to discipline soldiers in moderate drinking but also to restrict the civilian social spaces the soldier could mingle in and thus to further control the circulation of news and public opinion in and out of the military and through the empire's frontiers.[52] The illegal echoes of the mentidero were not only based on the dangerous political rumor and the unruly dissemination of news it engendered. As an outlet for stolen goods, the mentidero was also a node of the underworld networks of Madrid's picaresque, where soldiers such as Vicente, Mellado, and Magazo seem to have seamlessly merged.[53] In the urban spaces of popular publicity, petty crime and illegitimate political talk, thieving and ballad singing, must have been hard to distinguish.

In close contact with the underworld of Spanish cities, a particular subgenre of ballads known as *jácaras* emerged at the turn of the seventeenth century. Set in the mouth of thugs and the prostitutes (*coimas*) they exploited, jácaras were *romances* written in a poetic register that mimicked or elaborated the marginal jargon of the criminal world (*germanía, jacarandina*).[54] Their connection to the traditions of soldierly ballads remains unexplored, although many of these Spanish *rufianes, bravos, rufos, jaques,* or *valentones*, partially derived from the tradition of miles gloriosus in their literary representations, were indeed ex-combatants. Valentones shared a gestuality and a bodily hexis largely undistinguishable from the soldiers' *bizarría*. The public paid equal attention to the clothes of soldiers and those of the *jaques*, who organized themselves, like the pláticos, in camaradas. The world of prostitution in army life and soldierly culture must have had a role in the criminal structures that allowed *jaques* to exploit women as shown in multiple literary and historical sources.[55] Finally, ruffians shared with soldiers a military language, or a burlesque, mocking version of it. An author of *romances germanescos*, or "thuggish ballads," invoked Mars in the opening of a series on the life of criminals (*la vida airada*), and Lieutenant Mellado's face is crossed by *chirlos*—underground slang for the scars of a sword blow.[56] When Pablos follows the thugs into one of Seville's legendary taverns, they soon "started conversations about war" (empezaron pláticas de guerra) in which they toast the memory of fallen fellow criminals, mourn the death of popular urban poets, curse rival ruffians, and plead to kill agents of justice.[57] A debased metaphorics of war and the features of soldierly speech inform the language of the delinquents here and in other literary representations of the urban underworld of early modern Spain.

The army had always been "a fertile ground for underworld culture."[58] Recruiters frequently found in vagabonds and criminals a ready pool of human resources, while scrounging defined the everyday life of most campaigning soldiers. But when the veterans mixed with civilians at home the connections between servicemen and criminals were so tight that the soldiers' republic of letters became almost indistinguishable from that "otiose and vicious republic" of the urban underworld.[59] Whether as idling petitioners, hungry beggars, thieves, or pimps, disbanded soldiers were more often than not on the margins of society. The literature of veterans, often counted among the "gente de mal vivir," was intimately connected with the vivacious culture of the outcasts' world.[60] As civil society had little room for the myriad ex-combatants that filled the streets of Spain's towns and cities after being discharged or having deserted, returned soldiers found in the underworld of Spanish seventeenth-century cities a way of living not dissimilar from that of pícaros and thugs.

In the streets of some colonial cities such as Lima, by a very telling semantic mutation, groups of men characterized as dangerous idlers and threatening criminals, who had nothing to do with the monarchy's military machine, were actually known as *soldados*:

> A esta gente tal llaman soldados no porque lo sean, sino porque son bien andantes de unos lugares para otros, siempre con los naipes en las manos. . . . Son grandísimos fulleros que su cuidado no es otro más que entender en el arte de engañar. Esta gente es mucha la que anda por el Perú. Y todos por la mayor parte son enemigos de la gente rica y no desean sino novedades y alteraciones y alborotos en el Reino, por robar y meter en los codos en los bienes de que no pueden alcanzar sino con guerra y disensiones. . . . Todos andan bien vestidos, porque nunca les falta una negra o una india y algunas españolas, y no de las más pobres, que los visten y dan el sustento, porque de noche las acompañan y de día les sirven de bravos.[61]

> (They call these people soldiers, not because they are indeed soldiers, but because they wander around from one place to the other with a deck of cards in their hands. . . . They are terrible tricksters, and their only business is the art of swindling. There are a lot of these in Peru and the rich people are enemies to them; and they crave novelties, rebellion, and racketing in the kingdom, because this gives them chances to rob and to reach the goods that they can only attain thanks to war and discord. . . . They are all well dressed, because they never lack a black woman, or an Indian woman, and some Spanish ones—not the poorest—that dress them up and nourish them,

since [the soldiers] pimp them during the day and stay with them at night.)

It would be worth exploring whether it was the soldiers' usually antisocial behavior or their tendency toward organized resistance in the form of mutiny that led to this catachrestic metamorphosis of the word *soldado* in Peru—though it was probably both. In the early modern period, the popular protest of "the arrogant poor" (los pobres soberbios) is often hard to tell from apparently anomic social violence. In either case, however, soldiers appear linked to the urban underworlds of the Spanish monarchy and to different kinds of social or political protest (*novedades, alteraciones y alborotos*) that pits them clearly against "the rich." A century earlier, Machiavelli had insightfully warned that "the unarmed rich man is the reward of the poor soldier."[62]

It is perhaps not surprising that disenfranchised soldiers and the urban poor found ways to cooperate—if occasionally and in sharp contrast with their more frequent antagonism—in their common attempts to survive. In 1628, Madrid's local authorities confiscated all the bread that entered the city with the intention of distributing it from the Casa de la Panadería on the north side of Plaza Mayor. Two soldiers of the local Spanish Guard, Andrés García and Juan de Santa Cruz, grabbed "three loads of bread" only to be intercepted by one of the alcaldes, Don Miguel de Cárdenas, and admonished to "take what they needed and leave the rest." The guards replied that he had no jurisdiction over them because they were soldiers. Tension escalated after some mules, goaded by the soldiers, ran over the alcalde's horse. "There were heavy and rude words on both parts," to the point that the soldiers threatened the alcalde with their halberds. Later that day, and after a new exchange of insults, the alcalde managed to arrest Andrés, which prompted his companion, Juan, to go grab the company's drum and summon their comrades. To the alarm call, armed soldiers rapidly gathered in front of Madrid's main prison, the Cárcel de la Corte, forming a squadron, blocking the doors, and setting siege to the building:

> Luego intentaron traer un banco de Santa Cruz para romper puertas
> haciendo muchas amenazas a los alcaldes con palabras feas y descom-
> puestas, dichas a gritos para que las oyesen y que los habían de matar
> y sacar el soldado y los demás presos, a que se juntó gran tumulto
> de gente de la perdida y vagamunda, que pasaron de más de cuatro
> mil hombres alargándose a hablar mal de los primeros, mayores

ministros y del gobierno y falta de mantenimientos. Lo cual duró más de tres horas, teniendo sitiada y puesta la sala de los Alcaldes, hasta que de parte del presidente se asiguró a los sitiados y amotinados no se procedería contra el preso ni haría novedad sin dar cuenta al rey y expresar su resolución.[63]

(Then they brought a bench from [the church of] Santa Cruz to break the doors down, seriously threatening the alcaldes with ugly and offensive words, shouting that they would certainly kill them all to liberate the soldier and the rest of the prisoners. Then they were joined by a great number of rogues and vagabonds, totaling more than four thousand men who, for a long time, spoke ill of the highest ministers, the government, and the scarcity of foodstuffs. The siege to the Sala de los Alcaldes, which lasted for over three hours, was lifted when the soldiers were assured that neither the imprisoned soldier nor the mutinied would be prosecuted without consulting with the king himself.)

Narrated by the *alcalde* as the usual jurisdictional conflict between civilian and military justice, the incident is on the verge of developing into a full-scale popular uprising against the "government and the scarcity of foodstuffs." It is very likely that many soldiers were found among the "gente de la perdida y vagamunda" that gathered in "a great tumult," perhaps indistinguishably mixed with the flower of Madrid's picaresque and the lowest echelons of the subaltern townsfolk. Far from the anomic violence usually associated with the world of roguery and criminality, the unlikely association of soldiers and the urban poor gives way to organized, if ultimately failed, social protest. The warning of the anonymous soldier, "vagamundo y pobre," who was taken prisoner in front of the king's portrait was anything but inconsequential:

Yo lo vi, yo lo diré
Delito el ser pobre hicieron
Catad, rey, por vuestra causa,
Si la del pobre es la menos.[64]

(I saw it, I will say it: they have turned poverty into a crime. Beware, my king, for your own sake—since the poor's is not enough.)

When trying to picture the soldier-like "arrogant poor" of Lima and the soldier-led mass of "rogues and vagabonds" in Madrid's streets, I cannot help but be reminded of Marx's colorful description of the Parisian underclasses in 1852, which included ex-combatants alongside "discharged jailbirds, escaped galley slaves, swindlers, mountebanks, lazzaroni, pickpockets, tricksters, gamblers, *maquereaux* [pimps], brothel keepers, porters, literati, organ grinders, ragpickers, knife grinders, tinkers, beggars."[65] Had he known about the unlikely stories of the broken Spanish soldiers, he might have thought differently about the revolutionary potential of the lumpenproletariat, whether in his own time or in the longer history of class struggle.

Soldiers and their stories were troubling, and sometimes openly subversive, for the social order, and regardless of their content, the form and the material practices involved in their production and distribution were many times associated with crime, social and sexual violence, anticlericalism, and mutiny. The public voice of the soldier's ballad and the private one of the veteran's memoir shared not only the strong first-person enunciative structure but also the general indictment of the empire's military machine and of their motherland, which could not pay their salaries, recognize their service, or receive them, at least, as Cervantes wanted, with open arms. When reflexively examining and recounting their lives to an unlikely audience of civilians, broken soldiers made an ambiguous effort to dissociate themselves from the picaresque thugs with whom they otherwise had so much in common.

SOLDIERS AND PÍCAROS

El Escarramán se confundió con García de Paredes.

(Escarramán got mixed up with García de Paredes.)

—LUIS ROSALES

El soldado, como no muera de hambre, loor es morir peleando.

(The soldier's honor is to die fighting—unless he starves to death before.)

—PEDRO DE VALDIVIA

Scholars have often linked soldierly autobiographies and the picaresque tradition.[66] The literature of Golden Age Spain often includes soldiers, and particularly ex-combatants, among the most marginal and disenfranchised social groups. Before formally enrolling as infantrymen, many youths first entered the military as lackeys of veteran soldiers or officers. Rogues, therefore, found their place among the nonmilitary camp followers of every army, like Guzmán, the pícaro par excellence, who served a captain with his thievish wit. Berganza, the picaresque dog of Cervantes's *Coloquio de los perros*, written by the syphilitic veteran Campuzano, describes a roguish company of soldiers that behaved very much like Monipodio's criminal confraternity in *Rinconete y Cortadillo*; similarly, the gang of ruffians who rule the slaughterhouse in which the dog is born adopt the *bizarro* ways of discharged veterans. Soldier Píndaro rises to the top of Seville's criminal brotherhood while waiting for his armada to leave port. Soldier Domingo de Toral y Valdés, born to a family of grimly poor hidalgos, starts his narrative with an explicit reference to the discursive constellation of the picaresque—"I passed four years wandering through Spain like another Lazarillo de Tormes" (anduve otros cuatro peregrinando por España como otro Lazarillo de Tormes). The whole life of Estebanillo González, the last pícaro, is completely determined by the military context of the character's trajectory.[67]

Undoubtedly the discourse of poverty and the formal resemblance of an enunciative structure organized around a strong first person allow for the comparison of soldiers and pícaros as literary types and narrators.[68] More important, however, I would argue that this connection is made possible by a pervasive historiographical narrative that links the rise of the picaresque with the debauchment of the empire in the seventeenth century. Soldiers would narrate the military decay of the empire, just as pícaros had to deal with a world of social and economic ruin. As José Deleito y Piñuela once said with powerful clarity, "Epic was over; the picaresque novel was at its peak" (La epopeya había terminado. La novela picaresca estaba en su apogeo).[69] The history of literary genres simply accompanies the political history of the monarchy. It is an apparently self-evident argument: heroic soldier-poets such as Aldana and Ercilla sing the rise of the Spanish empire in epic verse while unworthy cynical veterans such as Contreras and Duque de Estrada mourn or mock its decline in picaresque autobiographies.

However, I would like to suggest a slightly different story, a messier one if we pay attention to the stories told by the soldiers themselves. On the one hand, rogues and soldiers were hardly distinguishable from the very beginning. The very origin of the word *pícaro* is related, in a number of ways, to the world of war and soldiering. In one of Covarrubias's imaginative etymologies, *pícaro* was linked to *pica* (pike) "because in the war, they sold them as slaves *ad hastam* ["subasta," "auction"]; and although pícaros belong to no one in particular, they are [slaves] of the republic for all those who want to rent them, occupying them in vile things" (porque en la guerra los vendían *ad hastam* por esclavos. Y aunque los pícaros no lo son en particular de nadie, sonlo de la república para todos los que los quieran alquilar, ocupándolos en cosas viles).[70] In a second hypothesis that gained currency in modern times, *pícaro* was related to "the inhabitants of Picardy, who were frequently fortune soldiers and who, when prevented from enlisting, lived as wanderers."[71] Furthermore, Covarrubias's reference in his entry on *pícaro* to his definition of *picaño*, which he defines as "the ragged and torn to pieces" (el andrajoso y despedazado), could be related to the image and the lexicon of broken soldiers. Perhaps influenced by the trope, developed by the servicemen themselves, of soldiering as slavery, Covarrubias's conceptualization of the rogue brings him closer to the military realm.

On the other hand, first-person, autobiographical narrative forms were available in soldierly traditions of writing well before the *Vida de Lazarillo de Tormes y de sus fortunas y adversidades* revolutionized the canons of Renaissance literature in the 1550s.[72] The autobiographical structure that is so congenial to picaresque stories belonged in the traditions of soldierly literature from the very first days of the military revolution. The text in which all soldiers' autobiographies of the early seventeenth century likely found inspiration is the *Breve suma de la vida y hechos de Diego García de Paredes, escrita por él mismo*. Paredes's *Suma* was first written in 1533, perhaps around the same time as *Lazarillo* was being composed, and first published in 1582, having a truly broad circulation, both in manuscript and in print.[73] The fascinating texts by Alonso de Contreras, Jerónimo de Pasamonte, Miguel de Castro, Diego Duque de Estrada, Catalina de Erauso, and other soldiers are thus the product of longstanding traditions of military writing and authorship in the soldiers' republic of letters.[74] And yet they are also a symptom of the partial failure of that republic and the brotherhood of the common soldiers. As appealing as they are, these texts certainly remained hidden for most of their comrades and the public at large. Contreras's, Castro's, Suárez Montañés's, and Pasamonte's are only kept in one single manuscript copy, autograph in the first two cases. Paredes's was the only soldierly memoir to ever see the light of print in the early modern period.

Paredes died unnecessarily at the age of sixty-five. In Bologna, in 1533, a few young gentlemen challenged the old soldier to a game that consisted of knocking down with your feet a straw stuck on a wall, which signaled the highest point reached by any of the contenders.

The legendary soldier would die a few days later from the injuries he sustained, but not before writing his short memoir on his deathbed. "Among the papers containing Diego García de Paredes's writings, there was one written and signed by his own hand" (Entre ciertos papeles que se hallaron en las escrituras de Diego García de Paredes se halló una de su letra y firmada de su nombre), according to one of its earlier copyists.[75] The genre of Paredes's scrawling in his *libros de memoria* may seem unstable and noncanonical, but it was patently related to the most honorable tradition of war writing. Next to Paredes's libros de memoria in his death inventory, as we saw in Chapter 1, lay a copy of Caesar's *Commentaries*. The editor of one Spanish translation of Caesar's war narratives explained that "*commentaries* refers to a book containing the deeds of someone briefly written, almost as in a book of memory or the somewhat longer register of everyday matters as in a diary, just as Caesar wrote his story in his book of memory every day little by little, as he went on conquering, which he called *commentaries*" (comentarios quiere decir libro en el cual contiene en sí los hechos de alguno sumariamente scritos, casi como en *libro de memorias* o registro algo largo de las cosas que cada día a manera de libro de jornales desta mesma suerte César escribió su historia poco a poco cada día como iba conquistando en su libro de memorias, el cual llamó comentarios).[76] The paratextual vocabularies of Renaissance writing cultures help us establish the connection between the classical model and the otherwise utterly different memoir by Paredes. Later on, Cabeza de Vaca would title the second, augmented edition of his first-person travel narrative *La relación y comentarios*, while Diego Duque de Estrada would also include a reference to Caesar's foundational narrative in the title of his *Comentarios del desengañado de sí mismo*.[77] Spanish soldiers such as Paredes and his successors transformed Caesar's detached third-person narrative of war into an engaged and eventually intimate first-person account of soldierly life, a formal transformation of wide-ranging consequences.

The tradition of military writing that I have aimed at reconstructing throughout this book turned soldiers into "cronistas de sí mismos" or chroniclers of themselves, a widespread phrase that refers to several modalities of self-writing in early modern Spain. Soldier and poet Gutierre de Cetina fears the Count of Feria's deeds will be forgotten unless he becomes his own chronicler ("si vos de vos no sois el coronista"). Vicente de la Roca recounted his own feats to the people in the village—"las hazañas que él de sí mismo había referido." Toral y Valdés is always tempted "to speak of himself" (hablar de sí) in his peculiar travelogue. And Diego García de Paredes is "his own chronicler" (coronista propio), according to the priest in *Don Quixote*.[78] The "discurso de sí mismo," as Sánchez Blanco referred to similar textual forms, is a variety of historical writing that found special resonance among the writers of the soldiers' republic of letters. Ortega's otherwise extremely insightful essay on Contreras's *Discurso de mi vida* was quite misled in asserting that "there is nothing less natural for the man of pure action than to write his memoir."[79] The retrospective writing of the autobiographical subject is an attempt to piece together a seemingly plotless life, a subject fragmented by war's lack of order and structure, the constant movement of soldierly life, and the strain of combat and death.[80]

This is how the life recorded by Paredes starts:

> En el año de mil y quinientos y siete hube una diferencia con Ruy Sánchez de Vargas sobre un caballo de Corajo, nuestro sobrino, que yo le tomé para venir en Italia. Vino tras mí Ruy Sánchez con tres de caballo y dímosnos tantas cuchilladas hasta que cayó Ruy Sánchez, y luego sus escuderos me acometieron de tal manera que me vi en grande aprieto, pero al fin los descalabré a todos y me fui mi camino.[81]

> (In the year of 1507 I had an argument with Ruy Sánchez de Vargas over one horse that belonged to Corajo, our nephew, which I took to come to Italy. Ruy Sánchez came after me with three other cavalrymen and we exchanged many sword blows until Ruy Sánchez fell, and then his squires attacked in a way that put me in a great predicament, but I finally split their heads open and went my way.)

The rest of Diego García de Paredes's narrative, after shockingly starting off with the maiming or murder of a few relatives, is not much different. During peacetime, Paredes wanders the streets of Rome, working as a hired thug and pimping women not unlike the Escarramán of the *jácaras*, as Luis Rosales melancholically remarked. With his first company as infantry captain he fights successfully in the papal armies, but at the slightest dispute with another captain he cuts his head after having surrendered, against aristocratic moral codes, military discipline, and Christian piety. Paredes is degraded and taken prisoner. In order to release himself, challenging no other than the pope, he kills the entire guard at the general's tent and deserts to the enemy's camp, where he fights as courageously as before.

The narration is not structured as a linear ascension up the chain of command to ever higher rank but rather as an anarchic succession of combats, deprived of their historical significance, and personal incidents that sharply contrast with his later public image and with his final exemplary gesture. He narrates insubordination, cold-blooded killing, desertion, and sacking with the same unenthusiastic, detached attitude as he recounts his leading role in crucial military campaigns of the Italian Wars or his individual chivalric duels.

Paredes dedicates one short sentence, at best, to some of the greatest Italian battles he helped win—when he does not squeeze into a single polisyndetic period several of them. Perhaps even more surprisingly, the text lacks significant technical or professional detail regarding the "matters of war," which had already become the most recognizable feature of soldierly writing. Paredes reveals very little of the vast experiential wisdom on how to wage war successfully that he and his comrades had already accumulated in that early stage. About the soldier's laconic idiom, a copyist remarked that "we can clearly gather from the style and way of speaking that the historian was also the owner [of these papers], because of the brevity with which he writes. He seems to have been more inclined to actions than to words, and very opposed to the amplification of his deeds with the arrogance and ostentation that others normally use" (bien claramente se conoce el estilo y manera de decir haber sido el historiador su propio dueño segúnd la brevedad con que se escribe. Parece bien cuanto más amigo debiera ser de obras que de palabras y cuán enemigo de ampliar mucho sus hechos con el blasón y fanfarronerías que otros lo suelen hacer).[82] Rhetorical *brevitas* (brevedad), here in the sense of a plain, condensed, and toned-down style that links it to the genre of the commentaries—as opposed to the excess and artifice of *amplificatio*—is an integral part of the *lengua soldada* cherished by the pláticos. However, I would disagree with the editor, who commends Paredes's decorous humbleness, and argue that the plain style associated with soldierly speech contributed greatly to the arrogant nonchalance characteristic of the *bizarro* ethos. Paredes's carefully understated braggadocio, inherent in the soldiers' public identity, will set the tone for the autobiographies that later imitated him, as we will soon see.

This reading is confirmed in the *Suma*'s recording of yet another memorable scene of the veteran's return home. Back in his native Extremadura, he stops at an inn in Coria with a page, closely followed by a group of twenty-five loyal arquebusiers from Italy. Because the captain dresses humbly as a road traveler, a group of *rufianes*, prostitutes, and sellers of indulgences (*bulderos*) poke fun at him, branding him a "hog dealer" (merchán de puercos) and a "Jew." Upon their arrival, the captain instructs his men to pretend they do not know him. Despite some warnings, the ruffians insist on the mockery and Paredes remains quiet, "to see how the party would end" (por ver en qué paraba la fiesta). Not being able to bear any longer the insults and the insinuation that his captain's weapons were stolen, one of his corporals reaches for his sword; it is only then that Paredes himself reacts:

> Me levanté de un banco en que estaba sentado y tomé el banco, y di con él al rufián y abríle la cabeza. Y al otro rufián y a las putas y a los bulderos eché al fuego unos sobre otros. La una puta que cayó debajo murió; los otros, quemadas las caras y las manos, salieron dando voces a la justicia, y el mesonero con ellos. Nosotros nos sentamos a cenar su cena hasta que todo el pueblo se juntó a la puerta.[83]

> (I stood up and took the bench upon which I was sitting, and I hit one ruffian and broke his head open. And the other ruffian, and the whores, and the indulgence sellers I threw into the fire, piling them up. The whore who fell underneath died; the others, with their faces and hands burning ran out calling for justice, and the innkeeper with them. We sat down to have their dinner until all the villagers gathered at the inn's door.)

As I have already pointed out, this is arguably the longest episode in Paredes's quite laconic memoir. Everything in this narrative passage—the characters, the atmosphere, the cynical inflection of the autobiographical voice—contrasts sharply with the unambiguously heroic image that both Paredes's contemporaries and later historians painted of the soldier. Yet we can see that, even in the unanimously missed days of a legendary emperor at the peak of his glory, the lives of the heroes who carried out his conquests could hardly be sung in the tone of epic when they were far from the battlefield. Already in 1533, the ethos and the representational logic of the soldiers' discourse would seem to belong in the world of *Celestina*, the life of Lazarillo, or the ballads of seventeenth-century underworld popular heroes.

Only a few days before Paredes wrote these lines, an unidentified group of people attacked him and his family's retinue at night in Friuli. Barely dodging the assault, he took revenge: "We killed so many that few escaped. I promise to God that on this day I was more cruel than I can ever before recall" (Matamos tantos que escaparon pocos. Prometo a Dios que este día fui más cruel que me acuerdo haber sido).[84] This is the closest Paredes's text comes to a confession, despite the fact that the context of writing may have invited him to offer one. None of the extant copies of the text registers the slightest remorse. Quite the contrary, lying on his deathbed after his most ridiculous war injury, Paredes justified the writing of his strange deeds by resorting to exemplarity: "I leave this memoir to Sancho de Paredes, my son, so that he can always act like a caballero in his defense and honor in the occasions to come, always placing God in front of his eyes, and trying to be right so that He can assist him" (Dejo esta memoria a Sancho de Paredes mi hijo, para que en las cosas que se ofrecieren en defensa y honra haga lo que debe como caballero, poniendo siempre a Dios delante de sus ojos y procurando tener razón para que él le ayude).[85] It was not only Paredes himself who considered his rather brutal account an unproblematic narration of the life of arms, worthy of being saved from oblivion as a treasure of exemplarity. The editor of the manuscript I have been quoting from confidently asserted that "it is not reasonable that such remarkable deeds be left in oblivion and the one who did them lost from memory" (no es razón que cosas tan señaladas se echen en olvido ni se pierda la memoria del que las hizo).[86]

Though later soldierly readers felt no less compelled to extol Paredes's legendary deeds, they pointed out a tension between his life as he wrote it and the epic models of Renaissance literary culture. According to the priest in Cervantes's *Don Quixote*, and in line with the copyist's opinion, Paredes wrote his life "with the modesty of a gentleman writing his own chronicle, but if another were to write about those feats freely and dispassionately, they would relegate all the deeds of Hector, Achilles, and Roland to oblivion" (que si, como él las cuenta y las escribe él asimismo, con la modestia de caballero y de cronista proprio, las escribiera otro libre y desapasionado, pusieran en su olvido las de los Hétores, Aquiles y Roldanes).[87] The issue of exemplarity is thus tightly linked to the problematics around the text's genre and style, and the tense relation, already discussed in the present book, between epic and autobiography as two privileged modes of war storytelling. Yet for Paredes, it seems that *vita* and *gesta* contribute in the same measure to his public image as a military hero. The private, illegitimate killings that occur far from the battlefield are indeed narrated with more detail than those carried out in combat action. The inflections of the autographical voice, which range from detached cruelty ("los descalabré a todos y me fui mi camino") to the cynical quipping about killing ("por ver en qué paraba la fiesta"), tell us that in fact that the speaker proudly values these ethically questionable deeds as crucial for his self-fashioning. Paredes made his way to war by severely injuring some older relatives and made it back home by ostentatiously killing some disrespectful compatriots—prostitutes and *Escarramanes* with whom he was all too familiar. Far from aristocratic modesty, what we find is the unrestrained *bizarría* of common soldiers who despised chivalric codes of behavior as contrary to their social aspirations and interests. Not unlike climbing *pícaros* showing off their clever ruses, the soldiers' first-person tales aimed at eliciting respect from civilians and military superiors alike through the threatening exposure of ruthlessness. Despite all the thieving and cheating, however, Guzmán never killed anyone; neither did Lázaro de Tormes. "Blood crimes are not picaresque matter,"[88] according to Marcel Bataillon. In contrast, the logic of violence that constitutes the soldier's means of subsistence informs most military autobiographies and lies at the core of all soldierly writing.

Paredes was universally recognized as one of the most outstanding soldiers of all times, and his legend represented the possibilities of soldiering. Unlike his comrade-in-arms Pedro Navarro, who was equally famous in early modern Europe, he was not a plain commoner but a petty hidalgo of very modest means from Trujillo.[89] By the time he died, in one of the most spectacular social flights of the era, he had served in every conceivable military office, he had been granted several nobility privileges, he had been knighted by the emperor himself into a chivalric order, and he was given a new heraldic crest.[90] And though at the peak of his glory he died a meaningless death, like a mock Icarus, motivated by the farcical hubris of the proud and cold-blooded soldier, Paredes's undisputed honor, based on feats both great and despicable, resonated exemplarily with the ambitions of young recruits and veterans alike.

THE LIVES OF HEROES

The opening scene in Alonso de Contreras's *Discurso de mi vida* vaguely resembles that of Paredes's *Suma* in its original, triggering violence.[91] On October 1, 1630, Captain Contreras sat down to write his life and the first memory that came to his mind, as he grabbed his pen, was the day in which he killed a classmate, the son of a rich constable, or *alguacil de corte*. The two kids had skipped school to go see a joust in the Puente Segoviana; yet presumably upon intervention of his classmate's father, "who was richer than my own" (que era más rico que el mío), Contreras was the only one to be publicly punished by the teacher, who made him bleed with "a whip of parchment" (un azote de pergamino). Alonso, the boy, took revenge with the same instrument that the adult writing these lines in his autograph manuscript had just used to sharpen his pen:

> Como tenía el dolor de los azotes, saqué el cuchillo de las escribanías y eché al muchacho en el suelo, boca abajo, y comencé a dar con el cuchillejo. Y como me parecía no lo hacía mal, le volví boca arriba y le di por las tripas, y diciendo todos los muchachos que le había muerto, me huí y a la noche me fui a mi casa como si no hubiera hecho nada.[92]

> (Still hurt by the lashes, I took out the sharpening knife and pushed the kid down to the floor, facing down, and I started to stab him. And since it seemed to me that I was not bad at it, turned him over, and stabbed him in his stomach; and the other kids saying that I had killed him, I fled and I went home at night as if nothing had happened.)

This original act of brutal violence, which he recounts nonchalantly and unapologetically, in the same manner as Paredes, is the ultimate beginning of his life story. The *escribanía* was a writing box or portable desk, and Contreras was probably looking at it while writing these lines. It is also remarkable how closely the instruments of writing—parchment, sharpening knife—are linked to the body of the future soldier and its traumas. The children's feud, moreover, and its tragic turn are caused by what both the boy Alonso and the writing captain perceive as a conspicuous injustice derived from social inequality. In the memory of the writing soldier, this foundational cruelty, the conquest of literacy in a local school (ultimately interrupted by the incident), and the adventurous beginning of life converge in the same originary scene. The intervention of the state's justice triggers Contreras's flight and the beginning of an adult life ceaselessly wounded by the omnipresence of this kind of socially motivated violence. Contreras's text will heretofore be, according to Beverly Jacobs's adequate wording, "a documentary of interclass antagonisms."[93]

After the first of his many imprisonments and forced exiles, Alonso returns to Madrid to serve as a silversmith's apprentice, which he readily abandons for the army, first as a lackey in the world of the kitchen's picaresque and then as a soldier. Tellingly, Contreras's first military action is desertion, which he blames on his most immediate officer, "who was no friend of fighting" (que no era amigo de pelear).[94] Here begins his successful piratical career for the Order of Malta in the Mediterranean world for which the *Discurso* is better known and a narrative ascension up the chain of command that, as in Paredes's case, is far from clean and straightforward.[95] However, the ambiguities and contradictions of a literary persona cast with epic, picaresque, and thuggish materials become clearer in the veterans' multiple returns to his home country.

Upon his first return to Spain from Malta, Contreras proudly narrates his appointment as lieutenant (alférez) and the reencounter with his mother. Later on, while recruiting soldiers in Écija, between Seville and Córdoba, a group of ruffians (*valientes*) steal some money from Contreras's company. The lieutenant responds to this defiance of his authority by arresting the braggarts and turning them over to the local governor (*corregidor*), who rewards him with the flashy clothes of the hanged. Shortly after, Contreras goes after some robbers who, pretending to be soldiers ("soldados que no lo eran"), were harassing the local population. The chase ends up in Córdoba's main brothel—"the first time I walked into this kind of place" (la primera vez que entraba en semejantes casas)—where he himself is taken for a thug when the local authorities arrive, and a fight breaks out. A fellow officer, captain Molina, appeases the corregidor and his police force, who grudgingly release Contreras after some explaining.[96]

Despite his efforts, the narrator is at pains to distinguish the main character from the rogues he officially fights. A few more ruffians ironically called "hidalgos" come to celebrate Contreras as the new hero of Córdoba's underworld, having on the same day killed some competing criminal lords and wounded a hated alguacil. Speaking in germanía's gangster slang, which Contreras claims not to understand while reproducing a lively dialogue among men who seem to be equals, they offer him a prostitute, the widow of another valentón, who becomes interested after seeing the lieutenant "so gallant and daring" (tan bizarro y alentado) in fighting cops and crooks alike. Once Contreras accepts Isabel under his protection, bringing her "with more authority than if she were a great lord's daughter" (con más autoridad que si fuera hija de un señor), the king's lieutenant is increasingly hard to distinguish from the swaggering pimp of the *germanesco* ballads and plays. And the narrator's half-hearted defense is again thwarted when a few days later, on their way to Lisbon, the reader learns that Contreras's fame as "the worst ruffian of Spain" (el mayor rufián que había en España) has quickly reached the ears of Badajoz's corregidor.[97]

His second return to Spain, after several years of service in the Medi-terranean, is preceded by one of the most intense moments in Contreras's autobiographical manuscript. Permanently deployed in a Sicilian presi-dio, the soldier marries a judge's widow from Palermo. They live happily together, according to his testimony, for a year and a half until one morn-ing Alonso finds his wife in bed with his best friend. The materiality of the soldier's autograph still keeps the traces of a conflicted writing and arguably a burdensome memory.

At first, the soldier writes: "I caught them together one morning and I killed them." Upon second thought, Contreras scratches out the seem-ingly painful *juntos* and effects a minimal grammatical intervention that turns the originally active sentence—"los maté"—into an impersonal one—"se murieron" (they died). Contreras refuses to expose the details (*las circunstancias*) of the incident and assures that "this I write very unwillingly" (esto lo escribo con mala gana). Far from a remorseful con-fession, the narrator does not regret having done it, as he only hopes that they repented on the spot ("téngalos Dios en el cielo si en aquel trance se arrepintieron").[98]

This correction, without significantly altering anything in the narra-tive, implies a certain detachment, a grammatical, if not legal, evasion of responsibility in the double murder. And yet what the materiality of the autograph actually reveals is a decisive claim to authorship, a careful attempt—in an otherwise very clean manuscript with few moments such as this one—to control the texture of the autobiographical subjectivity. The manipulation of the grammatical subject, rather than concealing it, highlights the elusive presence of the writing, historical subject. Again, the authority of the soldierly text is based on a tense, perhaps illegitimate, relation between the pen and sword that contradicts the most conven-tional formulations of the topos.

The only thing that the soldier saves from this domestic wreckage are his papers ("mis papeles de mis servicios"), and with these, Contreras heads to the court in Madrid to petition for a military office. Expect-ing to be appointed sergeant major of Sardinia, he is tricked by Lerma's omnipotent secretary, Rodrigo Calderón. After some palatine intrigues in El Escorial, where the king and his councils are staying, the soldier is accompanied by two men, neither of whom he trusts. So when he sees a suspicious gesture he reacts vehemently:

Uno que iba a mi lado derecho puso la mano detrás por debajo de la
capa, a quien yo miraba más a las manos que a la cara, y al punto saqué
la espada y di tan gran cuchillada en la cabeza que cayó en el suelo con

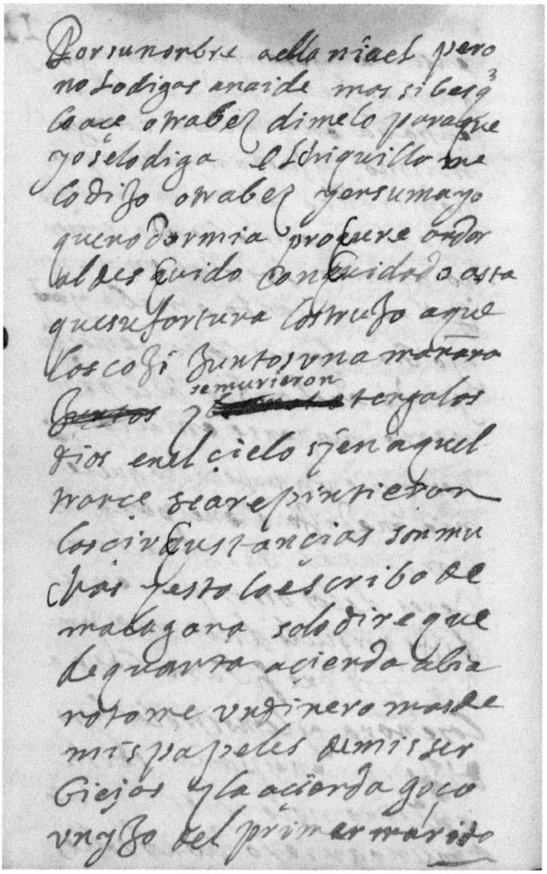

Figure 11. Alonso de Contreras, *Discurso de mi vida*, BNE Mss/7460, 81v. Autograph.

las escribanías en la mano, que si no se las veo le asegundo. El otro, que era el alguacil, metió mano al punto y, tirándome afuera, hice una raya en el suelo con la espada y dije "No me pase de ahí nadie, que lo haré pedazos."[99]

(The one on my right side, whose hands I watched more carefully than his face, reached underneath his cloak, and on that moment I drew my sword and slashed his head so badly that he fell on the ground holding his writing boxes, which stopped me from finishing him off. The other one, who was a constable, immediately drew on me; and dodging away, I traced a line on the floor with my sword and said: "No one dare to trespass, for I will tear him to pieces.")

The *escribanía*, mistakenly taken by Contreras to be a sword, saves the clerk from getting killed. Here the instruments of writing stand metonymically for the authority of the state, an authority that Contreras is nonetheless willing to challenge at every possible point in his autobiography. The soldier's escribanía, as shown in the opening school episode, is in direct opposition to this one of the secretary whose life Contreras spares at El Escorial. Although the adult Contreras is again antagonizing a constable and a secretary who is not too dissimilar from the schoolteacher, this episode entails an intriguing rehearsal of the opening scene. The soldier's penmanship is now displayed on the floor, writing with his sword a line that keeps the constable at bay and graphically signifies the conflict between the defying soldier and the state. In the typical language of valentones, Contreras uses the third instead of the second person and inserts a characteristic ethical dative ("No me pase de ahí nadie"). Pens and swords, *escribanías* and plebeian *cuchillejos*, killing and writing seem to be increasingly interchangeable in a text that intensely reflects on the power of both to authorize the soldiers' aspirations against the needs of the state that employs them.

This time he avoids prison but, disenchanted, he decides to withdraw from worldly life, soldierly or otherwise, and to become a hermit, only to find himself accused of being the leader of a Morisco rebellion in one of the most rocambolesque episodes of the narrative.[100] After proving his innocence, he is given an infantry company in Flanders and appointed captain. Once in the Low Countries, Contreras serves for the two first years of the truce and then is granted permission to leave for Spain to pursue his aspirations to a habit of the Order of Malta. On his way back from the Low Countries through Burgundian territory, a fellow soldier, "a Spaniard who got married there because he was banished from the king's territories, for he was one of Flanders' mutineers" (un español que estaba allí casado por no poder estar en los estados del rey, a causa de ser de los amotinados de Flandes), helps him dodge death again when he is accused of espionage by the French.[101] Again, corporate and class solidarity between serving soldiers and runaway deserters overshadows any other possible allegiances and loyalties. And upon his third return to Spain, he is newly imprisoned for a sexual affair in which two married women were involved, one of which gets her buttocks cut by the soldier—or rather knight of the Order of Malta. In the tumultuous trial that follows Contreras verbally defies again the judicial authority of the tribunal and he is banished from Madrid for three years.

Similar episodes occupy the rest of Contreras's autobiography: he is repeatedly imprisoned, he serves valiantly in the New World and back in the Mediterranean, and he fights the king's councillors and secretaries with the same determination with which he confronts his rowdy subordinate soldiers. As shown in the veterans' many returns, Contreras's relation with the state he is supposed to serve is tense throughout the narrative and he misses no opportunity to record the struggles between the proud soldier and the monarchy's civil servants. In a surprisingly consistent fashion, the veteran pits not only the trigger-happy attitude of the bizarro soldier but also the "raw language of the tavern, the gambling house, and the brothel" (un crudo vocabulario de tasca, timba y lupanar) against all forms of state authority.[102] The ambiguous camaraderie Contreras shows, on several occasions, with the poor, pícaros, and thugs contrasts sharply with the dismissive disrespect, if not open defiance, of his military and civilian superiors.

It is hard to impose a legible order in Contreras's collection of seemingly isolated life events. In one of the most insightful interpretations of Contreras's text, José Ortega y Gasset vividly compares the soldier's life writing to the calligraphy of a bird's flight in the air, a trajectory impossible to pin down. The "disjointed life" and "spasmodic destiny" (vida descoyuntada; destino espasmódico) of Alonso de Contreras was, according to the philosopher, resistant to meaning and emplotment.[103] Action is an end in itself and there seems to be no logical connection between one event and the next, between past, present, and future. For Lope de Vega, however, the captain's deeds "were worthy of a long history or a heroic poem" (digno sujeto fuera de larga historia o de poema heroico). In 1625, well before Contreras set out to write his own memoir, the playwright gave the soldier shelter in his own house and wrote a most enthusiastic panegyric in a comedy dedicated to him. The epic that Lope imagines for Contreras would trace his social ascension from a poor childhood in Madrid, "hurled in the arms of Fortune" (arrojado en los [brazos] de la fortuna), to the captaincy, the habit of Malta, the encomienda. Contreras's deeds, which Lope will be "honored to write in numerous verses" (pienso en dilatados versos honrarme de escribir sus valerosos hechos), are comparable to no less than those of Diego García de Paredes, among others. In the person of Alonso "natural valor" had successfully "sued inherited valor (or value)" (puso el valor natural / pleito al valor heredado).[104] The lives of soldiers seem to beg for an ultimately impossible reinscription into the epic mode in order to make proper sense of them, but the matters of war as they experienced and recounted them go against the grain of heroic literature—even in the peculiarly elaborated forms of soldierly gunpowder epic. The soldiers' *vitae* and the empire's *gesta*, like Alonso de Salamanca's autobiographical epic helped us see, often seem at odds with each other.

Scholars such as Jacobs have often emphasized, not unlike Lope, "the work's predominantly social thrust." In Contreras's autobiography, "every action would have the purpose of achieving social advancement, power, and respect." Jacobs's insightful reading also points out, however, that Contreras's epic ascension ended up collapsing into the usually circular structure of the soldier's social trajectory, which "prefigures the ultimate failure and lends the *Vida* a Sisyphean aura: the protagonist who alters the predetermined order by leaving his 'rightful' place to enter a higher stratum will unequivocally fail and sink to his original level."[105] It is indeed the climb of Sisyphus, or the flight of Icarus, after all. For, first, the last two parts of Contreras's autobiography, written years apart, have been shown to narrate Contreras's successive falls and his increasing disenchantment; second, because Lope writes no heroic poem singing Contreras's life; and third, because the autobiography that Contreras himself writes a few years later will remain forever unfinished and unpublished, like the "life" of the criminal rogue Ginés de Pasamonte in *Don Quijote* and Alonso de Salamanca's epic and autobiographical travails—yet unlike the extremely successful picaresque lives published by professional writers. The lives of heroes seem to stubbornly resist the linear forms of the epic, or even those of the picaresque, ironically ascensional, and bloodless narratives.

How are we to explain the soldiers' peculiar visions of the self in their autobiographical writing? How are we to understand why these authors would tell stories of cold-blooded murder and association with the criminal underworld, in their first-person, autographed memoirs without showing any kind of Christian—or even human—remorse? Scholars have repeatedly checked many of the events Contreras narrates against the documentary records of early modern Spain, often confirming the historical accuracy of his autobiography—some literary critics nevertheless insist on characterizing, whether dismissively or enthusiastically, as fictional or novelesque.[106] Yet what matters most is that, as shown by the peculiar dynamics of pen and sword in his text, he is fully responsible for the persona skillfully devised in his war memoir. It is his choice to present himself not only as a dutiful, courageous, and competent soldier but also as an insubordinate braggart, a fearsome killer, and a determined survivor.

The actions of these heroes may seem to us hardly heroic, but they are fully in agreement with the ethos and value system of Spain's soldiery, if not with our own. Plunder, desertion, crime, mutiny, and even assassination are the stuff of which the lives of soldiers are made. They belong fully in the lives of heroes together with their valor in combat and their professional discipline—not against them. Instilling fear in their military superiors and in their helpless civilian victims, soldiers seem to have found, was the only way for them to survive. They attained respect through the public display of toughness and a threatening virility flexibly articulated in the social, bodily, and discursive codes of bizarría. Their dubious reputation was not something to be ashamed of but instead something to brag about and to use advantageously. And their place in the social imagination of early modern Spain may be compared to the sometimes epic role of bandits or mafiosi in other historical contexts.[107]

It is certainly no wonder that the defiant autobiographies of soldiers such as Contreras, Pasamonte, Miguel de Castro, Catalina de Erauso, and Diego Duque de Estrada remained unpublished. Contreras's "cuchillo de escribanía" is the last and perhaps most revealingly subversive trope, in the long tradition that played metonymically with the materialities of writing and fighting. Garcilaso and Ercilla alternated, in the most conventional formulation, sword and pen; Cristóbal Rodríguez Alva told us that the lines of his Flemish epic were spilled with his own blood; Santiago de Tesillo inked his pen with gunpowder to shoot words. By conflating killing and writing, Contreras's sharpening knife, used against the son of a rich authority figure, shows a crucial paradox of soldiering and its representations in early modern Europe. Violence empowered soldiers and blood enabled writing. The authority of their narratives, like their professional, symbolic capital in the society of soldiers, relied largely on killing. Common men took up weapons and pens to escape poverty and to survive, but in so doing they pushed the lines that separated legitimate and illegitimate violence, the state's allegedly just wars and outright crime, ultimately questioning the most fundamental assumptions about soldiering, war, and empire.

In 1594, the soldiers of D. Antonio de Zúñiga's tercio in the army of Flanders had enough of payment delays and bad excuses. One morning, the soldiers of Namur posted a menacing, mutinous *cartel*:

> Cien pagas nos deben y me parece que no hacen caso de nosotros;
> no se espanten por cosas que viren, pus ansí nos tratan, pues no nos
> pagan lo que tanto trabajamos; aun de una miseria hambre que nos
> dan nos la van alargando de mes a mes. Tanto cargan al asno que a
> coces echan la carga, que por vida de Dios que nos lo han de pagar
> los que más cerca estuvieren pues tan poco se acuerdan de nosotros.
> Juro +++[108]
>
> (They owe us a hundred pays and it seems to me that they don't care
> about us. Let them not be shocked at what they may see, since they
> treat us this way and don't pay us who work so hard. They even drag
> out from one month to the next the pittance [and] hunger they give
> us. They load up the donkey so much that with kicks we will throw
> it away, because by God's life those who are nearest will pay for it,
> since they take so little thought of us. I swear +++)

The tone of this truly remarkable document is not dissimilar from the correspondence between the rebels of Mahdia and the imperial authorities in the 1550s, as we saw in Chapter 3. Nor is it that different from the large body of mutineers' papers masterfully analyzed by Geoffrey Parker, who also recovered this piece. It could be tempting to explain the strange calligraphy of the piece as a result of the partial literacies of the soldierly mass, but soldiers must have purposefully contorted their handwriting in order to avoid Londoño's ordinance to keep of track it, which was intended precisely to control mutiny. Again, writing signifies the soldiers' organized resistance, whether as a metaphor or as an actual material practice.

Perhaps more intriguing are the continuities between this *cartel* and the texts of the soldiers that have been discussed thus far. The themes of hunger and misery are never absent from the ballads of the broken soldiers or the autobiographies of rowdy veterans. The proud vindication of their professional work is the raison d'être of both the petition-like memoirs written by veterans and the *pláticos'* gunpowder epics—and it also resembles the imperious ways in which an "arrogant poor" such as Vicente de la Roca addressed his rich neighbors when he returned from war. The aggressively defiant language of the mutineers is fully in line with that of the literary thugs of the *jácaras* and with the rich public orality of the soldiers' republic. "Por vida de Dios," "lo han de pagar," "no se espanten por las cosas que viren": these blasphemous expletives and utterly offensive warnings intensely defy authority and are an integral part of the *bizarría* that informs both the sociability of the soldiery in the army and many

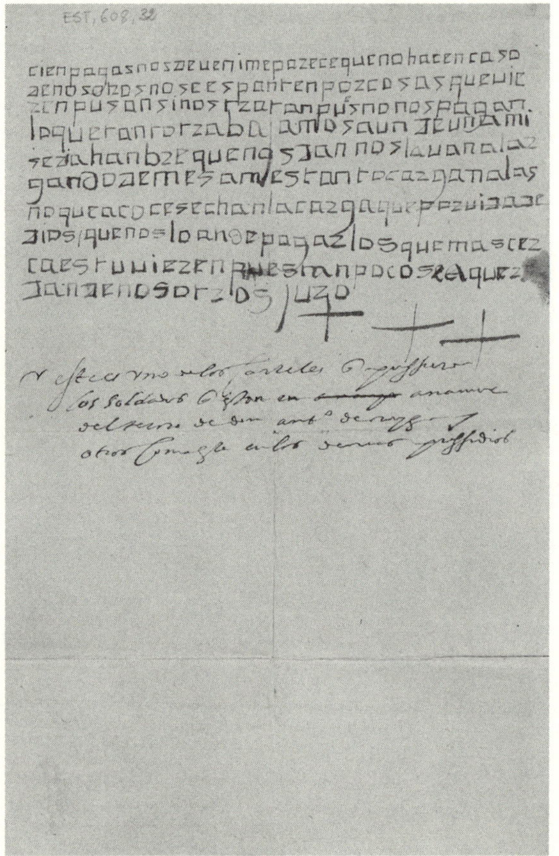

Figure 12. *Pasquín puesto en Namur por los soldados españoles en 1594.* España, Ministerio de Cultura,
AGS, Estado 608, fol. 32.

of the mutinous literary texts they proudly authored. Alonso de Contreras would have happily signed it. In fact, if we consider that what the soldier's autobiography does is transform the anonymous, collective crosses of the end into the bold, threatening individual signature of an *author*, I believe we may get closer to understanding what these puzzling texts are about.

Epilogue

Willingly or unwillingly, common soldiers end wars and ruin empires. This does not only mean that by succeeding in the battlefield they end political disputes. It means that the resistance of common soldiers, whether active or passive, uncovers the limits of the expansionist and militaristic logics of early modern empires and forces the state to reconsider foreign policy. Competent, proud, and unruly soldiers such as Contreras did as much to win battles for the Spanish Habsburgs as they did to shake the foundations of their power. Already in 1574, and referring to the first mutiny of Antwerp, Luis de Requesens, the governor-general of the Spanish Netherlands, wrote that "it was not the prince of Orange who had lost the Low Countries, but the soldiers born in Valladolid and Toledo."[1]

The exhaustion of the Catholic Mars was indeed apparent, even more than on the battlefield, in the extreme difficulties the state found in persuading new recruits to enroll voluntarily, the readiness with which they deserted, and the generalization of mutiny. In December 1654, Jerónimo de Barrionuevo recorded in his *Avisos*, referring to the war against rebel Catalonia, that "no one wants to leave the house to serve again; and from the five or six thousand veteran soldiers that are in Madrid, I hear only 350 have enrolled, and these lame, one-handed, and broken" (no quiere nadie salir de su casa, ni tornar a servir más; y con haber en Madrid de 5 a 6000 soldados viejos, me aseguran no se han registrado 350, y esos, cojos, mancos y estropeados). The next year, in a new attempt to recruit soldiers for the same war, "they announced that anyone who enrolled would receive six reales up front plus one pay and clothes. This is the necessity of recruits, for one single man cannot be found even if paid one arm and a leg" (pregonaron que a cualquiera persona que se quisiere alistar por soldado, le darían cada día 6 reales de socorro, y una paga y un vestido luego anticipadamente. Tal es la necesidad que hay de gente, que no se halla un hombre por un ojo de la cara).[2] It is hardly surprising that Castile's common folk would be unwilling to fight in a civil war where the soldiers of the crown's skeletal armies in Barcelona were "so poor that they go to the convents' kitchen soup, almost naked, and even the captains wear espadrilles for the lack of shoes" (tan pobres, que iban á la sopa de los Conventos, y que están desnudos, y que los Capitanes traen alpargatas por no tener zapatos). "Everyone complains to the king and he could not care less" (Todos se quejan al rey y él de nada se dolía), concludes Barrionuevo with a familiar reference, in the manner of the soldierly ballads, to a perennially popular *romance*.[3]

If the state appeared increasingly incapable of filling the ranks of its armies with new recruits, the veterans in service were not helping either. Attrition rates owed significantly more to desertion than to casualties on the battlefield. Between 1608 and 1619 more than four thousand soldiers deserted from Oran, sometimes preferring captivity over duty. In 1640, the troops raised in Extremadura with the occasion of the Portuguese rebellion reached wastage rates of 90 percent.[4] The naturalness with which one epistle by soldier-poet Andrés Rey de Artieda depicts two comrades discussing the futility of the soldier's life, their mistreatment by officers, and their intents to desert suggests the connection between rank-and-file gossiping, the lettered practices of the writing soldiers, and the less than dishonorable possibility of defection.[5]

Mutiny was so widespread in the Habsburg armies that in some periods it seemed that the fate of war and peace rested in the hands of rebel soldiers. There were forty-six mutinies between 1572 and 1607 in the army of Flanders, an average of two per year, and occasionally involving as many as seven thousand men.[6] Geoffrey Parker has brilliantly described the sophisticated practices that mutineers came to master in their organized protests against their superiors: the publication of *carteles*, the admittance of officers only if they were willing to give up their rank and serve on the same footing with the troops, the radically democratic election of their rank-and-file leadership, the practices of self-government, self-defense, and self-finance, and even the use of official seals from their soldierly "republics" in their written interlocution with their former commanders. This set of practices would seem to constitute a surprisingly radical political culture within the Spanish armies of the early modern period.[7] And yet most military historians have consistently concluded, with Parker, that "like most civilian revolts of the early modern period, the military mutinies of the Spanish army reveal no evidence of any revolutionary purpose of politically conscious agitators."[8] In terms similar to Hobsbawm's when discussing "primitive rebels," Parker has downplayed the political nature of mutinies because "they had no subversive political or social programme" while on the other hand he has described them as the "collective protest" of a striking "military proletariat." Parker is certainly right to be prudent about the *consciousness* and long-term *strategies* of mutinying soldiers, but "the fact that this was designed primarily to destroy the authority of the superordinate elite and carried no elaborate blueprint for its replacement, does not put it outside the realm of politics," as Ranajit Guha—otherwise sympathetic to and influenced by Hobsbawm's Gramscian turn— pointed out when questioning the "pre-political" nature and alleged primitivism of past popular revolts.[9] In fact, it is the soldiers' mutinous writings that have been discussed in this book that allow us to articulate more clearly a political subject and to see the radical nature of the soldiers' resistance.

The *pláticas* of the Muses' comrades, this book has shown, played no small role in bending the back of the once almighty monarchy of Spain. It is impossible not to see the link between the ballads of the returning soldiers, showing the material misery of soldierly life, or the starving petitioning soldiers in Madrid's streets, and the active resistance of the Castilian peasantry to the aggressive recruitment policies of a staggering state, as masterfully studied by Ruth MacKay.[10] At the turn of the seventeenth century, a high-level official of the Council of War attributed the difficulties in recruitment to "the many broken soldiers who come back from everywhere, and the miseries these and others tell about where they have been, and what they have seen others to suffer and the many honorable soldiers who remain unrewarded" (los muchos estropeados que acuden de todas partes, las miserias que estos y los que no lo son cuentan de donde vienen, ver padecer y quedar sin premio muchos soldados honrados).[11] In Diego Núñez de Alva's *Diálogos de la vida del soldado* a poor veteran returning home crosses paths with a young man who is going to war only to dissuade him from enlisting.[12] Many of the soldiers' texts explored in this book did a lot of cultural work to dethrone the "mythology of war" by offering absurd rather than heroic versions of death at war.[13] The monarchy could no longer mobilize its subaltern classes with the promise of social promotion and basic sustenance because the stories of broken soldiers, the deserters, and the reformed mutineers showed amply how hollow those promises were. The soldier's voice carried an authority difficult to counter. They had been there, they had been mistreated, starved, and wounded; and the reality of a scar on their skin or the lack of a limb was quite difficult to hide under the state's promise of reward or the crusading rhetoric of empire. By painting a grim portrait of soldierly life, myriad texts discouraged common men from enlisting and contrasted drastically with those texts that aimed at providing exemplary tales of war that would stir them to join the army. The moral economy of the traditional epic song, as we saw, could never fully accommodate the soldier's experience of modern war; but it would certainly cease to exist, even in the peculiar form of gunpowder epic, when confronted with the debased world of criminal veterans and ex-combatant beggars. After generations of veterans told their stories of hunger, disease, exploitation, and death, the commoners of Spain must have learned, as Torres Naharro knew already in 1517, that "to gamble one's life" is a foolishness only typical of soldiers (poner la vida al tabrero / bobería es de soldados).[14]

The literary practices of the plático soldiers were not simply a factor in resistance, desertion, and mutiny; in many cases, they were instrumental—they were the very condition enabling those practices. Londoño's restrictive ordinances about the soldiers' *pláticas*, the anti-aristocratic drive of soldierly epic, Hierro's ambiguous narration of his comrades' mutiny, Salamanca's unabashed criticism of military policy, Tesillo's blaming of imperial defeats on the centipede of writing soldiers, Ercilla's questioning of imperial certainties in the New World, the protesting ballads of the broken soldiers, the aggressive bizarría of Contreras's autobiography: all of these clearly show that the oppositional and self-defensive tactics of the resistant rank and file were intimately related to the literary culture of their republic of letters. Moreover, many of the Muses' comrades were themselves personally involved in serious conflicts with military and imperial authorities. Ercilla was sentenced to death for insubordination, a penalty he barely escaped. Diego Suárez Montañés, the writer of a brief memoir, chronicles, and *romances*, was imprisoned in Oran for being

the instigator and the leader of a mutiny (*electo*) against the governing Count of Alcaudete, an accusation that he vehemently denied.
The same happened to Alonso de Contreras, bizarrely indicted as the
organizer and commander of a failed Morisco uprising in Aragon.
Jerónimo de Pasamonte, for his part, saw the manuscript of his autobiographical text seized by the Inquisition for scrutiny on the potential charges of heresy.[15] Just as soldierly ballads were associated—and
dealt amply—with desertion, crime, and social violence, the voices
of these soldiers were often linked to indiscipline, mutiny, and social
disorder.

As García-Santo Tomás eloquently put it, "Writing about war
was no longer a matter of glorifying the nation, as the early modern
Spanish mercenary tried to find a balance between patriotism and the
temptation to blame the Crown for its overambitious enterprises."[16]
Against Weber's traditional thesis that war was the single most important factor in the rise of the modern state—or as Charles Tilly said,
"war made the state, and the state made war"—I. A. A. Thompson
has convincingly argued that "war was less a stimulant than a test of
the state."[17] For Thompson, the royal bureaucracies of early modern
Europe, and of Habsburg Spain in particular, were poorly equipped
to deal with immensely complex administrative operations required
to recruit, supply, deploy, and manage an army—only during the
three first decades of Philip II's government was the crown able to
efficiently centralize these operations. To this argument I would add
that the state's soldiers were among the most serious threats to its
authority. The state's management of war allowed for the paradox
that the very same institutions, practices, and structures that were
required to wage imperial war also enabled soldiers to compromise
the outcomes of military policy and even the political survival of the
monarchy. Against the harmonious historiographical picture that the
critical topos of "the pen and the sword" implies, the stories written
and read, sung and heard by soldiers, were often quite troublesome
for the empire.

Viewed from the ranks, warfare—its logics, its ethics, its
legitimacy—must look very different, and what the soldiers experience and witness has often motivated them to write and to resist.
Nevertheless, when considering the survival strategies of common
soldiers, including writing, a pervasive storyline in Spanish cultural
history has inscribed them in a narrative of decadence and decline.
La vida y hechos de Estebanillo González (Antwerp: Viuda de Juan

Cnobbart, 1646), the picaresque account of a rogue soldier, has been often seen as the perfect example, "the most significant testimony to the decline of Spanish military spirit."[18] The desertions of the *tornillo* soldiers, who defected right after enrolling in a company just to get the first pay, the engagement in illegal activities in both the military and civilian spheres, and the rebellious carnivalization of the most sacred military and political institutions, which become the very narrative regime of *Estebanillo González*, have all been interpreted as symptoms of the degradation of the military class, a consequence of the second proletarianization of a trade that was once honorable and prestigious. This is what some anxious historiographical narratives did, after somehow having failed to recognize that imperial warfare had always been conducted by "armies of poor men": "From an initially noble, or at least hidalgo, coloring, [the army] shades into a picaresque nuance, including soldiers and captains. The hypothesis is still to be verified, but there appears an increasing rarefaction of the traditionally dominant noble element. And evil feeds evil."[19]

Rather than as symptoms of decadence, we could instead read these practices of resistance and the writings that supported them, in search of a new heroics, as the ruses of the weak, the accumulated knowledge of the surviving and sometimes defiant subaltern—and again, it must be no coincidence that Gramsci's spatial metaphor to describe social relations in industrial societies, as in Marx, came from the military. Whether as picaresque everyday forms of resistance or, occasionally, in swaggering open defiance of the system as a whole, the soldiers' ploys were but the kit of survival strategies that they had developed through the years to avoid death, a wisdom largely reproduced in the lines written within the soldiers' republic of letters. Estebanillo's defensive cowardice, his devastating and self-serving cynicism, his venality and clever racketing, and even his willingness to betray his king and country can already be found in texts as early as Bartolomé Torres Naharro's *Comedia soldadesca*, written in the second decade of the sixteenth century. Avoidance, disobedience, delay, and outright rebellion were always there as tactics for the common soldier to use to get by, the everyday weapons of the weak, in the language of James Scott.[20] Yet perhaps the most valuable and sophisticated of his earlier comrades' legacies to Estebanillo is indeed his voice, his last ruse against death around the corner, in Cervantes's phrase. In Hispanic cultural traditions the legitimacy of the poor man's life as a matter of artistic elaboration is usually associated with the fictional world of the picaresque; yet the soldiers' republic of letters allowed for forms of popular authorship in which the poor or the humble folk were also successful personae for literary enunciation and the lives of these lowly heroes worthy writing matter. The legitimacy of the poor, common soldier to speak his life—regardless of the authorship debate in *Estebanillo*'s case—was enabled by the tradition of writing soldiers and their republic of letters.[21]

Soldierly epic, military treatises, and historiographical writing oftentimes emplotted the lives of soldiers as success stories. For the working classes of early modern Iberia, the military revolution had opened a road, never straightforward, to professional promotion and social recognition through the symbolic capital accumulated by their military and cultural practices. Promising monetary reward, social prestige, and even ennoblement, soldiering, for many reasons, presented itself as an ascensional trajectory for the poor of Spain. The soldiers who wrote their *vidas* occasionally show their progress but also, and more important, the limits of social advancement through soldiering and writing for the common folk and the déclassés, however meritorious. Pasamonte may have ended suffering from madness and religious prosecution after a life of captivity and physical pain. Catalina de Erauso, from a good Basque lineage, soldiered for decades before she got to personally meet the king and even the pope, only to seemingly end up driving mules in New Spain. Soldiering seems to have worked for Contreras, who would quite rapidly rise from kitchen boy—like Estebanillo and Duque de Estrada—to several captaincies and eventually an *encomienda* "for his deeds."[22] But in the last episode he narrates before his text is suddenly interrupted, Contreras is despised by the Marquis of Santa Cruz, who denies that he had ever been a cavalry captain. And one Alonso de Contreras, perhaps the homonymous captain, died poor in Madrid in 1653, his funeral and burial being paid with charitable donations.[23] What these autobiographies seem to tell is not so much the ruin of the empire but the relative failure of their class to secure social promotion, visibility, and ultimately a life not always threatened by poverty, injury, and madness.

It is true that the plático soldiers never acquired, for instance, the centrality and relevance of their Ottoman counterparts in a period that Baki Tezcan called "the age of the janissaries," when organized mutinying soldiers were capable of forcing grand viziers in and out, and even of executing disliked sultans such as Osman II in 1622.[24] The pláticos' protests could hardly secure soldierly privileges and long-term social advancement for the rank and file. The gunpowder discourses of the soldiery seem to have ultimately failed; the army became the site of satire and the arbitristas' scrutiny in the search for the causes of imperial decay. The process of rearistocratization and privatization of the military administration that Thompson called "devolution" may have contributed to block the ascension of the plático soldiers as a social group and potentially a political actor. González de León, for his part, has also argued that in the course of the Eighty Years' War the incipient meritocracy of the school of Alba was progressively eroded, again cutting the wings of Icarian soldiers.[25]

But the legacy of early modern writing soldiers is potentially vast and deserves further study. In 1917, while mutineers in the French army were being bitterly accused of pacifism and communism, Edward B. Osborn edited *The Muse in Arms*, "a collection of war poems, for the most part written in the field of action, by seamen, soldiers, and flying men who are serving, or have served in the Great War."[26] During the war that was going to end all wars, the voices of the British soldiers would provide the best "glimpses of the ultimate significance of warfare." Osborn's claim that "there has been nothing like it before in the history of English literature, nor, indeed, of any other literature," very much in harmony with the urgently nationalistic rhetoric of the prologue to his landmark anthology, cannot really be sustained.[27] It is my contention that common soldiers have long strived to understand the wars they fought through writing and reading. Modern conceptions and "frames of war," moreover, have been shaped by popular forms of storytelling adopted or developed by the Muses' comrades that may have a historical ancestry older than we think.[28] Our understanding of war owes much to the epic of authorship and the romance of survival featuring these common soldiers, to the stories they told themselves and others while struggling for a living, recognition, and remembrance. Among "the things they carried," in Tim O'Brien's phrase, there could always be found pens and paper, memoirs and sonnets, ballads and chronicles.

Moreover, the military languages of soldierly comradeship, resistance, class, and professional pride may have loomed large in the radical political cultures and practices of modernity. There are good reasons why Parker pointed out the mutineers' council's "superficial resemblance to a Soviet" and why the Spanish word *camarada*, for instance, gave way in different European languages to the usage of *comrade* as a stock phrase among popular and revolutionary movements since the late eighteenth century.[29] For the reader living in a permanently postwar America it is no longer shocking to think of soldiers writing and talking publicly or to imagine loyal servicemen turning their backs on, or actually fighting against, the state that employed them. In Vietnam soldiers pioneered the protests that later extended to civil society, helped to a great extent by the cultural practices associated with the different underground presses, as well as by the rich orality of the veterans' war stories. The instrumental role of the G.I. Movement and Veterans Against the War in ending the Vietnam War and the central place of their public pláticas in the subsequent revisions of America's war policies are now widely recognized.[30] The new Iraq syndrome has given way to an ever-rising number of novels and short stories, memoirs, poetic collections, and video-narratives, some of them highly critical of the state's military policies. On the other side of an ever-shifting frontline, the only deserter of the Iraqi army who survived the slaughter perpetrated by the Islamic State in the summer of 2014 made a public pledge never to soldier again.[31]

In the case of Spain, the political and cultural legacies of the soldiers' defiant voices and practices also deserve further study. The extensive Bourbon reforms in the military, which relatively improved the living conditions of common soldiers, are hardly understandable without the long history of successful organization and resistance among the troops. And yet raucous lampoons and ballads continued to accompany the soldiers' protests during the eighteenth century.[32] A mutinous and pamphletary political culture, moreover, traversed modern Spanish history in the nineteenth century during "the age of liberalism."[33] The anonymous artillery soldiers who joined the May 1 popular uprising against the Napoleonic invasion in Madrid and the deserters who joined the guerrillas in the same war invite us to reevaluate the political significance of the earlier mutinies and desertions that I have discussed in this book. Mutinous and outspoken soldiers led or supported repeated rebellions, first against absolutism and then against the conservative or liberal governments that failed to deliver the promises of political revolution. In 1820, General Rafael del Riego and the expeditionary army he was leading to bring the American colonies back to Spanish sovereignty rebelled in Cádiz against the king and forced him to accept the Cádiz constitution of 1812—yet another instantiation of how resisting soldiers kill empires.[34] The history of similar *pronunciamientos* led by liberal officers such as Espartero, Topete, or Prim that largely determined the political fights of the period is well-known; yet the role of the discontent rank and file in pushing or checking their commanders, as in circulating pamphlets, poems, and rumor that constitute the political culture of the period, merits more scholarly attention. Similarly, the protagonism of common soldiers in the creation of the army's literary societies, *ateneos*, academies, and military periodicals that fueled social, cultural, and political debates in the second half of the century remains to be explored.[35]

In the twentieth century, the long dictatorships of Primo de Rivera and Franco have brutally obscured our view of the relationship between the military and the history of modern democratization. The role of the clandestine Unión Militar Democrática—modeled after the Portuguese revolutionary Movimento das Forças Armadas—in countering the reactionary forces of the Francoist military during the transition to democracy is not clearly acknowledged.[36] Today, in the rapidly changing political landscape of current Spain, some soldiers who are resisting the institutional and political inertias of a largely conservative army structure have taken center stage. As I write these lines a Spanish lieutenant and his fiction and nonfiction writing have gained public notoriety for outspokenly denouncing the corruption of the military, the conditions of service, and the limits on the civil rights of many Spanish soldiers. After months of arrest and court-martial, Lieutenant Segura has been dishonorably discharged from the army, but media coverage of his case for over two years has only extended the reach of his grievances and the support of a large sector of public opinion.[37] In a similarly notorious case, Major Zaida Cantera has abandoned the army after years of fighting against the opaque and corrupt structures of an army that she denounced for sexual harassment and bullying, which she recounts in a coauthored book.[38]

The example of these modern plático soldiers might help us see the endeavors of their ancestral comrades in a new light. For the common soldiers of the Catholic monarchy there was hardly ever a Golden Age—it was indeed made of iron and gunpowder from the start. Yet their voices always played a substantial, defining role in the stories that organized the self-perception of Habsburg Spain and its global empire. "If the small voice of history gets a hearing at all," writes Ranajit Guha in an essay that pits history's undertones against the noise of what he calls statist discourse, "it will do so only by interrupting the telling of the dominant version, breaking up its storyline and making a mess of its plot." Indeed, if the soldiers' writings some-times provided metanarratives of Spanish imperial history structured around the tropes of ascension and decay, perhaps more frequently their stories tended toward the dissolution of "chronology itself" in favor of a "cyclicity" that was both enabling and frustrating.[39]

A few years after the emblematic defeat of Rocroi (1643), and on the distant battlefields of Chile, Santiago de Tesillo provided a power-ful mythological analogy for the Spanish empire that may help us in this attempt to rethink the narratives and chronologies of the empire and the Spanish Golden Age: "The Spanish Catholic Mars is a Sisy-phus of this heavy rock, bringing it up to the summit of ultimate victory and turning to fall with it to its lowest origins" (El Católico Marte Español es un Sísifo desta pesada peña, subiéndola casi a la cumbre de la última vitoria y volviendo a caer con ella a lo más infe-rior de sus primordios).[40] Tesillo's allegory was particularly appropri-ate for the context of the never-ending Chilean wars but also for the empire's military history broadly considered. For the fighting rank and file the myth may have fittingly incarnated the unending effort and eternal frustration of soldiering and may help us understand the narrative structures of texts such as Contreras's plotless life or Duque de Estrada's *Comentarios*, which has indeed been seen as tracing "a circular, and not a linear progression, one which eventually leads to recurrent failure."[41] Although it may seem to be a variation of the traditional descending narrative of decadence, the key to the myth of Sisyphus is its cyclical nature. It is not a one-directional, linear nar-rative but a circular one in which causality and precedence are hard to establish. The rock, like the empire, might ascend to the summit or fall to the bottom, but punishment remains the same for the Sisyph-ean and Icarian Spanish soldiers who carried out unending imperial wars and who once dared to fly too close to the sun. The only solu-tion would be, as the mutineers attempted many times, to topple the boulder, the burden of the empire.

Whether Tesillo was aware of it or not, the story of Sisyphus is truly fitting indeed, if we think about it. Although versions of the myth vary, it seems that Sisyphus was "the wiliest man alive," accord-ing to Homer, a consummate trickster who was able to outwit Thana-tos (Death) and even to put him in chains.[42] It was Ares (Mars) who brought Sisyphus back to the underworld and imposed the final pun-ishment on the conqueror of death. Those who lived dying, according to Torres Naharro's paradoxical formulation, enrolled, fought, killed, scrounged, sacked, deserted, mutinied, rebelled, and thieved, all in an attempt to out-trick death. They could certainly die unexpectedly, the end that a suddenly wise Don Quixote predicts for the poor lad who goes to war for want of money.[43] They could even die as some kind of mock Icarus who could not reach a straw in the wall, like Paredes. But before they died, many of them read about those who preceded them and wrote abundantly so that they themselves could be remembered, "a testament to [their] own survival."[44] The writings of those who lived "continuously flirting with death," in García-Santo Tomás's evocative wording, were "a continuous struggle against the physical and narrative fragmentation imposed by the unpredictability of war." When Orpheus descended to Hades, those punished with unending suffering like Tantalus, Ixion, and Tityos were moved and momentarily relieved by "the charms of his matchless lyre."[45] Among them, Sisyphus, the laborer of the underworld, dropped his stone, sat down on it, and listened. For the Muses' comrades, kicking away the rocky burden of the empire, like the mutinous donkey of that *cartel* in Namur, was hardly dissociable from the hearing and telling of stories about "weapons, wars, and the men who fight them."

INTRODUCTION

Epigraphs: Virgil, *Aeneid*, trans. Robert Fagles (New York: Penguin, 2006), 9.873–76. "Virgilio fue hijo de un ollero y fue el mejor poeta de los italianos." Pedro Mexía, *Silva de varia lección agora nuevamente enmendada y corregida por el autor* (Lyon: Herederos de Diego de Junta, 1556), 338. See also Suetonius, *Vita Vergili*, in *Lives of the Caesars, Volume II*, ed. and trans. J. C. Rolfe, Loeb Classical Library 38 (Cambridge, MA: Harvard University Press, 1914), 449. Translations throughout the book are my own unless otherwise noted.

1. "Pour le soldat roturier, les lettres ne sont pas un héritage, mais un conquête." Frédérique Verrier, *Les armes de Minerve: L'humanisme militaire dans l'Italie du XVIe siècle* (Paris: Presses de l'Université de Paris-Sorbonne, 1997), 102.

2. A generation of fascist intellectuals in postwar Spain devoted a lot of attention to this topic: Luis Rosales and Felipe Vivanco, *Poesía heroica del imperio* (Madrid: Ediciones Jerarquía, 1940); José María Hernández Rubio, *Poetas soldados españoles* (Madrid: Editora Nacional, 1945); José López de Toro, *Los poetas de Lepanto* (Madrid: Instituto Histórico de Marina, 1950); José Antonio Maravall, *El humanismo de las armas en Don Quijote* (Madrid: Instituto de Estudios Políticos, 1948), which he substantially revised in *Utopía y contrautopía en el Quijote* (Santiago de Compostela: Pico Sacro, 1976). In more recent times, the unproblematic identification of the politics of empire in early modern Spain with the discourse produced by its soldiers persists. In 1998 the director of the Spanish Royal Academy, Víctor García de la Concha, edited *Armas y letras en el Siglo de Oro español (Antología poética)* (Madrid: Ministerio de Defensa, 1998), a collection of texts depicting "soldiering as a chivalric exercise, valiant and honorable, to the service of three great ideals: homeland, monarchy, and Catholic faith" (17).

3. "La Fortuna envidiosa / hirió la mano de Miguel de Cervantes, / pero su ingenio en versos de diamantes / los de plomo volvió con tanta gloria." Lope de Vega, *Laurel de Apolo* (1630), ed. Antonio Carreño (Madrid: Cátedra, 2007), 413. Luis Astrana Marín titled his monumental biography of Cervantes *Vida ejemplar y heroica de Miguel de Cervantes*, 7 vols. (Madrid: Instituto Editorial Reus, 1948–58).

4. See especially Rafaelle Puddu, *El soldado gentilhombre: Autorretrato de una sociedad Guerrera, la España del siglo XVI*, trans. Enrique Lynch (Barcelona: Arcos Vergara, 1984); Margarita Levisi, *Autobiografías del Siglo de Oro: Alonso de Contreras, Jerónimo de Pasamonte y Miguel de Castro* (Madrid: Sociedad General Española de Librería, 1984); Verrier, *Les armes de Minerve*; Giovanni Caravaggi, ed., *La espada y la pluma: Il mondo militare nella Lombardia spagnola cinquecentesca* (Viareggio, Lucca: Mauro Baroni, 2000); Antonio Espino López, *Guerra y cultura en la época moderna* (Madrid: Ministerio de Defensa, 2001); Yuval Noah Harari, *Renaissance Military Memoirs: War, History, and Identity, 1450–1600* (Woodbridge: Boydell, 2004); David García Hernán, *La cultura de la guerra y el teatro del Siglo de Oro* (Madrid: Silex, 2006); Adam McKeown, *English Mercuries: Soldier Poets in the Age of Shakespeare* (Nashville: Vanderbilt University Press, 2009); and Stephen Rupp, *Heroic Forms: Cervantes and the Literature of War* (Toronto: University of Toronto, Press, 2014).

5. Michael Roberts, *The Military Revolution, 1550–1560* (Belfast: M. Boyd, 1956). Geoffrey Parker, *The Military Revolution: Military Innovation and the Rise of the West* (Cambridge: Cambridge University Press, 1996), 6–44, provides a useful historiographical revision of the concept, the chronology, the scope, and the geography of the military revolution as a historiographical paradigm, which he strongly defends against its critics. See also the afterword (155–76), which complements the essays collected by Clifford J. Rogers in *The Military Revolution Debate: Readings in the Military Transformation of Early Modern Europe* (Boulder, CO: Westview Press, 1995). For general evaluations of the military revolution debate and the influence of the "new military history" in Spanish historiography, see Enrique García Hernán and Davide Maffi, eds., *Guerra y sociedad en la Monarquía Hispánica: Política, estrategia y cultura en al Europa moderna (1500–1700)* (Madrid: CSIC, 2006), 885–900; and Luis Ribot, "Los ejércitos en la Europa moderna: El caso español," in *El arte de gobernar: Estudios sobre la España de los Austrias* (Madrid: Alianza, 2006), 17–56.

6. Michael Mallett, "The Transformation of War, 1494–1530," in *Italy and the European Powers: The Impact of War, 1500–1530*, ed. Christine Shaw (Leiden: Brill, 2006), 17.

7. Ibid., 5.

8. For some relevant figures regarding the size of Habsburg armies, see Parker, *The Military Revolution*, 24, 45. See also Frank Tallett, *War and Society in Early Modern Europe, 1495–1715* (London: Routledge, 1992), 4–13; Mallett, "The Transformation of War," 3–4; Fernando González de León, *The Road to Rocroi: Class, Culture and Command in the Spanish Army of Flanders, 1567–1659* (Leiden: Brill, 2009); and David Parrott, *The Business of War: Military Enterprise and Military Revolution in Early Modern Europe* (Cambridge: Cambridge University Press, 2012).

9. For the "society of soldiers," see John Hale, *War and Society in Renaissance Europe, 1450–1620* (Montreal: McGill-Queen's University Press, 1998), 127–78.

10. Parker, *The Military Revolution*, 24. See also René Quatrefages, *La revolución militar moderna: El crisol español* (Madrid: Ministerio de Defensa, 1996). For a critique of Parker's "rise of the West" approach to the military revolution, see Jeremy Black, *Rethinking Military History* (London: Routledge, 2004); and Peter Lorge, *The Asian Military Revolution* (Cambridge: Cambridge University Press, 2008), 7–10.

11. McKeown, *English Mercuries*, 64.

12. Ranajit Guha, "The Small Voice of History," in *Subaltern Studies IX: Writings on South Asian History and Society*, ed. Shahid Amin and Dipesh Chakrabarty (Delhi: Oxford University Press, 1996), 12.

13. See Michael Murrin, *History and Warfare in Renaissance Epic* (Chicago: University of Chicago Press, 1994), 12, 15.

14. James Amelang, *The Flight of Icarus: Artisan Autobiography in Early Modern Europe* (Stanford, CA: Stanford University Press, 1998), 164. See also his insightful "Popular Autobiography in Late Medieval and Early Modern Europe," in *1490: En el umbral de la modernidad. El Mediterráneo europeo y las ciudades en el tránsito de los siglos XV–XVI* (Valencia: Generalitat, 1994), 409, in which he already suggested a strong connection between the military revolution and the proliferation of soldierly writing.

15. Amelang, *The Flight of Icarus*, 150.

16. Fernand Braudel, *The Mediterranean and the Mediterranean World in the Age of Philip II* (New York: Harper and Row, 1972), 2:836.

17. Victor Davis Hanson, *The Father of Us All: War and History, Ancient and Modern* (New York: Bloomsbury, 2010), 10.

18. McKeown, *English Mercuries*, 14.

19. See also Judith Butler, *Frames of War: When Is Life Grievable?* (London: Verso, 2009).

20. Joan Scott, "The Evidence of Experience," *Critical Inquiry* 17.4 (1991): 773–97.

21. McKeown, *English Mercuries*, 14.

22. Arlette Farge, *Des lieux pour l'histoire* (Paris: Seuil, 1997), 54. Emphasis in the original.

23. Also important in her ethical proposal is the fact that "if there exists anti-militarism it comes from [the] disappointment and disillusion" of those who experience war. Ibid., 63.

24. Homer, *Iliad*, trans. Robert Fagles (New York: Penguin, 1990), 9.186–91. I thank my friend and colleague Jay Reed, from Brown University's Classics Department, for this and other references in these paragraphs.

25. Virgil, *Aeneid*, trans. Fagles, 9.873–76.

26. See E. J. Kenney and W. V. Clausen, eds., *The Cambridge History of Classical Literature* (Cambridge: Cambridge University Press, 1982), 2:53–76.

27. "Cómo los que de humildes padres y linajes nascen también deben procurar ser claros por sí, y traense muchos exemplos de hombres que de bajos principios subieron a grandes estados y lugares." Mexía, *Silva*, 333.

CHAPTER I

1. Miguel de Cervantes, *Don Quijote de la Mancha*, ed. Francisco Rico (Barcelona: Instituto Cervantes/Crítica, 1999), 445.

2. See Karl Marx and Friedrich Engels, *The Communist Manifesto* (Arlington Heights: AHM, 1955), 17.

3. Bernal Díaz del Castillo, *Historia verdadera de la conquista de la Nueva España*, ed. Joaquín Ramírez Cabañas (México: Porrúa, 1994), 7; Gaspar Correia, *Lendas da India*, ed. Rodrigo José de Lima Felner (Lisboa: Academia Real das Ciências, 1925), 2:912.

4. Quoted in Michael Mallet and John Hale, *The Military Organization of a Renaissance State: Venice c. 1400 to 1617* (Cambridge: Cambridge University Press, 1984), 387–88. For more on the motivations for enrollment in the Spanish case, see Lorraine White, "Spain's Early Modern Soldiers: Origins, Motivation, and Loyalty," *War and Society* 19.2 (2001): 19–46.

5. The class structure of the army is discussed in every major work of early modern military history. See, for instance, Hale, *War and Society*, 100–26; and Puddu, *Soldado gentilhombre*, 148–75 and passim. There were of course noblemen among the ranks of Spanish armies, particularly impoverished hidalgos and *segundones* of petty aristocratic families. But military scholars agree that "the type of the ordinary new recruit . . . was not that of the gentleman soldier" (soldado gentilhombre)—an allusion to Puddu's argument—but rather that of "a young commoner of around 22, single, unemployed, and living in a Castilian urban center of more than 5,000 inhabitants"; I.A.A. Thompson, "El soldado del imperio: Una aproximación al perfil del recluta español en el Siglo de Oro," *Manuscrits* 21 (2003): 37. See also Fernando González de León, "Doctors of the Military Discipline: Technical Expertise and the Paradigm of the Spanish Soldier in the Early Modern Period," *Sixteenth Century Journal* 27.1 (1996): 61–85; and Pierre Vilar's evocative pages in "El tiempo de los hidalgos," in *Hidalgos, amotinados y guerrilleros: Pueblo y poderes en la historia de España* (Barcelona: Crítica, 1982), 32–34.

6. Gianclaudio Civale, *Guerrieri di Cristo: Inquisitori, gesuiti e soldati alla battaglia di Lepanto* (Milano: Unicolpi, 2009), 151; Quatrefages, *Los tercios españoles*, 277–85.

7. Parker, *Military Revolution*, 47. The pikeman's monthly stipend, three ducados, or 350 maravedíes, remained stable for most of the period studied in this book. To this base salary supplements based on merit, exceptional accomplishments, and rank could be added, but it was overall a meager income. See also Quatrefages, *Los tercios*, 244–51. Mallett and Hale, *The Military Organization of a Renaissance State*, 494–501, carried out the most comprehensive analysis of the salary of Renaissance soldiers, which would largely apply to the situation in the Habsburg territories. After analyzing their evolution through the sixteenth century, contrasting salaries with other unskilled workers, and evaluating their purchasing power, Mallet and Hale concluded that "in terms of wages, soldiers came well towards the bottom of the social ladder" (496).

8. On rogues and vagabonds joining the armies of different European states, see Tallett, *War and Society*, 85–89; Hale, *War and Society*, 85–90. On the commanders' preference for peasant recruits, see Verrier, *Les armes de Minerve*, 49–56, 77–81. Thompson, "El soldado del imperio," proved, however, that the majority of Spanish soldiers were recruited in urban settings.

9. Davis, *Society and Culture*, 192. On soldierly culture as marginal, see Peter Burke, *Popular Culture in Early Modern Europe*, 3rd ed. (Burlington, VT: Ashgate, 2009), 42–43.

10. Marie-Christine Rodríguez and Bartolomé Bennassar, "Signatures et niveaux culturel des témoins et accusés dans les procès d'Inquisition du réssort du tribunal de Tolède (1525–1817) et du tribunal de Cordove (1595–1632)," *Caravelle* 31 (1978): 23. The authors' decision in this otherwise excellent study makes it impossible to propose any estimate about literacy rates among the soldiers who were brought before the Inquisition tribunals, for we do not know how many of the 50 percent of men who could sign their names—a significantly high rate for a group that includes vagabonds and beggars—were soldiers (30).

11. Juan Eloy Gelabert, "Lectura y escritura en una ciudad provinciana del siglo 16: Santiago de Compostela," *Bulletin hispanique* 84 (1982): 283. Gelabert already noted, although he did not pursue, the potential connection between literacy and soldierly leisure time, or military *otium*, and suggested that soldiers should constitute a special collective in studies of literacy.

12. See Sarah T. Nalle, "Printing and Reading Popular Religious Texts in Sixteenth-Century Spain," in *Culture and the State in Spain, 1500–1850*, ed. Tom Lewis and Francisco Sánchez (New York: Garland, 1999), 131, 135–36.

13. Claude Larquié, "L'alphabétisation à Madrid en 1650," *Revue d'histoire moderne et contemporaine* (1981): 143–45, see also 150–51. Larquié does not make any distinction of rank or social background under the rubric of "the army" (l'armée), which he includes together with the nobility and the monarchy's functionaries, all of which he considers "fully literate." In his conclusions, Larquié restricts literacy to the "superior ranks" of the army, but there is no evidence in his article supporting this distinction.

14. Miguel de Cervantes, *Novelas ejemplares*, ed. Harry Sieber (Madrid: Cátedra, 2001), 2:292, trans. Lesley Lipson, 246.

15. Hugh Thomas, *Who's Who of the Conquistadors* (London: Cassels, 2000), xxiv. Thomas also pointed out that many of the men claiming hidalgo status in *probanzas* and *informaciones* from the 1560s had not done so at an earlier date.

16. John F. Schwaller and Helen Nader, *The First Letter from New Spain: The Lost Petition of Cortés and His Company, June 20, 1519* (Austin: University of Texas Press, 2014), 109–15, 137–39.

17. Mario Góngora, *Los grupos de conquistadores en Tierra Firme (1509–1532)* (Santiago de Chile: Editorial Universitaria, 1962), 68–90. Similar estimates for Chile are found in Tomás Thayer Ojeda and Carlos Larraín, *Valdivia y sus compañeros* (Santiago: Imprenta universitaria, 1951); see the cautions raised by Peter Boyd-Bowman in his review of the latter, published

in the *American Historical Review* 31.4 (1950): 691–93. José Ignacio Avellaneda, *The Conquerors of the New Kingdom of Granada* (Albuquerque: University of New Mexico Press, 1995), 74, appendix 2.

18. Matthew Restall, *The Conquistadors* (Oxford: Oxford University Press, 2012), 43–45. More information can be found in James Lockhart, *The Men of Cajamarca: A Social and Biographical Study of the First Conquerors of Peru* (Austin: University of Texas Press, 1972), 135–57.

19. Lockhart, *The Men of Cajamarca*, 34–35.

20. Ibid., 268–70.

21. For a groundbreaking reassessment, see Sarah Nalle, "Literacy and Culture in Early Modern Castile," *Past and Present* 125 (November 1989): 65–96, and "Printing and Reading," which counter previous views in works such as Rodríguez and Bennsassar, "Signatures et niveaux culturel des témoins." On women's literacy, the figures for which are continually being revised upward, see Anne Cruz and Rosilie Hernández, eds., *Women's Literacy in Early Modern Spain and the New World* (Burlington, VT: Ashgate, 2011). See also Antonio Viñao Frago, "The History of Literacy in Spain: Evolution, Traits, and Questions," *History of Education Quarterly* 30.4 (1990): 573–99; and R. A. Houston, *Literacy in Early Modern Europe: Culture and Education, 1500–1800* (London: Longman, 1988).

22. John Frow's critique of Pierre Bourdieu's otherwise very powerful argument about the social distribution of cultural capital in *La Distinction: Critique Sociale du Jugement* (Paris: Minuit, 1979) also shows the risks of considering that the logic of cultural differentiation is exclusively determined by class. See Frow, *Cultural Studies and Cultural Value* (Oxford: Oxford University Press, 1995), especially 16–59.

23. Although Elizabeth Eisenstein's *The Printing Press as an Agent of Change* (Cambridge: Cambridge University Press, 1979) remains an influential and powerful account, some aspects of her argument have been challenged. A major debate with Adrian Johns, which usefully gathered and reviewed major contributions to the field, took place in the *American Historical Review* 107 (2002). See also David McKitterick, *Print, Manuscript and the Search for Order, 1450–1830* (Cambridge: Cambridge University Press, 2003); and Andrew Pettegree, *The Book in the Renaissance* (New Haven, CT: Yale University Press, 2010). Richard Kagan, *Students and Society in Early Modern Spain* (Baltimore: Johns Hopkins University Press, 1974), xvii, borrowed Lawrence Stone's concept of "educational revolution" ("The Educational Revolution in England, 1560 to 1640," *Past and Present* 28 [1964]: 41–80) to describe the rapid growth of learning institutions and the number of students in sixteenth-century Castile, which for Kagan was even more impressive than that in England.

24. Eisenstein largely sidestepped the problem of the impact of the printing revolution on literacy rates in *The Printing Press*, 60–63, 414–15. On print and literacy, see Kagan, *Students and Society*, xvii–xviii, 18; Davis, *Society and Culture*, 73; and Burke, *Popular Culture*, 342–52. See also Roger Chartier, *The Order of Books: Readers, Authors, and Libraries Between the Fourteenth and the Eighteenth Centuries* (Stanford, CA: Stanford University

Press, 1994); and Roger Chartier, *Cultural History: Between Practices and Representations*, trans. Lydia G. Cochrane (Cambridge: Polity Press, 1988). A contrasting argument can be found in Jeremy Lawrance, "The Spread of Lay Literacy in Late Medieval Castile," *Bulletin of Hispanic Studies* 62.1 (1985): 79–94.

25. See Antonio Rodríguez Moñino, *Pliegos poéticos de la Biblioteca Colombina* (Berkeley: University of California Press, 1974); and Clive Griffin, *The Crombergers of Seville: The History of a Printing Dynasty* (Oxford: Clarendon Press, 1988), xvii–xviii.

26. Against Einsenstein's argument that the gap between scribal and print cultures was "a major historical great divide" (*The Printing Press*, 33), Adrian Johns, among others, argued that "print needs to be seen less in terms of a radical break than in those of an environment combining speech, manuscript, and print in mutual interaction." Adrian Johns, "How to Acknowledge a Revolution," *American Historical Review* 107 (2002): 120. See also Fernando Bouza, *Corre manuscrito: Una historia cultural del Siglo de Oro* (Madrid: Marcial Pons, 2001).

27. Published in Miguel Muñoz de San Pedro, "Documentación familiar de Diego García de Paredes," *Revista de Estudios Extremeños* 12 (1956): 34–40.

28. According to Roger Chartier, *Inscription and Erasure: Literature and Written Culture from the Eleventh to the Eighteenth Century*, trans. Arthur Goldhammer (Philadelphia: University of Pennsylvania Press, 2007), 22, a *libro de memoria* "was a small notebook whose pages were covered with a coating on which one could write with a stylus carried in the binding; after being written on, the pages could be erased and reused." See also Peter Stallybrass, Roger Chartier, Frank Mowery, and Heather Wolfe, "Hamlet's Tables and the Technology of Writing in Renaissance England," *Shakespeare Quarterly* 55.4 (2004): 1–41.

29. For a social and cultural history of writing in early modern Spain, see the works of Antonio Castillo Gómez, *Escribir y leer en el siglo de Cervantes* (Barcelona: Gedisa, 1999); *Entre la pluma y la pared: Una historia social de la escritura en el Siglo de Oro* (Madrid: Akal, 2006).

30. Kagan, *Students and Society*, 5–30. Even higher learning was available to many students of commoner background through full-ride scholarships provided by some universities and colleges.

31. On this fascinating soldier, see Richard Kagan and Abigail Dyer, *Inquisitorial Inquiries: Brief Lives of Secret Jews and Other Heretics* (Baltimore: Johns Hopkins University Press, 2011), 87–115 (quotes from 90–91, 94, 108); and Richard Kagan, *Lucrecia's Dreams: Politics and Prophecy in Sixteenth-Century Spain* (Berkeley: University of California Press), 95–101.

32. Juan Claudio Aznar de Polanco, *Arte de escribir* (Madrid: Manuel Ruiz de Murga, 1719), 21v–23r and illustration on 24r. All three stories are in José María de Cossío, ed., *Autobiografías de soldados (siglo XVII)*, BAE 90 (Madrid: Atlas, 1956), 7, 77, 487.

33. Thompson, "El soldado del imperio."

34. Cervantes, *Novelas*, 2:46. See also Quatrefages, *Los tercios*; and Parker, *The Army of Flanders*, 91–100.

35. On the *bandos*, see Quatrefages, *Los tercios*, 321–35.

36. Francisco de Quevedo, *La vida del Buscón*, ed. Fernando Cabo (Barcelona: Crítica, 1993), 123–31. For the ballad, see Agustín Durán, *Romancero general*, BAE 10 and 16 (Madrid: Rivadeneira, 1861), no. 1739. See Chapter 5 for a discussion of this text.

37. See, for instance, Parker, *The Army of Flanders*, 151–52; and Tallett, *War and Society*, 134–38.

38. Sebastián de Covarrubias, *Tesoro de la lengua castellana* (Madrid: Luis Sánchez, 1611), s.v. "camarada." Commander Sancho de Londoño encouraged the practice because "they can support themselves better with their salary than if they were on their own, and also the good friendship and other benefits" (poderse sustentar con el sueldo mejor que estando cada uno de por sí y así mesmo grande amistad, con otras muchas utilidades). Sancho de Londoño, *Discurso sobre la forma de reducir la disciplina militar a mejor y antiguo estado* (Brussels: Velpius, 1589), 3v. See also Bernardo de Vargas Machuca, *Milicia y descripción de las Indias* (Madrid: Pedro Madrigal, 1599), 59r.

39. Cervantes, *Novelas*, 1:43, 47.

40. See José Lara Garrido, "Palma de Marte y lauro de Apolo: La poesía del 'oficio militar' en Francisco de Aldana y Cristóbal de Virués," in Caravaggi, *La espada y la pluma*, 295–97. Andrés Rey de Artieda, *Discursos, epístolas y epigramas de Artemidoro*, ed. Antonio Vilanova (Barcelona: Selecciones Bibliófilas, 1955), 171, originally published in Zaragoza by Angelo Tavanno, 1605.

41. See Francisco Martí Grajales, *Ensayo de un diccionario biográfico y bibliográfico de los poetas que florecieron en el Reino de Valencia hasta el año 1700* (Madrid, 1927), 376–88; and Eduardo Juliá Martínez, "Nuevos datos sobre Rey de Artieda," *Boletín de la RAE* 20 (1930): 667–86.

42. Rey de Artieda, *Discursos*, 210–11, 218, 220–21, 225. Londoño and other "doctors of military discipline" (González de León) allowed prostitutes in the army, *Discurso* (Brussels, 1596), 91, quoted by Quatrefages, *Los tercios*, 272. See also Parker, *The Army of Flanders*, 175–76; and Lorraine White, "The Experience of Spain's Early Modern Soldiers: Combat, Welfare, and Violence," *War in History* 9.1 (2002): 28–30.

43. Rey de Artieda, *Discursos*, 220–21, 224, 227.

44. Roger Chartier, "Culture as Appropriation: Popular Cultural Uses in Early Modern France," in *Understanding Popular Culture: Europe from the Middle Ages to the Nineteenth Century*, ed. Steven L. Kaplan (New York: Mouton Publishers, 1984), 250.

45. AGS, Contaduría Mayor de Cuentas, 2a/76, second bundle. The reference in Parker, *The Army of Flanders*, 151–53, led me to this set of documents.

46. Juan Rufo, *Las seiscientas apotegmas y otras obras en verso*, ed. Alberto Blecua (Madrid: Espasa-Calpe, 1972), no. 553.

47. Fray Juan de Toromazote in Santiago de Tesillo, *Epítome chileno, ideas contra la paz* (Lima: Jorge López de Herrera, [1648]), sig. ¶¶.

48. Garcilaso de la Vega, "Égloga III," *Obra poética y textos en prosa*, ed. Bienvenido Morros (Barcelona: Crítica, 2007), 311. On the trope of

writing as conquering, see also Mary Gaylord, "El lenguaje de la conquista y la conquista del lenguaje en las poéticas españolas del Siglo de Oro," in *Actas del IX Congreso de la Asociación Internacional de Hispanistas* (Frankfurt: Verwuert, 1989), 469–75.

49. See Quatrefages, *Los tercios*, 126–27.

50. Juan de Oznaya, *Historia de la Guerra de Lombardía, batalla de Pavía y prisión del rey Francisco de Francia*, CODOIN 38 (Madrid: Imprenta de la Viuda de Calero, 1861), 366.

51. Jerónimo de Vivar, *Crónica de los reinos de Chile*, ed. Angel Barral Gómez, Crónicas de América 41 (Madrid: Historia 16, 1988), 58.

52. Diego de Saavedra Fajardo, *República literaria*, ed. John Dowling (Salamanca: Anaya, 1967), 45; Nicholas Basbanes, *On Paper* (New York: Alfred Knopf, 2013), 131–35.

53. See facsimiles in Antonio Rodríguez Moñino, *Las fuentes del romancero general* (Madrid: Real Academia Española, 1957), 1:47r, 2:80r. Also collected in *Romancero general* (Madrid, 1600), 27r. The two lines written on the roll of Artieda's infantry company coincide with the *contrafacta* version "Romance al Nascimiento," in Biblioteca de la Universitat de Barcelona, Ms. 1146, 335r–v, Manuscrits Catalans de l'Edat Moderna (MCEM), http://mcem.iec.cat/veure.asp?id_manuscrits=2336, accessed August 11, 2014.

54. Francisco de Aldana, *Poesías castellanas completas*, ed. José Lara Garrido, 2nd ed. (Madrid: Cátedra, 1997), 109.

55. Cristóbal de Virués, *El Monserrate* (Madrid: Sancha, 1805), xxxi.

56. Martín García Cerezeda, *Tratado de las campañas y otros acontecimientos de los ejércitos del Emperador Carlos V en Italia, Francia, Austria, Berbería y Grecia, desde 1c521 hasta 1545* (Madrid: Sociedad de Bibliófilos Españoles, 1873), 1:3.

57. Ibid.

58. On the culture of *curiosidad*, see Javier Castro-Ibaseta, "Beware the Poetry: Political Satire and the Emergence of the Spanish Public Sphere (1600–1645)" (Unpublished manuscript, University of Michigan).

59. On Ávila y Zúñiga, see Ángel González Palencia, *Don Luis de Ávila y Zúñiga: Gentilhombre de Carlos V* (Madrid: Estanislao Maestre, 1932). Eugenio Mele, "Don Luis de Ávila, su 'Comentario' y los italianos," *Bulletin Hispanique* 24.2 (1922), 97–119, gives an idea of the centrality of this outstanding character in the culture and politics of Renaissance Europe, from Spain to Italy and Germany, during the first half of the century.

60. Luis Zapata, *Miscelánea*, ed. Pascual de Gayangos, Memorial Histórico Español 11 (Madrid: 1859), 184, qtd. in González Palencia, *Luis de Ávila*, 17.

61. Prudencio de Sandoval, *Historia de la vida y hechos del Emperador Carlos V* (Madrid: Atlas, 1955–56), bk. 29, chap. 1.

62. I have not been able to find the 1549 print, presumably a *relación de sucesos* in the popular *pliego* form, that Sandoval seems to have known. The battle of Mühlberg that ended the war took place on April 23, 1547. The *Comentario*'s princeps was published in Venice in 1548.

63. Bartolomé Leonardo de Argensola, *Conquista de las islas Malucas* (Madrid: Alonso Martín, 1609), 2.

64. Baltasar de Vargas, *Breve relación en octava rima de la jornada que ha hecho el Señor Duque de Alba* (Antwerp: Amato Tabernerio, 1568), A2r.

65. Ibid., fols. A6r, G4v.

66. Lorenzo de Zamora, *Primera parte de la Historia de Sagunto Numancia y Carthago* (Alcalá: Juan Iñiguez de Lequerica, 1589), prologue.

67. Luís de Camões, *Os Lusíadas*, ed. Álvaro Júlio da Costa Pimpão (Lisbon: Instituto Camões, 2000) 10.128; Luís de Camões, *The Lusiads*, trans. Landeg White (Oxford: Oxford World Classics, 2008).

68. Gaspar García de Alarcón, *La victoriosa conquista . . . de los Azores* (Valencia: Herederos de Joan Navarro, 1585), A4r.

69. See Díaz del Castillo, *Historia verdadera*, 1–2, 115.

70. Pedro Cieza de León, *La crónica del Perú* (Madrid: Historia 16, 1984), 59.

71. Alonso de Ercilla, *La Araucana*, ed. Isaías Lerner (Madrid: Cátedra, 1993) 69.

72. Ibid.

73. Rolena Adorno, *The Polemics of Possession in Spanish American Narrative* (New Haven, CT: Yale University Press, 2007), 7. Similarly, Ricardo Padrón, *The Spacious Word: Cartography, Literature and Empire in Early Modern Spain* (Chicago: University of Chicago Press, 2004), 227, has questioned this type of rhetorical authentication of Ercilla's poetic voice, particularly in the poet's narration of his expedition to Chiloé (*Araucana*, 36.29).

74. Adorno, *The Polemics of Possession*, 7.

75. José Toribio Medina, *La Araucana: Ilustraciones* (Santiago de Chile: Imprenta Elzeviriana, 1917–18), 1:72. Captain Juan Gómez, in turn, is recurrently depicted in *La Araucana* as a veteran and courageous Spanish soldier fighting the Mapuche. See, for instance, Ercilla, *Araucana*, 4.65, 4.72, 15.35.

76. Bartolomé Torres Naharro, *Comedia soldadesca*, in *Teatro renacentista*, ed. Alfredo Hermenegildo (Madrid: Austral, 1990), 174. On the likely military experience of this commoner, see Joseph Gillet, *Propalladia and Other Works of Bartolomé de Torres Naharro* (Menasha: George Banta, 1943–61), 4:402–5.

77. *La inquieta Flandes*, 1v. This interesting poem, now held at the BNE, MSS/22648, has gone completely unnoticed by literary critics. I found the reference in Parker, *The Army of Flanders*, 101, who in turn thanks Fernando Bouza for mentioning it to him. The poem, which covers the "events of Flanders" from 1585 to 1590, seems to have been finished in 1594. See Chapter 4.

78. Ercilla, *La Araucana*, 69–70.

79. See Medina, *La Araucana: Ilustraciones*, 2:412–13.

80. Irving Leonard, *Books of the Brave* (Berkeley: University of California Press, 1992), 164.

81. Miguel de Jaque, *Viaje de las Indias Orientales y Occidentales* (Seville: Renacimiento, 2008), 92. The Philippines were indeed considered a natural continuation of the West Indies rather than an eastern colony.

82. Parker, *The Army of Flanders*, is the most detailed account of the military structures and spaces associated with the Spanish road. Luis Ribot,

"Soldados españoles en Italia: El castillo de Milán a finales del siglo XVI," in *Guerra y sociedad,* ed. García Hernán and Maffi, 401–44, provides a good description of garrison life by focusing on the castle of Milan and the relationship between the garrisoned soldiers and the civil population.

83. Bronwen Wilson and Paul Yachnin, introduction to *Making Publics in Early Modern Europe: People, Things, Forms of Knowledge* (New York: Routledge, 2010), 4.

84. See Pettegree, *The Book in the Renaissance,* 136–44 and his *The Invention of News: How the World Came to Know About Itself* (New Haven, CT: Yale University Press, 2014).

85. See Antonio Rodríguez Moñino, *Nuevo diccionario bibliográfico de pliegos sueltos poéticos (siglo XVI),* ed. Arthur L.-F. Askins and Víctor Infantes (Madrid: Castalia, 1997), nos. 487, 1085, 1097; and Rodríguez Moñino, *Pliegos poéticos de la Biblioteca Colombina,* nos. 21, 35, 40, 41, 42, 64, 83, 123, 147, 183, 224, 249, for those chapbooks that have now disappeared but may have been composed by soldiers. See also Paolo Pintacuda, *La battaglia di Pavia nei "pliegos" poetici e nei "romanceros"* (Lucca: Mauro Baroni, 1997).

86. The ballad was added to Lorenzo Sepúlveda, *Romances nuevamente sacados de historias antiguas de la crónica de España* (Antwerp: Joannes Steelsius, 1551), 238r, which advertises the freshly arrived poem on the title page of a reprint. On the editorial history of this work, see Linde Brocato, "Publishing, Typography, and Politics: Mena's Works and the Parallel Editions of Antwerp, 1552" (CAS paper, directed by Prof. D. W. Krummel, University of Illinois at Urbana-Champaign, 2011), 10–11, which I thank her for sharing.

87. Hale, *War and Society,* 135.

88. Bernardino de Escalante, *Diálogos del Arte militar* (Seville: A. Pescioni, 1583), A2r.

89. Ibid., A2r–v.

90. Kagan, *Students and Society,* 39.

91. On the transatlantic book trade during the colonial period, in addition to Leonard, *Books of the Brave,* see Pedro Rueda Ramírez, *Negocio e intercambio cultural: El comercio de libros con América en la Carrera de Indias (siglo XVII)* (Seville: Universidad, 2005); and Carlos Alberto González Sánchez, *New World Literacy: Writing and Culture Across the Atlantic* (Lewisburg, PA: Bucknell University Press, 2011).

92. Melchor Xufré del Águila, *Compendio historial* (Santiago: Anales de la Universidad, 1897), 337, 340.

93. See Díaz del Castillo, *Historia verdadera,* 61, 323–24, 376. Winston A. Reynolds, *Romancero de Hernán Cortés: Estudio y textos de los siglos XVI y XVII* (Madrid: Ediciones Alcalá, 1967), compiled texts and fragments of *romances* on the matter of Hernán Cortés.

94. Diego de Rueda y Mendoza, *Relación verdadera de las xequias funerales que la insigne ciudad de Manila celebró a la muerte de la majestad del Rey Felipe Tercero y reales fiestas que se hicieron a la felice sucesión de su único heredero y señor nuestro Felipe 4,* 149r–v, a manuscript written in

Manila in 1625 and now kept at the HSA. A mention by soldier Alonso de Contreras to a soldierly *comedia* in Sicily, *Discurso de mi vida*, ed. Henry Ettinghausen (Madrid: Espasa-Calpe, 1988), 77, confirms that theatrical performances were a common practice in the society of soldiers.

95. Rueda y Mendoza, *Relación verdadera*,123r.

96. Miguel de Loarca, *Relación del viaje que hecimos a la China desde la ciudad de Manila en las del poniente año de 1575* (1575), 128. Quoted from Dolors Folch Fornesa's transcription of the RAH manuscript, in *La China en España*, http://www.upf.edu/asia/projectes/che/s16/loarca.htm, accessed June 5, 2014.

97. The phrase is in Baltasar del Hierro, *Destruición de África: Agora nuevamente por muy gentil estilo compuesta* (Seville: Sebastián Trujillo, 1560), 12v.

98. T. C. Price Zimmerman, *Paolo Giovio: The Historian and the Crisis of Sixteenth-Century Italy* (Princeton, NJ: Princeton University Press, 1995), 67–69, gives a thorough explanation of the story I recount here. Given the contradictions and obscurities of Giovio's explanations, Zimmerman offers two alternative hypotheses: either "his story about the lost books was merely a convenient fiction introduced years later to cover his failure to complete the history of the pontificates of Alexander VI and Julius II," or Giovio's excuses were due, more likely, "to his reluctance to write the history of the years leading to the sack of Rome, since so many of his patrons shared responsibility for it."

99. Pauli Iovii, *Opera* (Rome: Istituto poligrafico dello Stato, 1956–99), 3:170, in a note after book 4 of the *Historiarum tomus primus*. I take the reference from Zimmerman, *Giovio*, 311.

100. Iovii, *Opera*, 9:172, quoted in Zimmerman, *Giovio*, 68.

101. Antonio Joan Villafranca, in his prologue to his translation of Giovio's history, *Libro de las historias y cosas acontecidas en Alemaña, España, Francia, Italia, etc.*, trans. Antonio Joan Villafranca (Valencia: Juan Mey, 1562).

102. See, for instance, Fernando de Herrera, *Anotaciones a la poesía de Garcilaso*, ed. Inoria Pepe and José María Reyes (Madrid: Cátedra, 2001), 899. The most hostile criticism of Giovio's histories was written in the 1560s by the conqueror of New Granada, Gonzalo Jiménez de Quesada, *El Antijovio*, ed. Rafael Torres Quintero (Bogotá: Instituto Caro y Cuervo, 1952).

103. See Deoclezio Redig de Campos, "Il nome di Martin Lutero graffito sulla disputa del Sacramento," *Ecclesia* 6 (1947): 648–49; Deoclezio Redig de Campos, "Un altro graffito del Sacco nelle Stanze di Raffaello," *Ecclesia* 19.11 (1960): 552–54.

104. See Ramón Menéndez Pidal, *Romancero hispánico* (Madrid: Espasa-Calpe, 1953), 2:61.

105. Michel de Certeau, *The Practice of Everyday Life*, trans. Steven Rendall (Berkeley: University of California Press, 1988), 166.

106. Mikhail Bakhtin, *Rabelais and His World* (Bloomington: Indiana University Press, 1984), 21, 303–67.

107. Baldassarre Castiglione, *The Book of the Courtier*, ed. and trans. George Bull (London: Penguin, 2011), 92.

108. In one of many instances, he claims to have been a good friend of Captain Pedro Navarro, a plebeian soldier who reached the highest commanding posts in both the Habsburg and the Valois armies during the Italian wars: "I became friends with him because I wanted to have his account for the truth of my history." Paolo Giovio, *Diálogo de las empresas militares y amorosas*, trans. Alonso de Ulloa (Lyon: Guillem Rouville, 1561), 87v.

109. Tesillo, *Epítome chileno*, 3v.

110. See mainly Massimo Rospocher, "Versos desde las plazas: La poesía como lenguaje de comunicación política en los espacios públicos de las ciudades italianas del renacimiento," in *Opinión pública y espacio urbano en la Edad Moderna*, ed. Antonio Castillo Gómez, James Amelang, and Carmen Serrano Sánchez (Gijón: Trea, 2010), 185–210; Massimo Rospocher, "Songs of War: Historical and Literary Narratives of the 'Horrendous Italian Wars' (1494–1559)," in *Narrating War: Early Modern and Contemporary Perspectives*, ed. Marco Mondini and Massimo Rospocher (Bolonia: Il Mulino, 2012): 79–97; and Massimo Rospocher and Rosa Salzberg, "'El vulgo zanza': Spazi, pubblici, voci a Venezia durante le guerre d'Italia," *Storica* 48.16 (2010): 83–120.

111. Rospocher and Salzberg, "'El vulgo Zanza,'" 95.

112. Oznaya, *Historia de la Guerra de Lombardía*, 329, 335.

113. González Palencia, *Luis de Ávila*, 54.

114. Díaz del Castillo, *Historia verdadera*, 375–76; Bernal Díaz del Castillo, *The Conquest of New Spain*, trans. Alfred Maudslay (Nendeln: Kraus, 1967), 4:198, from which I quote with minimal modifications.

115. Díaz del Castillo, *The Conquest of New Spain*, trans. Maudslay, 4:199, original in *Historia verdadera*, 376.

116. See José Toribio Medina, *Romances basados en La Araucana* (Santiago: Imprenta Elzeviriana, 1918), xii–lxxvi, for some of these notices The *romance* about Lope de Aguirre can be found in "Relación de Gonzalo de Zúñiga," published by Beatriz Pastor and Sergio Callau, *Lope de Aguirre y la rebelión de los marañones* (Madrid: Castalia, 2011), 148–49.

117. On Lorenzo Martín, a soldier and poet praised by Castellanos, see his *Historia del Reino de Nueva Granada*, ed. Antonio Paz y Meliá (Madrid: Pérez Dubrull, 1886), 2:49–52, 1:365–68. See also Bakhtin, *Rabelais*, 20–21, 303–67.

118. Quevedo, *Buscón*, 130, and what follows in 127.

119. Pettegree, *The Book in the Renaissance*, 346.

120. Marcos de Isaba's *Cuerpo enfermo de la milicia española, con Discursos y avisos para que pueda ser curado, útiles y de provecho* (Madrid: Guillermo Druy, 1594) was actually published by his brother-in-law Miguel Guerrero de Casetà, who served as *teniente* of the Capua castle, where he found Isaba's papers and sent them to the Council of War for publication.

121. Isaba, *Cuerpo enfermo*, 1r–v. The substance of these soldierly pláticas closely resembles the language of a chapter in Mexía, *Silva*, 28–31.

122. Isaba, *Cuerpo enfermo*, 2v–3r.

123. See Parker, *The Military Revolution*, 162–71, who draws from Gaston Zeller, *Le Siège de Metz par Charles-Quint* (Nancy: Société d'impressions typographiques, 1943).

124. Arbolanche's poem *Las Abidas* was published in Zaragoza in 1566, when he was only twenty, but he must have already been serving in the army and very likely participated in the defense of Malta in 1565. He was back in his hometown by the beginning of 1571. He married the daughter of a prosperous local merchant with whom he started a company shortly before dying in 1572. For biographical details, see Fernando González Ollé, "Jerónimo de Arbolanche," in *Las Abidas*, by Jerónimo de Arbolanche (Madrid: CSIC, 1969), 1–25. Luis de Campo Jesús, *Jerónimo de Arbolanche, poeta del siglo XVI: Su vida y su obra* (Pamplona: La acción social, 1964), 117–40, speculates about Arbolanche's life in the years between 1566 and 1572, for which he found no documentation, but Arbolanche must have spent this period soldiering. For a study of his main poem, see Javier Irigoyen-García, "Jerónimo de Arbolanche's *Las Abidas* (1566) and the Mythical Origins of Spain," *Symposium* 67.2 (2013): 85–97.

125. J. García Morales, "Las trasnochadas de la pluma, de don Sancho de Londoño," in *Homenaje a don Agustín Millares Carlo* (Gran Canaria, 1975), 1:637–60, noted the existence of the manuscript, *Poesías del Maestre de Campo don Sancho de Londoño*, now at the BNE (MSS/21738). Geoffrey Parker mentioned the work in passing in *The Army of Flanders*, 101, and Enrique García Hernán, "Don Sancho de Londoño: Perfil biográfico," *Revista de Historia Moderna* (Alicante) 22 (2004): 7–72, has used it to recover some biographical information about the general.

126. Sancho de Londoño, *Poesías del Maestre de Campo don Sancho de Londoño*, BNE, MSS/21738, 121r.

127. Ibid., 116v.

128. Ibid., 120r–v.

129. Ibid., 112r.

130. Ibid., 150r.

131. Ibid., 122r.

132. Ibid., 154v.

133. Ibid., 155r–v.

134. I take the reference from Hale, *War and Society*, 84, but I quote more extensively from an earlier edition of the same English translation of Ambroise Paré's works: *The workes of that famous chirurgion Ambrose Parey*, trans. Thomas Johnson (London: Thomas Cotes, 1634), 1152–53.

135. The manuscript copy of the *Discurso* was written in 1568 and is held by the Leiden University Library, Codices Vulcaniani 92D. It was not printed, however, until 1587 in Brussels, by Roger Velpius (I quote from Brussels: Velpius, 1589). Martín de Eguiluz reissued it again, as an attachment to his *Milicia, discurso y regla militar* (Brussels, 1596). For the complex textual history and transmission of the *Discurso*, see Mazzocchi, "Nel testo del *Discurso* di Sancho de Londoño: Note bibliografiche ed ecdotiche," in *La espada y la pluma*, ed. Caravaggi, 563–79.

136. Londoño, *Discurso*, 33r.

137. Vargas Machuca, *Milicia y descripción de las Indias*, 55v.

138. Pierre Bourdieu, *Outline of a Theory of Practice*, trans. Richard Nice (Cambridge: Cambridge University Press, 1977), 87.

139. Santiago de Tesillo, *Guerra de Chile, causas de su duración, medios para su fin* (Madrid: Imprenta Real, 1647), 7v–8r; Tomás Rodaja, in *El licenciado Vidriera*, undergoes a similar transformation: Cervantes, *Novelas*, 2:47.

140. Londoño, *Discurso*, 36r.

141. Ibid., 33v.

142. Ibid., 36r.

143. Vargas Machuca, *Milicia indiana*, 53v–55r.

144. Pedro de Valdivia, *Cartas de Pedro de Valdivia que tratan del descubrimiento y conquista de Chile*, ed. José Toribio Medina and Jaime Eyzaguirre (Santiago de Chile: Fondo Histórico y Bibliográfico José Toribio Medina, 1953), 197–98.

145. See Covarrubias's definition of *corro* in his *Tesoro*.

146. Quoted in Fernando Bouza, "Servidumbres de la soberana grandeza: Criticar al rey en la corte de Felipe II," in *Imágenes históricas de Felipe II*, coord. Alfredo Alvar Ezquerra (Alcalá: Centro de Estudios Cervantinos, 2000), 162.

147. Londoño, *Discurso*, 36r.

CHAPTER 2

1. On the Wars of Italy, see Michael Mallett and Christine Shaw, *The Italian Wars, 1494–1559* (Harlow: Pearson, 2012); and Christine Shaw, ed. *Italy and the European Powers: The Impact of War, 1500–1530* (Leiden: Brill, 2006).

2. Oznaya, *Historia de la Guerra de Lombardía*, 396–97.

3. Tim O'Brien, *The Things They Carried* (New York: Broadway Books, 1998), 77.

4. Ariosto, *Orlando*, 9.28, trans. Barbara Reynolds.

5. Ibid., 9.90, 11.22, 11.27.

6. Fernando Bouza, *Palabra e imagen en la corte: Cultura oral y visual de la nobleza en el Siglo de Oro* (Madrid: Abada, 2003), 161–62.

7. See Mallett and Shaw, *The Italian Wars*, 148–59. Jean Giono's detailed account in *The Battle of Pavia*, trans. A. E. Murch (London: Owen, 1965) remains useful.

8. Parker, *The Military Revolution*, 159.

9. Covarrubias, *Tesoro*, 58r.

10. Ibid., 58v.

11. Ibid. This could have been taken from Mexía, *Silva*, 31.

12. Covarrubias, *Tesoro*, 58v.

13. Murrin, *History and Warfare*, 123. See his discussion of the "negative critiques" of gunpowder warfare on pp. 123–37. Cf. pp. 138–49 for opposing "positive evaluations" of the new technologies, particularly strong, Murrin argues, in Iberian epic.

14. Garcilaso de la Vega, "Elegía II," in *Obra poética y textos en prosa*, ed. Bienvenido Morros (Barcelona: Crítica, 2007), 185, and "Epístola a Boscán," lines 66–80, in *Obra poética*, 196–97. See soldier Diego Duque de

Estrada's praise of Naples in his *Comentarios del desengañado de sí mismo: Vida del mismo autor* (Madrid: Castalia, 1982), 187–88.

15. Cervantes, *Novelas*, 2:45–50. See also Frederick de Armas, "The Exhilaration of Italy," *Quixotic Frescoes: Cervantes and Italian Renaissance Art* (Toronto: University of Toronto Press, 2006), 3–13; and Frederick de Armas, "Cervantes and the Italian Renaissance," in *Cambridge Companion to Cervantes*, ed. Anthony J. Cascardi (Cambridge: Cambridge University Press, 2002), 32–57.

16. Valdivia, *Cartas de Pedro de Valdivia*, 25, 57, 63. In the middle of Peru's civil wars, Valdivia recognized a former comrade from his Italian days (165).

17. See this and other similar testimonies in Parker, *The Army of Flanders*, 182.

18. Benedetto Croce, *España en la vida italiana del Renacimiento* (Buenos Aires: Imán, 1945), explored the presence of Spanish soldiers, courtiers, diplomats, and common people in Renaissance Italy, particularly Naples. Joseph Fucilla collected in *Relaciones hispano-italianas* (Madrid: CSIC, 1953) a series of seminal essays on the cultural exchanges between the two peninsulas. See also Thomas Dandelet, *Spanish Rome, 1500–1700* (New Haven, CT: Yale University Press, 2001); and Thomas Dandelet, *Spain in Italy: Politics, Society, Religion, 1500–1700* (Leiden: Brill, 2007).

19. González Palencia, *Luis de Ávila*, 49.

20. Croce, *España en la vida italiana*, provided a still useful outline of the remarkable influence of Spanish books of chivalry in Italian Renaissance letters, while Maxime Chevalier, *L'Arioste en Espagne (1530–1650): Recherches sur l'influence du "Roland Furieux"* (Bordeaux: Institute d'Études Ibériques et Ibéro-Américaines, 1966), thoroughly explored the influence of Ariosto in the literary production of Golden Age Spain.

21. Paolo Giovio, *La vita del marchese di Pescara*, trans. Domenichi (Venezia, 1559), fol. 171, quoted by Croce, *España en la vida italiana*, 82.

22. Juan de Valdés, *Diálogo de la lengua*, ed. José Enrique Laplana (Barcelona: Crítica, 2010), 256–57.

23. Daniel Eisenberg, *Romances of Chivalry in the Spanish Golden Age* (Newark, DE: Juan de la Cuesta, 1982), 100. In Eisenberg's selection of Hernando Colón's entries prices range between 95 and 440. See also cautions by Griffin, *The Crombergers*, 137, and José Manuel Lucía Megías, *Imprenta y libros de caballerías* (Madrid: Ollero y Ramos, 2002).

24. See Cervantes, *Don Quijote*, 1.6.

25. For an extended version of this argument, and what follows, see Miguel Martínez, "The Heroes in the World's Marketplace: Translating and Printing Epic in Renaissance Antwerp," in *Translation and the Book Trade in Early Modern Europe*, ed. José María Pérez Fernández and Edward Wilson-Lee (Cambridge: Cambridge University Press, 2014), 81–106.

26. González Palencia, *Luis de Ávila*, 95. A useful summary and contextualization of Bernardo's *Amadigi* can be found in Jo Ann Cavallo, *The Romance Epics of Boiardo, Ariosto, and Tasso: From Public Duty to Private Pleasure* (Toronto: University of Toronto Press, 2004), 169–77.

27. Ludovico Ariosto, *Orlando furioso de Lodovico Ariosto nuevamente traducido en prosa castellana*, trans. Diego Vázquez de Contreras (Madrid: Juan Montoya, 1585).

28. On the copy given to Charles, see José Luis Gonzalo Sánchez-Molero, *La "librería rica" de Felipe II: Estudio histórico y catalogación* (Madrid: Ediciones Escurialenses, 1998), 138–41. On Urrea's life and literary production, which includes a translation of Olivier de la Marche's *Le Chevalier Délibéré*, an epic poem, a chivalric romance, and a military treatise, see Pierre Geneste, *Essai sur la vie et l'oeuvre de Jerónimo de Urrea* (Lille: Université de Lille III, 1975). Hernando de Alcocer, very likely a soldier as well (Chevalier, *L'Arioste*, 84), published in 1550 a translation that would be completely obliterated by Urrea's success: *Orlando furioso de Ludivico Ariosto nuevamente traducido de verbo ad verbum del vulgar Toscano en el nuestro Castellano* (Toledo: Juan Ferrer, 1550).

29. See Ariosto, *Orlando furioso*, trans. Jerónimo Jiménez de Urrea, ed. Cesare Segre and María de las Nieves Muñiz, 81.

30. See Juan Cristóbal Calvete de Estrella, *El felicísimo viaje del muy alto y muy poderoso Príncipe don Phelippe*, ed. Paloma Cuenca (Madrid: Sociedad Estatal para la Conmemoración de los Centenarios de Felipe II y Carlos V, 2001), 314–54. See also Miguel Martínez, "Género, imprenta y espacio social: Una poética de la pólvora para la épica quinientista," *Hispanic Review* 79.2 (2011): 163–87; and Martínez, "The Heroes in the World's Marketplace."

31. Mario Domenichelli, *Cavaliere e gentiluomo: Saggio sulla cultura aristocratica in Europa (1513–1915)* (Rome: Bulzoni, 2002), 152.

32. Baldassarre Castiglione, *The Book of the Courtier*, ed. Daniel Javitch (New York: Norton, 2002), 24.

33. Ibid., 21, 27–29.

34. Exceptions to this can be found in Angela Carella, "Urbino e le Marche," *Letteratura italiana*, ed. Alberto Asor Rosa (Torino: Einaudi, 1988), 506–8, and Verrier, *Les armes de Minerve*, 101, who also noticed the contradiction between the profession of arms as the alleged most defining feature of the courtier and the anecdote of the boasting soldier who does not know how to behave in society: "We could read this scene of humiliation as the aristocracy's revenge taunting the parvenu's coarseness, after being deprived of their military monopoly." See also John Najemy's thorough exploration of the unresolvable contradictions between arms and letters in Castiglione's text: "Arms and Letters: The Crisis of Courtly Culture in the Wars of Italy," in *Italy and the European Powers*, ed. Shaw, 207–38.

35. Castiglione, *Courtier*, ed. Javitch, 24.

36. Ibid., 25.

37. Ibid., 51.

38. See, in this respect, Verrier, *Les armes de Minerve*, 28.

39. Carella, "Urbino e le Marche," 504–5.

40. Hale, *War and Society*, 46.

41. Ariosto, *Orlando furioso*, trans. Jiménez de Urrea, ed. Segre and Nieves Muñiz, 3.29.

42. Puddu, *Soldado gentilhombre*, 31. See also Murrin, *History and Warfare*.

43. Hale, *War and Society*, 100–126; Vilar, "El tiempo de los hidalgos," 31–32.

44. Charles Oman, *A History of the Art of War in the Sixteenth Century* (New York: E. P. Dutton, 1937) is still useful. See also Bert S. Hall, *Weapons and Warfare in Renaissance Europe* (Baltimore: Johns Hopkins University Press, 1997). For the concomitant transformations of the social meanings of *caballería*, see Jesús Rodríguez-Velasco, "Esfuerço: La caballería de estado a oficio (1524–1615)," in *Amadís de Gaula quinientos años después. Estudios en homenaje a Juan Manuel Cacho Blecua*, ed. José Manuel Lucía Megías and María del Carmen Marín Pina (Alcalá: Centro de Estudios Cervantinos, 2008), 661–89.

45. Torres Naharro, *Comedia soldadesca*, 308.

46. Maxime Chevalier, *Lectura y lectores en la España de los siglos XVI y XVII* (Madrid: Turner, 1976), 65–103, and Eisenberg, *Romances of Chivalry*, 89–118, questioned the interpretation of books of chivalry as popular literature, arguing instead that they were mostly consumed by Spanish aristocrats. Nalle, "Literacy and Culture," and Sylvia Roubaud, "Los libros de caballerías," in Miguel de Cervantes, *Don Quijote de la Mancha*, ed. Francisco Rico (Barcelona: Instituto Cervantes/Editorial Crítica, 1999), 105–28, provided examples of the circulation of *Amadís* and its offspring among the popular classes of Spain.

47. Jerónimo Pasamonte, *Vida y trabajos de Jerónimo de Pasamonte*, in *Autobiografías de soldados (siglo XVII)*, ed. José María de Cossío, BAE 90 (Madrid: Atlas, 1956), chap. 40.

48. Contreras, *Discuso de mi vida de mi vida*, chap. 40.

49. Rospocher, "Songs of War," 81–83; Francesco Guicciardini, *Storie fiorentine* (Bari: Laterza, 1931), chap. 11.

50. "Mentre che io canto, o Iddio redentore, / Vedo la Italia tutta a fiama e a foco / Per questi Galli, che con gran valore/ Vengon per disertar non so che loco; / Però vi lascio in questo vano amore / De Fiordespina ardente a poco a poco; / Un'altra fiata, se mi fia concesso, / Racontarovi il tutto per espresso." Matteo Maria Boiardo, *Orlando innamorato*, ed. Riccardo Bruscagli (Torino: Einaudi, 1996), 3.9.26.

51. See David Abulafia, ed., *The French Descent into Renaissance Italy, 1494–95: Antecedents and Effects* (Aldershot: Variorum, 1995); Shaw, *Italy and the European Powers*.

52. The year 1494 becomes the beginning of the enduring metanarrative about the fall of Italy and the barbarian invasions of the French army, but it is also the starting point of the epic *narratio* of individual poems. Early poets such as Gerolamo Senese in his *La venuta del Re Carlo con la rotta del Taro* (Venice: Manfredo Bonelli, 1496–97) literally take up the pen at the exact moment that Boiardo drops it. Later compilations, such as the popular *Guerre orrende* (Venice: Paulo Danza, 1532), mark 1494, narratively and typographically, as the beginning of their historical summae of the wars of Italy. See Marina Beer et al., eds., *Guerre in ottava rima* (Modena: Panini, 1989), 3:856, 3:939.

53. The texts gathered in Beer et al., *Guerre*, recounted the wars of Italy and the Mediterranean from the fall of Constantinople in 1453 to the battle of Lepanto in 1571. Between 1471 and 1655, 365 titles in this distinct tradition were printed, a high percentage of which were published before 1550. Some of these texts were collected as "popular poetry" in a number of nineteenth- and twentieth-century anthologies and are considered "minor" and "marginal" by their modern editors. Beer et al., *Guerre*, 1:7. See also the works gathered in Klaus W. Hempfer, ed., *Ritterepik der Renaissance* (Stuttgart: Franz Steiner, 1989).

54. Rospocher, "Songs of War," 96.

55. By Rinuccini, see, for instance, *Istoria come il stato di Milano al presente è stato conquistato* (Venice: ca. 1510), in Beer et al., *Guerre*. On Celebrino, see Rospocher, "Songs of War," 84–85.

56. Since Chevalier's classic study on the influence of Ariosto, Ercilla's debt to the Italian poet is undeniable (*L'Arioste*, 144–58). The nature of this intertextual relationship, however, is subject to scholarly debate. See Frank Pierce, *La poesía épica del Siglo de Oro* (Madrid: Gredos, 1961); Antonio Prieto, "La poesía épica renacentista," in *La poesía española del siglo XVI*, vol. 2, *Aquel valor que respetó el olvido* (Madrid: Cátedra, 1987), 781–831; José Lara Garrido, *Los mejores plectros: Teoría y práctica de la épica culta en el Siglo de Oro* (Málaga: Analecta Malacitana, 1999); James Nicolopulos, *The Poetics of Empire in the Indies: Prophecy and Imitation in "La Araucana" and "Os Lusíadas"* (University Park: Pennsylvania State University Press), 2000; and Padrón, *The Spacious Word*, 185–230.

57. Murrin, *History and Warfare*, 12.

58. See, for instance, Beer et al., *Guerre*, 2:18, 29, 30, 50, 180.

59. Ibid., 2:34, 425, 427.

60. Rinuccini, *Istoria come il stato di Milano al presente è stato conquistato*, in Beer et al., *Guerre*, 2:132. José Lara Garrido, *Los mejores plectros: Teoría y práctica de la épica culta en el Siglo de Oro* (Málaga: Analecta Malacitana, 1999), 46, also emphasized this effort to construct "a historical epos of the present" as one of the most significant novelties of the genre.

61. *La guerra di Parma* (Parma: Seth Viotto, 1552), Aii, in Beer et al., *Guerre*, 3:207. See also *La memoranda presa de Peschera*, in *Guerre*, 2:297, and *Historia de la guerra del Piamonte*, in 3:137.

62. Nicolo di Agustini, *Li successi bellici seguiti nella Italia dal fatto d'arme* (Venice: Nicolo Zopino and Vincenzo da Venetia, 1521), Aiv, in Beer et al., *Guerre*, 3:592.

63. Verrier, *Les armes de Minerve*, 32.

64. Murrin, *History and Warfare*, 13.

65. Martí Grajales, *Ensayo de un diccionario*, 427, documented Sempere's commercial activities in his late years. Rafael Martí de Viciana, *Libro segundo de la crónica de la ínclita y coronada ciudad de Valencia y su reino* (Valencia: Joan Navarro, 1564) does not include any of the variants of his last name among the noble lineages of Valencia. Sempere knows the military world and the wars of Italy very well and had important relations with a family of ennobled Valencian soldiers, the Aldana. See Jerónimo Sempere,

Carolea (Valencia: Joan de los Arcos, 1560), 1:140v, 150r; and Enric Querol Coll, "Els Aldana, tortosins del segle XVI aveïnats a València: De les armes a les lletres," *Pedralbes* 27 (2007): 206.

66. Sempere, *Carolea*, Aiv–v.

67. Giovio quoted in Puddu, *Soldado gentilhombre*, 21. See also Francesco Guicciardini, *Storia d'Italia* (Torino: Einaudi, 1971), bk. 1, chap. 11.

68. Sempere, *Carolea*, 126v. The term *gallos* is frequently used in the *Guerre in ottava rima* to refer to the French, and it is likely that Sempere drew from them. See, for instance, Beer et al., *Guerre*, 2:357, 411.

69. Sempere, *Carolea*, 127r, 130r.

70. Ibid., 127v.

71. Ibid., 132r. Verrier made this point graphically: "The knight (chevalier) is to the soldier, historically, a class enemy" (*Les armes de Minerve*, 29).

72. In 1560, Baltasar del Hierro published another poem, *La destruición de África* (Seville: Sebastián Trujillo), which I will discuss in detail in Chapter 3.

73. Baltasar del Hierro, *Libro y primera parte de los victoriosos hechos del muy valeroso caballero Don Álvaro de Bazán* (Granada: René Rabut, 1561), Aiii.

74. Ibid.

75. Ercilla, *Araucana*, 69–70.

76. Ibid., 1.1.

77. See, for instance, Archangelo da Lonigo, *La gloriosa vittoria et presa d'Affrica* (Bologna: Bartholomeo Bonardo, ca. 1550), Aiv, in Beer et al., *Guerre*, 4:736, which starts with very similar lines: "Que non si cantera lascivi amori / ne fabulose eroi, ne finte imprese."

78. Ercilla, *Araucana*, 9.49 and passim.

79. Ibid., 25.43.

80. Hernando Álvarez de Toledo, *Purén indómito* (Leipzig: A. Franck, 1862), 8. As Michael Murrin put it when reading a stanza in Oña's *Arauco domado*, "a list of guns," or of weapons, "can tell us much and actually imply a sort of gunpowder poetics." Murrin, *History and Warfare*, 12.

81. We know almost nothing about Hipólito Sans, except that he was born in Xàtiva to a petty noble Catalan family. Vicente Ximeno, *Escritores del reino de Valencia* (Valencia: Dolz, 1746–49), 1:179.

82. Hipólito Sans, *La Maltea: En que se trata la famosa defensa de la Religión de Sant Joan en la isla de Malta* (Valencia: Joan Navarro, 1582), 71v. The poem does contain, however, a conventional, Ariostean dismissal of firearms as "diabolic machines" that ended true military virtue (23r).

83. On Rufo's important poem, see Elizabeth B. Davis, *Myth and Identity in the Epic of Imperial Spain* (Columbia: University of Missouri Press, 2000), 61–97; Murrin, *History and Warfare*, 179–96; and Lara Vilà, "Épica e imperio: Imitación virgiliana y propaganda política en la épica española del XVI" (PhD diss., Universidad Autónoma de Barcelona, 2001), 637–63. For Rufo's biography, see Rafael Ramírez de Arellano, *Juan Rufo, jurado de Córdoba: Estudio biográfico y crítico* (Madrid, 1912 [facsimile]; Valladolid: Maxtor, 2002).

84. The phrase is used by Martín Antonio del Río in the dedication of his *La crónica sobre don Juan de Austria/Die Chronik über Don Juan de Austria*, ed. Miguel Ángel Echevarría Bacigalupe and Friedrich Edelmayer (Oldenbourg: Verlag für Geschichte und Politik, 2003), originally written in 1600.

85. "Juan Rufo begs your majesty that Andrés de Prada, secretary of the Council of War, and formerly of our lord Don Juan, provide an authenticated testimony of how his highness [Don Juan] asked him [Juan Rufo] to write the *Austríada*, for which he received the means and the stipend; and also how in Flanders his highness instructed someone to write down everything as it happened in order to send it to Juan Rufo (cómo en Flandes mandó su alteza apuntar lo que iba sucediendo con fin de enviárselo)." AGS, GyM, leg. 343, fol. 82. In another petition to the Council of the Indies he claims to have started writing the poem in 1571 or 1572. AGI, Indiferente, 740n229 and AGI, Panamá, 1n33.

86. After the death of Don John, he must have tried, this time unsuccessfully, to find patronage for his second poem in the person of the fifth Duke of Alba, don Antonio. Rufo included the beginning of this new poem in *Las seiscientas apotegmas*, 333–36. In the same work he commented on Alba's disdain, apothegm no. 541.

87. See Geoffrey Parker, *The Dutch Revolt* (Ithaca, NY: Cornell University Press, 1977), 208–16.

88. See volumes R/13312 and R/9706 at the BNE.

89. See Parker, *The Army of Flanders*, 80–105.

90. Arxiu de la Corona d'Aragó, Consejo de Aragón, leg. 0254, n. 113, accessed through PARES. Many of Alba's men wrote now forgotten epics about the war in the Low Countries that deserve some critical attention. In addition to Giner and Baltasar de Vargas (*Breve relación*), Pedro Alfonso Pimentel, a soldier from Burgos, wrote *Guerras civiles de Flandes* in the 1580s and 1590s. The poem, in ottava rima, recounts, almost like a personal diary, over thirty years of campaigning in Flanders. See Fernando González Ollé, "*Guerras civiles de Flandes*: Poema épico inédito," *Boletín de la Real Academia Española* 45 (1965): 141–84.The manuscript seems to be now lost but was transcribed by María América Gómez Dovale in "Una fuente inédita sobre la guerra de Flandes" (PhD diss., Universidad Complutense de Madrid, 1957). See also the discussion of the poems of soldiers Cristóbal Rodríguez Alva and Emanuel Antunes later in the chapter.

91. The new epic was indeed printed in a distinct bibliographical format, cheaper and easier to distribute than that of the Italian *romanzo* or the Spanish *libro de caballerías*, which would in turn facilitate the creation of specific publics organized around the professional, social, and spatial links of the Habsburg military complex. See Martínez, "Género, imprenta y espacio social," and "The Heroes in the World's Marketplace."

92. Geneste, *Jerónimo de Urrea*, 266–68.

93. This prologue in verse only appears in the copy of *Vitorioso Carlos Quinto* (ca. 1569) held at the HSA (for full reference, see manuscript no. CLXVII in Antonio Rodríguez Moñino, *Catálogo de manuscritos poéticos*

en la biblioteca de The Hispanic Society of America [New York: HSA, 1965–66]) and does not figure in the BNE copy (MSS/1469).

94. See Ludovico Ariosto, *Orlando furioso*, trans. Jerónimo Jiménez de Urrea, ed. Cesare Segre and María de las Nieves Muñiz (Madrid: Cátedra, 2002), 3021–51, in the appendixes collected by the editor, María de las Nieves Muñiz.

95. On Urrea's modest noble background, see Geneste, *Jerónimo de Urrea*, 19–68; and Martínez, "Género, imprenta y espacio social."

96. See Luis Zapata, *Carlo famoso* (Valencia: Joan Mey, 1566), 7r; and Manuel Terrón Albarrán, introduction to his edition of *Carlo famoso* (Badajoz: Diputación Provincial, 1981), 1–173.

97. Martínez, "Género, imprenta y espacio social."

98. Joan Mey died in 1555 or 1556. His widow, Jerónima Gales, and her second husband, Pedro de Huete, must have been responsible for Zapata's edition. See Margarita Bosch Cantallops, "Contribución al estudio de la imprenta en Valencia en el siglo XVI" (PhD diss., Universidad Complutense de Madrid, 1989), 1:64–82.

99. Zapata, *Carlo famoso*, Aiv.

100. Ibid.

101. Matteo Maria Boiardo, *Los libros de Mattheo Maria Boyardo, llamados Orlando Enamorado, traducidos en Castellano*, trans. Francisco Garrico de Villena (Valencia: Mey, 1555). In the same year, and with the same printer, Garrido de Villena published yet another romance epic: *El verdadero suceso de la famosa batalla de Roncesvalles, con la muerte de los doce pares de Francia* (Valencia: Joan Mey, 1555). Many narrative poems were written in continuation or imitation of the wildly popular poem by Ariosto and its equally famous Spanish translation by Urrea from the middle of the 1550s: Nicolás Espinosa, *La segunda parte del Orlando* (Antwerp: Martinus Nutius, 1556); Martín Bolea de Castro, *Libro de Orlando determinado que prosigue la materia de Orlando el Enamorado* (Lérida: Miguel Prats, 1578); and Agustín Alonso, *Historia de las hazañas y hechos de Bernardo del Carpio* (Toledo: Pero López de Haro, 1585). See also those anthologized in Juan Carlos Pantoja Rivero, *Antología de poemas caballerescos castellanos* (Alcalá: Centro de Estudios Cervantinos, 2004). The most thorough studies of this corpus are Chevalier, *L'Arioste en Espagne* and Lara Vilà, "Épica e imperio."

102. Zapata, *Carlo famoso*, Aiv.

103. This is a very rare imprint. The only copy I have been able to find is currently at Paris's Bibliothèque Nationale, which also holds a second edition printed in Antwerp in 1622 by Giraldo Wolsschatio that I have not been able to consult. Jean Peeters-Fontainas, *Bibliographie des impressions espagnoles des Pays-Bas méridionaux* (Nieuwkoop: B. de Graaf, 1965), 1:60, considered the princeps lost.

104. Emanuel Antunes, *Primera parte de la baxada de los españoles de Francia en Normandía* (Rouen: George l'Oyselet, 1593), 1.

105. Ibid., 139.

106. Ibid., 159–61.

107. Ibid., 73.

108. Rufo, *Apotegmas*, no. 553.

109. Cervantes, *Novelas*, 2:45.

110. For the collective protagonism of "soldados pláticos," see, for instance, Sempere, *Carolea*, 39r; Hierro, *Destruición de África*, 6r; and Ercilla, *Araucana*, 2.65. Ercilla's long catalogues of fighters, both noble and plebeian, can be found everywhere in his epic. See also Puddu, *Soldado gentilhombre*, 78–80.

111. Horace, *Satires. Epistles. The Ars of Poetry*, LCL 194 (Cambridge, MA: Harvard University Press, 1929), line 73.

112. Pedro de Navarra, *Diálogos cual debe ser el chronista del príncipe, materia de pocos aún tocada* (Zaragoza: Juan Millán, 1567), 16v–17r.

113. Ibid., 5v. Similarly, Zimmerman, *Giovio*, 74, recounts how "Guicciardini was unable to reconcile eyewitness memoirs [of the battle of Pavia] to his own satisfaction and left his account unfinished."

114. Tesillo, *Guerra de Chile*, 75v.

CHAPTER 3

1. I have published earlier versions of the first two sections of this chapter as "'The Spell of National Identity': War and Soldiering on the North African Frontier (1550–1560)," *Journal of Spanish Cultural Studies* 12.3 (2011): 293–307; and "La vida de los heroes: Sobre épica y autobiografía en el Mediterráneo habsburgo," *Calíope* 19.1 (2014): 103–28.

2. Braudel, *The Mediterranean*, 2:836.

3. Virgil, *Aeneid*, trans. Fagles, 233.

4. The phrase was used by James Amelang, "Saving the Self from Autobiography," in *Selbstzeugnisse in der Frühen Neuzeit: Individualisierungsweisen in interdisziplinärer Perspektive*, ed. Kaspar von Greyerz unter Mitarbeit von Elisabeth Müller-Luckner (Munich: Oldenbourg, 2007), 129–40, who took it, with a different meaning, from Philippe Lejeune's "The Autobiography of Those Who Do Not Write," in *On Autobiography*, trans. Katherine Leary (Minneapolis: University of Minnesota Press, 1989).

5. Hale, *War and Society*, 44.

6. In addition to Hale, see mainly I. A. A. Thompson, *War and Government in Habsburg Spain, 1560–1620* (London: University of London Press, 1976); Tallett, *War and Society*, 188–216; and Ruth MacKay, *The Limits of Royal Authority: Resistance and Obedience in Seventeenth-Century Castile* (Cambridge: Cambridge University Press, 1999).

7. Braudel, *The Mediterranean*, 2:907–11 offers a useful historical account of what he called "the Africa affair."

8. See M. J. Rodríguez-Salgado, *Un imperio en transición: Carlos V, Felipe II y su mundo, 1551–1559* (Barcelona: Crítica, 1992), 176–96.

9. Most of these biographical data have been extracted from Baltasar del Hierro's hitherto unknown oeuvre, which will be discussed later. The information about his travel to the New World is in AGI, Contratación, 5537, L.3, fol. 57v.

10. To my knowledge, the only extant copy of these two epic poems is now kept at the Real Academia de la Historia in Madrid (2/2908), bound together by nineteenth-century bibliophile General Eduardo Fernández de San Román (1818–87). The *Libro de los valerosos hechos* was facsimilized by Archer M. Huntington, the founder of the HSA, using a copy necessarily different from San Román's, which probably belonged to Pascual de Gayangos, the location of which is unknown to me.

11. This work, in what again appears to be the only surviving copy, is held by the Biblioteca de la Universidad de Barcelona (B-44/3/13–2).

12. Andrew C. Hess, *The Forgotten Frontier: A History of the Sixteenth-Century Ibero-African Frontier* (Chicago: University of Chicago Press, 1978).

13. For Trujillo's workshop, see María del Carmen Álvarez Márquez, *La impresión y el comercio de libros en la Sevilla del quinientos* (Seville: Universidad, 2007), 275–78.

14. Domingo de Toral y Valdés, *Relación de la vida del capitán Domingo de Toral y Valdés, escrita por el mismo capitán*, CODOIN 71 (Madrid: Miguel Ginesta, 1879), 504.

15. Hierro, *Destruición de África*, Eiiii–v.

16. See, for instance, Ercilla's *romance* on the Azores battle in Arthur F. Askins, "El romance de Ercilla, A los veyntidos de Iulio," in *Homenaje a Eugenio Asensio* (Madrid: Gredos, 1988), 57–66.

17. John Keegan, *The Face of Battle* (New York: Barnes and Noble, 1976).

18. Hierro, *Destruición de África*, 5v.

19. The humanist chronicler Juan Cristóbal Calvete de Estrella wrote *De Aphrodisio expugnato quod vulgo Aphricam vocant: Commentarius* (Amberes: Martín Nucio, 1551), the first historical account of the capture of Mahdia, which was translated into Spanish by Diego Gracián in 1558 as *La conquista de la ciudad de África en Berbería* (Salamanca: Juan de Canova, 1558). The Roman Horatius Nucula offered his own version of the events, *Commentariorum de bello Aphrodisiensi libri quinque* (Rome: Valerium and Ludovicum fratres Brixienses) in 1552, the same year that Pedro de Salazar, a soldier himself, published *Historia de la guerra y presa de África con la destruición de la villa de Monaster y isla del Gozo y pérdida de Trípol de Berbería: Con otras muy nuevas cosas* (Naples: Mastre Matia, 1552). Other historical accounts of the events include Juan Lorenzo Otavanti, "Las felicísimas nuevas de la victoria que su majestad ha haido de la ciudad de África," in *Archivo y biblioteca de la casa de Medinaceli: Series de sus principales documentos, 2ª bibliográfica*, ed. Antonio Paz y Meliá (Madrid, 1922). Cornelius Scepper compiled several texts and fragments on the Africa affair in *Rerum a Carolo V Caesare Augusto in Africa Bello gestarum commentarij* (Antwerp: Ioan Bellerum, 1554), while Diego de Fuentes later wrote *Conquista de África donde se hallarán agora nuevamente recopiladas por Diego de Fuentes muchas y muy notables hazañas de particulares caballeros* (Anvers: Philippo Nutio, 1570). In addition to this rich historiographical corpus, *romances* and Italian popular epic contributed to the spectacular publicity of this event (Beer et al., *Guerre*, 4:727–42).

20. Hierro, *Destruición de África*, 6r.

21. Ibid., 6r–v.

22. On the daily life of North African presidios, see Braudel, *The Mediterranean*, 2:854–65.

23. See, for instance, AGS, Estado, leg. 1119, doc. 226, and AGS, Estado leg. 1120, docs. 6, 120.

24. Hierro, *Destruición de África*, 7r, 10r.

25. Ibid., 7v.

26. Ibid., 9v.

27. Ibid., 10v.

28. This popular use of *letijo* is also found in Mateo Brizuela's pliegos; see Pedro Cátedra, *Invención, difusión y recepción de la literatura popular impresa (siglo XVI)* (Mérida: Editora Regional, 2002), 368.

29. Hierro, *Destruición de África*, 8r–9v.

30. For re-creations of the naval battle in the epic tradition, see David Quint, *Epic and Empire: Politics and Generic Form from Virgil to Milton* (Princeton, NJ: Princeton University Press, 1993), 21–49.

31. Hierro, *Destruición de África*, 11v.

32. Ibid., 12v.

33. See mainly Quint, *Epic and Empire*; Davis, *Myth and Identity*; and Nicolopulos, *The Poetics of Empire*.

34. Braudel, *The Mediterranean*, 2:910. Fortunately, most of the documentation produced by the mutinied soldiers themselves has survived. Their letters and *capitulaciones* can be found in AGS, Estado, leg. 1120, docs. 84, 114, 151; leg. 1121, docs. 29, 49, 179, 190. On early modern soldierly mutinies, see Quatrefages, *Los tercios*, 263–68; Hale, *War and Society*, 171–72; and, above all, Parker, *The Army of Flanders*, 185–206. The most comprehensive contemporaneous account of the Mahdia mutiny, which differs from Hierro's in important respects, is Luis de Mármol Carvajal, *Libro tercero y segundo volumen de la Descripción general de África* (Granada: Rene Rabut, 1573), 2:278–85.

35. Hierro, *Destruición de África*, 12v.

36. Sancho de Leyva a Juan de Vega, 21 de julio 1552, AGS, Estado, leg. 1120, doc. 86. Juan de Vega appears to have believed the soldiers' accusations against Leyva and insists on the animosity that the captain aroused among the soldiery. Juan de Vega al emperador a 29 de septiembre 1552, AGS, Estado, leg. 1120, doc. 126.

37. Hierro, *Destruición de África*, 13r, 14v. For Leyva's version of the mutiny, which once more confirms the size and significance of the mutiny, see his letter of July 21, 1552, to Juan de Vega, AGS, Estado, leg. 1120, doc. 86.

38. Hierro, *Destruición de África*, 14v.

39. Ibid., 15v.

40. *Carta de los soldados de África al virrey de Sicilia. 21 de julio 1552*, AGS, Estado, leg. 1120, doc. 84.

41. Parker describes in detail the functioning of mutinies in the army of Flanders, which was no different from their North African counterparts. See Parker, *The Army of Flanders*, 157–76.

42. Mármol Carvajal, *Descripción de África*, 279v. Rodríguez-Salgado, *Un imperio en transición*, 402, insists on the political success of the rebels on a regional scale.

43. Hierro, *Destruición de África*, 17v.

44. Ibid., 21v.

45. Hale, *War and Society*, 171.

46. *Los soldados de África a Juan de Vega*, November 28, 1552, AGS, Estado, leg. 1120, doc. 151.

47. Hierro, *Destruición de África*, 22r.

48. Ibid., 24r.

49. Ibid., 24v.

50. *Los soldados de África a Juan de Vega*, July 7, 1553, AGS, Estado, leg. 1121, doc. 49.

51. The bitter *memorial* that Acuña sent to Philip recounting his lifelong military services to the crown insists on the fact that the soldiers of Africa maintained their vindictive attitude even after the mutiny had been appeased. See Narciso Alonso Cortés, *Don Hernando de Acuña: Noticias biográficas* (Valladolid: Biblioteca Studium, 1975), 83. The *capítulos* containing the soldiers' demands can be found in AGS, Estado, leg. 1121, doc. 29.

52. Hierro, *Destruición de África*, 28r.

53. Ibid., Aii.

54. On the politics of epic form, and particularly epic closure, see Quint, *Epic and Empire*.

55. Andrew Hess, "The Battle of Lepanto and Its Place in Mediterranean History," *Past and Present* 57 (1972): 53–73.

56. A comprehensive account of these events can be found in Gianclaudio Civale, "Tunisi spagnola tra violenza e coesistenza (1573–74)," *Mediterranea: Ricerche storiche* 21 (2011): 51–88; and Civale, *Guerrieri di Cristo*, 175–208. See also Enrique García Hernán, "La conquista y pérdida de Túnez por don Juan de Austria (1573–1574)," *Annali di Storia militare europea* 2 (2010): 39–95. More succinct but equally useful narratives are found in Andrew Hess, *Forgotten Frontier*, 90–95; and Braudel, *The Mediterranean*, 2:1133–42.

57. On Lepanto, 112 more publications would be issued during the following year. See Carl Göllner, *Turcica*, 3 vols. (Bucharest: Editura Academiei, 1961–68), nos. 1506–1609. For Tunis and La Goleta, in contrast, see nos. 1644, 1646. On the impact of Lepanto in the news culture of early modern Europe, see Pettegree, *The Invention of News*, 139–44.

58. On the literature of Lepanto, see López de Toro, *Los poetas de Lepanto*; Mary Gaylord, *The Historical Prose of Fernando de Herrera* (London: Tamesis, 1970); Davis, *Myth and Identity*, 61–97; Murrin, *History and Warfare*, 179–96; Lara Vilà, "Las más ricas prendas de poesía que tiene España: Cervantes y la épica sobre Lepanto," in *Cervantes y su tiempo: Lectura y signo*, ed. Juan Matas Caballero and José María Balcells Doménech (León: Universidad de León, 2008); and Elizabeth Wright, "Narrating the Ineffable Lepanto: The *Austrias Carmen* of Joannes Latinus (Juan Latino)," *Hispanic Review* 77.1 (Winter 2009): 71–91.

59. See Cervantes, *Quijote*, 1.39.

60. Cervantes, *Quijote*, 457, trans. Grossman, 339.

61. See his own testimony in Pasamonte, *Vida*, 9.

62. Pascual de Gayangos, *Memorias del cautivo de la Goleta de Túnez (el alférez Pedro de Aguilar)* (Madrid: Sociedad de Bibliófilos Españoles, 1875). The original manuscript is held by the HSA and deserves further study.

63. Jerónimo de Torres y Aguilera, *Crónica y recopilación de varios sucesos de guerra . . .* (Zaragoza: Juan Soler, 1579), 121v.

64. Civale, "Tunisi spagnola," 53 and Gayangos, *Memorias del cautivo de la Goleta*, 286–88, add other manuscript works on the same events.

65. See Paul de Man, "Autobiography as De-Facement," *MLN* 94.5 (1979): 919.

66. Philippe Lejeune, *Le pacte autobiographique* (Paris: Seuil, 1975), 313. See also Linda Anderson, *Autobiography* (London: Routledge, 2001).

67. Mikhail Bakhtin, *The Dialogic Imagination*, ed. Michael Holquist (Austin: University of Texas Press, 1981), 34.

68. Lejeune, *Le pacte autobiographique*, 14. On early modern autobiography in the Hispanic world, see mainly Nicholas Spadaccini and Jenaro Talens, eds., *Autobiography in Early Modern Spain* (Minneapolis: Prisma, 1988); and Francisco Sánchez-Blanco, "El marco institucional del discurso sobre sí mismo: Autobiografías del Renacimiento," in *Schwerpunkt Siglo de Oro: Akten des Deutschen Hispanistentages Wolfenbüttel*, ed. Hans-Josef Niederehe (Hamburg: Helmut Buske, 1986), 129–47.

69. For a useful discussion of the different forms of autobiographical discourse, see Amelang, *The Flight of Icarus*, 28–51. See also Harari, *Renaissance Military Memoirs*. Marcus Billson has defined the memoir as a type of text that "recounts a story of the author's witnessing a real past which he considers to be of extraordinary interest and importance. . . . The memorialist derives his personal identity, not from a sense of himself as a developing emotional, intellectual, or spiritual being, but rather from his posture among men, his role in society." Marcus Billson, "The Memoir: New Perspectives on a Forgotten Genre," *Genre* 10.2 (1977): 261.

70. This text, which remained unstudied even though Ricardo González Castrillo revealed its existence in "La pérdida de La Goleta y Túnez en 1574 y otros sucesos de historia otomana, narrados por un testigo presencial: Alonso de Salamanca," *Anaquel de Estudios Árabes* 3 (1992): 247–86, is soon to be edited by Ana María Rodríguez-Rodríguez. The manuscript is now at Madrid's Real Biblioteca, where it came as part of the bibliophilic Conde de Gondomar's lavish library; José María Díez Borque, "Libros de poesía en bibliotecas del Siglo de Oro (1600–1650)," *Revista de Filología Española* 90.1 (2010): 69–98. The production of the manuscript must have been discontinuous, since it is dated 1576 on the title page and the last canto is dated in 1577. Furthermore, the author announces in the prologue that the poem has 468 stanzas, instead of the actual 430.

71. Alonso de Salamanca, *Libro de cassos impensados*, 3r–v.

72. *Soldado particular* was an ambiguous phrase. It is usually understood as "noble," but instances can be found in which it means something closer

to "private," a soldier of no rank. Diego de Salazar, *Tratado de re militari* (Alcalá: Miguel de Eguía, 1536), 35r; Juan Ginés de Sepúlveda, *Diálogo llamado Demócrates*, trans. Antonio Barba (Seville: Juan Cromberger, 1541), 23v; Rodríguez Alva, *La inquieta Flandes*, 242r; Toral y Valdés, *Relación*, 528.

73. Salamanca, *Libro*, 81v.

74. Ibid.

75. María Antonia Garcés, *Cervantes in Algiers: A Captive's Tale* (Nashville: Vanderbilt University Press, 2002); Lisa Voigt, *Writing Captivity in the Early Modern Atlantic: Circulations of Knowledge and Authority in the English and Iberian Worlds* (Chapel Hill: University of North Carolina Press, 2009); Ana María Rodríguez-Rodríguez, *Letras liberadas: Cautiverio, escritura y subjetividad* (Madrid: Visor, 2013).

76. Salamanca, *Libro*, 3v.

77. See also, for instance, Pasamonte, *Vida*, 9; and Escalante, *Diálogos del Arte militar*, A2v.

78. Salamanca, *Libro*, 2r.

79. A highly critical evaluation of the global strategy can be found in Salamanca, *Libro*, 33r–34v, 41v–43r. The polemical attacks on the commanding officers' specific tactical and strategic decisions are, nonetheless, constant. See, for instance, 14v–16r, 20r, 22r–23r, 24r, 26v, 31r–v, 32r, 35r–v, 36v, 37v, 43r, 45r–v. Some soldiers in the *Libro*'s story even dare to point to King Philip's responsibility: "[decían] Felipe a grandes voces, ¿qué hacías / que no socorres fuerza tan amada?" *Libro*, 33r.

80. Salamanca, *Libro*, 8v.

81. Ibid., 6r.

82. González Castrillo, "La pérdida de la Goleta y Túnez," provides a useful and detailed summary of the main episodes narrated in each of the six cantos, to which I refer the reader.

83. Salamanca, *Libro*, 21v.

84. For the meticulous dating of specific military events, see, for instance, ibid., 16r, 18v, 23r, 26v, 28v, 29r, 30v, 35r, 45v, 46v, 49v, 52v.

85. Ibid., 35r.

86. Ibid., 42v.

87. Ibid., 49v.

88. Jonathan Culler, *The Pursuit of Signs: Semiotics, Literature, Deconstruction* (Ithaca, NY: Cornell University Press, 1981), 138, 142.

89. Salamanca, *Libro*, 50v–51r.

90. Culler, *The Pursuit of Signs*, 146.

91. On the attribution of the poem "Sobre nevados riscos levantado," from which the line "Llorad sin descansar, ojos cansados" is taken, see Christopher Maurer, *Obra y vida de Francisco de Figueroa* (Madrid: Istmo, 1988), 180–81. Vega, *Obra poética*, 202. I thank Elizabeth Davis for calling my attention to the Garcilasian connections of the most lyrical passages of the *Libro de cassos impensados*.

92. Salamanca, *Libro*, 61r–63r.

93. Ibid., 63r–69r.

94. Pasamonte mentions "the liberation of Xiban Bay's galley, whose slaves rebelled some years ago" (la libertad de la galera de Xiban Bay, que allí se había levantado los años atrás), in his autobiography, *Vida*, 18.

95. For the notion of "act of authorship," see Amelang, *The Flight of Icarus.*

96. Salamanca, *Libro*, 79v.

97. Ibid., 79v–80r.

98. Ibid., 80r–81r.

99. The document "Relación del suceso de La Goleta y fuerte de Túnez y ysla de Estaño, 1574" can be found in Enrique García Hernán in *La armada española en la monarquía de Felipe II y la defensa del Mediterráneo* (Madrid: Tempo, 1995), 61–62.

100. For a comprehensive critical discussion of the relevance of the proper name for autobiographical discourse, see Anderson, *Autobiography*, 80–81; and Spadaccini and Talens, *Autobiography*, 9–37, especially 25.

101. Amelang, *The Flight of Icarus.*

102. Hierro, *Destruición de África*, A1v.

103. Amelang, "Saving the Self," 137.

104. Amelang, *The Flight of Icarus*, 51.

105. Covarrubias, *Tesoro*, s.v. "autor."

106. Salamanca, *Libro*, 80r.

107. Lejeune, *On Autobiography*, 194; De Man, "Autobiography as De-facement," 922.

108. De Man, "Autobiography as De-Facement," 922.

109. Salamanca, *Libro*, 9r–v.

110. Ibid., 81v.

111. Ibid., 69r.

112. Michel Foucault, "What Is an Author?" in *The Essential Works of Michel Foucault, 1954–1984* (New York: New Press, 1997–2000), 2:205.

113. Ibid., 2:209.

114. Enrique García-Santo Tomás, "Ruptured Narratives: Tracing Defeat in Diego Duque de Estrada's *Comentarios del desengañado de sí mismo (1614–1645)*," *eHumanista* 17 (2011): 92.

115. On this corpus, see Chapter 5.

116. See, for instance, José María de Cossío, ed., *Autobiografías de soldados (siglo XVII)*, BAE 90 (Madrid: Atlas, 1956), xviii–xix.

117. AGS, GyM, leg. 262, fol. 51; leg. 270, fol. 158; leg. 276, fol. 231; leg. 309, fol. 103; and AGS, Estado, leg. 1156, fols. 231, 259.

118. See Daniel Hershenzon, "Early Modern Spain and the Creation of the Mediterranean: Captivity, Commerce, and Knowledge" (PhD diss., University of Michigan, Ann Arbor, 2011).

119. Alonso de Salamanca, maestro de artilleros, A 29 de abril 1590, AGS, GyM, leg. 306, doc. 123.

120. Al Consejo de Guerra, por Alonso de Salamanca, cabo maestro de los artilleros de Trápana a 10 de hebrero, 1589, AGS, GyM, leg. 262, fol. 51. More on Salamanca's negotiations of his overdue salary can be found in AGS, Estado (Sicilia), leg. 1156, fols. 259, 260.

121. AGS, GyM, leg. 262, fol. 51, and leg. 270, doc. 158.

122. Ibid.

123. AGS, GyM, leg. 306, doc. 123.

124. On both Álava y Viamont and Tartaglia, see González de León, "Doctors of the Military Discipline," 70–71; and Espino López, *Guerra y cultura*, 216–18.

125. AGS, GyM, leg. 306, doc. 123.

126. Salamanca's dismissal of Álava y Viamont's work also indicates the competition among writing soldiers at "the most creative [moment] in the history of Spanish military thought." González de Léon, "Doctors of the Military Discipline," 70. There were earlier and briefer treatises on artillery that are only known in manuscript. See Espino López, *Guerra y cultura*, 212–15.

127. AGS, GyM, leg. 276, fol. 231.

128. See Espino López, *Guerra y cultura*, 216.

129. Julio César Firrufino, *Plático manual y breve compendio de artillería* (Madrid: Viuda de Alonso Martín, 1626), fol. ¶6r.

130. See Hierro, *Don Álvaro de Bazán*, title page and canto 2.

131. Alonso de Salamanca, maestro de artilleros, A 29 de abril 1590, AGS, GyM, leg. 306, doc. 123.

132. I borrow the expression from Elizabeth Wright, *Pilgrimage to Patronage: Lope de Vega and the Court of Philip III (1598–1621)* (Lewisburg, PA: Bucknell University Press, 2001).

133. Michael Warner, *The Letters of the Republic: Publication and the Public Sphere in Eighteenth-Century America* (Cambridge, MA: Harvard University Press, 1990), xi.

134. Ibid., 5–9.

135. Ibid., xi.

136. Tesillo, *Epítome chileno*, preliminaries ¶¶ and ¶2.

137. Warner, *The Letters of the Republic*, 11.

CHAPTER 4

The epigraph is Diego de Hojeda's preliminary poem to Pedro de Oña's *Arauco domado* (Lima: Antonio Ricardo, 1596). I consulted most of the primary sources for this chapter, some unique, at the JCB. The argument here is deeply in debt to its fantastic archive and to the fellows of 2013–14.

1. Diego de Rosales, *Historia general del reino de Chile: Flandes indiano*, ed. Benjamín Vicuña Mackenna (Valparaíso: Imprenta del Mercurio, 1877), 1:18–19. The analogy linking Flanders and Chile can be found earlier in Tesillo, *Guerra de Chile*, which refers to Flanders as "the parade ground of the world" and "the center of war" (plaza de armas, centro de la guerra), while Chile is "the Flanders of the Indies" (42v).

2. Vargas Machuca, *Milicia y descripción de las Indias*, iv–2r, translated in *The Indian Militia and the Description of the Indies*, ed. Kris Lane and trans. Timothy F. Johnson (Durham, NC: Duke University Press, 2008), 18. I usually quote from Johnson's translation, also providing the folio number of

the original. I have, however, introduced some translations or minor modifications of my own without note.

3. Vargas Machuca, *Indian Militia*, 24; *Milicia y descripción*, 6r.

4. Kris Lane, "Introductory Study," *Indian Militia*, xi.

5. It is likely this brutality motivated the censorship: "certain things have been scratched . . . once these are removed, it seems to me that the book can be printed" (algunas cosas van tildadas . . . las cuales quitadas me parece que se puede imprimir). Vargas Machuca, *Milicia y descripción*, ¶3v. On the same page, censor Antonio Osorio confirms that the book has been "emended."

6. For a succinct but very comprehensive and useful biography of Vargas Machuca, see Lane, "Introductory Study," xxxvii–lx. A previous, book-length biography of Vargas Machuca is María Luisa Martínez de Salinas, *Castilla ante el Nuevo Mundo: La trayectoria indiana del gobernador Bernardo de Vargas Machuca* (Valladolid: Diputación, 1991).

7. See Lane, "Introductory Study" and AGI, Chile, 1, n. 41; AGI, Patronato, 164, r. 1, containing the *Información* of 1600; AGI, Indiferente, 746, n. 8; AGI, Santa Fe, 1, nn. 203–5.

8. Vargas Machuca, *Indian Militia*, 14; ¶¶5v, ¶¶6r.

9. Ibid., 26; 7r.

10. Ibid., 47 and 56; 24r and 32r.

11. Ibid., 26; 7r.

12. Ibid., 26; 7r–v.

13. Ibid. 19; 3r.

14. Ibid., 53; 29v.

15. Ibid., 38; 17r.

16. Ibid., 45, 56; 22r, 32r, 70v.

17. The detailed attention that Vargas Machuca devotes to the arquebus and to gunpowder contradicts the accounts of the conquest wars that emphasized the older technologies and tactics of pre-Renaissance cavalry and chivalric warfare, such as Alberto Mario Salas, *Las armas de la Conquista* (Buenos Aires: Emecé Editores, 1950), 127–58. The *Milicia* is full of details about how to make gunpowder from scratch, how to preserve it against humidity or accidental detonation, how to march with the fuses on fire, how to use guns in ambushes, and how to exploit the dissuasive power it had over fearful indigenous warriors still not familiar with the technology. In Vargas Machuca's account of American warfare, the material culture of the conquistador is fully determined by the culture of gunpowder. See Vargas Machuca, *Indian Militia*, 70–75; 43v–49r.

18. Escalante, *Diálogos del Arte militar*, A2v.

19. See Rolena Adorno and Patrick Charles Pautz, *Álvar Núñez Cabeza de Vaca: His Account, His Life, and the Expedition of Pánfilo de Narváez* (Lincoln: University of Nebraska Press, 1999), 1:360–72.

20. Lockhart, *The Men of Cajamarca*, 17–22; Avellaneda, *The Conquerors of the New Kingdom of Granada*, 78.

21. See Thomas, *Who's Who of the Conquistadors*, 6, 20–21, 25, 29, 88, 122, 123, 133.

22. Matthew Restall, *Seven Myths of the Spanish Conquest* (Oxford: Oxford University Press, 2003), 27–43, 43; see also Matthew Restall and Felipe Fernández-Armesto, *The Conquistadors* (Oxford: Oxford University Press, 2012), 52–60.

23. A useful sample of this corpus can be found in José Promis's anthology *La literatura del reino de Chile* (Valparaíso: Universidad de Playa Ancha Editorial, 2002). See also Francisco Esteve Barba, *Crónicas del reino de Chile*, BAE 131 (Madrid: Atlas, 1960); and Cedomil Goic, *Letras del Reino de Chile* (Madrid: Iberoamericana/Vervuert, 2006).

24. *Carta al emperador Carlos V*, October 15, 1550, in Valdivia, *Cartas de Pedro de Valdivia*, 147.

25. Valdivia, *Cartas de Pedro de Valdivia*, 97. Valdivia repeatedly refers to his experience and prudence "in the matters of war" in a way that links them to his Italian experience at least as much as it does to his American *baquiano* skills. See page 119.

26. Valdivia, *Cartas de Pedro de Valdivia*, 135 and, with minor variants, 202.

27. Ibid., 135.

28. Ibid., 157.

29. Machiavelli, *Art of War*, trans. Christopher Lynch (Chicago: University of Chicago Press, 2003), 35–36.

30. Ibid., 61.

31. Vivar, *Crónica de los reinos de Chile*, 263. On the textual history of this unique manuscript, now kept at Chicago's Newberry Library, see Leopoldo Sáez Godoy, ed., *Gerónimo de Vivar: Crónica y relación copiosa y verdadera de los Reinos de Chile (1558)* (Berlin: Coloquium Verlag, 1979). For a comprehensive study of the text in relation to other chroniclers of Chile, see Giorgio Antei, *La invención del reino de Chile: Gerónimo de Vivar y los primeros cronistas chilenos* (Bogotá: Instituto Caro y Cuervo, 1989).

32. Parker, *The Military Revolution*, 41.

33. Vivar, *Crónica de los reinos de Chile*, 265.

34. Valdivia, *Cartas de Pedro de Valdivia*, 99.

35. Ercilla, *Araucana*, 69. The translations are my own, although I have found support in Charles Maxwell Lancaster and Paul Thomas Manchester's version: *The Araucaniad* (Nashville: Vanderbilt University Press, 1945). I provide page numbers for the prologue, while referring to canto and stanza everywhere else throughout.

36. Ercilla, *Araucana*, 77.

37. Ibid., 1.13–32.

38. Ibid., 5.12.

39. Ibid., 8.6, 12.8. Virgilian warriors also lean on spears in *Aeneid*, 9.229–30.

40. See, for instance, Ercilla, *Araucana*, 9.43, 34.53.

41. Ibid., 33.70, 33.84.

42. Ibid., 2.16.

43. Ibid., 16.43.

44. Ibid., 1.47. Other writers on Chile spoke naturally of the *republican* constitution of Mapuche polities. Valdivia himself, in *Cartas de Pedro de*

Valdivia, 44, understood Mapuche confederations as *behetrías*, the word for Castilian communities where local leaders, if any, were elected by the people and were not subject to any kind of lordship. Alonso de Góngora Marmolejo, *Historia de todas las cosas que han acaecido en el reino de Chile*, ed. Miguel Donoso Rodríguez (Madrid: Iberoamericana/Vervuert, 2010), 232, linked the Araucanian *behetría*, "a manera de república," to the meritocratic and egalitarian institutions of Araucanian warfare. Vargas Machuca similarly said of the Araucanians that they were "gente de behetría." *Milicia Indiana*, 5r. See also Imogen Sutton's excellent analysis of republicanism in Ercilla: "'De gente que a ningún rey obedecen': Republicanism and Empire in Alonso de Ercilla's *La Araucana*," *Bulletin of Hispanic Studies* 91.4 (2014): 417–35.

45. In his *Art of War*, Machiavelli situates the Venetians as an almost perfect model in military matters. Also, according to John Hale, "no other governing class had so informed an interest in military affairs as did the Venetian patriciate." *Renaissance War Studies* (London: Hambledon, 1983), 445.

46. Niccolò Machiavelli, *The Prince*, ed. Quentin Skinner and Russell Price (Cambridge: Cambridge University Press, 1988), 18.

47. Ercilla, *Araucana*, 25.1–3.

48. Alonso de Góngora Marmolejo, *Historia de Chile desde su descubrimiento hasta 1575*, in *Crónicas del reino de Chile*, ed. Francisco Esteve Barba, BAE 131 (Madrid: Atlas, 1960), 76.

49. Alonso de Ovalle, *Histórica relación del reino de Chile* (Roma: Francisco Caballo, 1646), 83, 205.

50. Scholars of *La Araucana* have paid a lot of attention to these prophetic episodes. See mainly Isaías Lerner, "Ercilla y Lucano," in *Hommage á Robert Jammes*, ed. Francis Cerdan (Toulouse: Presses Universitaires du Mirail, 1994), 683–91; Murrin, *History and Warfare*, 138–46; Nicolopulos, *The Poetics of Empire*; Vilà, "Épica e imperio," 604–35; Paul Firbas, "El sueño en la trama épica: La visión corográfica de San Quintín en *La Araucana* de Ercilla," in *Los sueños en la cultura iberoamericana: Siglos XVI–XVIII*, ed. Sonia Rose, Peer Schmidt, and Gregor Weber (Seville: CSIC, 2011), 385–407.

51. See Adorno, *The Polemics of Possession*, 113–47; and Rolena Adorno, "Arms, Letters, and the Native Historian in Early Colonial Mexico," in *1492–1992: Re/discovering Colonial Writing*, ed. René Jara and Nicholas Spadaccini (Minneapolis: Prisma Institute, 1989), 201–24.

52. Juan Ginés de Sepúlveda, *Tratados políticos de Juan Ginés de Sepúlveda*, ed. Ángel Losada (Madrid: Instituto de Estudios Políticos, 1963), 34–35. Originally published as *De conuenientia militaris disciplinae cum christiana religione dialog., qui inscribitur Democrates* (Romae: Antonium Bladu, 1535), Sepúlveda's dialogue was translated into Spanish by Antonio Barba as *Diálogo llamado Demócrates* (Sevilla: Juan Cromberger, 1541).

53. Adorno, *The Polemics of Possession*, 118.

54. Mary Gaylord, "Spain's Renaissance Conquests and the Retroping of Identity," *Journal of Hispanic Philology* 16 (1992): 127, 129.

55. See Salas, *Las armas de la conquista*, 250–57, 417–18.

56. Vargas Machuca, *Milicia indiana*, 85r, my translation.

57. See Álvaro Jara, *Guerra y sociedad en Chile* (Santiago: Editorial Universitaria, 1971), 44–112.

58. Ercilla, *Araucana*, 11.50–51, 12.19–21.

59. Jara, *Guerra y sociedad*, 59–60; Sergio Villalobos, *La vida fronteriza en Chile* (Madrid: MAPFRE, 1992), 246–47.

60. Tesillo, *Guerra de Chile*, 18v–19r.

61. Antei shows convincingly that Ercilla learned about this episode from Vivar, whether reading his 1558 manuscript chronicle or just through the everyday soldierly pláticas of the time they spent together in the war. See Antei, *La invención del reino de Chile*, 182.

62. Ercilla, *Araucana*, 8.13–14.

63. Isaías Lerner pointed out that this episode is related to the literary codes of classical epos and to the Renaissance imitation of Roman parades with the spoils of the vanquished, "a manera de triunfos," as Ercilla himself suggests in the stanza that follows the last quoted. See Ercilla, *Araucana*, 259n16.

64. Rosales, *Historia de Chile*, 2:459, quoted by Jara, *Guerra y sociedad*, 64.

65. Pedro Mariño de Lobera, *Crónica del reino de Chile*, bk. 2, chap. 4, in *Crónicas del reino de Chile*, ed. Francisco Esteve Barba, BAE 131 (Madrid: Atlas, 1960).

66. Barbara Fuchs, *Mimesis and Empire: The New World, Islam, and European Identities* (Cambridge: Cambridge University Press, 2001), 5–6.

67. Homi Bhabha, "Of Mimicry and Man: The Ambivalence of Colonial Discourse," *October* 28 (1984): 128.

68. Ercilla, *Araucana*, 8.16.

69. Quoted in Jara, *Guerra y sociedad*, 127.

70. Beatriz Pastor, *Discursos narrativos de la conquista: Mitificación y emergencia* (Hanover: Ediciones del Norte, 1988), 387.

71. In a twofold argument, Fuchs, *Mimesis and Empire*, 45, reads Caupolicán's threat as both a comic parody of the Spaniards' imperialist rhetoric and practice *and* a revealing acknowledgment of the empire's vulnerability.

72. Quint, *Epic and Empire*, 13.

73. Ibid., 9.

74. "The idea of an 'anti-imperialist,' Chilean national interpretation in opposition to an older, pro-Habsburg 'Spanish national' reading of Ercilla's text creates the impression of a divide in the scholarship surrounding this, the most-read Spanish-language epic of the period." Davis, *Myth and Identity*, 20.

75. Nicolopulos, *The Poetics of Empire*, and Vilà, "Épica e imperio" studied in depth the relation between the imitative practices of the epic tradition in relation to the discursive articulation of the empire, while Elizabeth Davis incorporated a reflection on the political, ethnic, and gender identities to the discussion of epic as the "master narrative of the program of imperial monarchy" (*Myth and Identity*, 19). See also Fuchs, *Mimesis and Empire*, 35–49; Lara Garrido, *Los mejores plectros*, 11–95; Isaías Lerner, "Felipe II y Alonso de Ercilla," *Edad de Oro* 18 (1999): 87–101; and Padrón, *The Spacious Word*, 185–230.

76. Quint, *Epic and Empire*, 34.

77. Historian Stuart Schwartz explicitly raised "the question of how to judge who are the winners and losers historically." Faced with the ultimately ethical dilemma of identifying winners and losers, of emphasizing "the resilience of indigenous culture or the disruption and exploitation that the conquest represented," the historian suggests adding a question mark to his own title, which can no longer be considered exclusively "a description of a permanent condition." Schwartz, preface to *Victors and Vanquished: Spanish and Nahua Views of the Conquest of Mexico* (New York/Boston: Berdford/St. Martin's, 2000), vi. See also Rolena Adorno, "Discourses on Colonialism," 255.

78. All quotes in Ercilla, *Araucana*, 1.1–2.

79. Pedro de Oña, *Arauco domado*, ed. J. T. Medina (Santiago, 1917), 26. Also quoted in Quint, *Epic and Empire*, 390n47.

80. Ercilla, *Araucana*, cantos 3–7.

81. See, for instance, Ercilla, *Araucana*, 9.37, 9.109.

82. Quint reads this passage ironically: "The incongruity of this picture of the poet as a flag-waving Araucanian hints that it needs to be read with irony, an irony, however, that extends to the larger epic where the Spaniards are more generally victorious: the poem should not be read as an opportunistic endorsement of their conquest or as a taking of sides with might regardless of right" (*Epic and Empire*, 178).

83. Ercilla, *Araucana*, 12.46.

84. Ibid., 22.10.

85. Ibid., 26.2.

86. Ibid., 26.25; see also 31.28.

87. Ibid., 34.36.

88. Ercilla, *Araucana*, 34.36–38.

89. Quint, *Epic and Empire*, 166. For discussion of the inconclusive structures and unfulfilling endings of *La Araucana*'s main storyline, see Ramona Lagos, "El incumplimiento de la programación épica en *La Araucana*," *Cuadernos Americanos* 238 (1981): 157–91; Padrón, *The Spacious Word*, 217; Fuchs, *Mimesis and Empire*, 38; and Fuchs, *Romance* (New York: Routledge, 2004), 83–85.

90. See Leonard, *Books of the Brave*, 290–99; and Teodoro Hampe Martínez, *Bibliotecas privadas en el mundo colonial* (Frankfurt: Iberoamericana/Vervuert, 1996), 70–72.

91. Xufré del Águila, *Compendio historial*, 43–44. Martín del Barco Centenera, who spent twenty-four years in South America, refuses to narrate anything Chilean, arguing that the matter belongs exclusively to Ercilla; see his *Argentina y conquista del Río de la Plata* (Lisbon: Pedro Craesbeck, 1602), 205v.

92. Miguel de Aguirre, *Población de Valdivia: Motivos y medios para aquella fundación* (Lima: Jorge López de Herrera, 1647), fols. 32r–v; Santiago de Tesillo, *Guerra de Chile*, 86r.

93. Jorge de Eguía y Lumbe, *Último desengaño de la guerra de Chile* (Madrid, 1664), quoted in Luis Vitale, *Interpretación marxista de la historia de Chile* (Santiago: Ediciones de Prensa Latinoamericana, 1967), 1:175–76.

94. Rosales, *Historia de Chile*, 1:liv.

95. Juan López de Velasco, *Demarcación y división de las Indias* (ca. 1575), JCB Ms. 61r–63v.

96. Pedro de León Portocarrero, *Descripción del virreinato del Perú*, ca. 1620 (Lima: Universidad Ricardo Palma, 2009), 58–59.

97. This can be seen in *Relación de los servicios que hizo a su magestad del Rey don Felipe Segundo y Tercero, don Alonso de Sotomayor* (Madrid: Viuda de Cosme Delgado, 1620), 85r, in which King Philip III appoints Alonso de Sotomayor, a veteran from Flanders, as governor and captain general of Chile in 1604.

98. On the "real situado" and "guerra defensiva," see Jara, *Guerra y sociedad*.

99. Alonso González de Nájera, *Desengaño y reparo de la guerra del reino de Chile*, ed. José Toribio Medina (Santiago: Imprenta Ercilla, 1889); Francisco Núñez de Pineda y Bascuñán, *Cautiverio feliz y razón de las guerras dilatadas de Chile* (Santiago: Imprenta del Ferrocarril, 1863).

100. Tesillo, *Guerra de Chile*, 10r–v. See also his *Epítome chileno*.

101. In addition to those gathered here, see Jara, *Guerra y sociedad*, 113–27.

102. Santiago de Tesillo, *Guerra de Chile*, 9r.

103. *Carta de Francisco de Quiñones a SM*, in Medina, *Colección de documentos inéditos para la historia de Chile: Segunda Serie*, 5 (Santiago: Fondo Histórico y Bibliográfico J. T. Medina, 1957–61), 117.

104. *Relación de la vitoria que Dios nuestro señor fue servido de dar en el Reino de Chile a los 13. de enero de 1631* (Lima: Francisco Gómez Pastrana, 1631), A2r.

105. *Relación verdadera de las paces que capituló con el Araucano rebelado, el marqués de Baides* (Madrid: Francisco Maroto, 1642), A1r. It has been attributed to Alonso de Ovalle.

106. The same names are in Tesillo, *Guerra de Chile*, 8r, who reports about *relaciones* arriving in Lima with news from Chile in September 1629. González de Nájera confirms the Mapuche practice of shouting out their names before engaging in combat, which explains the fame of the warriors and the precision of Chilean onomastics in Spanish sources, beginning with Ercilla. See Salas, *Las armas de la Conquista*, 290–91.

107. Aguirre, *Población de Valdivia*, 31v–32r.

108. Pekka Hämäläinen, *Comanche Empire* (New Haven, CT: Yale University Press, 2008), 7. Hämäläinen's book, which "tells the familiar tale of expansion, resistance, conquest, and loss, but with a reversal of usual historical roles: it is a story in which Indians expand, dictate, and prosper and European colonists resist, retreat, and struggle to survive" (1), has provided crucial inspiration for my own argument, and I believe that fruitful comparisons can be drawn between what happens in the northern- and southernmost frontiers of the Spanish empire.

109. Ercilla, *Araucana*, 8.30.

110. Vargas Machuca, *Milicia Indiana*, 27r.

111. Ibid., 140v.

112. Vargas Machuca, *Indian Militia*, 34; Vargas Machuca, *Milicia indiana*, 13v. The passage is again loaded with Ercillian overtones, cf. *Araucana*, 3.4. The commonplace gained new currency and positive values in Bernardo de Balbuena's *Grandeza Mexicana*, where *interest* is indeed a virtuous "pegajosa liga" (sticky lasso) (*Araucana* 3.1) that holds society together.

113. Vargas Machuca, *Indian Militia*, 37; 16r. See Ercilla, *Araucana*, 3.3: "Codicia fue ocasión de tanta guerra / y perdición total de aquesta tierra." See Virgil's classical topos in *Aeneid*, 3.57.

114. Vargas Machuca, *Indian Militia*, 23; 5v.

115. Galbarino's story in Ercilla, *Araucana*, cantos 22, 23, and 26, especially 25.35–41. Mutilation of hands and noses was as common a practice in the conquest of Chile as anywhere else in the Indies. Valdivia himself reports doing it repeatedly, sometimes to as many as two hundred Mapuche soldiers. See Valdivia, *Cartas de Pedro de Valdivia*, 137, 204.

116. Bernardo de Vargas Machuca's *Discurso de guerra . . . para la pacificación y allanamiento de los indios del reino de Chile* (AGI, Patronato, 227, r. 34), from which I quote, was transcribed by José Toribio Medina in *Colección de documentos inéditos para la historia de Chile,* Segunda Serie, 5, 119–32.

117. Vargas Machuca, *Discurso de guerra*, 4r.

118. Ibid.

119. See Jara, *Guerra y sociedad*, 113–43. On the crucial figure of Alonso de Ribera, governor of Chile from 1601 to 1605 and from 1612 to 1617, see also Diego Barros Arana, *Historia general de Chile* (Santiago: Centro de Estudios Barros Arana, 1999), 3:251–28. For the school of Alba and for the institutional, military, and cultural history of the war of Flanders in general, see González de León, *The Road to Rocroi*.

120. Ercilla, *Araucana*, 17.52, 18.47.

121. See, for example, the remarkable story about how he managed to recover a clean copy of his historiographical work, ready for the printer, that had been lost in a tavern by his drunken scrivener only to end up in the hands of the Fuggers' young horse keeper. Esteban de Garibay, *Discurso de mi vida*, ed. Jesús Moya (Bilbao: Euskal Herriko Unibertsitatea, 1999), 166.

122. This fragment had already been pointed out by Chevalier, *Lectura y lectores*, 119, who found it extracted in Medina, *Documentos*, 525.

123. Ovalle, *Histórica relación*, 83. Also quoted by Medina, *Ilustraciones*, 2:414. For a bibliography of *La Araucana*'s editions, see August J. Aquila, *Alonso de Ercilla y Zúñiga: A Basic Bibliography* (London: Grant and Cutler, 1975), 15–16, which completes the previous one by Medina in *Ilustraciones*.

124. Medina, *Ilustraciones*, 1:7.

125. Ibid., 1:73.

126. Antunes, *Primera parte de la baxada de los españoles de Francia en Normandía*, fol. 3v of the preliminaries, not foliated.

127. Benjamin Schmidt, "Exotic Allies: The Dutch-Chilean Encounter and the (Failed) Conquest of America," *Renaissance Quarterly* 52.2 (1999): 440–73; Benjamin Schmidt, *Innocence Abroad: The Dutch Imagination*

and the New World, 1570–1670 (Cambridge: Cambridge University Press, 2001), xvii–xxviii.

128. For all the quotes preceding this note, see Schmidt, "Exotic Allies," 461–62, 466, 469.

129. *Historiale beschrijvinghe*, 1, 60. My thanks to César Manrique Figueroa, who translated for me the Dutch original at the JCB.

130. Barbara Fuchs, "Traveling Epic: Translating Ercilla's *La Araucana* in the Old World," *Journal of Medieval and Early Modern Studies* 36.2 (2006): 379. In the same study, Fuchs explores the first, partial English translation of *La Araucana*, done by George Carew, an English colonial official in Ireland, where the author makes ample use of a similar "American Analogy" (386–91).

131. This interesting poem, now held at the BNE, MSS/22648, has gone completely unnoticed by literary critics. I found the reference in Parker, *The Army of Flanders*, 101, who in turn thanks Fernando Bouza for mentioning it to him.

132. Rodríguez Alva, *La inquieta Flandes*, 397r–398r.

133. Ibid., 10r–v.

134. Far from barbarism, the heretic Dutch would be "equalled by no one in their way of living" if it were not for their fondness for intemperate drinking (ninguno en su vivir les igualara; ibid., 12v). The political language of the Dutch rebels in Rodríguez Alva's poem is tightly linked to the sophisticated republican vocabularies displayed by Ercilla in his depiction of Araucanian senatorial deliberations. Motherland (*patria*) and liberty (*libertad*) versus oppression and tyranny constitute the pillars of Dutch political discourse in *La inquieta Flandes* (102r and following, 158v and passim).

135. Rodríguez Alva, *La inquieta Flandes*, 116v–117r; Ercilla, *Araucana*, 23.12–13.

136. Rodríguez Alva, *La inquieta Flandes*, 117r.

137. Fuchs, *Mimesis and Empire*, 42.

138. Xufré del Águila, *Compendio historial*, 2.

139. Tesillo, *Guerra de Chile*, 3r.

CHAPTER 5

The chapter epigraph comes from Miguel de Cervantes, *Poesías completas*, ed. Vicente Gaos (Madrid: Castalia, 1981), 365. The two epigraphs following the heading come from, respectively, Verrier, *Les armes de Minerve*, 100, and Ricardo Palma, quoted by José Toribio Medina, *Romances basados en La Araucana* (Santiago: Imprenta Elzeviriana, 1918), vii.

1. Enrique García-Santo Tomás has reminded us repeatedly of the richness and relevance of the body of writings by and the images of ex-combatants. See mainly "Ruptured Narratives" but also *Espacio urbano y creación literaria en el Madrid de Felipe IV* (Madrid: Iberoamericana/Vervuert, 2004), 86–88, and *Modernidad bajo sospecha: Salas Barbadillo y la cultura material del siglo XVII* (Madrid: CSIC, 2008), 139–45.

2. For these different meanings, in addition to the texts commented on here, see Paredes's *Suma* in Antonio Sánchez Jiménez, *El Sansón de*

Extremadura: Diego García de Paredes en la literatura española del siglo XVI (Newark, DE: Juan de la Cuesta, 2006, 42–43; Díaz del Castillo, *Historia verdadera*, 375; Mateo Alemán, *Guzmán de Alfarache*, ed. José María Micó (Madrid: Cátedra, 2001) 2:465; and Diego Núñez de Alva, *Diálogos de la vida del soldado* (Cuenca: Juan Alonso de Tapia, 1589), A7r.

3. In Xufré del Águila, *Compendio historial*, sig. ¶4r.

4. On the soldiers' wounds, see White, "The Experience of Spain's Early Modern Soldiers," 20–27; and García-Santo Tomás, "Ruptured Narratives."

5. Luis de Góngora, "Pensó rendir la mozuela," in *Romances*, ed. Antonio Carreño (Madrid: Cátedra, 2000), 286.

6. *La vida y hechos de Estebanillo González*, ed. Antonio Carreira and Jesús Antonio Cid (Madrid: Cátedra, 1990), 1:286.

7. AGS Estado 558, 51, article 18, quoted in Parker, *The Army of Flanders*, 169.

8. "¿Puédese más decir sino que cuando / despido el salso humor yo de mi boca, / antes que llegue al suelo, ya en el aire, / va congelado en cuerpo espeso y duro?" Aldana, "Respuesta a su hermano Cosme desde Flandes," in *Poesías*, 281.

9. Toral y Valdés, *Relación*, 501, trans. Guy Sawyer, 36.

10. *Cancionero de Juan de Escobedo (Ms. 330 Biblioteca Real Academia Española)*, ed. Marcial Rubio Arquez (Pisa: ETS, 2004), no. 96. See pages 15–36 of Rubio Arquez's introduction. The poem was also copied and largely modified in the 1586 *Cancionero de poesías varias: Ms. Reginensis Latini 1635 de la Biblioteca Vaticana*, ed. José Labrador Herraiz, Ralph A. DiFranco, Carmen Parrilla García (Almería: Universidad de Almería, 2008), no. 133 (see also p. 20).

11. BNE MSS/17951; Pedro de Padilla, *Romancero en el qual se contienen algunos sucesos que en la jornada de Flandes*, ed. José J. Labrador Herraiz and Ralph A. DiFranco (México: Frente de Afirmación Hispanista, 2010), 148. The stanzas are actually *quintillas*, not *redondillas*.

12. Correia, *Lendas da India*, tome 2, vol. 2:912; Vargas Machuca, *Milicia Indiana*, 23v–24r; Pastor and Callau, *Lope de Aguirre*, 62.

13. *Tristo/tristi, trista/triste* occur 41 times in Petrarch's *Canzionere*. See, for instance, nos. 277 ("alma trista"), 148 ("cor tristo"), 323 ("trista vita"), 23 ("lagrime triste"), 15 ("tristi pianti"). Francesco Petrarca, *Cancionero*, ed. Jacobo Cortines (Madrid: Cátedra, 1989).

14. Lope de Vega in Vicente Espinel, *Diversas rimas* (Madrid: Luis Sánchez, 1591), A8v. See, for instance, in this same volume, 2r, 4r, 5r.

15. See the exhaustive *recensio* of the original texts for these lines in *Cancionero Vaticana*, 373–83. For an accessible version of the *romances* mentioned here, see Giusseppe di Stefano, *Romancero* (Madrid: Castalia, 2010), nos. 16, 33, 108, 142, 150, 151. The collage of lines from well-known ballads was a common practice in popular satire. See, for instance, the anonymous *coplas* received by King Philip II in October 1575 as recorded by Fray Juan de San Gerónimo in his *Memorias*, in CODOIN, 7:151–55.

16. Marqués de Santillana, *Obras completas*, ed. Ángel Gómez Moreno and Maxim P. A. M. Kerkhof (Barcelona: Planeta, 1988), 444.

17 All quotes in *Cancionero de Juan Escobedo*, n. 96.

18. I quote from Alfred Morel-Fatio's edition in "La plainte du soldat esp-agnol," *Romanische Forschungen* 23 (1907): 160–61, which he copied from a manuscript at Paris's Bibliothèque Nationale, although I amend some of his errors using the 1586 *Cancionero Vaticana*, no. 316. The names of Philip II's secretaries in the Councils of Italy and War—Eraso, Vargas, Gaytán—date the composition of the poem to the late 1570s.

19. See Emily Francomano, "'Puse un sobreescripto': Manuscript, Print and the Material Epistolarity of *Cárcel de Amor*," *Fifteenth-Century Studies* 36 (2011): 25–48.

20. Morel-Fatio, "La plainte," summarily identifies these characters. For the commanders of "the school of Alba," see González de León, *The Road to Rocroi*.

21. See Parker, *The Army of Flanders*, 141–43; and L. Van Meerbeeck, "L'hôpital royal de l'armée espagnole a Malines en l'an 1637," *Bulletin du Cercle royal archéologique, littéraire et artistique de Malines* 54 (1950): 81–125.

22. It was first printed in *Laberinto amoroso*, ed. Juan de Chen (Barce-lona: Sebastián de Cormellas, 1618), 84–87, and reprinted in *Primavera y flor de romances* (Lisbon: Mattheus Pinheiro, 1626), but it has precedents and later iterations in several pliegos. Also collected by Agustín Durán, *Romancero general*, BAE 16 (Madrid: Rivadeneyra, 1851), 2:575–76, no. 1739. For the complex editorial history of this poem and its intertexts, see Edward Wilson, "Samuel Pepys' Spanish Chapbooks, Part II," *Transactions of the Cambridge Bibliographical Society* 2.3 (1956): 229–68. Its popularity is confirmed by Juan de Zabaleta's re-creation of the poem in *Día de fiesta por la mañana y por la tarde* (Madrid: Diego Pacheco, 1885), 72–74.

23. This can be found in a letter to the Count-Duke of Olivares sent from the Netherlands in 1629, quoted by Marcelin Defourneaux, *Vida cotidiana en la España del Siglo de Oro* (Barcelona: Arcos Vergara, 1983), 200.

24. Diego Ximénez de Ayllón, *Sonetos a illustres varones este felicísimo y católico ejército y corte* (Antwerp: Viuda de Juan Lacio, 1569).

25. Cervantes, *Don Quijote*, 446, trans. Grossman, 331.

26. Rey de Artieda, *Discursos*, 221. "Enemigo mortal del trato humano" is a line from Garcilaso's "Égloga II," line 918. Garcilaso de la Vega, *Obra poética*, 266.

27. Cervantes, *Don Quijote*, 835, trans. Grossman, 619. On this episode, see Barbara Fuchs, "Dismantling Heroism: The Exhaustion of War in Don Quijote," *PMLA* 124.5 (2009): 1842–46; and Rupp, *Heroic Forms*.

28. All the quotes in these paragraphs are in Cervantes, *Don Quijote*, 577–80, trans. Grossman, 434–38.

29. Virgil, *The Eclogues*, trans. Guy Lee (New York: Penguin, 1984), 34–34. Octavian Augustus confiscated land to pay veterans of Philippi in 41 B.C.E. See Richard Hunter, "Virgil's Ecl. I and the Origins of Pastoral," in *Brill's Companion to Greek and Latin Pastoral*, ed. Marco Fantuzzi and Theodore Papanghelis (Leiden: Brill, 2006), 264; and Richard Thomas and

Jan Ziolkowski, *The Virgil Encyclopedia* (Chichester: Wiley-Blackwell, 2014), 1:785.

30. Eugenio, the storytelling shepherd, closely resembles his Virgilian counterpart. Meliboeus, like Eugenio, is a goatherd, and Eugenio runs into Don Quixote's party while chasing one of his strayed she-goats, just like Meliboeus finds Daphnis, Corydon, and Thyrsis in search of his billy goat in *Ecl.* 7, when he reappears in Virgil's series. Virgil, *Eclogues*, 78–79.

31. Stanislav Zimic, "Sobre los amores de Leandra y Vicente de la Roca (*Don Quijote*, I, caps. 50–52)," *Anales cervantinos* 30 (1992): 67–76, suggested a reading of Vicente's behavior along class terms, as a revenge of the long-humiliated poor peasant against the wealthy families of his hometown.

32. Paul Fussell, *The Great War and Modern Memory* (Oxford: Oxford University Press, 1975), 231–69.

33. *Quixote*, 439; *Quijote*, 583–84.

34. *Quixote*, 438; *Quijote*, 582.

35. Quevedo, *Buscón*, 124. *Entretenimiento* means "entertainment," in addition to the military institution. *Ventaja*, which meant both "wage-supplement" of a soldier's salary and "advantage" in card games, entails a similarly untranslatable wordplay.

36. Javier Castro-Ibaseta, "Monarquía satírica: Poética de la caída del Conde-Duque de Olivares" (PhD diss., Universidad Autónoma de Madrid, 2008), especially 230–74, and 591ff., which I follow in my own account, together with his "Mentidero de Madrid: La Corte como comedia," in *Opinión pública y espacio urbano en la Edad Moderna*, ed. Antonio Castillo Gómez, James Amelang, and Carmen Serrano Sánchez (Gijón: Trea, 2010), 43–58. Castro-Ibaseta is currently finishing a book on similar topics under the title "Beware the Poetry: Political Satire and the Emergence of the Spanish Public Sphere (1600–1645)."

37. Robert Darnton, *The Great Cat Massacre and Other Episodes in French Cultural History* (New York: Vintage, 1984), 36.

38. For the comparable role of soldiers in English news culture, see McKeown, *English Mercuries*, 32–36.

39. Castro-Ibaseta, "Monarquía satírica," 211, 237–45.

40. Jean Canavaggio, *Cervantes* (Madrid: Espasa-Calpe, 2003), 209–68; Cervantes's *memorial*, from which I quote, on 223.

41. AGS, GyM, leg. 343, fol. 301.

42. Ramírez de Arellano, *Juan Rufo*, 57–63; Rufo, *Apotegmas*, no. 572.

43. Contreras, *Vida*, 133, 214–19.

44. Rufo, *Apotegmas*, no. 477.

45. See M. Cruz García de Enterría, *Sociedad y poesía de cordel en el Barroco* (Madrid: Taurus, 1973), 115.

46. See Alessandro Cassol, *Vita e scrittura: Autobiografie di soldati spagnoli del Siglo de Oro* (Milano: LED, 2000), 219–33, who finds the *pliego* in BNE R/4512(5), 18r–21v.

47. Antonio Rodríguez Moñino, "El alférez Francisco de Segura, autor y colector de romances," *Revista del Instituto "José Cornide" de Estudios Coruñeses* 4.4 (1968): 185–204. *Catálogo de pliegos sueltos poéticos de la*

Biblioteca Nacional: Siglo XVII (Madrid: Universidad de Alcalá, 1998) provides an idea of the sheer volume of this traffic in broadsheets of all kinds. See also Henry Ettinghausen, "Informació, comunicació i poder a l'Espanya del segle XVII," *Manuscrits* 23 (2005): 45–58; and Henry Ettinghausen, *La guerra dels Segadors a través de la premsa de l'època*, 4 vols. (Barcelona: Curial, 1993).

48. Francesco Andreini, *Le bravure del capitano Spavento* (Venice: Giacomo Antonio Somasco, 1609), [5v, preliminaries].

49. Quevedo, *Buscón*, 166.

50. Quoted in Castro-Ibaseta, "Monarquía satírica," 250.

51. See ibid., 239–241.

52. Londoño, *Discurso*, 33v.

53. See Castro-Ibaseta, "Monarquía satírica," 251, and Covarrubias, *Tesoro*, s.v. "corrillo" and "baratillo."

54. Emilio Cotarelo y Mori's historical and linguistic study of the *jácara* traditions in *Colección de entremeses, loas, jácaras, mojigangas* (Madrid: Bailly-Bailliére, 1911), 1:cclxxiv–ccxc, is still very useful. José Hesse, ed., *Romancero de germanía* (Madrid: Taurus, 1967), published Juan Hidalgo's work by the same title, originally printed in Barcelona in 1609, while John M. Hill, ed., *Poesías germanescas* (Bloomington: Indiana University Press, 1945), added earlier and later examples to the corpus.

55. Andrés Rey de Artieda wrote poems to camp prostitutes, *Discursos*, 194, 212–17, 220. Common soldier Miguel de Castro gives ample coverage of the topic in his bawdy autobiography, in Cossío, *Autobiografías de soldados*, 487–627.

56. Hill, *Germanescas*, 67; Quevedo, *Buscón*, 125.

57. Quevedo, *Buscón*, 224.

58. Mary Elizabeth Perry, "Soldiers and Pícaros," in *Crime and Society in Early Modern Seville* (Hanover, NH: University Press of New England, 1980), 111.

59. The words belong to arbitrista González de Cellórigo, quoted in I. A. A. Thompson, "A Map of Crime in Sixteenth-Century Spain," *Economic History Review* 21 (1968): 244.

60 Perry, *Crime and Society*, 19. For the European subcultures of the licensed veteran soldiers, see Burke, *Popular Culture*, 72–79.

61. León Portocarrero, *Descripción del virreinato del Perú*, 58–59. See also AGI, Lima, Lima 36: n. 1, lib. IV, fols. 98–101v; AGI, Lima 35: n. 31, lib. II, fols. 118–119v; AGI, Lima 34: n. 30, lib. IV, fols, 57–64v. I owe these references to Guillermo García Montúfar, who generously shared this archival material with me.

62. Machiavelli, *Art of War*, 159.

63. All quotes from *Motín y levantamiento de los soldados de la Guarda contra la Sala de Alcaldes*, BNE, MSS/2360, 336r–v. Barrionuevo reports similar riots supported by both soldiers and the urban poor in Málaga and Seville. Jerónimo de Barrionuevo, *Avisos* (Madrid: Impresor de Cámara, 1892), 2:178–79.

64. Durán, *Romancero*, 2:576.

65. Karl Marx, *The Eighteenth Brumaire of Louis Bonaparte* (Moscow: Progress Publishers, 1937), chap. 5, *Marxist Internet Archive*, https://www.marxists.org/archive/marx/works/1852/18th-brumaire/, accessed July 15, 2015. For a different characterization of the lumpen proletariat, see Marx, *Capital Vol. 1*, trans. Ben Fowkes (London: Penguin, 1976), 797.

66. The sources of the epigraphs following the heading are: Rosales, "El desengaño del imperio," in *Poesía heroica del imperio*, lxxii; and Valdivia, *Cartas de Pedro de Valdivia*, 201.

Carlos Pereyra, "Soldadesca y picaresca," *Boletín de la Biblioteca Menéndez Pelayo* 19 (1927): 352–61 and 20 (1928): 74–96, 150–63, 243–50; Cossío, *Autobiografías de soldados*, xviii, xxvi; Levisi, *Autobiografías del Siglo de Oro*, 103; Anne Cruz, "From Pícaro to Soldier," in *Discourses of Poverty: Social Reform and the Picaresque Novel in Early Modern Spain* (Toronto: University of Toronto Press, 1999), 160–206; Lane's introduction to Vargas Machuca, *Indian Militia*, xxii, xxv.

67. Alemán, *Guzmán*, 357–71; Cervantes, *Novelas*, 1:191–240, 2:332–34; Gonzalo de Céspedes y Meneses, *Varia fortuna del soldado Píndaro*, ed. Arsenio Pacheco (Madrid: Espasa-Calpe, 1975), 1:137–57; Toral y Valdés, *Relación*, 497, trans. Sawyer, 29.

68. For a characterization of the "literature of the poor," which would encompass those texts where "the legitimacy [is] given by the enunciation of a free and poor 'I,'" see Juan Carlos Rodríguez, *La literatura del pobre* (Granada: Comares, 2001), 23–47, quote on 25.

69. José Deleito y Piñuela, *El declinar de la monarquía española* (Madrid: Espasa-Calpe, 1947), quoted in Defourneaux, *Vida cotidiana*, 204.

70. Covarrubias, *Tesoro*, s.v.

71. See Alberto del Monte, *Itinerario de la novela picaresca española* (Barcelona: Lumen, 1971), 12, which provides a thorough discussion of the term *pícaro*.

72. On the complex chronology of the *Lazarillo*'s composition and its textual history, see also Monte, *Itinerario*, 17–25, and Francisco Rico's introduction to *Lazarillo de Tormes* (Madrid: Cátedra, 1990), 13–30.

73. A relatively large number of copies have come down to us in sixteenth- and seventeenth-century manuscripts. See, for instance, MSS/1752, 186r–189v, MSS/5602, 40v–48r, and MSS/12931(15) at the BNE, and Instituto Valencia de Don Juan (IVdDJ), E17,44, 150r–154v, a hitherto unknown copy from which I quote, for I believe it is among the oldest testimonies. The Real Academia Española's library keeps another copy that I have not been able to consult, RM Caja 84/13, according to the Catálogo de Patrimonio Bibliográfico, http://www.mecd.gob.es/cultura-mecd/areas-cultura/bibliotecas/mc/ccpb/portada.html, accessed August 29, 2014. For the print tradition, see *Crónica del Gran Capitán Gonzalo Hernández de Córdoba y Aguilar; con la vida del caballero Diego García de Paredes* (Seville: Andrea Pescioni, 1580, 1582; Alcalá, 1584). The best modern edition is Sánchez Jiménez, *El Sansón de Extremadura*, 41–65, but given its complex textual history, the *Suma* still merits a critical edition.

74. On this corpus, see Cossío, *Autobiografías*; Levisi, *Autobiografías del Siglo de Oro*; Margarita Levisi, "Golden Age Autobiography: The Soldiers," in *Autobiography in Early Modern Spain*, ed. Nicholas Spadaccini and Jenaro Talens (Minneapolis: Prisma Institute, 1988), 97–117; Cassol, *Vita e scrittura*; and Harari, *Renaissance Military Memoirs*.

75. Paredes, *Breve suma*, IVdDJ, 150r.

76. Julius Caesar, *Los comentarios de Gayo Iulio Cesar*, trans. Diego López de Toledo (Paris: Arnold Burkmann, 1549), first printed in Toledo by Petrus Hagenbach, 1498, and in Alcalá by Miguel de Eguía in 1529.

77. Alvar Núñez Cabeza de Vaca, *La relación y comentarios del gobernador de lo acaescido en las dos jornadas que hizo a las Indias* (Valladolid: Francisco Fernández de Córdoba, 1555); Duque de Estrada, *Comentarios*; see the author's comments on genre and purpose, in terms similar to Paredes's, on pp. 462 and 469.

78. Cetina in Adolfo de Castro, *Poetas líricos de los siglos XVI y XVII*, BAE 42 (Madrid: Rivadeneyra, 1854), 48; Toral y Valdés, *Relación*, 547; Cervantes, *Quijote*, 372, 579.

79. Sánchez-Blanco, "El marco institucional del discurso sobre sí mismo"; José Ortega y Gasset, "Prólogo" to Alonso de Contreras, *Discurso de mi vida* (Madrid: Alianza, 1967), 34.

80. See Robert Jay Lifton, *Home from War: Learning from Vietnam Veterans* (Boston: Beacon Press, 1973), 38; and García-Santo Tomás, "Ruptured Narratives."

81. Paredes, *Suma*, IVdDJ ms., 154v.

82. Ibid.

83. Ibid., 153v.

84. Ibid.

85. Ibid., 154v. In other copies of the text Paredes calls his memoir a "mirror" for his son's conduct, but Paredes's text is far from the *instrucciones de heredero* studied by Fernando Bouza in *Imagen y propaganda: Capítulos de historia cultural del reinado de Felipe II* (Madrid: Akal, 1998), 197–245.

86. Paredes, *Breve suma*, IVdDJ ms., 150r.

87. Cervantes, *Don Quixote*, 372, trans. Grossman, 269.

88. Marcel Bataillon, *Pícaros y picaresca* (Madrid: Taurus, 1969), 14.

89. Struggling to make virtue out of necessity, Tomás Tamayo de Vargas, the first biographer of Paredes, said that "nobility is undoubtedly more venerable when its origins are unknown," *Diego García de Paredes i relación breve de su tiempo* (Madrid: Luis Sánchez, 1621), 5. Similarly, Paredes's modern biographer, Pedro Muñoz de San Pedro, Count of Canilleros, claimed to be himself a descendant of the "Sansón de Extremadura." His family connections to the character and Lockhart's accurate caution that he "makes all the people he writes about seem equally noble" (Lockhart, *The Men of Cajamarca*, 136) should warn us against some of his conclusions about the social standing of Paredes, which he utterly exaggerates. In a highly idealizing interpretation of this forefather, Muñoz de San Pedro had a hard time assimilating some of the episodes in the *Breve suma* into the general narrative of high nobility, chivalric prowess, and moral integrity that

frames his reading of the figure, who actually belonged to the lower layers of local hidalguía. Miguel Muñoz de San Pedro, *Diego García de Paredes, Hércules y Sansón de España* (Madrid: Espasa Calpe, 1946), 51.

90. Miguel Muñoz de San Pedro, "Documentación histórica de Diego García de Paredes," *Revista de Estudios Extremeños* 12 (1957): 307–37.

91. The beginning of several autobiographies written by veterans may serve as a token of the influence Paredes's brief memoir had in later soldierly texts. Toral y Valdés, *Relación*, 497–98, enrolled in the army after killing a fellow servant in a nobleman's house, while Duque de Estrada, *Comentarios*, 102–3, killed his wife and his best friend, whom he found together in bed, which triggered his flight and first enlistment in the military.

92. Contreras, *Discurso de mi vida*, 70.

93. Beverly Jacobs, "Social Provocation and Self-Justification in the *Vida* of Captain Alonso de Contreras," *Hispanic Review* 51.3 (1983): 319.

94. Contreras, *Discurso de mi vida*, 75.

95. Levisi, *Autobiografías del Siglo de Oro*, 112–29, offered a perceptive reading of the narrative structure of the text's three parts, respectively finished in 1630, 1633, and after 1641, which nonetheless contrasts with José Ortega y Gasset's characterization of Contreras's life as plotless in his "Prólogo" to *Discurso de mi vida*.

96. Contreras, *Discurso de mi vida*, 131–39.

97. Ibid., 139, 147. Later in the narrative, he will comment on the deliberate usage of a phrase in germanía: "ojo avizor, como dicen los lampones," 241.

98. Contreras, *Discurso de mi vida*, 158. Ettinghausen was the only editor to note the author's important revisions. In an analogous situation, Duque de Estrada makes similar metanarrative comments: "I have dropped my pen more than four times to avoid writing it"; "it costs me a lot of pain to write it" (he dejado más de cuatro [veces] la pluma para no escribirlo; me cuesta dolores el escribirlo). *Comentarios*, 102, 103.

99. Contreras, *Discurso de mi vida*, 160.

100. Similar religious retreats are found in a number of soldierly autobiographies. See, for instance, Duque de Estrada, *Comentarios*, 456.

101. Contreras, *Discurso de mi vida*, 187.

102. Ortega y Gasset, "Prólogo," 41.

103. Ibid., 29–30, 9, 18.

104. Lope de Vega, *El rey sin reino*, in *Parte veinte de las comedias* (Madrid: Viuda de Alonso Martín, 1625), 226v–228v.

105. Jacobs, "Social Provocation," 304, 308, 314–15.

106. Eric Naylor, "La encomienda del capitán Contreras," *Revista de Filología Española* 53.1 (1970): 305–8; Henry Ettinghausen, "Alonso de Contreras: Un épisode de sa vie," *Bulletin Hispanique* 77.3–4 (1975): 293–318; María Antonia Domínguez Flores, "Alonso de Contreras: Discurso de mi vida. Edición y estudio" (PhD diss., Universidad Complutense de Madrid, 2007), 55–78.

107. See Eric Hobsbawm, *Primitive Rebels: Studies in Archaic Forms of Social Movement in the 19th and 20th Centuries* (New York: Frederick Praeger, 1963).

108. This mutiny *cartel*, the only surviving one, was published by Julián Paz, "Pasquín puesto en Namur por los soldados españoles en 1594," *Revista de Bibliotecas, archivos y museos* 1, tercera época (1897): 118, and by Geoffrey Parker, "Mutiny and Discontent in the Spanish Army of Flanders, 1572–1607," *Past and Present* 58 (1973): 38–52. I have largely transcribed Parker's translation, with only one significant variation of his rendition "they load the donkey so much that they have to do it with kicks." The apparent grammatical disagreement between *asno* and *echan* in "tanto cargan al asno que a coces echan la carga" can be explained by the collective nature of the "donkeys" who endorse and sign this note, ready to kick away the load. The phrase echoes with proverbial idioms and popular culture.

EPILOGUE

1. Quoted in Parker, *The Army of Flanders*, 157.

2. Jerónimo de Barrionuevo, *Avisos*, 4 vols. (Madrid: Impresor de Cámara, 1892), 1:156, 2:212. See similar testimonies elsewhere: 1:162–63, 2:223, 237.

3. Ibid., 2:337, March 25, 1656. Barrionuevo ironically refers to "Mira Nero de Tarpeya," in Giusseppe di Stefano, ed., *Romancero* (Madrid: Castalia, 2010), 217.

4. Parker, *The Military Revolution*, 56–58. More telling figures are in Parker, *The Army of Flanders*, 177–89, and White, "The Experience of Spain's Early Modern Soldiers," 4–5.

5. Rey de Artieda, *Discursos*, 168–71.

6. Parker, "Mutiny and Discontent," 39; Parker, *The Army of Flanders*, 157–76, 253–56.

7. For a contrasting view of the relationship between class and mutiny in the Dutch army of Flanders, see David Trim, "Ideology, Greed, and Social Discontent in Early Modern Europe: Mercenaries and Mutinies in the Rebellious Netherlands, 1568–1609," in *Rebellion, Repression, Reinvention: Mutiny in Comparative Perspective*, ed. Jane Hathaway (Westport, CT: Praeger, 2001), 47–61.

8. Parker, "Mutiny and Discontent." Hale, *War and Society*, 172, offers a similar assessment of the apolitical and nonideological character of early modern mutinies.

9. Parker, *The Army of Flanders*, 174. See Ranajit Guha's classic critique of Hobsbawm's characterization of peasant revolts as pre-political in *Elementary Aspects of Peasant Insurgency in Colonial India* (Durham, NC: Duke University Press, 1999), 1–17, quote on 9. See also James Scott, *The Weapons of the Weak* (New Haven, CT: Yale University Press, 1984).

10. MacKay, *The Limits of Royal Authority*.

11. Quoted by I. A. A. Thompson, "El soldado, la sociedad y el Estado en la España de los siglos XVI y XVII," in *Historia militar de España*, vol. 3.2, coord. Luis Ribot (Madrid: Ministerio de Defensa, 2009), 447–69.

12. Núñez de Alva, *Diálogos*, A7r.

13. See Lifton, *Home from War*, 18, 30.

14. Torres Naharro, *Comedia soldadesca*, in *Teatro renacentista*, ed. Hermenegildo, 184.

15. For Ercilla, see José Toribio Medina, *Vida de Ercilla* (México: FCE, 1948), 86–94; and Diego Suárez Montañés, "Discurso verdadero de la naturaleza, peregrinación, vida y partes del autor de la presente historia," in Alfred Morel-Fatio, "Soldats espagnols du XVIIe siècle: Alonso de Contreras, Miguel de Castro et Diego Suárez," *Bulletin Hispanique* 3.2 (1901): 153. Contreras, *Discurso de mi vida*, 159–80; Pasamonte, *Vida*, 5.

16. García-Santo Tomás, "Ruptured Narratives," 80.

17. Thompson, *War and Government*, 287. Tilly quoted in Tallett, *War and Society*, 188. See also MacKay's argument confirming Thompson's view in *The Limits of Royal Authority*, 11–12.

18. Marcelin Defourneaux, *Vida cotidiana en la España del Siglo de Oro* (Barcelona: Arcos Vergara, 1983), 201.

19. Quatrefages, *Los tercios*, 319.

20. Scott, *Weapons of the Weak*; see especially xv–xxii, 28–47, 304–50. I also draw from the language and theorization of de Certeau, *The Practice of Everyday Life*.

21. Antonio Carreira and Jesús Antonio Cid, in their edition of *La vida y hechos de Estebanillo González* (Madrid: Cátedra, 1990), have solidly proved the historical existence of "Estebanillo" but attributed the homonym picaresque text to Gabriel de la Vega, a clerk of commoner background who worked for the army of Flanders.

22. Contreras, *Discurso de mi vida*, 227.

23. See Ettinghausen, "Alonso de Contreras."

24. Baki Tezcan, *The Second Ottoman Empire: Political and Social Transformation in the Early Modern World* (Cambridge: Cambridge University Press, 2010). Tezcan argues that what has traditionally been considered as decline in Ottoman historiography is in fact a complex set of profound transformations that entailed a redistribution of power among different sectors and corporations of Ottoman society. The prestige and privileges of the army, as a part of the *askeri* or ruling class as opposed to the ruled or *re'aya*, attracted many individuals who paid their way into the army instead of being recruited by the traditional *devşirme* system. The social, political, and financial opportunities the army corps afforded turned the soldiers into one of the main political actors, and certainly one of the most privileged social groups, of early modern Turkey.

25. See Thompson, *War and Government*, particularly 146–59; González de León, *The Road to Rocroi*, 159–213.

26. E. B. Osborn, ed., *The Muse in Arms* (New York: Frederick A. Stokes, 1917). References to the French mutineers are in Parker, foreword to Jane Hathaway, ed., *Rebellion, Repression, Reinvention: Mutiny in Comparative Perspective* (Westport, CT: Praeger, 2001), viii.

27. Parker, foreword, vii. On the poetry of the Great War's soldiers, see Fussell's masterful *The Great War and Modern Memory*.

28. Butler, *Frames of War.*

29. See Parker, *The Army of Flanders*, 174.

30. See, for instance, David Cortright, *Soldiers in Revolt: GI Resistance During the Vietnam War* (Chicago: Haymarket Books, 2005); and the excellent films *Winter Soldiers* (1972) and *Sir! No Sir!* by David Zeiger (USA, Mindbomb Films, 2005).

31. George Packer, "Home Fires: How Soldiers Write Their Wars," *New Yorker*, April 7, 2014; Tim Arango, "Escaping Death in Northern Iraq," *New York Times*, September 3, 2014.

32. See the *pasquines* reproduced in Manuel Danvila y Collado, *Reinado de Carlos III* (Madrid: El Progreso, 1893), 5:196–97 and attached images. I take the reference from Cristina Borreguero Beltrán, "Al servicio de Su Majestad el rey de España: Soldados, reclutamiento y vida cotidiana," in *Historia militar de España III: Los Borbones*, ed. Carmen Iglesias (Madrid: Ministerio de Defensa, 2014), 3:148–79.

33. Josep Fontana, *Historia de España*, vol. 6, *La época del liberalismo* (Madrid: Crítica-Marcial Pons, 2007).

34. Ibid., 38, 53, 95–106. See also Stanley G. Payne, *Politics and the Military in Modern Spain* (Stanford, CA: Stanford University Press, 1967); and Geoffrey Jensen, *Irrational Triumph: Cultural Despair, Military Nationalism and the Ideological Origins of Franco's Spain* (Reno: University of Nevada Press, 2002), 1–30.

35. See Jensen, *Irrational Triumph*, 23–30.

36. For an insider's point of view, see Gabriel Cardona, *El problema militar en España* (Madrid: Historia 16, 1990).

37. Luis Gonzalo Segura's first novel is *Un paso al frente* (Madrid: Tropo, 2014). See Carlos del Castillo, "El ejército expulsa al teniente Segura," *Público*, June 11, 2015, http://www.publico.es/politica/ejercito-expulsa-al-teniente-luis.html, and his blog, "Un paso al frente," http://blogs.publico.es/un-paso-al-frente/, accessed June 13, 2015.

38. Zaida Cantera and Irene Lozano, *No, mi general* (Barcelona: Plaza y Janés, 2015). For news on the case, see *El País*, http://elpais.com/tag/caso_zaida_cantera/a/, accessed June 13, 2015.

39. Guha, "The Small Voice of History," 12.

40. Tesillo, *Guerra de Chile*, 1r.

41. See Ortega, "Prólogo" to *Discurso de mi vida*; and García-Santo Tomás, "Ruptured Narratives," 84.

42. Homer, *Iliad*, trans. Fagles, 200; Homer, *Odyssey*, trans. Robert Fagles (New York: Penguin, 1996), 269, 512n. See also Christiane Sourvinou-Inwood, "Sisyphus," in *The Oxford Classical Dictionary*, 3rd rev. ed., ed. Simon Hornblower and Antony Spawforth (New York: Oxford University Press, 2005).

43. "It is all dying and end of the story" (todo es morir y acabóse la obra). Cervantes, *Don Quijote*, 1:833.

44. García-Santo Tomás, "Ruptured Narratives," 81.

45. Ovid, *Metamorphoses*, trans. Horace Gregory (New York: New American Library, 1958), 274.

BIBLIOGRAPHY

Abulafia, David, ed. *The French Descent into Renaissance Italy, 1494–95: Antecedents and Effects.* Aldershot: Variorum, 1995.

Adorno, Rolena. "Arms, Letters, and the Native Historian in Early Colonial Mexico." In *1492–1992: Re/discovering Colonial Writing,* ed. René Jara and Nicholas Spadaccini. Minneapolis: Prisma Institute, 1989. 201–24.

———. *The Polemics of Possession in Spanish American Narrative.* New Haven, CT: Yale University Press, 2007.

Adorno, Rolena, and Patrick Charles Pautz. *Álvar Núñez Cabeza de Vaca: His Account, His Life, and the Expedition of Pánfilo de Narváez.* 3 vols. Lincoln: University of Nebraska Press, 1999.

Aguirre, Miguel de. *Población de Valdivia: Motivos y medios para aquella fundación.* Lima: Jorge López de Herrera, 1647.

Aldana, Francisco de. *Poesías castellanas completas.* Ed. José Lara Garrido. 2nd ed. Madrid: Cátedra, 1997.

Alemán, Mateo. *Guzmán de Alfarache.* Ed. José María Micó. Madrid: Cátedra, 2001.

Alonso, Agustín. *Historia de las hazañas y hechos de Bernardo del Carpio.* Toledo: Pero López de Haro, 1585.

Alonso Cortés, Narciso. *Don Hernando de Acuña: Noticias biográficas.* Valladolid: Biblioteca Studium, 1975.

Álvarez Márquez, María del Carmen. *La impresión y el comercio de libros en la Sevilla del quinientos.* Seville: Universidad, 2007.

Álvarez de Toledo, Hernando. *Purén indómito.* Leipzig: A. Franck, 1862.

Amelang, James. *The Flight of Icarus: Artisan Autobiography in Early Modern Europe.* Stanford, CA: Stanford University Press, 1998.

———. "Popular Autobiography in Late Medieval and Early Modern Europe." In *1490: En el umbral de la modernidad. El Mediterráneo europeo y las ciudades en el tránsito de los siglos XV–XVI.* Valencia: Generalitat, 1994. 405–23.

———. "Saving the Self from Autobiography." In *Selbstzeugnisse in der Frühen Neuzeit: Individualisierungsweisen in interdisziplinärer Perspektive*, ed. Kaspar von Greyerz unter Mitarbeit von Elisabeth Müller-Luckner. Munich: Oldenbourg, 2007. 129–40.

Anderson, Linda. *Autobiography*. London: Routledge, 2001.

Andreini, Francesco. *Le bravure del capitano Spavento*. Venice: Giacomo Antonio Somasco, 1609.

Antei, Giorgio. *La invención del reino de Chile: Gerónimo de Vivar y los primeros cronistas chilenos*. Bogotá: Instituto Caro y Cuervo, 1989.

Antunes, Emanuel. *Primera parte de la baxada de los españoles de Francia en Normandía*. Rouen: George l'Oyselet, 1593; Antwerp: Giraldo Wolsschatio, 1622.

Aquila, August J. *Alonso de Ercilla y Zúñiga: A Basic Bibliography*. London: Grant & Cutler, 1975.

Arango, Tim. "Escaping Death in Northern Iraq." *New York Times*, September 3, 2014.

Arbolanche, Jerónimo de. *Las Abidas*. Zaragoza: Juan Millán, 1566.

Argensola, Bartolomé Leonardo de. *Conquista de las islas Malucas*. Madrid: Alonso Martín, 1609.

Ariosto, Ludovico. *Orlando furioso*. Trans. Jerónimo Jiménez de Urrea. Ed. Cesare Segre and María de las Nieves Muñiz. Madrid: Cátedra, 2002.

———. *Orlando furioso*. Trans. Barbara Reynolds. 2 vols. Baltimore: Penguin, 1975–77.

———. *Orlando furioso traduzido en Romance Castellano*. Trans. Jerónimo Jiménez de Urrea. Antwerp: Martinus Nutius, 1549.

———. *Orlando furioso de Lodovico Ariosto nuevamente traducido en prosa castellana*. Trans. Diego Vázquez de Contreras. Madrid: Juan Montoya, 1585.

———. *Orlando furioso de Ludivico Ariosto nuevamente traducido de verbo ad verbum del vulgar Toscano en el nuestro Castellano*. Trans. Hernando Alcocer. Toledo: Juan Ferrer, 1550.

———. *Roland Furieux, composé premierement en ryme Thuscane par messir Loys Arioste, noble Ferraroys, et maintenant traduict en prose Françoyse*. Lyon: Sulpice Sabon, 1543.

Askins, Arthur F. "El romance de Ercilla: A los veyntidos de Iulio." In *Homenaje a Eugenio Asensio*. Madrid: Gredos, 1988. 57–66.

Astrana Marín, Luis. *Vida ejemplar y heroica de Miguel de Cervantes*. 7 vols. Madrid: Instituto Editorial Reus, 1948–58.

Avellaneda, José Ignacio. *The Conquerors of the New Kingdom of Granada*. Albuquerque: University of New Mexico Press, 1995.

Ávila y Zúñiga, Luis de. *Comentario de la guerra de Alemaña*. Venice: Thomás de Gornoça, 1548.

Aznar de Polanco, Juan Claudio. *Arte de escribir*. Madrid: Manuel Ruiz de Murga, 1719.

Bakhtin, Mikhail. *The Dialogic Imagination*. Ed. Michael Holquist. Austin: University of Texas Press, 1981.

———. *Rabelais and His World*. Bloomington: Indiana University Press, 1984.

Barco Centenera, Martín del. *Argentina y conquista del Río de la Plata*. Lisbon: Pedro Craesbeck, 1602.

Barrionuevo, Jerónimo de. *Avisos*. 4 vols. Madrid: Impresor de Cámara, 1892.

Barros Arana, Diego. *Historia general de Chile*. 16 vols. Santiago: Centro de Estudios Barros Arana, 1999–.

Basbanes, Nicholas. *On Paper*. New York: Alfred Knopf, 2013.

Bataillon, Marcel. *Pícaros y picaresca*. Madrid: Taurus, 1969.

Beer, Marina, Amedeo Quondam, et al., eds. *Guerre in ottava rima*. 4 vols. Modena: Panini, 1989.

Bhabha, Homi. "Of Mimicry and Man: The Ambivalence of Colonial Discourse." *October* 28 (1984): 125–33.

Billson, Marcus. "The Memoir: New Perspectives on a Forgotten Genre." *Genre* 10.2 (1977): 259–82.

Black, Jeremy. *Rethinking Military History*. London: Routledge, 2004.

Boiardo, Matteo Maria. *Orlando innamorato*. Ed. Riccardo Bruscagli. Torino: Einaudi, 1996.

———. *Los tres libros de Mattheo Maria Boyardo, llamados Orlando Enamorado, traducidos en Castellano*. Trans. Francisco Garrido de Villena. Valencia: Joan Mey, 1555.

Bolea de Castro, Martín. *Libro de Orlando determinado que prosigue la materia de Orlando el Enamorado*. Lérida: Miguel Prats, 1578.

Bosch Cantallops, Margarita. "Contribución al estudio de la imprenta en Valencia en el siglo XVI." 2 vols. PhD diss., Universidad Complutense de Madrid, 1989.

Bourdieu, Pierre. *La Distinction: Critique Sociale du Jugement*. Paris: Minuit, 1979.

———. *Outline of a Theory of Practice*. Trans. Richard Nice. Cambridge: Cambridge University Press, 1977.

Bouza, Fernando. *Corre manuscrito: Una historia cultural del Siglo de Oro*. Madrid: Marcial Pons, 2001.

———. *Imagen y propaganda: Capítulos de historia cultural del reinado de Felipe II*. Madrid: Akal, 1998.

———. *Palabra e imagen en la corte: Cultura oral y visual de la nobleza en el Siglo de Oro*. Madrid: Abada, 2003.

———. "Servidumbres de la soberana grandeza: Criticar al rey en la corte de Felipe II." In *Imágenes históricas de Felipe II*. Coordinated by Alfredo Alvar Ezquerra. Alcalá: Centro de Estudios Cervantinos, 2000.

Braudel, Fernand. *The Mediterranean and the Mediterranean World in the Age of Philip II*. 2 vols. New York: Harper and Row, 1972.

Brocato, Linde. "Publishing, Typography, and Politics: Mena's Works and the Parallel Editions of Antwerp, 1552." CAS paper, directed by Prof. D. W. Krummel. University of Illinois at Urbana-Champaign, 2011.

Burke, Peter. *Popular Culture in Early Modern Europe*. 3rd ed. Burlington, VT: Ashgate, 2009.

Butler, Judith. *Frames of War: When Is Life Grievable?* London: Verso, 2009.

Caesar, Julius. *Los comentarios de Gayo Iulio Cesar*. Trans. Diego López de Toledo. Paris: Arnold Burkmann, 1549.

Calvete de Estrella, Juan Cristóbal. *De Aphrodisio expugnato quod vulgo Aphricam vocant: Commentarius*. Amberes: Martín Nucio, 1551.

———. *La conquista de la ciudad de África en Berbería*. Trans. Diego Gracián. Salamanca: Juan de Canova, 1558.

———. *El felicíssimo viaje del muy alto y muy poderoso Príncipe don Phelippe*. Ed. Paloma Cuenca. Madrid: Sociedad Estatal para la Conmemoración de los Centenarios de Felipe II y Carlos V, 2001.

Camões, Luís de. *Os Lusíadas*. Ed. Álvaro Júlio da Costa Pimpão. Lisbon: Instituto Camões, 2000.

———. *The Lusiads*. Trans. Landeg White. Oxford: Oxford World Classics, 2008.

Campo Jesús, Luis de. *Jerónimo de Arbolanche, poeta del siglo XVI: Su vida y su obra*. Pamplona: La acción social, 1964.

Canavaggio, Jean. *Cervantes*. Madrid: Espasa-Calpe, 2003.

Cancionero de Juan de Escobedo. (Ms. 330 Biblioteca Real Academia Española). Ed. Marcial Rubio Arquez. Pisa: ETS, 2004.

Cancionero de poesías varias: Ms. Reginensis Latini 1635 de la Biblioteca Vaticana. Ed. José Labrador Herraiz, Ralph A. DiFranco, and Carmen Parrilla García. Almería: Universidad de Almería, 2008.

Cantera, Zaida, and Irene Lozano. *No, mi general*. Barcelona: Plaza y Janés, 2015.

Caravaggi, Giovanni, ed. *La espada y la pluma: Il mondo militare nella Lombardia spagnola cinquecentesca*. Viareggio, Lucca: Mauro Baroni, 2000.

Cardona, Gabriel. *El problema militar en España*. Madrid: Historia 16, 1990.

Carella, Angela. "Urbino e le Marche." In *Letteratura italiana*. Ed. Alberto Asor Rosa. Torino: Einaudi, 1988. 2.1:473–520.

Cassol, Alessandro. *Vita e scrittura: Autobiografie di soldati spagnoli del Siglo de Oro*. Milano: LED, 2000.

Catálogo de pliegos sueltos poéticos de la Biblioteca Nacional: Siglo XVII. Madrid: Universidad de Alcalá, 1998.

Cátedra, Pedro. *Invención, difusión y recepción de la literatura popular impresa (siglo XVI)*. Mérida: Editora Regional, 2002.

Castellanos, Juan de. *Historia del Reino de Nueva Granada*. 2 vols. Ed. Antonio Paz y Meliá. Madrid: Pérez Dubrull, 1886.

Castiglione, Baldassarre. *The Book of the Courtier*. Ed. and trans. George Bull. London: Penguin, 2011.

———. *The Book of the Courtier*. Ed. Daniel Javitch. New York: Norton, 2002.

Castillo, Carlos del. "El ejército expulsa al teniente Segura." *Público*, June 11, 2015. http://www.publico.es/politica/ejercito-expulsa-al-teniente-luis.html, accessed June 13, 2015.

Castillo Gómez, Antonio. *Entre la pluma y la pared: Una historia social de la escritura en el Siglo de Oro*. Madrid: Akal, 2006.

———. *Escribir y leer en el siglo de Cervantes*. Barcelona: Gedisa, 1999.

Castro, Adolfo de. *Poetas líricos de los siglos XVI y XVII*. BAE 42. Madrid: Rivadeneyra, 1854.

Castro-Ibaseta, Javier. "Beware the Poetry: Political Satire and the Emergence of the Spanish Public Sphere (1600–1645)." Unpublished manuscript, University of Michigan.

———. "Mentidero de Madrid: La Corte como comedia." In *Opinión pública y espacio urbano en la Edad Moderna*, ed. Antonio Castillo Gómez, James Amelang, and Carmen Serrano Sánchez. Gijón: Trea, 2010.

———. "Monarquía satírica: Poética de la caída del Conde-Duque de Olivares." PhD diss., Universidad Autónoma de Madrid, 2008.

Cavallo, Jo Ann. *The Romance Epics of Boiardo, Ariosto, and Tasso: From Public Duty to Private Pleasure*. Toronto: University of Toronto Press, 2004.

Certeau, Michel de. *The Practice of Everyday Life*. Trans. Steven Rendall. Berkeley: University of California Press, 1988.

Cervantes, Miguel de. *Don Quijote de la Mancha*. Ed. Francisco Rico. Barcelona: Instituto Cervantes/Editorial Crítica, 1999.

———. *Don Quixote*. Trans. Edith Grossman. New York: Harper Collins, 2003.

———. *Exemplary Stories*. Trans. Lesley Lipson. Oxford: Oxford University Press, 1998.

———. *Novelas ejemplares*. Ed. Harry Sieber. Madrid: Cátedra, 2001.

———. *Poesías completas*. Ed. Vicente Gaos. Madrid: Castalia, 1981.

Céspedes y Meneses, Gonzalo de. *Varia fortuna del soldado Píndaro*. 2 vols. Ed. Arsenio Pacheco. Madrid: Espasa-Calpe, 1975.

Chartier, Roger. *Cultural History: Between Practices and Representations*. Trans. Lydia G. Cochrane. Cambridge: Polity Press, 1988.

———. "Culture as Appropriation: Popular Cultural Uses in Early Modern France." In *Understanding Popular Culture: Europe from the Middle Ages to the 19th Century*. Ed. Steven L. Kaplan. The Hague: 1984. 229–54.

———. *Inscription and Erasure: Literature and Written Culture from the Eleventh to the Eighteenth Century*. Trans. Arthur Goldhammer. Philadelphia: University of Pennsylvania Press, 2007.

———. *The Order of Books: Readers, Authors, and Libraries in Europe Between the Fourteenth and Eighteenth Centuries*. Stanford, CA: Stanford University Press, 1994.

Chevalier, Maxime. *L'Arioste en Espagne (1530–1650): Recherches sur l'influence du "Roland furieux."* Bordeaux: Institute d'Études Ibériques et Ibéro-Américaines, 1966.

———. *Lectura y lectores en la España de los siglos XVI y XVII*. Madrid: Turner, 1976.

Cieza de León, Pedro. *La crónica del Perú*. Madrid: Historia 16, 1984.

Civale, Gianclaudio. *Guerrieri di Cristo: Inquisitori, gesuiti e soldati alla battaglia di Lepanto*. Milano: Unicolpi, 2009.

———. "Tunisi spagnola tra violenza e coesistenza (1573–74)." *Mediterranea: Ricerche storiche* 21 (2011): 51–88.

Contreras, Alonso de. *Discurso de mi vida*. Ed. Henry Ettinghausen. Madrid: Espasa-Calpe, 1988.

Correia, Gaspar. *Lendas da India*. Ed. Rodrigo José de Lima Felner. Lisbon: Academia Real das Ciências, 1925.

Cortright, David. *Soldiers in Revolt: GI Resistance During the Vietnam War*. Chicago: Haymarket Books, 2005.

Cossío, José María de, ed. *Autobiografías de soldados (siglo XVII)*. BAE 90. Madrid: Atlas, 1956.

Cotarelo y Mori, Emilio. *Colección de entremeses, loas, jácaras, mojigangas*. 2 vols. Madrid: Bailly-Bailliére, 1911.

Covarrubias y Orozco, Sebastián de. *Tesoro de la lengua castellana o española*. Madrid: Melchor Sánchez, 1611. http://www.rae.es, July 20, 2015.

Croce, Benedetto. *España en la via italiana del Renacimiento*. Buenos Aires: Imán, 1945.

Crónica del Gran Capitán Gonzalo Hernández de Córdoba y Aguilar; con la vida del caballero Diego García de Paredes. Seville: Andrea Pescioni, 1580, 1582; Alcalá, 1584.

Cruz, Anne. *Discourses of Poverty: Social Reform and the Picaresque Novel in Early Modern Spain*. Toronto: University of Toronto Press, 1999.

Cruz, Anne, and Rosilie Hernández, eds. *Women's Literacy in Early Modern Spain and the New World*. Burlington, VT: Ashgate, 2011.

Culler, Jonathan. *The Pursuit of Signs: Semiotics, Literature, Deconstruction*. Ithaca, NY: Cornell University Press, 1981.

Dandelet, Thomas. *Spain in Italy: Politics, Society, Religion, 1500–1700*. Leiden: Brill, 2007.

———. *Spanish Rome, 1500–1700*. New Haven, CT: Yale University Press, 2001.

Danvila y Collado, Manuel. *Reinado de Carlos III*. Madrid: El Progreso, 1893.

Darnton, Robert. *The Great Cat Massacre and Other Episodes in French Cultural History*. New York: Vintage, 1984.

Davis, Elizabeth B. *Myth and Identity in the Epic of Imperial Spain*. Columbia: University of Missouri Press, 2000.

Davis, Natalie Zemon. *Society and Culture in Early Modern France: Eight Essays*. Stanford, CA: Stanford University Press, 1975.

Defourneaux, Marcelin. *Vida cotidiana en la España del Siglo de Oro*. Barcelona: Arcos Vergara, 1983.

Deleito y Piñuela, José. *El declinar de la monarquía española*. Madrid: Espasa-Calpe, 1947.

De Armas, Frederick. "Cervantes and the Italian Renaissance." In *Cambridge Companion to Cervantes*, ed. Anthony J. Cascardi. Cambridge: Cambridge University Press, 2002. 32–57.

———. "The Exhilaration of Italy." In *Quixotic Frescoes: Cervantes and Italian Renaissance Art*. Toronto: University of Toronto Press, 2006. 3–13.

De Man, Paul "Autobiography as De-Facement." *MLN* 94.5 (1979): 919–30.

Díaz del Castillo, Bernal. *The Conquest of New Spain*. Trans. Alfred Maudslay. Nendeln: Kraus, 1967.

———. *Historia verdadera de la conquista de la Nueva España*. Ed. Joaquín Ramírez Cabañas. Mexico: Porrúa, 1994.

Díez Borque, José María. "Libros de poesía en bibliotecas del Siglo de Oro (1600–1650)." *Revista de Filología Española* 90.1 (2010): 69–98.

Domenichelli, Mario. *Cavaliere e gentiluomo: Saggio sulla cultura aristo-cratica in Europa (1513–1915)*. Roma: Bulzoni, 2002.

Domínguez Flores, María Antonia. "Alonso de Contreras: Discurso de mi vida. Edición y estudio." PhD diss., Universidad Complutense de Madrid, 2007.

Duque de Estrada, Diego. *Comentarios del desengañado de sí mismo: Vida del mismo autor*. Madrid: Castalia, 1982.

Durán, Agustín. *Romancero general*. 2 vols. BAE 10, 16. Madrid: Rivad-eneyra, 1851.

Eguiluz, Martín de. *Milicia, discurso y regla militar*. Brussels, 1596.

Eisenberg, Daniel. *Romances of Chivalry in the Spanish Golden Age*. New-ark, DE: Juan de la Cuesta, 1982.

Eisenstein, Elizabeth. *The Printing Press as an Agent of Change*. Cambridge: Cambridge University Press, 1979.

Ercilla, Alonso de. *La Araucana*. Ed. Isaías Lerner. Madrid: Cátedra, 1993.

———. *The Araucaniad*. Trans. Charles Maxwell Lancaster and Paul Thomas Manchester. Nashville: Vanderbilt University Press, 1945.

———. *Historiale beschrijvinghe der goudtrijcke landen in Chile ende Arauco, ende andere provincien in Chili ghelegen*. Trans. Isaac Janszo-nius. Rotterdam: J. v. Waesberghe, 1619.

Escalante, Bernardino de. *Diálogos del Arte militar*. Seville: A. Pescioni, 1583.

Espinel, Vicente. *Diversas rimas*. Madrid: Luis Sánchez, 1591.

Espino López, Antonio. *Guerra y cultura en la época moderna*. Madrid: Ministerio de Defensa, 2001.

Espinosa, Nicolás. *La segunda parte del Orlando*. Antwerp: Martinus Nutius, 1556.

Esteve Barba, Francisco, ed. *Crónicas del reino de Chile*. BAE 131. Madrid: Atlas, 1960.

Ettinghausen, Henry. "Alonso de Contreras: Un épisode de sa vie." *Bulletin Hispanique* 77.3–4 (1975): 293–318.

———. *La guerra dels Segadors a través de la premsa de l'època*. 4 vols. Bar-celona: Curial, 1993.

———. "Informació, comunicació i poder a l'Espanya del segle XVII." *Manuscrits* 23 (2005): 45–58.

Farge, Arlette. *Des lieux pour l'histoire*. Paris: Seuil, 1997.

Firbas, Paul, ed. *Épica y colonia: Ensayos sobre el género épico en Latinoa-mérica (siglos XVI y XVII)*. Lima: Universidad Nacional Mayor de San Marcos, 2008.

———. "El sueño en la trama épica: La visión corográfica de San Quintín en *La Araucana* de Ercilla." In *Los sueños en la cultura iberoamericana: Siglos XVI–XVIII*, ed. Sonia Rose, Peer Schmidt, and Gregor Weber. Seville: CSIC, 2011. 385–407.

Firrufino, Julio César. *Plático manual y breve compendio de artillería.* Madrid: Viuda de Alonso Martín, 1626.

Fontana, Josep. *Historia de España. Vol. 6, La época del liberalismo.* Madrid: Crítica-Marcial Pons, 2007.

Foucault, Michel. "What Is an Author?" In *The Essential Works of Michel Foucault, 1954–1984.* New York: New Press, 1997–2001. 2:205–22.

Francomano, Emily. "'Puse un sobreescripto': Manuscript, Print and the Material Epistolarity of *Cárcel de Amor.*" *Fifteenth-Century Studies* 36 (2011): 25–48.

Frow, John. *Cultural Studies and Cultural Value.* Oxford: Oxford University Press, 1995.

Fuchs, Barbara. "Dismantling Heroism: The Exhaustion of War in Don Quijote." *PMLA* 124.5 (2009): 1842–46.

———. *Mimesis and Empire: The New World, Islam, and European Identities.* Cambridge: Cambridge University Press, 2001.

———. *Romance.* New York: Routledge, 2004.

———. "Traveling Epic: Translating Ercilla's *La Araucana* in the Old World." *Journal of Medieval and Early Modern Studies* 36.2 (Spring 2006): 379–95.

Fucilla, Joseph. *Relaciones hispano-italianas.* Madrid: CSIC, 1953.

Fuentes, Diego de. *Conquista de África donde se hallarán agora nuevamente recopiladas por Diego de Fuentes muchas y muy notables hazañas de particulares caballeros.* Anvers: Philippo Nutio, 1570.

Fussell, Paul. *The Great War and Modern Memory.* Oxford: Oxford University Press, 1975.

Garcés, María Antonia. *Cervantes in Algiers: A Captive's Tale.* Nashville: Vanderbilt University Press, 2002.

García de Alarcón, Gaspar. *La victoriosa conquista que don Álvaro Bazán marqués de Sancta Cruz, General dela armada, y ejército de su Mag. hizo en las Islas de los Azores, el año de 1583.* Valencia: Herederos de Joan Navarro, 1585.

García Cerezeda, Martín. *Tratado de las campañas y otros acontecimientos de los ejércitos del Emperador Carlos V en Italia, Francia, Austria, Berbería y Grecia, desde 1521 hasta 1545.* 3 vols. Madrid: Sociedad de Bibliófilos Españoles, 1873.

García de la Concha, Víctor, ed. *Armas y letras en el Siglo de Oro español: Antología poética.* Madrid: Ministerio de Defensa, 1998.

García de Enterría, M. Cruz. *Sociedad y poesía de cordel en el Barroco.* Madrid: Taurus, 1973.

García Hernán, David. *La cultura de la guerra y el teatro del Siglo de Oro.* Madrid: Silex, 2006.

García Hernán, Enrique. *La armada española en la monarquía de Felipe II y la defensa del Mediterráneo.* Madrid: Tempo, 1995.

———. "La conquista y pérdida de Túnez por don Juan de Austria (1573–1574)." *Annali di Storia militare europea* 2 (2010): 39–95.

———. "Don Sancho de Londoño: Perfil biográfico." *Revista de Historia Moderna* (Alicante) 22 (2004): 7–72.

García Hernán, Enrique, and Davide Maffi, eds. *Guerra y sociedad en la Monarquía Hispánica: Política, estrategia y cultura en al Europa moderna (1500–1700).* Madrid: CSIC, 2006.

García Morales, J. "Las trasnochadas de la pluma, de don Sancho de de Londoño." In *Homenaje a don Agustín Millares Carlo.* Las Palmas de Gran Canaria: Confederación Española de Cajas de Ahorros, 1975. 1:637–60.

García de Paredes, Diego. *Breve suma de la vida y hechos de Diego García de Paredes la qual él mismo escribió y la dejó firmada de su nombre, como al fin della parece.* Zaragoza: 1582. Also in *Crónicas del Gran Capitán.* Ed. Antonio Rodríguez Villa. BAE 10. Madrid: 1908. 235–69.

García-Santo Tomás, Enrique. *Espacio urbano y creación literaria en el Madrid de Felipe IV.* Madrid: Iberoamericana/Vervuert, 2004.

———. *Modernidad bajo sospecha: Salas Barbadillo y la cultura material del siglo XVII.* Madrid: CSIC, 2008.

———. "Ruptured Narratives: Tracing Defeat in Diego Duque de Estrada's *Comentarios del desengañado de sí mismo* (1614–1645)." *eHumanista* 17 (2011): 78–98.

Garibay, Esteban de. *Discurso de mi vida.* Ed. Jesús Moya. Bilbao: Euskal Herriko Unibertsitatea, 1999.

Garrido de Villena, Francisco. *El verdadero suceso de la famosa batalla de Roncesvalles, con la muerte de los doce pares de Francia.* Valencia: Joan Mey, 1555.

Gayangos, Pascual de. *Memorias del cautivo de la Goleta de Túnez (el alférez Pedro de Aguilar).* Madrid: Sociedad de Bibliófilos Españoles, 1875.

Gaylord, Mary. *The Historical Prose of Fernando de Herrera.* London: Tamesis, 1970.

———. "El lenguaje de la conquista y la conquista del lenguaje en las poéticas españolas del Siglo de Oro." In *Actas del IX Congreso de la Asociación Internacional de Hispanistas.* Frankfurt: Verwuert, 1989. 469–75.

———. "Spain's Renaissance Conquests and the Retroping of Identity." *Journal of Hispanic Philology* 16 (1992): 125–36.

Gelabert, Juan Eloy. "Lectura y escritura en una ciudad provinciana del siglo 16: Santiago de Compostela." *Bulletin hispanique* 84 (1982): 264–90.

Geneste, Pierre. *Essai sur la vie et l'oeuvre de Jerónimo de Urrea.* Lille: Université de Lille III, 1975.

Gillet, Joseph. *Propalladia and Other Works of Bartolomé de Torres Naharro. 4 vols.* Menasha: George Banta, 1943–61.

Giner, Miguel. *El sitio y toma de Anvers.* Milán: Pacífico Poncio, 1587.

Giono, Jean. *The Battle of Pavia.* Trans. A. E. Murch. London: Owen, 1965.

Giovio, Paolo. *Diálogo de las empresas militares y amorosas.* Trans. Alonso de Ulloa. Lyon: Guillem Rouville, 1561.

———. *Libro de las historias y cosas acontecidas en Alemaña, España, Francia, Italia, etc.* Trans. Antonio Joan Villafranca. Valencia: Juan Mey, 1562.

———. *Pavli Iovii novocomensis episcopi nvcerini historiarvm svi temporis Tomus Primus.* Florencia: In officina Laurentii Torrentini Dvcalis Typographi, 1550.

Goic, Cedomil. *Letras del Reino de Chile.* Madrid: Iberoamericana/Vervuert, 2006.

Göllner, Carl. *Turcica.* 3 vols. Bucharest: Editura Academiei, 1961–68.

Gómez Dovale, María América. "Una fuente inédita sobre la guerra de Flandes." PhD diss., Universidad Complutense de Madrid, 1957.

Góngora, Luis de. *Romances.* Ed. Antonio Carreño. Madrid: Cátedra, 2000.

Góngora, Mario. *Los grupos de conquistadores en Tierra Firme (1509–1532).* Santiago de Chile: Editorial Universitaria, 1962.

Góngora Marmolejo, Alonso de. *Historia de Chile desde su descubrimiento hasta 1575.* In Esteve Barba, 75–224.

———. *Historia de todas las cosas que han acaecido en el reino de Chile.* Ed. Miguel Donoso Rodríguez. Madrid: Iberoamericana/Vervuert, 2010.

González Castrillo, Ricardo. "La pérdida de La Goleta y Túnez en 1574 y otros sucesos de historia otomana, narrados por un testigo presencial: Alonso de Salamanca." *Anaquel de Estudios Árabes* 3 (1992): 247–86.

González de León, Fernando. "Doctors of the Military Discipline: Technical Expertise and the Paradigm of the Spanish Soldier in the Early Modern Period." *Sixteenth Century Journal* 27.1 (1996): 61–85.

———. *The Road to Rocroi: Class, Culture and Command in the Spanish Army of Flanders, 1567–1659.* Leiden: Brill, 2009.

———. "*Soldados pláticos* and *caballeros*: The Social Dimensions of Ethics in the Early Modern Spanish Army." In *The Chivalric Ethos and the Development of Military Profesionalism,* ed. D. J. B. Trim. Boston: Brill, 2003. 235–68.

González de Nájera, Alonso. *Desengaño y reparo de la guerra del reino de Chile*. Ed. José Toribio Medina. Santiago: Imprenta Ercilla, 1889.

González Ollé, Fernando. "*Guerras civiles de Flandes*: Poema épico inédito." *Boletín de la Real Academia Española* 45 (1965): 141–84.

———. "Jerónimo de Arbolanche." In *Las Abidas*. By Jerónimo de Arbolanche. Madrid: CSIC, 1969. 1–25.

González Palencia, Ángel. *Don Luis de Ávila y Zúñiga: Gentilhombre de Carlos V*. Madrid: Estanislao Maestre, 1932.

González Sánchez, Carlos Alberto. *New World Literacy: Writing and Culture Across the Atlantic*. Lewisburg, PA: Bucknell University Press, 2011.

Griffin, Clive. *The Crombergers of Seville: The History of a Printing Dynasty*. Oxford: Clarendon Press, 1988.

Guha, Ranajit. *Elementary Aspects of Peasant Insurgency in Colonial India*. Durham, NC: Duke University Press, 1999.

———. "The Small Voice of History." In *Subaltern Studies IX: Writings on South Asian History and Society*, ed. Shahid Amin and Dipesh Chakrabarty. Delhi: Oxford University Press, 1996.

Guicciardini, Francesco. *Storia d'Italia*. Torino: Einaudi, 1971.

———. *Storie fiorentine*. Bari: Laterza, 1931.

Hale, John. *Renaissance War Studies*. London: Hambledon, 1983.

———. *War and Society in Renaissance Europe, 1450–1620*. Montreal: McGill-Queen's University Press, 1998.

Hall, Bert S. *Weapons and Warfare in Renaissance Europe*. Baltimore: Johns Hopkins University Press, 1997.

Hämäläinen, Pekka. *Comanche Empire*. New Haven, CT: Yale University Press, 2008.

Hampe Martínez, Teodoro. *Bibliotecas privadas en el mundo colonial*. Frankfurt: Iberoamericana/Vervuert, 1996.

Hanson, Victor Davis. *The Father of Us All: War and History, Ancient and Modern*. New York: Bloomsbury, 2010.

Harari, Yuval Noah. *Renaissance Military Memoirs: War, History, and Identity, 1450–1600*. Woodbridge: Boydell, 2004.

Hathaway, Jane, ed. *Rebellion, Repression, Reinvention: Mutiny in Comparative Perspective*. Westport, CT: Praeger, 2001.

Hempfer, Klaus W., ed. *Ritterepik der Renaissance*. Stuttgart: Franz Steiner, 1989.

Hernández Rubio, José María. *Poetas soldados españoles*. Madrid: Editora Nacional, [1945].

Herrera, Fernando de. *Anotaciones a la poesía de Garcilaso*. Ed. Inoria Pepe and José María Reyes. Madrid: Cátedra, 2001.

Hershenzon, Daniel. "Early Modern Spain and the Creation of the Mediterranean: Captivity, Commerce, and Knowledge." PhD diss., University of Michigan, Ann Arbor, 2011.

Hess, Andrew C. "The Battle of Lepanto and Its Place in Mediterranean History." *Past and Present* 57 (1972): 53–73.

———. *The Forgotten Frontier: A History of the Sixteenth-Century Ibero-African Frontier.* Chicago: University of Chicago Press, 1978.

Hesse, José, ed. *Romancero de germanía.* Madrid: Taurus, 1967.

Hierro, Baltasar del. *Destruición de África.* Seville: Sebastián Trujillo, 1560.

———. *Libro y primera parte de los victoriosos hechos del muy valeroso caballero Don Álvaro de Bazán.* Granada: René Rabut, 1561.

———. *Triumphos y grandes recebimientos de la insigne ciudad de Barcelona a la venida del famosíssimo Phelipe rey de las Españas &c., con la entrada de los sereníssimos príncipes de Bohemia.* Barcelona: Jaime Cortey. Véndese en casa de Joan Trinxer, 1564.

Hill, John M., ed. *Poesías germanescas.* Bloomington: Indiana University Press, 1945.

Hobsbawm, Eric. *Primitive Rebels: Studies in Archaic Forms of Social Movement in the 19th and 20th Centuries.* New York: Frederick Praeger, 1963.

Homer. *Iliad.* Trans. Robert Fagles. New York: Penguin, 1990.

———. *Odyssey.* Trans. Robert Fagles. New York: Penguin, 1996.

Horace. *Satires. Epistles. The Ars of Poetry.* LCL 194. Cambridge, MA: Harvard University Press, 1929.

Houston, R. A. *Literacy in Early Modern Europe: Culture and Education, 1500–1800.* London: Longman, 1988.

Hunter, Richard. "Virgil's Ecl. I and the Origins of Pastoral." In *Brill's Companion to Greek and Latin Pastoral,* ed. Marco Fantuzzi and Theodore Papanghelis. Leiden: Brill, 2006.

Iglesias, Carmen, ed. *Historia militar de España III: Los Borbones.* Madrid: Ministerio de Defensa, 2014.

Irigoyen-García, Javier. "Jerónimo de Arbolanche's *Las Abidas* (1566) and the Mythical Origins of Spain." *Symposium* 67.2 (2013): 85–97.

Isaba, Marcos de. *Cuerpo enfermo de la milicia española, con Discursos y avisos para que pueda ser curado, útiles y de provecho.* Madrid: Guillermo Druy, 1594.

Jacobs, Beverly. "Social Provocation and Self-Justification in the *Vida* of Captain Alonso de Contreras." *Hispanic Review* 51.3 (1983): 303–19.

Jaque, Miguel de. *Viaje de las Indias Orientales y Occidentales.* Seville: Renacimiento, 2008.

Jara, Álvaro. *Guerra y sociedad en Chile.* Santiago: Editorial Universitaria, 1971.

Javitch, Daniel. *Proclaiming a Classic: The Canonization of "Orlando furioso."* Princeton, NJ: Princeton University Press, 1991.

Jensen, Geoffrey. *Irrational Triumph: Cultural Despair, Military Nationalism and the Ideological Origins of Franco's Spain.* Reno: University of Nevada Press, 2002.

Jiménez de Quesada, Gonzalo. *El Antijovio.* Ed. Rafael Torres Quintero. Bogotá: Instituto Caro y Cuervo, 1952.

Jiménez de Urrea, Jerónimo, trans. *Orlando furioso dirigido al Príncipe don Philipe nuestro señor, traducido en Romance Castellano.* Amberes: Martín Nucio, 1549.

———. *Vitorioso Carlos Quinto.* Ca. 1569. BNE MSS/1,469.

Johns, Adrian. "How to Acknowledge a Revolution." *American Historical Review* 107 (2002): 120.

Juliá Martínez, Eduardo. "Nuevos datos sobre Rey de Artieda." *Boletín de la RAE* 20 (1930): 667–86.

Kagan, Richard. *Lucrecia's Dreams: Politics and Prophecy in Sixteenth-Century Spain.* Berkeley: University of California Press, 1995.

———. *Students and Society in Early Modern Spain.* Baltimore: Johns Hopkins University Press, 1974.

Kagan, Richard, and Abigail Dyer. *Inquisitorial Inquiries: Brief Lives of Secret Jews and Other Heretics.* Baltimore: Johns Hopkins University Press, 2011.

Keegan, John. *The Face of Battle.* New York: Barnes and Noble, 1976.

Kenney, E. J., and W. V. Clausen, eds. *The Cambridge History of Classical Literature.* Vol. 2. Cambridge: Cambridge University Press, 1982.

Laberinto amoroso. Ed. Juan de Chen. Barcelona: Sebastián de Cormellas, 1618.

Lagos, Ramona. "El incumplimiento de la programación épica en *La Araucana.*" *Cuadernos Americanos* 238 (1981): 157–91.

Lara Garrido, José. *Los mejores plectros: Teoría y práctica de la épica culta en el Siglo de Oro.* Málaga: Analecta Malacitana, 1999.

———. "*Palma de Marte y lauro de Apolo*: La poesía del 'oficio militar' en Francisco de Aldana y Cristóbal de Virués." In Caravaggi, 281–346.

Larquié, Claude. "L'alphabétisation à Madrid en 1650." *Revue d'histoire moderne et contemporaine* 28 (1981): 132–57.

Las Casas, Bartolomé de. *Brevísima relación de la destruición de las Indias.* Ed. José Miguel Martínez Torrejón. Barcelona: Galaxia Gutenberg, 2009.

Lawrance, J. N. H. "The Spread of Lay Literacy in Late Medieval Castile." *Bulletin of Hispanic Studies* 62.1 (1985): 79–94.

Lazarillo de Tormes. Ed. Francisco Rico. Madrid: Cátedra, 1990.

Lejeune, Philippe. *On Autobiography*. Trans. Katherine Leary. Minneapolis: University of Minnesota Press, 1989.

———. *Le pacte autobiographique*. Paris: Seuil, 1975.

León Portocarrero, Pedro de. *Descripción del virreinato del Perú*. Lima: Universidad Ricardo Palma, 2009.

Leonard, Irving. *Books of the Brave*. Berkeley: University of California Press, 1992.

Lerner, Isaías. "Ercilla y Lucano." In *Hommage á Robert Jammes*. 3 vols. Ed. Francis Cerdan. Toulouse: Presses Universitaires du Mirail, 1994. 683–91.

———. "Felipe II y Alonso de Ercilla." *Edad de Oro* 18 (1999): 87–101.

———. Introduction to *La Araucana*. By Alonso de Ercilla. Madrid: Cátedra, 1998.

Levisi, Margarita. *Autobiografías del Siglo de Oro: Alonso de Contreras, Jerónimo de Pasamonte y Miguel de Castro*. Madrid: Sociedad General Española de Librería, 1984.

———. "Golden Age Autobiography: The Soldiers." In *Autobiography in Early Modern Spain*, ed. Nicholas Spadaccini and Jenaro Talens. Minneapolis: Prisma Institute, 1988.

Lifton, Robert Jay. *Home from War: Learning from Vietnam Veterans*. Boston: Beacon Press, 1973.

Lloyd, Howell A. *The Rouen Campaign, 1590–1592: Politics, Warfare and the Early Modern State*. Oxford: Clarendon Press, 1973.

Loarca, Miguel de. *Relación del viaje que hecimos a la China desde la ciudad de Manila en las del poniente año de 1575*. In *La China en España*, ed. Dolors Folch Fornesa. http://www.upf.edu/asia/projectes/che/s16/loarca.htm, accessed June 5, 2014.

Lockhart, James. *The Men of Cajamarca: A Social and Biographical Study of the First Conquerors of Peru*. Austin: University of Texas Press, 1972.

Londoño, Sancho de. *Discurso sobre la forma de reducir la disciplina militar a mejor y antiguo estado*. Brussels: Velpius, 1589.

———. *Poesías del Maestre de Campo don Sancho de Londoño*. BNE, MSS/21,738.

López de Toro, José. *Los poetas de Lepanto*. Madrid: Instituto Histórico de Marina, 1950.

López de Velasco, Juan. *Demarcación y división de las Indias*. Ca. 1575. JCB Ms.

Lorge, Peter. *The Asian Military Revolution*. Cambridge: Cambridge University Press, 2008.

Lucía Megías, José Manuel. *Imprenta y libros de caballerías*. Madrid: Ollero y Ramos, 2002.

Machiavelli, Niccolò. *Art of War.* Trans. Christopher Lynch. Chicago: University of Chicago Press, 2003.

———. *The Prince.* Ed. Quentin Skinner and Russell Price. Cambridge: Cambridge University Press, 1988.

MacKay, Ruth. *The Limits of Royal Authority: Resistance and Obedience in Seventeenth-Century Castile.* Cambridge: Cambridge University Press, 1999.

Mallett, Michael. "The Transformation of War, 1494–1530." In Shaw.

Mallett, Michael, and John Hale. *The Military Organization of a Renaissance State: Venice c. 1400 to 1617.* Cambridge: Cambridge University Press, 1984.

Mallett, Michael, and Christine Shaw. *The Italian Wars, 1494–1559.* Harlow: Pearson, 2012.

Maravall, José Antonio. *El humanismo de las armas en Don Quijote.* Madrid: Instituto de Estudios Políticos, 1948.

———. *Utopía y contrautopía en el Quijote.* Santiago de Compostela: Pico Sacro, 1976.

Mariño de Lobera, Pedro. *Crónica del reino de Chile.* In Esteve Barba, 225–562.

Mármol Carvajal, Luis de. *Libro tercero y segundo volumen de la Descripción general de África.* Granada: Rene Rabut, 1573.

Martí Grajales, Francisco. *Ensayo de un diccionario biográfico y bibliográfico de los poetas que florecieron en el Reino de Valencia hasta el año 1700.* Madrid: Tipografía de la Revista de Archivos, Bibliotecas y Museos, 1927.

Martí de Viciana, Rafael. *Libro segundo de la crónica de la ínclita y coronada ciudad de Valencia y su reino.* Valencia: Joan Navarro, 1564.

Martínez, Miguel. "Género, imprenta y espacio social: Una poética de la pólvora para la épica quinientista." *Hispanic Review* 79.2 (2011): 163–87.

———. "The Heroes in the World's Marketplace: Translating and Printing Epic in Renaissance Antwerp." In *Translation and the Book Trade in Early Modern Europe,* ed. José María Pérez Fernández and Edward Wilson-Lee. Cambridge: Cambridge University Press, 2014. 81–106.

———. "'The Spell of National Identity': War and Soldiering on the North African Frontier (1550–1560)." *Journal of Spanish Cultural Studies* 12.3 (2011): 293–307.

———. "La vida de los heroes: Sobre épica y autobiografía en el Mediterráneo habsburgo." *Calíope* 19.1 (2014): 103–28.

Martínez Millán, José, ed. *La corte de Felipe II.* Madrid: Alianza, 1994.

Martínez de Salinas, María Luisa. *Castilla ante el Nuevo Mundo: La trayec-

toria indiana del gobernador Bernardo de Vargas Machuca. Valladolid: Diputación, 1991.

Marx, Karl. *Capital Vol. 1*. Trans. Ben Fowkes. London: Penguin, 1976.

———. *The Eighteenth Brumaire of Louis Bonaparte*. Moscow: Progress Publishers, 1937. Digital edition by *Marxist Internet Archive*. https:// www.marxists.org/archive/marx/works/1852/18th-brumaire/, accessed July 15, 2015.

Marx, Karl, and Friedrich Engels. *The Communist Manifesto*. Arlington Heights, IL: AHM, 1955.

Maurer, Christopher. *Obra y vida de Francisco de Figueroa*. Madrid: Istmo, 1988.

McKeown, Adam. *English Mercuries: Soldier Poets in the Age of Shakespeare*. Nashville: Vanderbilt University Press, 2009.

McKitterick, David. *Print, Manuscript and the Search for Order, 1450–1830*. Cambridge: Cambridge University Press, 2003.

Medina, José Toribio. *La Araucana: Documentos*. Santiago de Chile: Imprenta Elzeviriana, 1918.

———. *La Araucana: Ilustraciones*. 2 vols. Santiago de Chile: Imprenta Elzeviriana, 1917–18.

———. *Colección de documentos inéditos para la historia de Chile*. Segunda Serie. 7 vols. Santiago: Fondo Histórico y Bibliográfico J. T. Medina, 1957–61.

———. *Romances basados en La Araucana*. Santiago: Imprenta Elzeviriana, 1918.

———. *Vida de Ercilla*. México: FCE, 1948.

Meerbeeck, L. Van. "L'hôpital royal de l'armée espagnole a Malines en l'an 1637." *Bulletin du Cercle royal archéologique, littéraire et artistique de Malines* 54 (1950): 81–125.

Mele, Eugenio. "Don Luis de Ávila, su 'Comentario' y los italianos." *Bulletin Hispanique* 24.2 (1922): 97–119.

Menéndez Pidal, Ramón. *Romancero hispánico*. 2 vols. Madrid: Espasa-Calpe, 1953.

Mexía, Pedro. *Silva de varia lección agora nuevamente enmendada y corregida por el autor*. Lyon: Herederos de Diego de Junta, 1556.

Monte, Alberto del. *Itinerario de la novela picaresca española*. Barcelona: Lumen, 1971.

Morel-Fatio, Alfred. "Soldats espagnols du XVIIe siècle: Alonso de Contreras, Miguel de Castro et Diego Suárez." *Bulletin Hispanique* 3.2 (1901): 135–58.

———. "La plainte du soldat espagnol." *Romanische Forschungen* 23 (1907): 155–61.

Muñoz de San Pedro, Miguel. *Diego García de Paredes, Hércules y Sansón de España*. Madrid: Espasa Calpe, 1946.

———. "Documentación familiar de Diego García de Paredes." *Revista de Estudios Extremeños* 12 (1956): 34–40.

———. "Documentación histórica de Diego García de Paredes." *Revista de Estudios Extremeños* 12 (1957): 307–37.

Murrin, Michael. *History and Warfare in Renaissance Epic*. Chicago: University of Chicago Press, 1994.

Najemy, John. "Arms and Letters: The Crisis of Courtly Culture in the Wars of Italy." In Shaw, 207–38.

Nalle, Sara T. "Literacy and Culture in Early Modern Castile." *Past and Present* 125 (November 1989): 65–96.

———. "Printing and Reading Popular Religious Texts in Sixteenth-Century Spain." In *Culture and the State in Spain, 1500–1850*, ed. Tom Lewis and Francisco Sánchez. New York: Garland, 1999. 126–56.

Navarra, Pedro de. *Diálogos cual debe ser el chronista del príncipe materia de pocos aún tocada*. Zaragoza: Juan Millán, 1567.

Naylor, Eric. "La encomienda del capitán Contreras." *Revista de Filología Española* 53.1 (1970): 305–8.

Nicolopulos, James. *The Poetics of Empire in the Indies: Prophecy and Imitation in "La Araucana" and "Os Lusíadas."* University Park: Pennsylvania State University Press, 2000.

Nucula, Horatius. *Commentariorum de bello Aphrodisiensi libri quinque*. Rome: Valerium and Ludovicum fratres Brixienses, 1552.

Núñez de Alva, Diego. *Diálogos de la vida del soldado*. Cuenca: Juan Alonso de Tapia, 1589.

Núñez Cabeza de Vaca, Alvar. *La relación y comentarios del gobernador de lo acaescido en las dos jornadas que hizo a las Indias*. Valladolid: Francisco Fernández de Córdoba, 1555.

Núñez de Pineda y Bascuñán, Francisco. *Cautiverio feliz y razón de las guerras dilatadas de Chile*. Santiago: Imprenta del Ferrocarril, 1863.

O'Brien, Tim. *The Things They Carried*. New York: Broadway Books, 1998.

Oman, Charles. *A History of the Art of War in the Sixteenth Century*. New York: E. P. Dutton, 1937.

Oña, Pedro de. *Arauco domado*. Lima: Antonio Ricardo, 1596.

———. *Arauco domado*. Ed. J. T. Medina. Santiago, 1917.

Ortega y Gasset, José. "Prólogo." *Discurso de mi vida*. By Alonso de Contreras. Madrid: Alianza, 1967.

Osborn, E. B., ed. *The Muse in Arms*. New York: Frederick A. Stokes, 1917.

Otavanti, Juan Lorenzo. "Las felicísimas nuevas de la victoria que su majestad ha haido de la ciudad de África." In *Archivo y biblioteca de la casa de Medinaceli: Series de sus principales documentos, 2ª bibliográfica*, ed. Antonio Paz y Meliá. Madrid: 1922. 369–70.

Ovalle, Alonso de. *Histórica relación del reino de Chile*. Rome: Francisco Caballo, 1646.

Ovid. *Metamorphoses*. Trans. Horace Gregory. New York: New American Library, 1958.

Oznaya, Juan de. *Historia de la Guerra de Lombardía, batalla de Pavía y prisión del rey Francisco de Francia*. CODOIN 38. Madrid: Imprenta de la Viuda de Calero, 1861. 289–403.

Packer, George. "Home Fires: How Soldiers Write Their Wars." *New Yorker*, April 7, 2014.

Padilla, Pedro de. *Romancero en el qual se contienen algunos sucesos que en la jornada de Flandes*. Ed. José J. Labrador Herraiz and Ralph A. DiFranco. México: Frente de Afirmación Hispanista, 2010.

Padrón, Ricardo. *The Spacious Word: Cartography, Literature and Empire in Early Modern Spain*. Chicago: University of Chicago Press, 2004.

Pantoja Rivero, Juan Carlos. *Antología de poemas caballerescos castellanos*. Alcalá: Centro de Estudios Cervantinos, 2004.

Paré, Ambroise. *The workes of that famous chirurgion Ambrose Parey*. Trans. Thomas Johnson. London: Thomas Cotes, 1634.

Parker, Geoffrey. *The Army of Flanders and the Spanish Road, 1567–1659*. 2nd ed. Cambridge: Cambridge University Press, 2004.

———. *The Dutch Revolt*. Ithaca, NY: Cornell University Press, 1977.

———. *The Military Revolution: Military Innovation and the Rise of the West, 1500–1800*. Cambridge: Cambridge University Press, 1996.

———. "Mutiny and Discontent in the Spanish Army of Flanders, 1572–1607." *Past and Present* 58 (1973): 38–52.

Parrott, David. *The Business of War: Military Enterprise and Military Revolution in Early Modern Europe*. Cambridge: Cambridge University Press, 2012.

Pasamonte, Jerónimo de. *Vida y trabajos de Jerónimo de Pasamonte*. In *Autobiografías de soldados (siglo XVII)*, ed. José María de Cossío. BAE 90. Madrid: Atlas, 1956.

Pastor, Beatriz. *Discursos narrativos de la conquista: Mitificación y emergencia*. Hanover: Ediciones del Norte, 1988.

Pastor, Beatriz, and Sergio Callau. *Lope de Aguirre y la rebelión de los marañones*. Madrid: Castalia, 2011.

Payne, Stanley G. *Politics and the Military in Modern Spain*. Stanford, CA: Stanford University Press, 1967.

Paz, Julián. "Pasquín puesto en Namur por los soldados españoles en 1594." *Revista de Bibliotecas, archivos y museos* 1, tercera época (1897): 118.

Peeters-Fontainas, Jean. *Bibliographie des impressions espagnoles des Pays-Bas méridionaux.* 2 vols. Nieuwkoop: B. de Graaf, 1965.

Pereyra, Carlos. "Soldadesca y picaresca." *Boletín de la Biblioteca Menéndez Pelayo* 19 (1927): 352–361; 20 (1928): 74–96, 150–63, 243–50.

Perry, Mary Elizabeth. *Crime and Society in Early Modern Seville.* Hanover, NH: University Press of New England, 1980.

Petrarca, Francesco. *Cancionero.* Ed. Jacobo Cortines. Madrid: Cátedra, 1989.

Pettegree, Andrew. *The Book in the Renaissance.* New Haven, CT: Yale University Press, 2010.

———. *The Invention of News: How the World Came to Know About Itself.* New Haven, CT: Yale University Press, 2014.

Pierce, Frank. *La poesía épica del Siglo de Oro.* Madrid: Gredos, 1961.

Pintacuda, Paolo. *La battaglia di Pavia nei "pliegos" poetici e nei "romanceros."* Lucca: Mauro Baroni, 1997.

Prieto, Antonio. "La poesía épica renacentista." In *La poesía española del siglo XVI. Vol. 2, Aquel valor que respetó el olvido.* Madrid: Cátedra, 1987. 781–831.

Primavera y flor de romances. Lisbon: Mattheus Pinheiro, 1626.

Promis, José. *La literatura del reino de Chile.* Valparaíso: Universidad de Playa Ancha Editorial, 2002.

Puddu, Raffaele. *El soldado gentilhombre: Autorretrato de una sociedad guerrera, la España del siglo XVI.* Trans. Enrique Lynch. Barcelona: Arcos Vergara, 1984.

Quatrefages, René. *La revolución militar moderna: El crisol español.* Madrid: Ministerio de Defensa, 1996.

———. *Los tercios españoles, 1567–1577.* Trans. Carlos Batal Batal. Madrid: Fundación Universitaria Española, 1979.

Querol Coll, Enric. "Els Aldana, tortosins del segle XVI aveïnats a València: De les armes a les lletres." *Pedralbes* 27 (2007): 199–218.

Quevedo, Francisco de. *La vida del Buscón.* Ed. Fernando Cabo. Barcelona: Crítica, 1993.

Quint, David. *Epic and Empire: Politics and Generic Form from Virgil to Milton.* Princeton, NJ: Princeton University Press, 1993.

Ramírez de Arellano, Rafael. *Juan Rufo, jurado de Córdoba: Estudio biográfico y crítico.* Madrid, 1912. Facsimile. Valladolid: Maxtor, 2002.

Redig de Campos, Deoclezio. "Un altro graffito del Sacco nelle Stanze di Raffaello." *Ecclesia* 19.11 (1960): 552–54.

———. "Il nome di Martin Lutero graffito sulla disputa del Sacramento." *Ecclesia* 6 (1947): 648–49.

Relación de los servicios que hizo a su magestad del Rey don Felipe Segundo y Tercero, don Alonso de Sotomayor. Madrid: Viuda de Cosme Delgado, 1620.

Relación verdadera de las paces que capituló con el Araucano rebelado, el marqués de Baides. Madrid: Francisco Maroto, 1642.

Relación de la vitoria que Dios nuestro señor fue servido de dar en el Reino de Chile a los 13. de enero de 1631. Lima: Francisco Gómez Pastrana, 1631.

Restall, Matthew and Felipe Fernández-Armesto. *The Conquistadors.* Oxford: Oxford University Press, 2012.

———. *Seven Myths of the Spanish Conquest.* Oxford: Oxford University Press, 2003.

Rey de Artieda, Andrés. *Discursos, epístolas y epigramas de Artemidoro.* Ed. Antonio Vilanova. Barcelona: Selecciones Bibliófilas, 1955.

Reynolds, Winston A. *Romancero de Hernán Cortés: Estudio y textos de los siglos XVI y XVII.* Madrid: Ediciones Alcalá, 1967.

Ribot, Luis. *El arte de gobernar: Estudios sobre la España de los Austrias.* Madrid: Alianza, 2006.

———. "Soldados españoles en Italia: El castillo de Milán a finales del siglo XVI." In *Guerra y sociedad*, ed. García Hernán and Maffi, 401–44.

Río, Martín Antonio del. *La crónica sobre don Juan de Austria/Die Chronik über Don Juan de Austria.* Ed. Miguel Ángel Echevarría Bacigalupe and Friedrich Edelmayer. Oldenbourg: Verlag für Geschichte und Politik, 2003.

Roberts, Michael. *The Military Revolution, 1550–1560.* Belfast: M. Boyd, 1956.

Rodríguez, Christine, and Bartolomé Bennassar. "Signatures et niveaux culturel des témoins et accusés dans les procès d'Inquisition du réssort du tribunal de Tolède (1525–1817) et du tribunal de Cordove (1595–1632)." *Caravelle* 31 (1978): 17–46.

Rodríguez, Juan Carlos. *La literatura del pobre.* Granada: Comares, 2001.

Rodríguez Alva, Cristóbal. *La inquieta Flandes . . . Debaxo de la qual se cuentan verdaderamente los sucesos de Flandes desde el año de mil y quinientos ochenta y cinco hasta el de noventa.* BNE, MSS/22648.

Rodríguez Moñino, Antonio. "El alférez Francisco de Segura, autor y colector de romances." *Revista del Instituto "José Cornide" de Estudios Coruñeses* 4.4 (1968): 185–204.

———. *Catálogo de manuscritos poéticos en la biblioteca de The Hispanic Society of America.* New York: HSA, 1965–66.

———. *Las fuentes del romancero general.* Madrid: Real Academia Española, 1957.

———. *Nuevo diccionario bibliográfico de pliegos sueltos poéticos (siglo XVI).* Ed. Arthur L.-F. Askins and Víctor Infantes. Madrid: Castalia, 1997.

———. *Pliegos poéticos de la Biblioteca Colombina.* Berkeley: University of California Press, 1974.

Rodríguez-Rodríguez, Ana María. *Letras liberadas: Cautiverio, escritura y subjetividad.* Madrid: Visor, 2013.

Rodríguez-Salgado, M. J. *Un imperio en transición: Carlos V, Felipe II y su mundo 1551–1559.* Barcelona: Crítica, 1992.

Rodríguez-Velasco, Jesús. "Esfuerço: La caballería, de estado a oficio (1524–1615)." In *Amadís de Gaula quinientos años después: Estudios en homenaje a Juan Manuel Cacho Blecua,* ed. José Manuel Lucía Megías and María del Carmen Marín Pina. Alcalá: Centro de Estudios Cervantinos, 2008. 661–89.

Rogers, Clifford J. *The Military Revolution Debate: Readings in the Military Transformation of Early Modern Europe.* Boulder, CO: Westview Press, 1995.

Rosales, Diego de. *Historia general del reino de Chile: Flandes indiano.* 3 vols. Ed. Benjamín Vicuña Mackenna. Valparaíso: Imprenta del Mercurio, 1877–1878.

Rosales, Luis, and Luis Felipe Vivanco. *Poesía heroica del imperio.* Madrid: Ediciones Jerarquía, 1940.

Rospocher, Massimo. "Songs of War: Historical and Literary Narratives of the 'Horrendous Italian Wars' (1494–1559)." In *Narrating War: Early Modern and Contemporary Perspectives,* ed. Marco Mondini and Massimo Rospocher. Bolonia: Il Mulino, 2012. 79–97.

———. "Versos desde las plazas: La poesía como lenguaje de comunicación política en los espacios públicos de las ciudades italianas del renacimiento." In *Opinión pública y espacio urbano en la Edad Moderna,* ed. Antonio Castillo Gómez, James Amelang, and Carmen Serrano Sánchez. Gijón: Trea, 2010. 185–210.

Rospocher, Massimo, and Rosa Salzberg. "'El vulgo zanza': Spazi, pubblici, voci a Venezia durante le guerre d'Italia." *Storica* 48.16 (2010): 83–120.

Roubaud, Sylvia. "Los libros de caballerías." In Cervantes, *Quijote,* cv–cxxviii.

Rueda y Mendoza, Diego de. *Relación verdadera de las xequias funerales que la insigne ciudad de Manila celebró a la muerte de la majestad del Rey Felipe Tercero y reales fiestas que se hicieron a la felice sucesión de su único heredero y señor nuestro Felipe 4.* 1625. Ms. HSA.

Rueda Ramírez, Pedro. *Negocio e intercambio cultural: El comercio de libros con América en la Carrera de Indias (siglo XVII)*. Seville: Universidad, 2005.

Rufo, Juan. *La Austríada*. Madrid: Alonso Gómez, 1584.

———. *Las seiscientas apotegmas y otras obras en verso*. Ed. Alberto Blecua. Madrid: Espasa-Calpe, 1972.

Rupp, Stephen. *Heroic Forms: Cervantes and the Literature of War*. Toronto: University of Toronto Press, 2014.

Saavedra Fajardo, Diego de. *República literaria*. Ed. John Dowling. Salamanca: Anaya, 1967.

Saavedra Guzmán, Antonio de. *El peregrino indiano*. Ed. María José Rodilla León. Madrid/Frankfurt: Iberoamericana/Vervuert, 2008.

Sáez Godoy, Leopoldo, ed. *Gerónimo de Vivar: Crónica y relación copiosa y verdadera de los Reinos de Chile (1558)*. Berlin: Coloquium Verlag, 1979.

Salamanca, Alonso de. *Libro de cassos impensados*. 1576. Ms. Real Biblioteca.

Salas, Alberto Mario. *Las armas de la Conquista*. Buenos Aires: Emecé Editores, 1950.

Salazar, Diego de. *Tratado de re militari*. Alcalá: Miguel de Eguía, 1536.

Salazar, Pedro de. *Historia de la guerra y presa de África con la destruición de la villa de Monaster y isla del Gozo y pérdida de Trípol de Berbería: con otras muy nuevas cosas*. Naples: Mastre Matia, 1552.

Sánchez-Blanco, Francisco. "El marco institucional del discurso sobre sí mismo: Autobiografías del Renacimiento." In *Schwerpunkt Siglo de Oro: Akten des Deutschen Hispanistentages Wolfenbüttel*, ed. Hans-Josef Niederehe. Hamburg: Helmut Buske, 1986. 129–47.

Sánchez Jiménez, Antonio. *El Sansón de Extremadura: Diego García de Paredes en la literatura española del siglo XVI*. Newark, DE: Juan de la Cuesta, 2006.

Sánchez-Molero, José Luis Gonzalo. *La "librería rica" de Felipe II: Estudio histórico y catalogación*. Madrid: Ediciones Escurialenses, 1998.

Sandoval, Prudencio de. *Historia de la vida y hechos del emperador Carlos V*. Madrid: Atlas, 1955–56.

Sans, Hipólito. *La Maltea: En que se trata la famosa defensa de la Religión de Sant Joan en la isla de Malta*. Valencia: Joan Navarro, 1582.

Santillana, Marqués de. *Obras completas*. Ed. Ángel Gómez Moreno and Maxim P. A. M. Kerkhof. Barcelona: Planeta, 1988.

Scepper, Cornelius. *Rerum a Carolo V Caesare Augusto in Africa Bello gestarum commentarii*. Antwerp: Ioan Bellerum, 1554.

Schmidt, Benjamin. "Exotic Allies: The Dutch-Chilean Encounter and the (Failed) Conquest of America." *Renaissance Quarterly* 52.2 (1999): 440–73.

———. *Innocence Abroad: The Dutch Imagination and the New World, 1570–1670*. Cambridge: Cambridge University Press, 2001.

Schwaller, John F., and Helen Nader. *The First Letter from New Spain: The Lost Petition of Cortés and His Company, June 20, 1519*. Austin: University of Texas Press, 2014.

Schwartz, Stuart. *Victors and Vanquished: Spanish and Nahua Views of the Conquest of Mexico*. New York/Boston: Berdford/St. Martin's, 2000.

Scott, James. *The Weapons of the Weak*. New Haven, CT: Yale University Press, 1984.

Scott, Joan. "The Evidence of Experience." *Critical Inquiry* 17.4 (1991): 773–97.

Segura, Luis Gonzalo. *Un paso al frente*. Madrid: Tropo, 2014.

———. "Un paso al frente." http://blogs.publico.es/un-paso-al-frente/, accessed June 13, 2015.

Sempere, Jerónimo. *Carolea*. Valencia: Joan de los Arcos, 1560.

Sepúlveda, Juan Ginés de. *Diálogo llamado Demócrates*. Trans. Antonio Barba. Seville: Juan Cromberger, 1541.

———. *Tratados políticos de Juan Ginés de Sepúlveda*. Ed. Ángel Losada. Madrid: Instituto de Estudios Políticos, 1963.

Sepúlveda, Lorenzo. *Romances nuevamente sacados de historias antiguas de la crónica de España*. Antwerp: Joannes Steelsius, 1551.

Shaw, Christine, ed. *Italy and the European Powers: The Impact of War, 1500–1530*. Leiden: Brill, 2006.

Sir! No Sir! Dir. David Zeiger. Mindbomb Films, 2005. DVD.

Spadaccini, Nicholas, and Jenaro Talens, eds. *Autobiography in Early Modern Spain*. Minneapolis: Prisma, 1988.

Stallybrass, Peter, Roger Chartier, Frank Mowery, and Heather Wolfe. "Hamlet's Tables and the Technology of Writing in Renaissance England." *Shakespeare Quarterly* 55.4 (2004): 1–41.

Stefano, Giusseppe di, ed. *Romancero*. Madrid: Castalia, 2010.

Stone, Lawrence. "The Educational Revolution in England, 1560 to 1640." *Past and Present* 28 (1964): 41–80.

Sutton, Imogen. "'De gente que a ningún rey obedecen': Republicanism and Empire in Alonso de Ercilla's *La Araucana*." *Bulletin of Hispanic Studies* 91.4 (2014): 417–35.

Tallett, Frank. *War and Society in Early Modern Europe, 1495–1715*. London: Routledge, 1992.

Tamayo de Vargas, Tomás. *Diego García de Paredes y relación breve de su tiempo*. Madrid: Luis Sánchez, 1621.

Terrón Albarrán, Manuel. Introduction to *Carlo famoso*. By Luis Zapata. Badajoz: Diputación Provincial, 1981. 1–173.

Tesillo, Santiago de. *Epítome chileno, ideas contra la paz*. Lima: Jorge López de Herrera, [1648].

———. *Guerra de Chile, causas de su duración, medios para su fin*. Madrid: Imprenta Real, 1647.

Tezcan, Baki. *The Second Ottoman Empire: Political and Social Transformation in the Early Modern World*. Cambridge: Cambridge University Press, 2010.

Thayer Ojeda, Tomás, and Carlos Larraín. *Valdivia y sus compañeros*. Santiago: Imprenta universitaria, 1951.

Thomas, Hugh. *Who's Who of the Conquistadors*. London: Cassels, 2000.

Thomas, Richard, and Jan Ziolkowski. *The Virgil Encyclopedia*. 3 vols. Chichester: Wiley-Blackwell, 2014.

Thompson, I. A. A. "A Map of Crime in Sixteenth-Century Spain." *Economic History Review* 21 (1968): 244–67.

———. "El soldado del imperio: Una aproximación al perfil del recluta español en el Siglo de Oro." *Manuscrits* 21 (2003): 17–38.

———. "El soldado, la sociedad y el Estado en la España de los siglos XVI y XVII." In *Historia militar de España*, vol. 3.2, coordinated by Luis Ribot. Madrid: Ministerio de Defensa, 2009. 447–69.

———. *War and Government in Habsburg Spain, 1560–1620*. London: University of London Press, 1976.

Toral y Valdés, Domingo de. *The Life of Captain Domingo de Toral y Valdés*. Trans. Guy Sawyer. BA thesis, Bard College, 2013.

———. *Relación de la vida del capitán Domingo de Toral y Valdés, escrita por el mismo capitán*. CODOIN 71. Madrid: Miguel Ginesta, 1879.

Torres y Aguilera, Jerónimo de. *Crónica y recopilación de varios sucesos de guerra que ha acontescido en Italia y partes de Levante y Berbería, desde que el Turco Selin rompió con Venecianos y fue sobre la isla de Chipre año de M.D.LXX. hasta que se perdió la Goleta y fuerte de Túnez en el de M.D.LXXIIII*. Zaragoza: Juan Soler, 1579.

Torres Naharro, Bartolomé. *Comedia soldadesca*. In *Teatro renacentista*, ed. Alfredo Hermenegildo. Madrid: Austral, 1990.

Trim, David. "Ideology, Greed, and Social Discontent in Early Modern Europe: Mercenaries and Mutinies in the Rebellious Netherlands, 1568–1609." In *Rebellion, Repression, Reinvention: Mutiny in Comparative Perspective*, ed. Jane Hathaway. Westport, CT: Praeger, 2001. 47–61.

Valdés, Juan de. *Diálogo de la lengua.* Ed. José Enrique Laplana. Barcelona: Crítica, 2010.

Valdivia, Pedro de. *Cartas de Pedro de Valdivia que tratan del descubrimiento y conquista de Chile.* Ed. José Toribio Medina and Jaime Eyzaguirre. Santiago de Chile: Fondo Histórico y Bibliográfico José Toribio Medina, 1953.

Vargas, Baltasar de. *Breve relación en octava rima de la jornada que ha hecho el Señor Duque de Alba.* Antwerp: Amato Tabernerio, 1568.

Vargas Machuca, Bernardo de. *Discurso de guerra . . . para la pacificación y allanamiento de los indios del reino de Chile.* AGI, Patronato, 227, r. 34.

———. *The Indian Militia and the Description of the Indies.* Ed. Kris Lane, trans. Timothy F. Johnson. Durham, NC: Duke University Press, 2008.

———. *Milicia y descripción de las Indias.* Madrid: Pedro Madrigal, 1599.

Vega, Garcilaso de la. *Obra poética y textos en prosa.* Ed. Bienvenido Morros. Barcelona: Crítica, 2007.

Vega, Lope de. *Laurel de Apolo.* Ed. Antonio Carreño. Madrid: Cátedra, 2007.

———. *El rey sin reino.* In *Parte veinte de las comedias.* Madrid: Viuda de Alonso Martín, 1625.

Verrier, Frédérique. *Les armes de Minerve: L'humanisme militaire dans l'Italie du XVIe siècle.* Paris: Presses de l'Université de Paris-Sorbonne, 1997.

La vida y hechos de Estebanillo González. Ed. Antonio Carreira and Jesús Antonio Cid. Madrid: Cátedra, 1990.

Vilà, Lara. "Épica e imperio: Imitación virgiliana y propaganda política en la épica española del XVI." PhD diss., Universidad Autónoma de Barcelona, 2001.

———. "Las más ricas prendas de poesía que tiene España: Cervantes y la épica sobre Lepanto." In *Cervantes y su tiempo: Lectura y signo,* ed. Juan Matas Caballero and José María Balcells Doménech. León: Universidad de León, 2008.

Vilar, Pierre. "El tiempo de los hidalgos." In *Hidalgos, amotinados y guerrilleros: Pueblo y poderes en la historia de España.* Barcelona: Crítica, 1982. 19–59.

Villagrá, Gaspar Pérez de. *Historia de la Nueva México.* Alcalá: Luys Martínez Grande, 1611.

Villalobos, Sergio. *La vida fronteriza en Chile.* Madrid: MAPFRE, 1992.

Virgil. *Aeneid.* Trans. Robert Fagles. New York: Penguin, 2006.

———. *The Eclogues.* Trans. Guy Lee. New York: Penguin, 1984.

Virués, Cristóbal de. *El Monserrate.* Madrid: Sancha, 1805.

———. *Obras trágicas y líricas del capitán Cristóbal de Virués*. Madrid: Alonso Martín, 1609.

Vitale, Luis. *Interpretación marxista de la historia de Chile*. 7 vols. Santiago: Ediciones de Prensa Latinoamericana, 1967.

Vivar, Jerónimo de. *Crónica de los reinos de Chile*. Ed. Angel Barral Gómez. Crónicas de América 41. Madrid: Historia 16, 1988.

Voigt, Lisa. *Writing Captivity in the Early Modern Atlantic: Circulations of Knowledge and Authority in the English and Iberian Worlds*. Chapel Hill: University of North Carolina Press, 2009.

Warner, Michael. *The Letters of the Republic: Publication and the Public Sphere in Eighteenth-Century America*. Cambridge, MA: Harvard University Press, 1990.

———. *Publics and Counterpublics*. New York: Zone Books, 2002.

White, Lorraine. "The Experience of Spain's Early Modern Soldiers: Combat, Welfare, and Violence." *War in History* 9.1 (2002): 1–38.

———. "Spain's Early Modern Soldiers: Origins, Motivation, and Loyalty." *War and Society* 19.2 (2001): 19–46.

Wilson, Bronwen, and Paul Yachnin, eds. *Making Publics in Early Modern Europe: People, Things, Forms of Knowledge*. New York: Routledge, 2010.

Wilson, Edward. "Samuel Pepys' Spanish Chapbooks, Part II." *Transactions of the Cambridge Bibliographical Society* 2.3 (1956): 229–68.

Winter Soldier. Winter Film Collective, 1972. DVD.

Wright, Elizabeth. "Narrating the Ineffable Lepanto: The *Austrias Carmen* of Joannes Latinus (Juan Latino)." *Hispanic Review* 77.1 (Winter 2009): 71–91.

———. *Pilgrimage to Patronage: Lope de Vega and the Court of Philip III (1598–1621)*. Lewisburg, PA: Bucknell University Press, 2001.

Ximénez de Ayllón, Diego. *Sonetos a illustres varones este felicísimo y católico ejército y corte*. Antwerp: Viuda de Juan Lacio, 1569.

Ximeno, Vicente. *Escritores del reino de Valencia*. 2 vols. Valencia: Dolz, 1746–49.

Xufré del Águila, Melchor. *Compendio historial*. Santiago: Anales de la Universidad, 1897.

———. *Compendio historial del descubrimiento, conquista, y guerra del reino de Chile*. Lima: Francisco Gómez Pastrana, 1630.

Zamora, Lorenzo de. *Primera parte de la Historia de Sagunto, Numancia y Carthago*. Alcalá: Juan Íñiguez de Lequerica, 1589.

Zabaleta, Juan de. *Día de fiesta por la mañana y por la tarde*. Madrid: Diego Pacheco, 1885.

Zapata, Luis. *Carlo famoso*. Ed. facsímil de Manuel Terrón Albarrán. Badajoz: Diputación Provincial, 1981.

———. *Miscelánea*. Ed. Pascual de Gayangos. Memorial Histórico Español 11. Madrid, 1859.

Zatti, Sergio. *The Quest for Epic: From Ariosto to Tasso*. Ed. Dennis Looney, trans. Sally Hill and Dennis Looney. Toronto: University of Toronto Press, 2006.

Zeller, Gaston. *Le Siège de Metz par Charles-Quint*. Nancy: Société d'impressions typographiques, 1943.

Zimic, Stanislav. "Sobre los amores de Leandra y Vicente de la Roca (*Don Quijote*, I, caps. 50–52)." *Anales cervantinos* 30 (1992): 67–76.

Zimmermann, T. C. Price. *Paolo Giovio: The Historian and the Crisis of Sixteenth-Century Italy*. Princeton, NJ: Princeton University Press, 1995.

ACKNOWLEDGMENTS

My much-missed mentor Isaías Lerner once said, with his usual wittiness, that writing the acknowledgments of a book was very much like dictating a testament. My own settling of intellectual accounts thus starts with my deep gratitude to him for his contagious enthusiasm, large philological knowledge, and sharp intelligence. Without his support and encouragement, I would very likely not be writing these lines. I am also deeply in debt to Lía Schwartz, José Miguel Martínez-Torrejón, Ottavio DiCamillo, and José del Valle, who have always been models of rigorous and passionate scholarship and invaluable supporters. Barbara Fuchs has provided all kinds of help, including tireless intellectual and professional guidance. I thank my most veteran interlocutors, David Rodríguez-Solás, Alex Alonso Nogueira, Marta Albalá Pelegrín, Javier Castro-Ibaseta, Mayte Green-Mercado, and Javier Irigoyen-García, for largely shaping, through years of fraternal conversation, the way I think about history and literature.

My home institution, the University of Chicago, has generously funded the research necessary for this book, mostly through the Humanities Visiting Committee. During my first and most important talk at Chicago, David Nirenberg posed, as usual, the crucial question, which is very much in the origin of the present book. My gratitude goes to my colleagues—in Romance Languages and elsewhere—Frederick de Armas, Ramón Gutiérrez, Mauricio Tenorio, Larissa Brewer-García, and Michael Murrin, who at different points read parts of this book and provided feedback and encouragement. Daisy Delogu has consistently guided me through some intricacies of the institution and the profession. Mario Santana, Agnes Lugo-Ortiz, Emilio Kourí, Larry Norman, Martha Lilia Tenorio, and the rest of the Department of Romance Languages and Literatures have proven to be great colleagues and brilliant interlocutors. Rocco Rubini and Laura Gandolfi are, within and beyond the walls of Wieboldt and Classics, my most reliable fellows-in-arms, intellectually and otherwise. Last but not least, during these years in Hyde Park, my dear friends Txinto, Pedro, Helena, Justin, Toni, Diana, Anne-Laure, Nacho, and Sun have heard more about soldiers than they needed to. Thanks for being there.

Archives in both Spain and the United States have offered the most pleasurable, enjoyable moments while working on this project. I am truly grateful to my friends John O'Neill and Vanessa Pintado at the Hispanic Society of America, Isabel Aguirre at the Archivo General de Simancas, and the librarians at Biblioteca Nacional, Real Biblioteca, Real Academia de la Historia, Harvard's Houghton Library, New York Public Library, the Newberry Library, and the Regenstein's Special Collections in Chicago.

This book would not really exist had I not had access to the holdings and the intellectual community of the John Carter Brown Library (JCB), where I spent the most productive year of my academic life as an NEH and Donald L. Saunders Fellow. Most of the actual writing took place in that little carrel in the basement, wonderfully escorted by my friends Elvira Vilches, Matthew Restall, and Amara Solari, who listened patiently, read chapters, and provided all kinds of human and intellectual support. Thanks also to the rest of the fellows of 2013–14, particularly Ana Hontanilla, César Manrique Figueroa, Guillermo García Montúfar, Adam Jasienski, and Pepa Hernández, as well as Ken Ward, Neil Safier, and the outstanding staff at the JCB. Since my time at Brown, Joseph Reed's classicist expertise has often gotten me out of trouble and has inspired one of the stories at the beginning of this book.

The University of Pennsylvania Press has provided all the help that a *bisoño* author might need. Jerry Singerman supported the project from the beginning, and I am grateful to him for bringing it, patiently, to successful completion. I would like to thank the first anonymous reader for her/his very useful feedback on the manuscript. Michael Armstrong-Roche's detailed and extraordinarily insightful second report helped me see some important blind spots in the argument. Linde Brocato and Jenn Backer contributed greatly to improve the quality of my non-native English writing.

The unfailing support of my parents, Ana and Miguel, and my sister, María, comes so naturally and generously that sometimes one tends to take it for granted. That I do for a living what I just love doing is only thanks to my parents' hard work, which they also taught me—with varying degrees of success—by example. With the same gracious example they raised me and my sister to learn how to put aside work and enjoy life—and in this they have succeeded beyond any reasonable expectation. Without this, and their unconditional love, what is the point of writing books?

During Christmas 2014, when this book had already been finished, my uncle Luis went to the attic of the family home in Máñores, a hamlet in Tinéu, Asturias, and found an old notebook from 1950. The elegant, proud handwriting was my grandfather's, and it recounted his mandatory military service in what was still the Spanish protectorate of Morocco. A peasant who would eventually become a bank clerk after the *mili*, my grandfather educated himself through reading, voraciously, all his life—including *War and Peace*. His writing, however, he never mentioned to anyone. But there it was: the countryside recruit's excitement about the world out there, the detached, commonsensical view of the nonsense of war and colonialism, the muted yet self-reliant critical voice and ruses of the common soldier that the reader will find in the pages of this book. It is to the memory of my grandfather, Lito, and my grandmothers Amparo and Otilia, who also saw and decried war, that I would like to dedicate this book.